THE NEWTON ABBOT TO MORETONHAMPSTEAD RAILWAY

by

Anthony R. Kingdom & Mike Lang

ARK PUBLICATIONS (RAILWAYS)

First published in 2004 by ARK PUBLICATIONS (RAILWAYS), an imprint of FOREST PUBLISHING, Woodstock, Liverton, Newton Abbot, Devon TQ12 6JJ

British Library Cataloguing in Publication Data
A catalogue record for this book is available from the British Library
ISBN 1–873029–09–8

Prairie tank No. 4117 taking water at Moretonhampstead on 28th February 1959, the final day of regular passenger trains on the branch.

Peter W. Gray

ARK PUBLICATIONS (RAILWAYS)
Editorial by:
E. R. Shepherd

Design and layout by:
Mike Lang

Typeset by:
Carnaby Typesetting, Torquay, Devon TQ1 1EG

Printed and bound in Great Britain by:
Wotton Printers Limited, Newton Abbot, Devon TQ12 4PJ

Cover photographs:

Front — (Top) 0-4-2T No. 1466 about to depart from platform 9 at Newton Abbot with the 2.15 p.m. service to Moretonhampstead on 18th July 1956.

R. C. Riley

(Lower) A study of Moretonhampstead Station on the morning of 19th February 1959, with Prairie tank No. 4150 waiting to leave with the 10.15 a.m. service to Newton Abbot.

Peter W. Gray

Back — A view of the line and surrounding countryside immediately to the north-west of Pullabrook (Hawkmoor) Halt, showing 0-4-2T No. 1466 tackling the 1 in 61 gradient beyond Letford Bridge with the 12.50 p.m. service from Newton Abbot to Moretonhampstead on 21st February 1959.

Peter W. Gray

CONTENTS

INTRODUCTION

A much-loved line and, in parts, one of great sylvan beauty, the Newton Abbot to Moretonhampstead Railway served the communities through which it passed for nearly a century and for many people, especially in its early years, was the only means of communication with the outside world.

It commenced life in 1866 as a single-line track in Brunel's broad gauge after being constructed by the Moretonhampstead & South Devon Railway Company, and between Ventiford (Teigngrace) and the south-eastern outskirts of Bovey Tracey followed much of the route of the Haytor Granite Tramway. Running in a predominantly north-westerly direction, the line was over 12 miles long and climbed more than 500 feet to its terminus situated amidst the foothills of eastern Dartmoor. Initially, there were only two intermediate stations – Bovey and Lustleigh. However, in 1867 another station was constructed at Teigngrace, and this was followed, in 1874, by the opening of Chudleigh Road Station (renamed Heathfield immediately prior to it becoming a junction for the Teign Valley line in 1882). During these early years there were also two changes of ownership. First, in 1872, the Moretonhampstead & South Devon Railway Company was amalgamated with the South Devon Railway Company, which had worked the line from

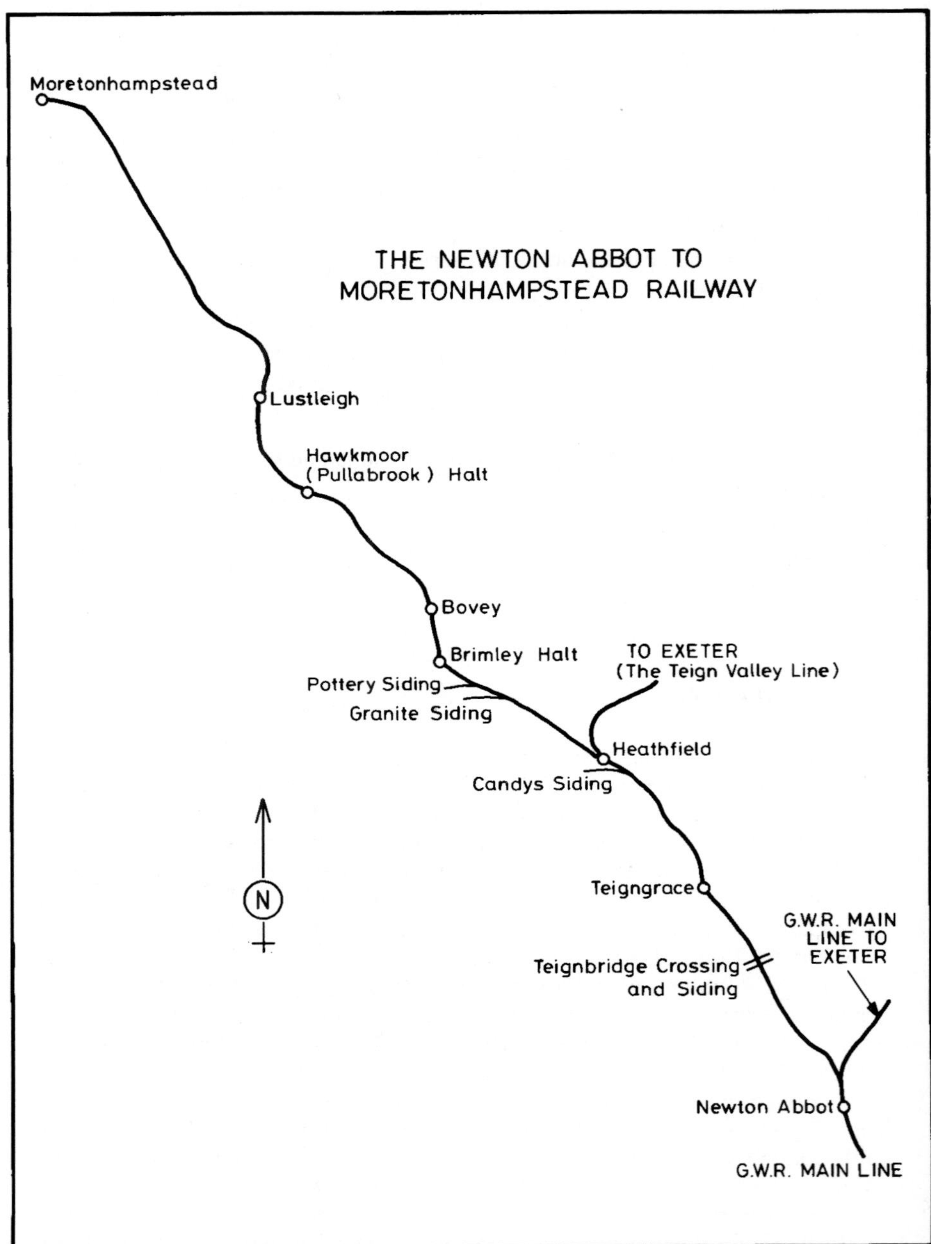
THE NEWTON ABBOT TO
MORETONHAMPSTEAD RAILWAY
Moretonhampstead
Lustleigh
Hawkmoor
(Pullabrook) Halt
Bovey
Brimley Halt
TO EXETER
(The Teign Valley Line)
Pottery Siding
Granite Siding
Heathfield
Candys Siding
N
Teigngrace
G.W.R. MAIN
LINE TO
EXETER
Teignbridge Crossing
and Siding
Newton Abbot
G.W.R. MAIN LINE

the outset, and then, just four years later, this latter company was itself absorbed by the Great Western Railway Company. As a result, from thereon the line became an integral part of the GWR system in Devon.

Conversion to standard gauge was a foregone conclusion once the GWR's superior broad gauge had to be surrendered to the nation's predominant 'coal truck' gauge of the north, in the quest for uniformity, and this was duly carried out over the weekend of 21st/22nd May 1892. At that time passenger traffic was still proving slow to develop, but within a few more years there was a noticeable improvement as ever-increasing numbers of visitors started travelling over the branch, particularly during the summer months. This, in turn, quickly prompted the GWR into steadily increasing the level of service and gradually introducing various other means of attracting business, which included providing omnibuses in conjunction with the trains for trips across Dartmoor (initially from Moretonhampstead and later from Bovey), the opening of two more stopping places along the branch – Brimley Halt (1928) and Hawkmoor Halt (1931) – and the purchase of the Manor House at North Bovey for use as a luxury hotel. Indeed, such became the popularity of the line that by the mid-1930s the weekday summer service consisted of no less than eleven trains in each direction between Newton Abbot and Moretonhampstead, of which seven were through workings from Totnes, Kingswear or Paignton, plus a further seven trains between Newton Abbot and Bovey.

That, sadly, proved to be the line's pinnacle. Road competition and increasing private car ownership was already starting to take its toll, and after the war little serious effort was made to retrieve the situation, which steadily worsened until, eventually, British Railways withdrew the passenger service on 2nd March 1959 – even before the Beeching Report! Furthermore, a recommendation that the position should be reviewed when diesel railcars became available in the area in 1961 fell upon deaf ears, as did attempts by a small group of enthusiasts to preserve the line as a private railway. The goods service, on the other hand, was initially left unaltered, but before long that, too, was gradually cut back until, after July 1970, the only part of the line still in use was the section between Newton Abbot and Heathfield. Surprisingly, at the time of writing, this still remains the case, although the only traffic nowadays is a once-weekly clay train.

In the pages that follow we sincerely hope that we have succeeded in bringing back happy memories to all those old enough to have known and loved this railway. To enable those of younger lineage, and future generations denied it delights, to appreciate it, this book was written and dedicated.

Anthony R. Kingdom & Mike Lang
July 2004

An aerial view of the northern side of Newton Abbot Station clearly showing (to the left of the photograph) platform 9 and the Moretonhampstead line as it runs alongside the extensive warehouse complex of Tucker's Maltings before veering north-westwards beyond the power station of the C.E.G.B.

Courtesy of Herald Express Publications, Torquay

THE ROUTE DESCRIBED

Newton Abbot to Moretonhampstead. A journey on the line in the mid-1950s.

The scene is set, it is a fine summer's day and the outside air is hazy and still, whilst inside a pair of autocoaches there is a soothing murmur of quiet, multiple conversations. There is also a general atmosphere of peace and tranquility as other sounds begin to add themselves to the scene: the gentle hiss of steam from leaking joints and then the sound of the fireman shovelling coal and applying the blower to the loco's fire, forcing the emission of semi-transparent, blue sulphurous fumes which spiral upwards from its chimney.

Our location is platform 9 of a large, busy and complex station, namely Newton Abbot, where the tranquility of our immediate surroundings is interrupted only by the sudden arrival of an express from Paddington or, maybe, The Midlands. Roaring into the station with its 13 coaches, this express loco sheds an air of disdain towards our little engine and its two autocoaches. And, as suddenly as it arrives, it departs for Plymouth or Torbay with a whistle and a staccato bark, shedding an air of superiority to all who observe it.

Suddenly our driver and fireman cease to chat to the guard; their last words to one another louden as they drift apart to attend to their respective duties. There is a lurch as the brakes are released, the creaking springs protest their reply, the 'down starting' signal for the branch drops and we are slowly pressed into motion as the driver eases the regulator open. We are on our way!

Digressing from our journey, the branch's 'main line terminus', Newton Abbot, must be described. However, to do this in detail is well outside the confines of this book and, instead, it is considered that an overall description of the station layout as at the date of our journey will suffice.

First, and foremost, it needs to be stated that at this time the station itself is still comparatively new, having been formally opened by Lord Mildmay of Flete on 11th April 1927. Prior to that event, since September 1923, work had been in progress on a major rebuilding/expansion programme of the old South Devon Railway station, which dated back to 1861 and had, itself, been a replacement of the original built for the opening of the line in 1846. This work had not only included extending and remodelling the track layout, but also replacing the former Brunelian-type station building, with its characteristic overall wooden roof, by a new, imposing three-storey block of red Somerset brick and Portland stone, topped with a stylish Mansard roof in Welsh slate. Sited a little further to the north than its rather austere-looking predecessor, but still alongside the road leading to Torquay, and facing Courtenay Park, it also features a large and handsome clock: this had been donated by the townspeople of Newton Abbot as an acknowledgment of the vastly improved facilities, and adorns the facade of the building on its centre pediment.

The main station building and forecourt at Newton Abbot, as seen on 28th June 1952 after it had been specially decorated for the queen's forthcoming visit to the Royal Show at Stover.

E. R. Shepherd

The station's other most prominent feature is its two wide, 1,375-feet long island platforms, both sporting an overall canopy some 570 feet in length. These canopies are of triangular section throughout their entire length and are constructed of lattice steel girders, supported by larger girders sunk into their respective platforms, and corrugated iron sheeting for the roofs, into which numerous glazed panels are incorporated in their inner sections in order to effect light reaching the platform centres. Below the canopies the accommodation is constructed wholly of timber in the form of horizontal planking, the only exception to this being some of the buildings on the 'down relief' platform; these are of cement block construction and were built to replace wooden structures damaged during an air raid on the station on 20th August 1940. Within this accommodation, on both platforms, are refreshment rooms, centrally heated waiting rooms, attractive bookstalls, staff offices and storerooms. Outside, uncharacteristic concrete lamp standards with twin arms and enamel parabolic reflectors adorn the platforms in their profusion, but the light from their filament lamps is not deemed to be very good!

The platforms cater for all the main line 'up' and 'down' traffic and, because of their length, are effectively both divided into two for operational purposes and numbered accordingly: the 'up main' platform (nearest the station building) is numbered 7 and 8, the 'up relief' platform is 5 and 6, the 'down main' platform is 3 and 4, and, finally, the 'down relief' platform is 1 and 2, the lower numbers in each instance being utilised for the platforms'

Main line activity at Newton Abbot:–
Above: County class 4–6–0 No. 1015 *County of Gloucester* pulling out of platform 7 with the 12.20 p.m. Penzance to Kensington milk train on 27th March 1954, as an unidentified 45xx class 2–6–2T waits in platform 9 at the head of the 6.5 p.m. train to Moretonhampstead.

Peter W. Gray

Below: Hall class 4–6–0 No. 4980 *Wrottesley Hall* standing at platform 7 with an 'up' train to Cardiff on 27th May 1958, while 0–6–0PT No. 3606 awaits departure from platform 9 with the 4.35 p.m. train to Exeter via the Teign Valley line.

R. A. Lumber

A busy scene at Newton Abbot on 6th August 1957 with all three 'up' roads and the bay platform in use. To the left of the picture Castle class 4–6–0 No. 5053 *Earl Cairns* stands at platform 5 with the 5.45 p.m. goods train from Goodrington, platforms 7 and 8 have just become occupied by BR standard class 5 4–6–0 No. 73029 and pilot engine 4–6–0 No. 6938 *Corndean Hall* with the 4.25 p.m. Plymouth Millbay to Paddington perishables train, and in the bay platform are two of the 14xx class 0–4–2Ts. In the foreground No. 1472 has just taken water and is now about to run around her train (at present in the siding beyond the platform end) before propelling it back into platform 9 in readiness for the 6.5 p.m. departure to Moretonhampstead, while sister engine No. 1468 is at the head of the 6.15 p.m. departure to Exeter via the Teign Valley line.

Peter W. Gray

northern sections. With regard to the running lines, there are actually six in all as there is also an 'up through' line lying parallel to the 'up main' line, and linked to it by a scissors crossing situated intermediately along the outer face of the 'up main' platform, and, similarly, there is a 'down through' line lying parallel to the 'down relief' line, these two, once again, linked at an intermediate point by a scissors crossing. The 'up relief' and 'down main' lines, incidentally, are also linked intermediately, only in this instance by a 'trailing' crossover. The result is that the overall layout affords a great deal of flexibility, particularly as regards the transfer of carriages between main line trains and those operating on the Kingswear branch, when the need arises.

In order to gain access to the two island platforms, passengers first have to enter the booking hall, situated on the ground floor of the station building, purchase their tickets and climb one of two stone stairways. Then, after showing their tickets to a ticket inspector, and passing through a sliding, metal trellis, ticket barrier, they proceed along a large covered walkway constructed of steel girders paved with heavy timber planking and numerous glazed panels. This, in turn, leads to two more, wooden, stairways, each leading down to the platform to which it is connected. However, for passengers intending to travel on the Moretonhampstead or Teign Valley lines (unless they are joining the morning through trains from Totnes or Paignton to Moretonhampstead, which use one of the 'up' main platforms) the procedure is somewhat different: once they have purchased their tickets they have to walk back out to the station forecourt, turn right and continue round to the side of the building in order to gain access to a separate 320-feet long bay platform (platform 9), also constructed during the rebuilding work and where the facilities for passengers are limited to a brick-built waiting room.

Beyond the platforms and running lines are five carriage sidings, a 65-feet manually-operated turntable, a stone-built coal stage (43 x 22 feet), a massive 56,000-gallon water tank and the extensive motive power depot. This, with Newton Abbot being a divisional headquarters, is not only responsible for upwards of 80 engines of its own, but also for major repairs to most of the small engines in the divisional boundaries (an area from Taunton to Penzance) and for minor repairs to many of the larger engines. The depot itself (still gaslit!) consists, essentially, of a standard straight road shed – built of stone walls and with a 'northlight' pattern roof – measuring 180 x 150 feet

Two more views of Moretonhampstead-bound trains about to depart from platform 9 at Newton Abbot:–

Above: 2–6–2T No. 5533 on a fine summer's day in 1957.

Geoff Howells

Overleaf: 0–4–2T No. 1470 with its single autocoach on 14th February 1959.

E. R. Shepherd

(10 bays at 15 feet) and sporting six accommodation roads; a locomotive factory (310 x 140 feet), this being situated directly behind the shed and, similarly, built of stone walls, but with a conventional pitched roof divided into six bays; and an adjoining office block (90 x 30 feet). Amongst its other facilities, the station also boasts a large carriage & wagon works, located further to the south on its far side, and two significant, timber-framed, signal boxes – West, located directly opposite the carriage & wagon works and containing 153 levers, and East, located at the northern extremity of the station and containing 206 levers. Indeed, at the time of its construction during the station rebuild, East was the second largest manual box on the GWR system.

Finally, before we revert to the commencement of our journey, it is interesting to note that two of the large signal gantries that span the tracks around the station are still equipped with GWR 1922-pattern wooden experimental signal arms.

As our train eases out of its bay, heading northwards and running parallel to the 'up' main line, it almost immediately (and imperceptibly) passes over the Quay Road 'tunnel', before drawing alongside the extensive warehouse complex of Tucker's Maltings: this lies on the left-hand side of the line and backs on to the station from Teign Road. Soon, on the opposite side, the outline of the massive Newton Abbot East Signal Box comes into view and, as it does, so we reach the far end of the warehouses and part company with the 'up' main line by veering north-westwards on a curve of just 12 chains radius. Whilst negotiating this severe curve our train provides us with our first views of the River Teign, the famous racecourse beyond and, to our left, the power station of the C.E.G.B., with its huge cooling tower and twin chimneys. It also encounters two substantial bridges in quick succession. Both of them are over 150 feet in length, have three spans and consist of very large plate girder superstructures supported on piers and abutments of dressed limestone. Situated at 25½ chains and 31¾ chains respectively from the terminus, they carry the line over the River Lemon – just short of its confluence with the River Teign – and over the Whitelake, a man-made channel linking the now-disused Stover Canal with the Teign estuary. This channel, incidentally, was needed so that in times past ball clay from the Bovey Basin could be transported in barges all the way from the canal basin at Ventiford to the port of Teignmouth, although its original purpose had been to drain Jetty Marsh.

Between the two bridges – appropriately named Lemon Bridge and Whitelake Bridge – we have also just passed the point where a line veers off to the left and leads to the power station sidings on Devon Wharf. But now, just beyond the second bridge, where the route ahead straightens and our loco can enjoy the additional benefit of a falling gradient of 1 in 132, we are passing Newton Abbot goods depot, again situated on the left-hand side of the line. Opened for traffic on 10th May 1911, after having been moved from its original site in the vicinity of where our journey commenced, this is based around a very impressive-looking goods shed built of red brick, with a 'through' siding. The adjoining goods yard, still known as 'New Yard', is also a very spacious affair, and amongst its many facilities are nine lengthy sidings which extend almost to the foot of the southern embankment of the Kingsteignton Road Bridge.

Having passed the goods shed, coincidental with m.p. (milepost) ½, our train now goes under the central arch of the aforementioned bridge – an imposing five-span structure of dressed limestone (piers, abutments and wings) and granite (arches), built slightly askew to the railway. From here it immediately passes a facing connection giving access to a private siding equipped with a ground frame and an adjoining loading ramp. Opened for traffic on 21st April 1938, and owned by Newton Abbot Clays Ltd, this siding is used for the transportation of ball clay from the bleak expanse of East Gold Marshes, away to our right. Meanwhile, to our left, we are now lying almost parallel to the milky grey coloured waters of the Whitelake channel in Jetty Marsh, although a more attractive viewpoint is provided by the north-eastern slopes of the hill beyond, Knowles Hill, which is surmounted by scattered dwellings and tall, majestic fir trees. At this point the line is on the level and at its lowest altitude anywhere along the branch. But, after passing the first platelayers' hut on our journey only a moment or so later, and also m.p. ¾, it begins to rise at the rate of 1 in 100 on a gentle right-hand curve and continues on a steepening embankment until reaching two, almost adjoining, bridges associated with the Stover Canal. The first, a fine, single arch, masonry bridge at 69½ chains, carries the line over water flowing from a bywash above the upper of the two Jetty Marsh locks into the Whitelake, while the second, a 46-feet long plate girder bridge supported on dressed limestone abutments, carries it over the canal itself – directly above the remains of the lock just mentioned.

On the far side of the two bridges the line immediately starts to descend at the same rate until, just after crossing a stone drainage culvert and passing m.p. 1 in quick succession, it runs on the level once more. It is then that the Stover Canal appears almost right alongside the line, on the eastern side, and the two proceed to run parallel to one another for some considerable distance. It is also at this point that the line straightens and settles for a north by west direction before crossing another stone drainage culvert at 1 mile $16\frac{1}{2}$ chains and reaching m.p. $1\frac{1}{4}$. The scenery along this stretch is dull to the extreme and not helped by the line, now starting to rise on a very gentle gradient of 1 in 937, being 'hemmed in' on both sides by a liberal scattering of trees and brushwood. Indeed, such is the nature of this low-lying and marshy terrain that shortly after our train passes the 'down distant' signal for Teignbridge Crossing yet another stone drainage culvert is encountered, at 1 mile 34 chains. By now, though, the monotony has already been broken somewhat by a sharp blast from the loco's whistle announcing our impending arrival at Teignbridge, just beyond m.p. $1\frac{1}{2}$.

Here again, the presence of the local ball clay industry is all too evident: on either side of the running line is a siding with an adjoining clay loading ramp, while on the far side of the Stover Canal are the remains of a long terrace of stone-built clay cellars from the days when the clay was transported by water. These sidings are actually of different length, that on the eastern side of the line being the shorter and capable of accommodating only 20 wagons, compared to the 30 of its counterpart. It is also the older, having been opened to traffic in 1893 as the result of an Agreement made between the GWR and Mr William Herbert Whiteway-Wilkinson of Whiteway & Co. The second siding, on the other hand, had not been opened

The new clay loading ramp on the eastern side of the line at Teignbridge, as photographed in 1948.
Watts Blake Bearne & Company Plc

until 22nd January 1914, when it was needed to help cope with the increase in the amount of clay being produced in the area. Both of their adjoining loading ramps, however, are of much more modern date. This is because in 1947 the firm of Watts, Blake, Bearne & Co. had replaced the original ramp on the eastern side of the line in order to improve the facilities for transferring clay from lorries into wagons, and, for similar reasons, the other ramp had been reconstructed in 1950.

Immediately beyond the two loading ramps and sidings, which are controlled by ground frames, is Teignbridge Crossing, with its adjacent crossing-keeper's cottage, at 1 mile 50¾ chains. The cottage, a single-storey building with stone walls and a conventional pitched roof of grey slate, with plain ridge tiles, is situated on the western side of the line and, up until 1947, had been occupied by a resident crossing keeper. However, on 19th September

Watched by the crossing keeper, who had opened the gates only a few minutes earlier, 0–4–2T No. 1427 approaches Teignbridge Crossing with the 2.15 p.m. service from Newton Abbot to Moretonhampstead on 19th October 1957. The new clay loading ramp shown in the previous photograph can clearly be seen in the background, as can the huge cooling tower and twin chimneys of the C.E.G.B power station at Newton Abbot.

Peter W. Gray

of that year it had been condemned as unfit for habitation and, thereafter, restricted in its use to that of a 'cabin'. From here, apart from the obvious responsibility of opening and closing the single level-crossing gates on either side of Old Exeter Road, the crossing-keeper's duties include operating the levers for each of the 'distant' signals that guard the crossing from both directions and also the points at the northern end of the two sidings. These

Having safely negotiated the level crossing at Teignbridge, 2–6–2T No. 5570 continues its journey from Moretonhampstead to Newton Abbot with the daily goods train by proceeding past the remains of the stone-built clay cellars situated on the far side of the disused Stover Canal, 19th October 1957.

Peter W. Gray

levers, incidentally, are all contained within a small, adjoining wooden lever cabin adorned with a nameplate proclaiming it to be 'Teignbridge Crossing Box' and which also serves as a platelayers' hut.

Once over the level crossing, the views from our train change dramatically as we enter open countryside and are bounded on both sides by a vast expanse of wet grassland, dotted with trees and very susceptible to flooding. The overgrown depression of the disused Stover Canal, which still lies immediately to the eastern side of the line, is now also clearly visible, while in the distance fleeting glimpses are to be had of the River Teign as it nears the end of its tortuous journey to the sea. Away to the south, added variety to the landscape is provided by the lush-green slopes of the hills around Highweek, where the 15th century parish church of All Saints is etched against the sky. At this point the line is running on a slightly stiffer gradient of 1 in 513 and on a very gentle curve towards the north-west. In so doing it crosses a small plate girder bridge at 1 mile $55\frac{1}{2}$ chains, under which water flows from the upper bywash for Teignbridge Lock, and continues on past m.p. $1\frac{3}{4}$ towards another such bridge at 1 mile $74\frac{3}{4}$ chains. Once again, this carries the line over water flowing from a bywash for one of the canal's locks, Graving Dock Lock, and just beyond it both the rear of the 'up distant' signal for Teignbridge Crossing and m.p. 2 are passed in quick succession. It is also in this vicinity that the gradient steepens to 1 in 100 and the grey, squat tower of the parish church of St Peter and St Paul, Teigngrace, comes into view. Unlike the other church that we have just seen, this one is of more modern date and was, in fact, designed and built in the late 1780s by James Templer II (and his two brothers) – the same person responsible for the construction of the Stover Canal only a few years later.

Our train is now only a short distance away from its first stopping point on the branch, Teigngrace Halt. Just before reaching it, however, a stone drainage culvert is encountered at 2 miles 7 chains and this marks the spot where another sharp blast from the loco's whistle is needed, as immediately beyond m.p. 2¼ there is an 'accommodation' crossing where a small trackway from the village bisects the line. Situated there are two stone buildings, one on either side of the running line, which are associated with the adjacent Stover Canal and were once used in connection with barge building and repair work.

With the line now on a gentle right-hand curve, and running on the level once more, it is only a matter of seconds before we are drawing alongside Teigngrace Halt, at 2 miles 28 chains, and stopping for a couple of passengers. At one time this was the first intermediate station on the branch, having been opened as such on 16th December 1867. But, with only modest goods traffic and passenger numbers – never very high in this rather isolated location – steadily declining from around the early 1920s, all that had changed. First, on 9th May 1925, Teigngrace had lost its own stationmaster when the post was amalgamated with Heathfield. Then, on 8th May 1939, it

Teigngrace Halt lies deserted as 0–4–2T No. 1427 arrives there with a Moretonhampstead-bound train on a warm summer's day in 1957.

Geoff Howells

Two contrasting views of Teigngrace Halt, looking northwards:–
Above: A photograph taken on 15th June 1950 from the eastern side of the line.

E. R. Shepherd

Below: A later photograph, taken on 13th July 1957 from the southern end of the platform.

D. Cullum

had become totally unstaffed and the word 'Halt' added to the existing station nameboard. At this point it is worth recalling that, in its 'heyday', Teigngrace had been fully signalled and even boasted its own little wooden signal box, with an 11-lever frame. That, though, had been only a short-lived situation, as with the advent of the electric train staff system of signalling in November 1901 all the signals were removed. It is also worth mentioning that in part, at least, the station had only come about because of a gesture on the part of the Moretonhampstead & South Devon Railway Company to the then Duke of Somerset of nearby Stover House, who, as a condition of selling land required by the company for the branch, had acquired the right to stop any train at Teigngrace on which he wished to travel!

To return to the date of our journey, the halt consists of a 252-feet long single platform on the western side of the line constructed of stone filling partly faced with brick. The covering, now partially masked by weeds and grass following years of neglect, is of brick at the front of the 'station' building and loose stone chippings edged, mainly, with concrete slabs with rounded shoulders on the lineside. It is backed by wooden palings or, at least, where these have not had to be replaced by wire fencing, and is accessed, towards its northern end, from an attractive tree-lined avenue leading off the byroad that serves the village. In earlier days the platform was illuminated by ornate glass lanterns containing oil lamps, but at around the time that the station was reduced to a halt these had been removed and superseded by hurricane lamps during the hours of darkness – and usually only one at that! Gone, too, are the attractive summertime floral displays of pre-World War II days, along with the hitherto well-kept station garden.

The 'station' building is situated a little to the north of a cast iron nameboard mounted on two short lengths of old rails and with an adjacent iron post from which a hurricane lamp can be hung. It is constructed of red brick and has a chimney protruding from a conventional pitched roof of grey slate, with plain ridge tiles. However, the only part of the building still in use is its integral, open-fronted waiting area, as the ticket/parcels office and toilets situated on either side had both been closed in 1939. This recess, apart from providing shelter for waiting passengers, is used for the posting of timetables and has a hooked bracket above its entrance from which another hurricane lamp can be hung.

Just beyond the platform, to the north, there is a timber-built platelayers' hut and also a facing connection giving access to a siding which has a short, southerly, spur and is capable of accommodating 12 wagons. Despite having been equipped with a new loading ramp in 1947 so that ball clay and other minerals from the nearby Stover Estate could be transferred from lorries into wagons, however, it appears never to have had a great deal of use. The points for it are operated from an open two-lever ground frame situated partway down the nearby platform ramp, and the siding itself, which dates back to 1872, lies on the western side of the line.

With the two new passengers safely aboard one of the autocoaches, and the 'right away' given by the guard, the driver once more releases the

In this view of 0–4–2T No. 1466 at Teigngrace Halt on 21st February 1959, the guard has just hung a hurricane lamp above the entrance to the recessed waiting area of the 'station' building as this, the 5.10 p.m. service from Moretonhampstead to Newton Abbot, will be the last train of the day before darkness descends.

Peter W. Gray

regulator and our little train lurches forward to continue the journey. The line ahead is now straight and still running on the level but, in the vicinity of m.p. $2\frac{1}{2}$ and the first of two stone drainage culverts that follow shortly afterwards, it begins to rise at the rate of 1 in 98 on a steepening embankment. This, in turn, leads to the scattered little hamlet of Ventiford and to two, almost identical, plate girder bridges with granite abutments. The first of these, at 2 miles $56\frac{3}{4}$ chains, carries the line over a farm track and the Ventiford Brook (a one-time feeder of the Stover Canal, which runs down from Stover Lake and now on into the nearby Teign), while the second, just beyond m.p. $2\frac{3}{4}$ and another stone drainage culvert, crosses a lane leading to some rather isolated cottages and Brock's Farm. It is the first bridge, however, that is of particular interest, for this lies adjacent to the now-overgrown upper terminus of the Stover Canal and denotes the approximate spot at which the unique, 8-mile long, Haytor Granite Tramway terminated. Completed in 1820 by George Templer (the son of James Templer II), after he had secured a contract for the supply of granite for use in the construction of London Bridge, this tramway had been used as a means of transporting the required material from quarries high up on Haytor Down to Ventiford. Here, it had then been transferred, by crane, from open, flat-topped, horse-drawn wagons to canal barges and taken to the port of Teignmouth, prior to being transported in sea-going vessels to its final destination. Unfortunately, there is now little evidence to show that such activity ever took place here, for this part of the tramway lies beneath the railway embankment and all of the buildings associated with the canal, which included clay cellars, have either long since been demolished or are ruinous. However, apart from the canal basin itself, the remains of the crane base are still partly visible and the house on the western side of the bridge, besides being an inn at that time, the Union Inn, was a smithy, where, it is believed, horses employed on the tramway were shod.

Continuing onwards, the line, already veering gently around to the north-west and now running on the level for a short distance, next passes the rear of Ley Green Farm (on the western side) and enters the solitary confines of Summerlane Copse. In so doing it also passes the site where Messrs Brassey & Ogilvie had a temporary yard and an array of workshops from which they manufactured much of the plant needed for the construction of the line in the 1860s. Hereafter the line starts to rise again on a gradient of 1 in 70, re-emerges from the trees and begins to curve around more towards the north. It then proceeds past m.p. 3, goes under the sturdy, granite-built, Summer Lane Bridge and immediately enters a shallow, tree-lined, clay cutting, where our train encounters a platelayers' hut, the 'down fixed distant' signal for Heathfield Station and m.p. 3¼, all in quick succession. It is whilst our train is still negotiating this cutting that the line starts to run on the level once more, before again altering course towards the north-west and continuing over a low embankment bounded, on both sides, by a combination of rather featureless pastureland and scrubland. Here also are two stone culverts that pass under the railway at a very acute angle. One is again for drainage purposes, but the furthermost houses two, large-diameter, cast-iron pipes which carry water from the Hennock reservoirs, high up in the hills to the north, to Torquay.

At the far end of the embankment the line passes under the Shilston Lane Bridge, which is almost an exact replica of the one previously encountered, and enters an extensive area of flat woodland, comprising Lower Brock's Plantation (to the right) and Higher Brock's Plantation (to the left). From this point, apart from minor deviations, the line follows the same route as that of the former Haytor Granite Tramway for the next 1½ miles or so, rising, in the first instance, at the rate of 1 in 172 until, just beyond m.p. 3½, when the ruling gradient becomes 1 in 2,024. It is then that our train passes the 'down main home' signal for Heathfield, a facing connection giving access to Timber Siding (now a private clay siding), the pointwork that marks the commencement of the double track section through the station and the rear of the 'up main advanced starting' signal. This, in turn, is followed on a short, gentle left-hand curve by m.p. 3¾, the 'down main intermediate home/down main to Candy's Siding' signals and the 'trailing' north end connection with the clay siding. Finally, as our train enters the station, it goes under the A38 road between Plymouth and Exeter by means of a substantial, granite-built,

Two photographs taken from the A38 overbridge at Heathfield on 11th July 1957:–
Above: The view south-eastwards showing Timber Siding, with its clay loading ramps, and the running line curving away towards Teigngrace between Lower Brock's Plantation (left) and Higher Brock's Plantation (right).
Below: The view north-westwards showing, in the foreground, the main station building and goods lock-up, and also the siding leading into the factory of Candy & Co.

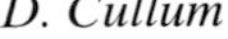

D. Cullum

A view of the main station building and goods lock-up at Heathfield from the 'down' platform, as 0–4–2T No. 1466 arrives with a train from Newton Abbot on 20th September 1955.

Courtesy of Peter W. Gray

bridge and passes both the facing connection for Candy's Siding and the rear of the 'up main starting' signal, before drawing to a halt adjacent to the 'down main inner home/down main to up branch inner home' signals on the 'down' platform.

Heathfield, at 3 miles 70 chains, is a fairly complex and, at times, quite a busy little station because, in addition to being the first crossing place on the branch, it is the junction for the Teign Valley Railway. It is also a somewhat unusual station inasmuch as the layout, as at the date of our journey, is the result of progressive modifications carried out down through the years, which are described in the next chapter. However, it needs to be mentioned here that of these, some of the most significant had been carried out in June 1927, for it was then that Heathfield had first become a crossing place for two passenger trains and the 'down' platform, at which we have just arrived, had been constructed. The platform itself is 320 feet long and 12 feet wide, it is backed by a wire fence supported by concrete posts and has a finished surface of tarmac chippings edged with granite slabs with rounded shoulders on the lineside. The only facilities for passengers using it, though, are a small, round-topped, waiting shelter of corrugated iron, which is situated at about the midway point, and a timber foot crossing; this provides access to and from the 'up' platform and lies at the base of the ramp at the northern end.

The 'up' platform, whilst bearing a strong resemblance to its 'down' counterpart as regards construction, except for the surface in front of the main station building being partly paved, is both longer and, for the major part, at least twice as wide (25 feet). This is because it incorporates a 270-feet long

A mid-morning scene at Heathfield on 7th July 1956. The crew of BR standard class 3 2–6–2T No. 82001, which has arrived with the 10.15 a.m. train from Moretonhampstead, are enjoying a brief rest before continuing the journey to Newton Abbot, while 0–4–2T No. 1427 is about to depart from the 'down' platform with the 10.32 a.m. service from Newton Abbot to Moretonhamptead and 0–6–0PT No. 5412 is waiting in the bay platform for the 10.50 a.m. departure to Exeter via the Teign Valley.

Peter W. Gray

bay platform on its eastern side for the Teign Valley trains and commences at a point adjacent to the A38 road bridge, giving it a total length of 413 feet. Here, set back only a relatively short distance from the bridge, are two buildings in very close proximity: the first is the main station building, complete with a canopy and an adjoining wing on either side, while the second is the goods lock-up. In both instances they are constructed of horizontal timber planking under a conventional pitched roof of grey slate (as are the two wings, which serve as the gents' toilet and a store/parcels room respectively), but immediately differ by the main station building having a brick-built chimney at either end of its roof. Apart from the lack of any chimneys, the goods lock-up also has no windows, but it is equipped with a sliding door on the platform side and another at the rear in order to facilitate the transfer of goods to and from road vehicles.

Further along the platform, at about the midway point, stands the station nameboard – proudly proclaiming Heathfield to be the junction for Chudleigh, Trusham, Ashton, Christow, Longdown, Ide and Exeter – while at the far, northern end, adjacent to the timber foot crossing, is the signal box. Appropriately, this is built of the buff-coloured bricks produced at the

Two more scenes at Heathfield, during the summer of 1957:–
Above: A busy moment on 10th June following the arrival of 2–6–2T No. 4145 with the 10.15 a.m. train from Moretonhampstead to Newton Abbot and 2–6–2T No. 4568 with the 10.5 a.m. through working from Paignton to Moretonhampstead. As can be seen, several passengers are now making their way towards the connecting Teign Valley train waiting in the bay platform and in the charge of 0–4–2T No. 1450.

E. R. Shepherd

Below: A somewhat quieter occasion as 0–4–2T No. 1427 waits at the 'up' platform whilst on a routine service between Moretonhampstead and Newton Abbot.

Geoff Howells

adjoining factory of Candy & Co., has a hipped roof of grey slate and contains 58 levers.

Having arrived at Heathfield, where the local landscape is dominated by the immense chimneys of Candy's factory, our driver is unable to proceed until he has received the 'electric train token' (or key token) for the next section of the single line branch – Heathfield to Bovey. This is necessary to ensure that only one train is in the section at a time and involves our fireman relinquishing the key token for the Newton Abbot to Heathfield section to the signalman and, in return, receiving the key token for the section ahead. At times this can mean a delay of several minutes until an 'up' train has arrived at Heathfield, but on this occasion the section ahead is unoccupied. So, with the 'down main starting' signal in the 'off' position, and the 'right away' given by the guard (which is acknowledged by a blast from the whistle), our train gently eases away from the platform, passes the signal box, with its adjoining foot crossing, and proceeds over the junction for the Teign Valley trains. This is followed by m.p. 4, the 'down main starting' signal and the points at the northern end of the 'down' loop, where our train rejoins the single line track by the 'up main home' signal. In so doing, it now starts to gather speed and soon encounters a wooden footbridge, which is situated near the southern end of quite a long row of brick-built terraced houses. Known as Heathfield Cottages, these houses had been constructed in the late 1800s by Candy & Co. for some of their employees, while the bridge, together with a footpath lying just beyond the western boundary of the railway line, is there to provide a means of access to the factory.

Continuing in a north-westerly direction, and still gathering speed on a rising gradient of 1 in 462, our train next passes the 'down main advanced starting' signal. It then proceeds past m.p. 4¼, and the stop blocks at the end of the goods siding, at the start of a gentle right-hand curve, before going under the central span of a fine, three-arched, granite-built bridge that carries the minor road to Little Bovey over the line. From here the route ahead lies across the open, mainly gorse-covered, expanse of Bovey Heath, which, initially, involves crossing over two small stone drainage culverts and tackling a rising gradient of 1 in 69 on a low embankment. As it continues on this embankment, the line also changes direction again and passes m.p. 4½, with its accompanying platelayers' hut, on a gentle left-hand curve. At this stage of our journey, where our view northwards extends to the distant rolling hills above Bovey Tracey and away towards Hennock, our train is still climbing at the rate of 1 in 69. However, soon afterwards the embankment is replaced by a shallow cutting and it is here, on the eastern flanks of White Hill, that the line reaches its highest point along this particular section. As an aside, White Hill carries some significance for being the site of a battle during the latter stages of the English Civil War. This had taken place on 9th January 1646 and resulted in the Parliamentarians, under the leadership of Lieutenant Oliver Cromwell, achieving an overwhelming victory over Lord Wentworth's troops, who were killed, captured or left fleeing for their lives.

By the time that our train emerges from the cutting below the summit of

A view of the open, mainly gorse-covered, expanse of Bovey Heath, showing 0–4–2T No. 1466 tackling the 1 in 69 gradient on the eastern flanks of White Hill with the 4.25 p.m. auto train from Newton Abbot on 26th February 1959. The tall chimneys in the background, to the right of the picture, are those of Candy's factory at Heathfield.

Peter W. Gray

White Hill the rear of the 'up fixed distant' signal for Heathfield and m.p. $4^3/_4$ have been passed in quick succession, and the line is on a falling gradient of 1 in 72. It has also straightened somewhat and is now bounded, on both sides, by tall pine and silver birch trees in what is quite a picturesque setting. As our train continues through this little wooded area, where the line starts to run on the level once more, on a low embankment, m.p. 5 is passed and this is followed, shortly afterwards, by a stone culvert carrying a minor tributary of the nearby River Bovey under the line and also by the facing connection for the now-disused Granite Siding – the point at which the route of the Haytor Granite Tramway diverges away to the west. Situated on the southern side of the line, this siding, together with an adjoining loading platform at its western end, had originally been provided by the Moretonhampstead & South Devon Railway Company as a condition of acquiring the lower section of the Haytor Granite Tramway from the Duke of Somerset for part of its railway. At around that time he had insisted that the siding was needed so that granite quarried on Haytor Down could still be transported out of the area, using the surviving section of the tramway for the initial stage of the journey. However, whilst production at the quarries was destined to continue for

Above: The rather picturesque setting near m.p. 4¾, as 0–6–0PT No. 3796 runs between the tall pine trees with the returning Moretonhampstead goods train on 27th February 1959. *Peter W. Gray*

Below: The somewhat overgrown Granite Siding and, in the distance, the eastern side of the double-arched Pottery Bridge. *M. C. Ewans*

another 50 years or so, it tended to be spasmodic and no evidence exists to suggest that the original purpose of Granite Siding was ever fulfilled. Instead, the siding had eventually been brought into use almost exclusively as a coal distribution point, both for the Bovey Gas Works (operational between 1884 and the late 1930s) and the local potteries. It had then continued as such until a few years before the date of our journey, when the coal assignments required by the potteries began arriving by road.

After running parallel to Granite Siding (about 300 feet in length), where the line starts to rise again at the rate of 1 in 69, our train next goes under the A382 road from Newton Abbot by passing through the southern span of Pottery Bridge, a substantial double-arched, oblique, structure of limestone, with brick spiral arches. It then immediately encounters a platelayers' hut and the facing connection to another siding, again on the southern side of the line. Situated directly opposite m.p. 5¹/₄, and known as Pottery Siding, this had originally been installed shortly after the previous siding for Messrs Divett, Buller and Company (the then owners of Bovey Pottery) as a means of despatching finished earthenware products direct from the pottery. However, due to a combination of a shift of emphasis towards road transportation and falling demand for these products from around the late 1940s, the siding has now virtually fallen into disuse. The points for it are operated by a two-lever

A fine overhead view of Bovey Pottery looking towards Pottery Bridge and the A382 road from Newton Abbot. Unfortunately, when this photograph was taken in the 1960s the siding into the pottery had been lifted and the pottery itself closed.

Courtesy of Claude & Margaret Steer

Two photographs of Brimley Halt taken on 31st January 1959:–
Above: The view southwards from the adjoining road bridge.
Below: The view northwards from the western side of the line.

E. R. Shepherd

ground frame housed in a small, timber-built 'cabin', the same arrangement as for Granite Siding.

Whilst passing the pottery, with its vast array of buildings and kilns, the view from our train westwards momentarily extends to the foothills of south-eastern Dartmoor, and almost to the well-known Haytor Rocks, situated some 1,500 feet above sea level. A few seconds later, however, the open aspect disappears as our train, now tackling an even stiffer gradient of 1 in 53, enters the first significant cutting along the branch. With the cutting still deepening, and the line starting to veer around to the north, m.p. 5½ and the 'down fixed distant' signal for Bovey Station are passed in quick succession. Then, almost before realising it because of being hidden from view until the last moment by the curvature of the line, our next stopping point, Brimley Halt, is reached at 5 miles 46 chains.

In common with many others provided throughout the GWR system, Brimley Halt had been opened (on 21st May 1928) in a bid to stem increasing road competition and on the basis that there would be sufficient passengers to make it viable. It consists of quite a substantially-built platform on the eastern side of the line, which is faced with stone blocks and has a covering of rolled stone chippings edged with concrete slabs throughout its entire length – a little over 100 feet. On the platform is a nameboard, an open-fronted waiting shelter built of horizontal timber planking under a sloping corrugated iron roof, two bench-type seats (one more or less at either end) and two

Another photograph taken at Brimley Halt on 31st January 1959 showing 2–6–2T No. 5183 accelerating away towards Newton Abbot with the 10.15 a.m. service from Moretonhampstead.

E. R. Shepherd

cylindrical metal posts with a hook near the top of each on which a hurricane lamp can be hung. These posts are again situated on either side of the waiting shelter, next to the seats, and the northernmost also lies at the bottom of a sloping cinder path that descends from the sole access gate. This, in turn, lies just beyond the eastern side of the nearby Ashburton Road Bridge and beside one of the perimeter walls to Bovey Tracey's recreation ground.

Leaving Brimley Halt, our train now passes under the aforementioned bridge, which is a single-arched, granite-built structure, and quickly gathers speed on a falling gradient of 1 in 66. The cutting at this point is at its deepest, but hereafter it gradually subsides until, just beyond a modern prefabricated concrete platelayers' hut on the eastern side of the line, it gives

0–4–2T No. 1439, in charge of the 10.5 a.m. through working from Paignton, runs down the 1 in 66 gradient towards Bovey on 30th August 1954, having just passed the modern prefabricated concrete platelayers' hut on the eastern side of the line.

R. C. Riley

way to a low embankment. In so doing, the views from our train are instantly transformed and the line becomes bounded, on both sides, by lush green fields. Beyond them, to the west and north-west, are vast areas of open countryside and woodland, where the foothills of Dartmoor form the backcloth, whilst on the opposite side nearly the whole of Bovey Tracey lies before us, part of it rising away towards the north-east before giving way to more pastureland and wooded hilltops. Our train, meanwhile, is making steady progress over what has now become a straight section of track, and,

The approach to Bovey Station from the direction of Newton Abbot c.1952. Note the station garden to the right.

Arthur Yendall

besides passing m.p. $5^3/_4$, is soon negotiating an accommodation crossing for pedestrians and farm vehicles going between Challabrook and the nearby market town. At this same spot a tributary of the River Bovey also flows under the line, through a stone culvert, and not far beyond it a small stream does likewise. By this stage the line is running on the level once more and our train is fast approaching Bovey Station, which it enters after passing a row of houses known as Blenheim Terrace and the 'down home' signal bracket (both situated on the western side of the line), and proceeding across the road to Haytor and Manaton by means of a level crossing. Once inside the station confines it immediately passes m.p. 6, as well as the wooden 'cabin' containing the two-lever ground frame for controlling the crossing. It then continues over the pointwork at the commencement of the double section of track that runs through the station until arriving adjacent to the 'up' platform, having by now also passed the rear of the 'up starting' signal.

Two general views of Bovey Station:–
Above: Looking towards Newton Abbot in the summer of 1957.

Geoff Howells

Below: Looking towards Lustleigh on 28th February 1959.

Peter F. Bowles

Always known simply as Bovey, as opposed to the town's full name of Bovey Tracey, the station (at 6 miles 6 chains) is very picturesque and well maintained, with floral displays, some in hanging baskets below the canopy, and a rose garden – just inside the level crossing and wicket gates on the eastern side of the line – adding to its overall charm. There are two platforms, both 300 feet long, although the 'down' platform is normally used only if a goods or passenger train from the Moretonhampstead direction is being crossed. It is connected to the 'up' platform by a timber foot crossing similar to the arrangement at Heathfield, except for being located at the southern end of the platform ramps, and has a finished surface of tarmac chippings edged with concrete slabs with rounded shoulders on the lineside. Throughout most of its length the facing is of granite, but when the platform had been extended in the 1890s the additional 110 feet was faced with bricks supplied by Candy & Co. At about the midway point stands one of the two station nameboards,

The rear of the main station building at Bovey.

Authors' Collection

together with a tall concrete post from which an oil lamp can be hung, while just beyond it is an open-fronted waiting shelter, again built of bricks supplied by Candy & Co., and equipped with seating and a hearth. This has a pitched roof of grey slate, with plain ridge tiles, that extends towards the lineside in order to provide extra protection from the elements, and a single chimney of matching Candy brick. A flat-roofed extension at the northern end of the building once served as the gents' toilet, but this had been sealed off in the 1930s. Finally, beyond this point the rear of the platform has a white-painted, wooden fence of four-feet high slats, their tops cut to an apex, which is in complete contrast to the southern side of the waiting room, where the platform is backed by a natural hedge.

The main station building is situated at the southern end of the 'up' platform, immediately beyond a round-topped, corrugated iron, store that had originated as a waiting shelter for bus passengers taking day trips across Dartmoor during the 1920s and 1930s. It is constructed in a most attractive manner of partly dressed granite blocks and, apart from the wings at either end, which are both flat-roofed, has a conventional pitched roof of grey slate, with plain ridge tiles, and two squat chimneys; unusually, these are octagonal in shape and immediately differ from one another inasmuch as the chimney at the southern end has only one flue compared to the two of its more northern counterpart. On the platform side, the building's many interesting features include arched window recesses, a doorway (also arched) in the Gothic style and a wide, timber canopy supported by six ornamental wrought iron wall brackets, while, at the rear, part of the roof extends outwards in a similar manner to that of the waiting shelter on the 'down' platform. This, in turn, provides a small porchway, or canopy, shielding two of the five arched windows on this side of the building and also the entrance doorway (again in the Gothic style) which leads into the booking hall and general waiting room, the station office, parcels room and ladies' toilet. The gents' toilet, on the other hand, is situated in the northern wing and can only be reached from the platform by entering a prefabricated concrete lean-to with a sloping corrugated roof.

The goods shed, situated a little to the north of the main station building, is a substantial structure built in a similar manner. Its walls, however, consist of a smaller proportion of granite and more grey and brown shillet, the roof is of corrugated iron and it has only one chimney; this protrudes from near the south-eastern corner of the roof. There are three large openings provided with heavy wooden sliding doors, one at either end and another on the eastern side, and three windows. Two of these, both with arched recesses, are on the platform side to give added light inside the shed when the doors are closed, and the third is to be found at the southern end to allow light into the office of the goods clerk, where there is also a hearth. Inside the shed, apart from this office, is a wide, full-length loading platform served by a goods siding (this terminates by a multi-purpose loading dock situated immediately beyond the southern end of the shed), a two-ton crane and, lastly, a goods loading bay for road traffic, which is accessed from the adjoining station yard.

The yard itself is quite a spacious affair and is served by a second goods siding. Known as 'Back Siding', this is connected to the other by facing points near the permanent way department and sleeper-built coal store at the northern end of the station site. From there, it continues past the station's platform-mounted four-ton crane, which is used for transferring timber and other heavy items between road vehicles and railway wagons, runs alongside the premises of R. E. Glanville & Son (a firm of agricultural merchants and engineers) and terminates just short of Station Road by the premises of another firm using the railway, Wyatt & Bruce (grain millers and seedsmen).

Returning now to the 'up' platform (constructed to the same specification as that of the original part of the 'down', except for the finished surface being of paving stones around the front of the main station building), the northernmost structure is the 17-lever frame signal box. This is situated next

Above: Another view of the station, this time from the driver's vestibule of W241W as it is being propelled into Bovey by 0–4–2T No. 1466 on the 1.35 p.m. service from Moretonhampstead, 19th February 1959.
Below: The same train leaving Bovey for Newton Abbot a few minutes later.

Peter W. Gray

Above: 0–4–2T No. 1427 brings its Moretonhampstead-bound train over the level crossing into Bovey on a routine service during the summer of 1957.

Geoff Howells

Below: BR standard class 3 2–6–2T No. 82034 pauses at Bovey with the 5.15 p.m. train from Moretonhampstead to Newton Abbot on 14th August 1956.

Hugh Ballantyne

Above: The Bovey signalman exchanges single line tablets with the fireman of Prairie tank No. 5183 on the 9.20 a.m. service from Newton Abbot to Moretonhampstead, 26th February 1959.
Below: The same train on the 10.15 a.m. return working from Moretonhampstead, now seen leaving Bovey, sending a column of condensing steam high into the branches of the avenue of trees which flanks the 'down' platform.

Peter W. Gray

Above: Southbrook House.
Below: Southbrook Bridge and a short section of the line running north-westwards through Parke Wood.

Peter George, Southbrook House

to the goods shed and is built mainly of timber under a pitched roof covered with slate and finished with ridge tiles. The rear wall, however, is of brick, as are parts of the end elevations and also its tall chimney stack which protrudes from near the south-eastern corner of the roof. All-round vision, apart from the rear, of course, is accomplished by multi-panelled sliding windows that run the whole length of the western (platform) side and by further windows at either end; the latter are completed to the apex with lateral wooden planking. At the northern end there is a partly glaze-panelled wooden door and a step, and at the front, below the sliding windows, is a standard GWR cast-iron nameplate.

Beyond the signal box, the rest of the platform is backed by a white-painted, wooden fence in like manner to that on part of the 'down' platform. This same type of fencing has also been used to bridge the gap between the main station building and the goods shed, where a gated recess leads down to the loading dock in the goods yard. Here also stands the other station nameboard and another tall concrete post from which an oil lamp can be hung.

Our train has now been standing at the 'up' platform for about a minute, during which time some passengers have alighted and others climbed aboard. A further exchange of key tokens between the fireman and the signalman has also taken place, so that our driver can enter the Bovey to Moretonhampstead section. The guard, meanwhile, is now busy ensuring that all the doors of the two autocoaches are closed, but moments later, with the 'down starting' signal having dropped, he finally gives the 'right away' once more. We are then on the move, almost immediately clearing the points into the two goods sidings and crossing over the Mill Leat, which runs under the double section of track through a stone culvert. With the line already starting to sweep gently around to the north-west, the pointwork at the recommencement of the single line track is next encountered, and just beyond this the 'up home' signal guarding the approach to the station from the Moretonhampstead direction is passed, viewed from the rear. The line at this point is still on the level but, as the 'down advanced starting' signal and m.p. 6¼ are approached, it begins to rise at the rate of 1 in 61 on a low embankment, before proceeding over the River Bovey by means of a substantial oblique granite bridge of elliptical form, the arch of which is built in spiral courses.

On the far side of the bridge the line continues to curve around to the north-west on an embankment until just beyond an accommodation crossing, when it suddenly dives into a shillet cutting at Staddon's Hill. Although quite deep, this cutting is also relatively short and soon gives way to another embankment that carries the line past Southbrook, with its picturesque and richly-wooded little dell. At the same time the line also crosses a minor tributary of the nearby River Bovey, which runs through a brick-built culvert at this point, as well as a granite-built bridge over the trackway connecting Southbrook Farm to Parke House – the ancestral home of the Hole family, who had been heavily involved in the original promotion of the railway. Even before we can fully appreciate the views here, however, the line, having now straightened, plunges into a second shillet cutting immediately beyond m.p. 6½ and then enters an extensive area of attractive woodland, consisting, predominantly, of oak trees and known as Parke Wood. Continuing in this most tranquil of settings, where cuttings are constantly being interspersed by embankments due to the undulating nature of the land hereabouts, the line starts to run on the level once more and soon leads our train past the rear of the 'up fixed distant' signal for Bovey. This, in turn, is quickly followed by m.p. 6¾ and the first of two accommodation crossings in close proximity, which are there to allow the local farmer access through the woodland on either side of the line and to his fields beyond. It is also in this vicinity that the line rises again at the rate of 1 in 66 and continues as such for the next quarter of a mile, during the course of which it starts to deviate towards the north and enters one of the deeper cuttings along this stretch. In so doing our train then encounters a platelayers' hut and m.p. 7, before passing under a granite-built accommodation bridge, known as Harris's Bridge, on the level.

Approaching m.p. 7¼ and an old masonry platelayers' hut, the line not only starts to climb again – at the rate of 1 in 67 – but also begins to change direction once more at the commencement of quite a long left-hand curve. This, in turn, soon leads to Wilford Bridge, which consists of a plate girder

A scene captured at m.p. 7¼ in the woods between Bovey and Pullabrook Halt, opposite an old masonry platelayers' hut, almost certainly dating from the opening of the line in 1866. The train is the 4.25 p.m. departure from Newton Abbot on 27th February 1959.

Peter W. Gray

Two photographs of the picturesque countryside around Wilford Bridge, showing *(above)* 0–4–2T No. 1466 on 4th August 1955 with the 11.35 a.m. train from Moretonhampstead to Newton Abbot and *(below)* the same service some two years later, on 9th July 1957.

D. Cullum

superstructure supported on granite abutments and passes over one of several lanes that meet in the vicinity. After crossing this bridge, the line then almost immediately enters another of the numerous cuttings being encountered and runs along the side of a very steep hill from where, down below us to our left, we can enjoy fleeting glimpses of the River Bovey and the adjoining countryside – a combination of fields and scattered woodlands. In addition, a little lane leading to Lustleigh can be seen running below and parallel to the line at this point. However, just beyond m.p. 7½, where a gradient of 1 in 311 commences over the Yeo embankment, the lane suddenly swings to the right and passes beneath the railway through a very oblique granite-built bridge, with a spiral arch and sprawling wings. Known as Yeo Bridge, this also marks the spot at which the long curve towards the west finally comes to an end. Almost immediately, though, this is followed by a gentle right-hand curve that continues over the remainder of the Yeo embankment and on into the Yeo cutting, wherein lies m.p. 7¾, our next stopping point (the recently renamed Pullabrook Halt) and, just beforehand, the site of Yeo Farm – a casualty of the railway due to the lie of the land and extremely hard nature of the rock in this locality rendering it impossible to make a deviation.

Situated in a rather secluded spot at 7 miles 61 chains, Pullabrook Halt dates back to 1st June 1931 and had been opened by the GWR partly for the

Viewed from the south-east, 0–4–2T No. 1466 propels the 3.15 p.m. auto train from Moretonhampstead towards m.p. 7¾ and out of Pullabrook Halt on 3rd January 1959.

Peter W. Gray

Hawkmoor Halt *(above)* which, on 13th June 1955, was renamed Pullabrook Halt *(below)*. The two photographs were taken on 10th October 1950 and 2nd May 1956 respectively.

E. R. Shepherd

Two views from the north-western side of Pullabrook Halt:–

Above: 0–4–2T No. 1427 calls briefly at the halt on a summer service to Moretonhampstead in 1957. *Geoff Howells*

Below: 0–4–2T No. 1466, also bound for Moretonhampstead, seen making a somewhat dramatic start on 31st January 1959. *E. R. Shepherd*

benefit of moorland walkers and for visitors to patients at Hawkmoor Hospital (a sanatorium for sufferers of tuberculosis) and partly to appease one of its directors, who lived in the nearby settlement known as Lower Knowle. At that time it was called Hawkmoor Halt, but on 13th June 1955 the name was changed to Pullabrook – derived from a farm and a wood situated a little over a quarter of a mile away to the south and west respectively. Almost certainly following complaints, this had been done to avoid confusion amongst the visitors to patients at Hawkmoor Hospital, who assumed that the halt was situated close to the hospital only to discover that it was about two miles away, along winding country lanes! The halt itself consists of a single platform on the western side of the line, which is almost exactly 80 feet long and constructed in like manner to that at Brimley Halt except for being faced with wooden sleepers instead of stone blocks and the surface being edged with boards rather than concrete slabs. It is backed by a low grassy bank which has been cut away at the southern end to accommodate a timber-built waiting shelter (virtually identical to that at Brimley Halt), and at the top of this bank is a wire boundary fence with wooden posts. At about the midway point of the platform, next to the waiting shelter, stands the usual GWR–type nameboard, and just beyond it is a small wooden bench, the two separated by a metal post from which a hurricane lamp can be hung. Another such post also stands at the base of the northern platform

A view just beyond Pullabrook Halt looking north-westwards towards Letford Bridge, as 0–4–2T No. 1466 continues its journey to Moreton-hampstead with the 10.30 a.m. train from Newton Abbot on 4th August 1955.
D. Cullum

The Moretonhampstead branch in all its glory, as captured by this superb view of 0–4–2T No. 1466 approaching Letford Bridge with the 12.50 p.m. departure from Newton Abbot on 21st February 1959. The waiting shelter at Pullabrook Halt can just be seen to the extreme right of the picture, and the houses are those comprising Lower Knowle.

Peter W. Gray

ramp, from where a wire fence with concrete posts runs between the railway line and a footpath for a distance of approximately 85 feet. Depending on their destinations, passengers can, at the far end of this fence, either climb a stile and continue along a footpath behind the halt that leads down to the lane at Yeo Bridge, or proceed over the line by means of a wooden foot crossing and walk up to an iron gateway built into the side of the lane at Lower Knowle.

On leaving Pullabrook Halt, where, on this trip, no-one boards or alights from our train, the line immediately starts to rise at the rate of 1 in 53 on a steepening embankment that swings in a wide arc to the west, towards a platelayers' hut and Letford Bridge. Here, the views from our train on a clear summer's day are awe-inspiring and of seemingly infinite variety. This is particularly true to our left, where, not far below us, we catch our first glimpse of the Wray Brook, meandering through open pastureland just above its confluence with the River Bovey. Beyond it is the river itself, now about to swing sharply away to the west and disappear amongst a range of delightfully wooded hills that lie between us and the partly visible frontier heights of eastern Dartmoor. To our right, the overall scene, no less attractive, is more domesticated. Here, the little lane that we passed over at Yeo Bridge is still in close attendance and, beyond it, lie the elegant and scattered dwellings comprising Lower Knowle, set amongst trees and backed by lush green fields bounded with neat hedgerows, before yet more woodlands take over to fill the skyline. Continuing in this sylvan scenery, our train now crosses the aforementioned Letford Bridge, which is a tall, double-

0–4–2T No. 1427, with its two-coach train to Moretonhampstead, makes an impressive sight as it crosses the three-arched Knowle viaduct on 4th August 1958.

E. R. Shepherd

Two views of trains crossing Lustleigh Mill viaduct:–
Above: BR standard class 3 2–6–2T No. 82033 in charge of the 2.15 p.m. train from Newton Abbot on 3rd September 1956.
D. Cullum

Below: 0–4–2T No. 1466 propelling the 3.15 p.m. auto train from Moretonhampstead to Newton Abbot on 27th December 1958.
Peter W. Gray

arched structure of granite with wide wings: its southern arch passes over another of the many winding lanes in this locality and the other over a farm track leading to fields. From here the gradient eases slightly to 1 in 61, m.p. 8 is passed and the line proceeds along a short cutting of extremely hard rock on the southern side of Knowle Hill. In so doing the line also starts to swing northwards on a tight right-hand curve of just 16½ chains radius, and continues as such until after bisecting a little footpath running through the adjoining woods and also crossing the Knowle viaduct, a magnificent three-arched structure of granite and elvan masonry that towers some 40 feet above the Wray Brook. Thereafter the curvature becomes less severe and our train continues its rather sinuous journey through another cutting named after nearby Rudge, wherein lies m.p. 8¼ and a granite-built bridge of the same name that carries a farm track over the line. Still veering northwards at this point, the line then begins to rise at the rate of 1 in 50 on a steepening embankment, crosses a plate girder bridge with granite abutments, below which lies a footpath-cum-farm track to Wrayland, and continues on towards m.p. 8½, with its accompanying platelayers' hut. However, before reaching this spot, the line momentarily straightens and undergoes a subtle change of direction in order to achieve the correct approach to Lustleigh Mill viaduct. Situated just beyond the milepost, this is of similar height and construction to that at Knowle, except for being composed of just two arches, and, once again, crosses over the Wray Brook, which, at this point, flows alongside another footpath to Wrayland.

Soon after passing over the viaduct the line continues its rather erratic behaviour by making a further deviation towards the north and also by

The extremely picturesque village of Lustleigh, centred around the 13th century Church of St John the Baptist.

Courtesy of Mrs M. Marsham

Two studies of Lustleigh Station:–
Above: Looking northwards towards Moretonhampstead on 28th February 1959.
Peter F. Bowles
Below: Looking southwards from the adjoining road overbridge on 4th August 1958.
E. R. Shepherd

entering a deep cutting of decomposed granite, interspersed with large granite boulders. This, in turn, is superseded by another embankment from where one of the most picturesque villages in the whole of Devon comes into full view, Lustleigh, complete with its little grey granite Church of St John the Baptist. At this point the station is less than a quarter of a mile away, but before reaching it our train has, first of all, to make a third crossing of the Wray Brook and also an adjoining footpath connecting the village to Wrayland. This is by means of a sturdy granite-built bridge, which is almost immediately followed by a plate girder bridge on granite abutments that carries the line over a trackway passing in front of the nearby Cleave Hotel to a meadow. The final run into the station is then completed by crossing over the Mill Leat, which runs under the line at an acute angle through a long stone culvert, and also by passing m.p. 8¾, together with the ground frame and facing connection for the goods siding.

Every bit as picturesque as the village it serves, the station at Lustleigh (8 miles 66 chains) consists of a 245-feet long platform on the western side of the line constructed of stone filling partly faced with brick. The covering is mainly of tarmac chippings edged with concrete slabs with rounded shoulders on the lineside, and it is backed throughout most of its length by a neat, white-painted, wooden fence of four-feet high slats, their tops cut to an apex. Only at the extreme northern end does it differ, where the fence gives way to a natural hedge of similar height. At approximately the midway point of the platform, where the finished surface is of paving stones, stands the main station building, smaller but otherwise almost an exact replica of that at Bovey. Indeed, the only differences of any significance are the building having only one wing instead of two, a small porchway built in matching stone under a pitched roof of grey slate

Another study of Lustleigh Station, as viewed from the driver's compartment of the 3.15 p.m. auto train from Moretonhampstead on 25th February 1959.

R. A. Lumber

immediately in front of the entrance from the forecourt, and no canopy. Inside, it consists of a waiting room/booking hall, the station office (once the domain of the stationmaster until the post had been amalgamated with Moretonhampstead in 1930) and the ladies' toilet, the gents' toilet being located in the flat-roofed wing on the southern side and accessed from the platform.

Apart from the main station building, the only other structure on the platform is the goods lock-up, which is almost identical to that at Heathfield except that its timber cladding is vertical rather than horizontal. It is situated just beyond the usual GWR-type station nameboard and set well back on the platform in such a way that one side is next to part of the southern wall of the gents' toilet and the other is adjacent to the stop blocks at the end of the goods siding. Consequently, as it has sliding doors front and rear, the transfer of small goods and parcels traffic can often be carried out from the platform, thereby avoiding the need for goods trains to enter the siding. During the summer months, in particular, this can be extremely useful because, in common with a number of other rural stations in the Westcountry, Lustleigh boasts a camping coach, and this is berthed at the end of the goods siding.

The camping coach at Lustleigh in 1935.

E. R. Shepherd

The goods yard, lying immediately to the south of the station forecourt, is a comparatively small and simple affair with just one building - a coal store. Constructed of stone under a pitched roof of corrugated iron, it is tucked away at the southern extremity of the station site, near the commencement of the siding. Apart from that, the only other structure on this entire side of the station is an oil store-cum-lamp room, which also has a corrugated iron, but sloping, roof and is built of unfaced concrete blocks. It is situated just outside the entrance to the goods yard and set well back from the gated entrance to a post and wire-fenced footpath leading to the village. This footpath is actually one of two means by which passengers can enter, or leave, the station, the other being by way of a flight of steps on the northern side that provides a connection to the road leading into, and out of, the village. Here, they are built up against the western side of the embankment of the adjoining, granite-built, road overbridge which is named after The Bishop's Stone – a huge, engraved granite boulder (thought to be the pedestal of an ancient wayside cross) that lies at the far side of the road a little further to the west and almost directly opposite the vehicular entrance to the station.

On a historical note Lustleigh had once had its own platform-mounted, timber-clad, signal box, with a 13-lever frame, and been fully signalled. However, like Teigngrace, the advent of the electric staff system of signalling in November 1901 had led to all the signals being removed and to the signal box, sited next to the goods lock-up, being used as an extra storeroom for a few years until it, too, had eventually been dismantled. More recently, in 1931, the station had also undergone a temporary change of name – to 'Baskerville'. This had been in connection with the production of an early film version of Sir Arthur Conan Doyle's well-known novel, *The Hound of the Baskervilles*, which featured 2–4–0 'Metro' tank No. 3590 as well as 2–6–2T No. 5530 in charge of what was portrayed as a Paddington express! Such fame had been followed by more later that same year, when the station began a sequence of winning 'garden certificates' in the annual competition organised by the GWR. Indeed, the well-tended station garden, situated on the eastern side of the line on land originally earmarked for a second platform and crossing loop, had, over the years, become a major feature. In it are buried two cats, 'Jemina James', whose life had been curtailed by a train, and his rather more celebrated predecessor, Jumbo, for whom a small gravestone had been provided, bearing the epitaph:–

Beneath this slab and stretched out flat,
Lies Jumbo, once our station cat.

According to Cecil Torr, in his book *Small Talk at Wreyland*, that cat had many lives: jumped in and out between the wheels of trains, and yet died in its bed.

The attractiveness of the village and nearby beauty spots, including the well-known Lustleigh Cleave with its famous Nutcracker Rock (a logan stone which, sadly, can no longer be made to oscillate), means that several passengers have now completed their journey. As a result, with some of them laden down with picnic hampers and the like, the platform momentarily becomes rather congested and a hive of activity. Before long, though, peace returns, our guard is able to carry out his usual ritual of slamming the carriage doors shut and giving the 'right away', and our train is on its way once more.

Overleaf: A selection of other views at Lustleigh from the 1950s.

BR standard class 3 2–6–2T No. 82033 with the mid-morning through working from Goodrington Sands Halt on 31st July 1955.

D. Cullum

The same class of locomotive as above, No. 82032, with the returning goods train from Moretonhampstead on 8th August 1955.

D. Cullum

0–6–0PT No. 3600 in charge of the 4.30 p.m. service from Newton Abbot on 6th September 1956.

D. Cullum

The same locomotive as in the preceding photograph, only now in charge of the daily goods train to Moretonhampstead on 19th July 1957.

D. Cullum

Passengers eagerly waiting to board the 12.50 p.m. train from Newton Abbot on a dull winter's day, 27th December 1958.

Peter W. Gray

Prairie tank No. 5183 after arriving with the 9.20 a.m. train from Newton Abbot on 26th February 1959.

Peter W. Gray

The line through the station is on the level but, after passing under Bishopstone Bridge, it starts to rise at the rate of 1 in 49 – the steepest gradient along the entire branch – in a cutting of decomposed granite and boulders. Known as the Bishopstone cutting, this quickly gives way to a relatively long and high embankment, where our train encounters m.p. 9 and a platelayers' hut, and passes over a tall, granite-built accommodation bridge. From here passengers can now see their motor-bound counterparts moving to and from Moretonhampstead along the A382 road just to the north of the line and the even closer waters of the Wray Brook on its meandering course through lush green meadowland on the valley floor. Further afield, on either side of the line, a high range of hills dominate the overall scene, their rugged slopes a mass of fresh green foliage of the beautiful woods that adorn this area. Here and there, too, can be seen the odd scattered dwelling, such as Kelly (after which the embankment is named, to the east) and Caseley Court (to the west).

Before reaching m.p. $9^{1}/_{4}$ the line, at this point running a little to the east of north, begins to veer sharply around to the north-west on a curve of about 16 chains radius. It is then that our train enters the very steep-sided Caseley cutting which, by towering some 70 feet above both sides of the line at one point, makes it by far the deepest cutting to be encountered. However, it is also quite short and, at its extremity, the line passes over the Caseley embankment and bridge, the latter built at a very acute angle of 30 degrees to accommodate the lane over which it crosses: it consists of an arch constructed in spiral courses and has massive wings and retaining walls, all of solid granite. After crossing the bridge, the line enters another short cutting and continues, in a circuitous course, along the hillside here for some considerable distance. In so doing it passes through a series of more cuttings, alternating with embankments, in an extremely picturesque wooded setting, the Wray Brook, flowing over its boulder-strewn course below us to our right, adding to the charm. At the same time our train also encounters the first of two accommodation bridges consisting of plate girders on granite abutments, m.p. $9^{1}/_{2}$, a platelayers' hut, m.p. $9^{3}/_{4}$, the second of the two accommodation bridges and numerous little stone culverts that carry water into the Wray Brook from the wooded hillside through which we are passing.

Near m.p. 10 the line passes close to East Wray, once the home of Thomas Wills, who had been one of the directors of the Moretonhampstead & South Devon Railway. It is here, too, that the line, although still on a rising gradient of 1 in 49, starts to run much lower along the hillside and not far above the level of its seemingly constant companion, the Wray Brook. All the while the extremely pleasant scenery is staying largely unchanged and continues as such after Higher Combe Wood, through which we have been travelling, is superseded by Sanduck Wood. The line, at this point, is now passing through property that had once belonged to another of the directors of the Moretonhampstead & South Devon Railway, the Earl of Devon, and going past the site where, in the 1870s, he had managed to persuade the South Devon Railway to install a temporary, 120-feet long, siding so that cut timber could be transported away from his woodland for commercial gain. Although

Above: Prairie tank No. 4145, with the 10.15 a.m. train from Moretonhampstead, passes through the Bishopstone cutting on the northern outskirts of Lustleigh, 9th July 1957.
Below: Another photograph taken later the same day, showing 0–6–0PT No. 3600 passing over the Kelly embankment with the 7 p.m. departure from Moretonhampstead.

D. Cullum

The heavily-wooded hillsides of the Wray valley are clearly evident from these two photographs of 0–4–2T No. 1466 hauling its two-coach train from Paignton to Moretonhampstead up the steep 1 in 49 gradient on 30th August 1956. In the top picture the train can be seen crossing the granite-built Caseley Bridge, while the lower picture shows it a little further up the line after having just crossed an accommodation bridge.

D. Cullum

no longer discernible, the siding had actually been quite close to m.p. 10¼, and it is not far beyond this point that the line starts to follow the original course of the Wray Brook for the next quarter of a mile or so. This is because the brook had had to be diverted during the building of the railway and deepened by several feet so as to avoid the possibility of floods during the winter months rising to, or above, the level of the line. As a result, for the time being it flows parallel and even closer to the line in an artificial channel that continues beyond m.p. 10½ and ends almost at the exact spot where a platelayers' hut stands (10 miles 48 chains). This is also near to where the gradient of 1 in 49, that commenced just beyond Lustleigh Station, finally eases to 1 in 87.

Just beyond m.p. 10¾ the gradient changes again, to 1 in 75, and the line finally emerges from the woodland to run on a low embankment between open pastureland, close to the A382 road (to the east) and the wooded slopes of Wray Cleave beyond. Along this stretch our train encounters a small stone

A view looking down the Wray valley from near Wray Barton, showing the close proximity of the A382 road and the bridge under which flow the waters of the Wray Brook. The train is the 2.15 p.m. service from Newton Abbot on 26th February 1959, consisting of the familiar combination of 0–4–2T No. 1466 and autocoach W241W.

Peter W. Gray

drainage culvert, an accommodation bridge of plate girders on granite abutments and m.p. 11, all in quick succession. This, in turn, is followed almost immediately afterwards by two more stone drainage culverts in close proximity, a further change of gradient – to 1 in 83 – and the start of a cutting which is named after Wray Barton, a Tudor mansion situated on the far side

A bird's eye view northwards from the road overbridge at Wray Barton of the 11.35 a.m. auto train from Moretonhampstead to Newton Abbot approaching m.p. $11^1/_4$ on 1st September 1956. It is being propelled by 14xx class of locomotive, probably No. 1427.

D. Cullum

of the adjoining road and since developed into a large farm complex. Continuing in this cutting for a short distance, our train goes under a particularly fine granite-built bridge which, unlike all the others encountered, has a partition parapet wall to divide the lane passing over the line from a cattle path. Hereafter, the cutting quickly gives way to another embankment, although not before m.p. $11^1/_4$ is passed.

Continuing on its journey north-westwards through more open pastureland, our train next passes over a farm track by means of a plate girder bridge on granite abutments and then enters a short cutting at the lower end of a small wood. Here, with the line starting to curve around a little more towards the north, it encounters a platelayers' hut and m.p. $11^1/_2$, before re-emerging on another embankment, passing over a stone drainage culvert and crossing the A382 road, also by means of a plate girder bridge. Known as Steward Bridge, and situated at 11 miles 55 chains, this is an oblique structure with extremely sturdy abutments and recessed wings, all of solid granite: on the Moretonhampstead side, the eastern wing extends over a culvert containing the waters of the Wray Brook, which had earlier passed under the road, on the other side of Wray Barton. Meanwhile, it is just prior to this point that the line not only starts to change direction again on a left-hand curve of 30 chains radius, but also steepens slightly to 1 in 82. Then, just beyond the bridge, it goes through a shallow cutting between Steward Farm and Steward Wood, past m.p. $11^3/_4$ and the 'down fixed distant' signal for Moretonhampstead Station, and on over another embankment up to the gated, but unmanned, 'accommodation'-type level crossing below Budleigh Farm. Much to the relief of our driver and fireman, it is here that the long sequence of rising gradients finally comes to an end.

Once the crossing is negotiated our train immediately enters a deep cutting, thence proceeding westwards past m.p. 12 and the rear of the Moretonhampstead 'up advanced starting' signal. Thereafter the line straightens, our train re-emerges from the cutting on another, short, embankment and makes a second crossing of the A382 road by means of King's Bridge, a similar structure to that of its immediate predecessor. This, in turn, is quickly followed by another crossing of the Wray Brook, which, here, runs under the line through a stone culvert, and by the 'down home' signal, before the start of the pointwork for the loop line and sidings at the incoming end of the station. The last stage of this extremely pleasant journey then takes our train past the gasworks, over an adjoining 'accommodation' crossing and on towards the rear of the 'up starting' signal, m.p. 12¼ and the former engine shed with its lean-to signal box, where, on reaching it, our fireman relinquishes the key token to the waiting signalman. Finally, after passing over a second 'accommodation' crossing and going over another culvert, through which flow the waters of the Wadley Brook, our train pulls alongside the platform and stops just short of the stop blocks, from where, one day, it had been hoped to continue the line to Chagford. Instead, we are now at journey's end – almost 40 minutes after leaving Newton Abbot and some 500 feet higher in surroundings of an entirely different nature.

Having just arrived at Moretonhampstead with the 12.50 p.m. auto train from Newton Abbot on 19th February 1959, the crew take a moment to pose for the camera.

Peter W. Gray

Two studies of Moretonhampstead Station from near the stop blocks:–
Above: The view looking south-eastwards on 25th February 1959, which includes the sleeper-built lock-up for the station's coal supply (in the foreground) and also the goods shed beyond the main station building and overall wooden roof.

R. A. Lumber

Below: The view looking eastwards a few days earlier, with the cattle dock to the right and the corrugated iron lamp hut to the left.

E. R. Shepherd

Two further studies of Moretonhampstead Station, showing:–
Above: The overall wooden roof viewed from a south-westerly direction, beyond the station's vegetable garden, during the summer of 1957.
Below: The view from inside the overall wooden roof looking eastwards, as 0–4–2T No. 1466 waits with its train alongside the station nameboard, again on a summer's day in 1957.

Geoff Howells

A general view of Moretonhampstead Station looking northwards on 28th February 1959, showing, from left to right, the main station building and overall wooden roof, the station nameboard, the platform-mounted six-ton crane and the goods shed.

Peter F. Bowles

Moretonhampstead Station is situated at 12 miles 28 chains from Newton Abbot and on the south-eastern outskirts of the little moorland town that it serves. The main station building is constructed of granite walls containing arched windows and doorways, and has a low pitched roof of grey slate from which two chimneys protrude. Inside, the accommodation consists of the usual facilities expected at a branch line terminus – booking hall-cum-waiting room, station office, parcels office and toilets – and is lit throughout by gas lamps, using gas supplied by the local gasworks.

Backing out onto the platform side of the building is the overall wooden roof, covering both the platform and the 'main' and loop lines at this point. It consists of lateral wooden planking supported by nine upright timbers set in granite plinths on the far side of the loop line. The northern wall of this overall roof is formed by the rear wall of the main station building and an open-arched masonry wing at either end, which provide a similar number of supports for the rafters of the roof and, together with the nine timber supports already mentioned, hold the roof in place. The roof fabric is also of timber, diagonally planked, and the whole construction is strengthened by a network of iron struts and tie bars. Because the original skylights had fallen into disrepair a few years earlier, leading to the removal of all the glazing, the resulting aperture is covered with corrugated iron, leaving a ventilation gap on either side of the ridge. Apart from that, the roof covering is entirely of roofing felt and battens. Under the roofed section the platform is covered with paving stones, but elsewhere the surface is of tarmac chippings edged with concrete slabs with rounded shoulders on the lineside. It is backed by iron railings except at its western extremity, on the far side of the main station building, where a white-painted, wooden fence of four-feet high slats, their tops cut to an apex, is utilised. Throughout its entire length – 300 feet – the platform is faced with granite.

Beyond the far (western) end of the platform stands a corrugated iron hut, which is used for the storage of paraffin and lamps, and, set back from it, a small, sleeper-built, lock-up for the station's coal supply. Opposite, and built alongside what is effectively a short siding beyond the end of the run-round loop, is a cattle dock with an adjacent brick building used for the storage of hay and sawdust; the latter kept as a floor covering in order to prevent the animals from slipping in their pens. Next to the south-western corner of the cattle pens there is also a white-painted, five-barred, wooden gate. This is there to provide access for cattle lorries and the suchlike, and is reached by a fenced trackway which runs above and to the rear of the stop blocks from the nearby A382 road, close to the stationmaster's house at the north-western corner of the station site.

To the east of the cattle dock, on the other side of the main station building, a siding off the loop line passes a whitewashed granite platelayers' hut with an adjoining timber-built storage shed, a now-redundant coal stage and a water tower, the latter feeding a water crane below it and another situated on the northern side of the running line, directly opposite. After also passing some modern, brick-built, coal bunkers, the siding then terminates at the former engine shed, which, like the coal stage, had been taken out of use

Above: A photograph of the water tower at Moretonhampstead, which was gravity fed from nearby Budleigh Farm, and 2–6–2T No. 4150 taking water prior to working the 10.15 a.m. service to Newton Abbot on 19th February 1959. Also visible, beyond the locomotive, are the two goods sidings and some of the various structures in the goods yard.

Peter W. Gray

Below: The former engine shed, now being used by the local coal merchant, and lean-to signal box as seen on 6th June 1960. The person stood by the entrance is the photographer's father, Wilfrid Shepherd.

E. R. Shepherd

Moretonhampstead Station as seen from the road entrance on 11th August 1955.
D. Cullum

in November 1947, when Moretonhampstead had ceased to be a sub-shed of Newton Abbot. Now used as a store by the local coal merchant, this is a substantial granite-built structure under a low-pitched slate roof surmounted by a full-length ventilator. On either side there are four large arched windows, and at the front there is an arched entrance large enough to accommodate one of the broad-gauge saddle tank locomotives that were in use at the time that the shed was built: for many years, up until 1949, this entrance had been equipped with a pair of heavy wooden sliding doors. At the rear of the building there is another arched 'entrance' of similar size, although almost totally sealed off, and partly attached to its north-eastern corner is a gas-lit enginemen's cabin constructed of granite under a low-pitched roof of grey slate, from which a brick-built chimney protrudes. Finally, on the northern wall, is the most unusual, lean-to, signal box, which is built of brick and timber, has a slate roof and a tall brick chimney stack, and contains a 12-lever (originally 15-lever) frame.

Almost directly opposite the signal box is the entrance to the goods yard. This is reached by means of a connection off the loop line and a diamond crossing over the running line (from which there is no direct connection), and is served by two sidings connected by facing points just beyond a loading gauge. Of these, the northernmost terminates just short of a corrugated iron office, with an adjoining metal weighbridge, and the southernmost leads to the goods shed, which it then passes through before terminating close to the main station building, adjacent to the northern face of the platform. The shed itself is almost an exact replica of that at Bovey and, similarly, contains a two-ton crane. Immediately to the front (eastern face) of the building stands a corrugated iron warehouse for a local firm of agricultural feed merchants and a somewhat smaller corrugated iron goods office, while at the rear is the station's platform-mounted six-ton crane, which is used for transferring timber and other heavy items between road vehicles and railway wagons. Other structures include a small wooden hut containing the meter for the station's gas supply (set back from the north-western corner of the goods shed), another, quite large, pitched roof building of granite and corrugated iron, which is situated directly behind the weighbridge and office and used as a local coal merchant's store, and, of particular interest, an upright granite slab commemorating the opening of the line. Mounted on a granite plinth at the foot of a sloping path used by passengers to gain access to the main station building from the A382 road, this had been erected on 26th June 1925 by the son of one of the directors of the Moretonhampstead & South Devon Railway Company, Elias Cuming, and is inscribed: 'Moreton-hampstead and South Devon Railway – 1866 – Directors – Earl of Devon – Thomas Wills, William R. Hole – John Divett, Elias Cuming – Thomas Woollcombe'.

The upright granite slab commemorating the opening of the line in 1866.

E. R. Shepherd

The complete mapping of the line that follows is based on the 1906 edition of the County Map series (25 inches to the mile), copies of which were kindly provided by Mr James Cadoux-Hudson of Little Woolleigh, Bovey Tracey, Devon. Each sheet has been reproduced at 42% of actual size to give a revised scale of 10.5 inches to the mile.

Newton Abbot to Moretonhampstead.

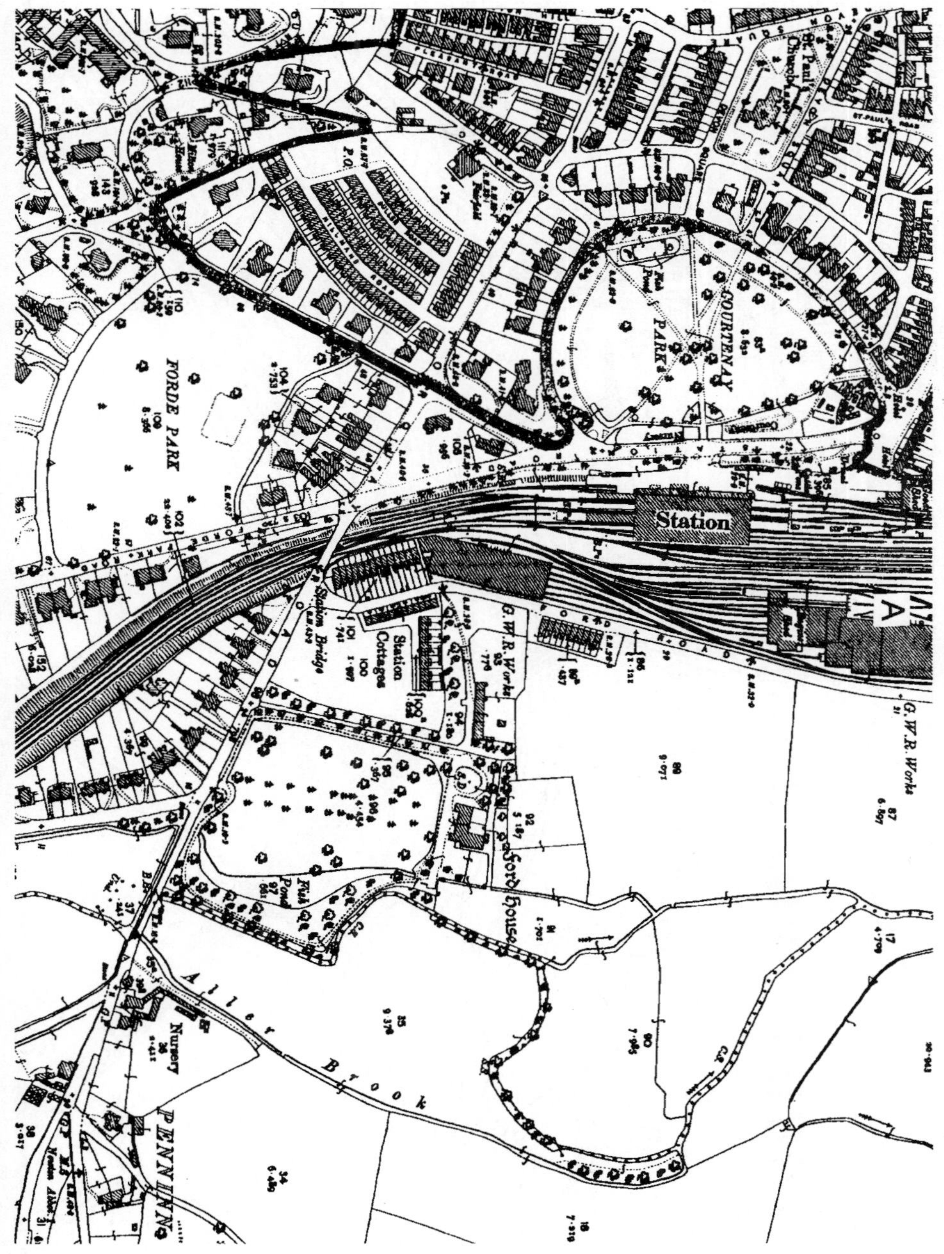

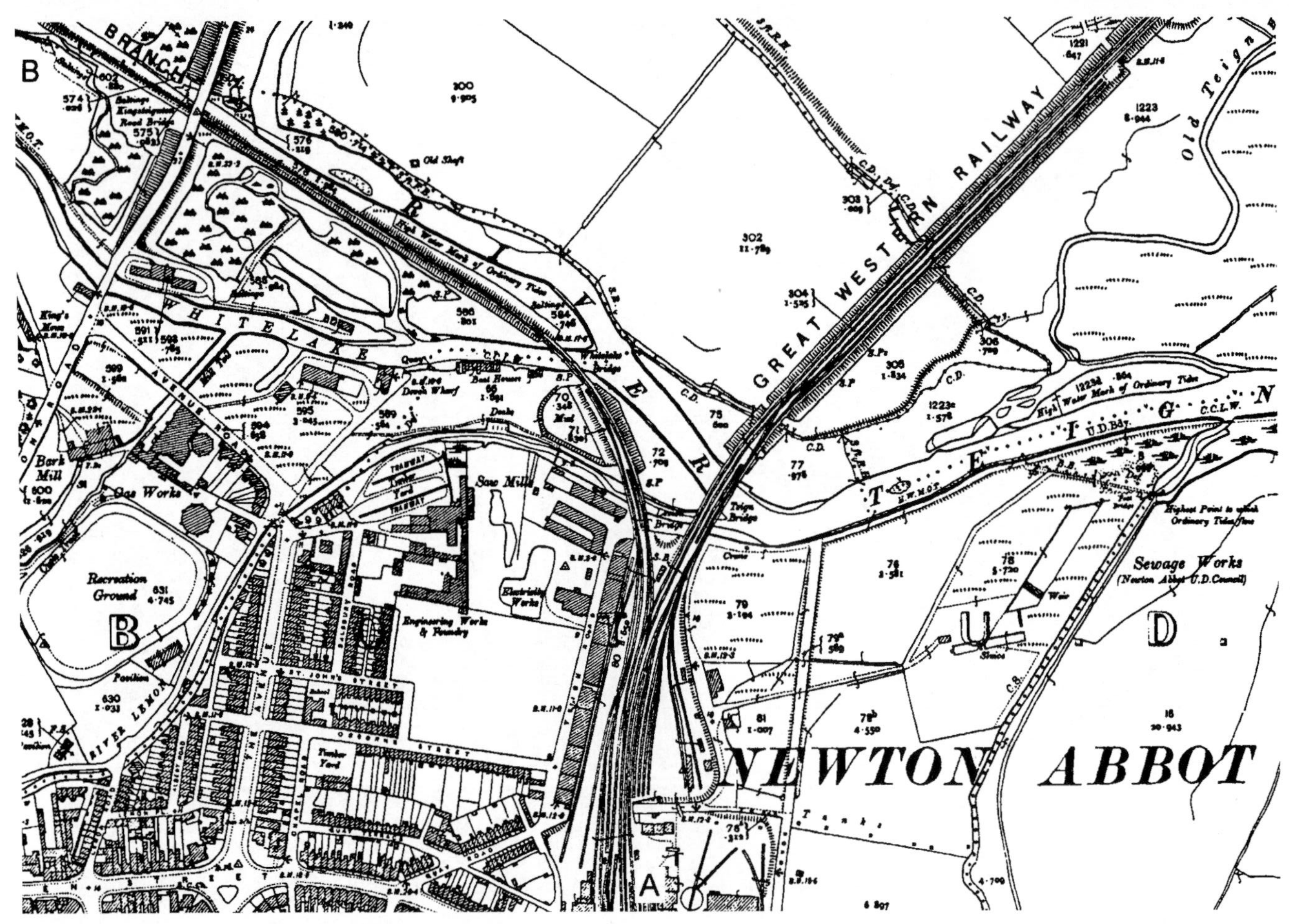
NEWTON ABBOT
GREAT WESTERN RAILWAY
WHITELAKE
RIVER TEIGN
Old Teign
Recreation Ground
Gas Works
Saw Mill
Engineering Works & Foundry
Electricity Works
Timber Yard
Sewage Works
(Newton Abbot U.D.Council)
Teign Bridge
Whitelake Bridge
Bark Mill
King's Kiln
Old Shaft
High Water Mark of Ordinary Tides
Highest Point to which Ordinary Tides flow
RIVER LEMON
AVENUE ROAD
THE AVENUE
ST. JOHN'S STREET
OSBORNE STREET
Pavilion
Weir
Sluice
Boat House
Devon Wharf

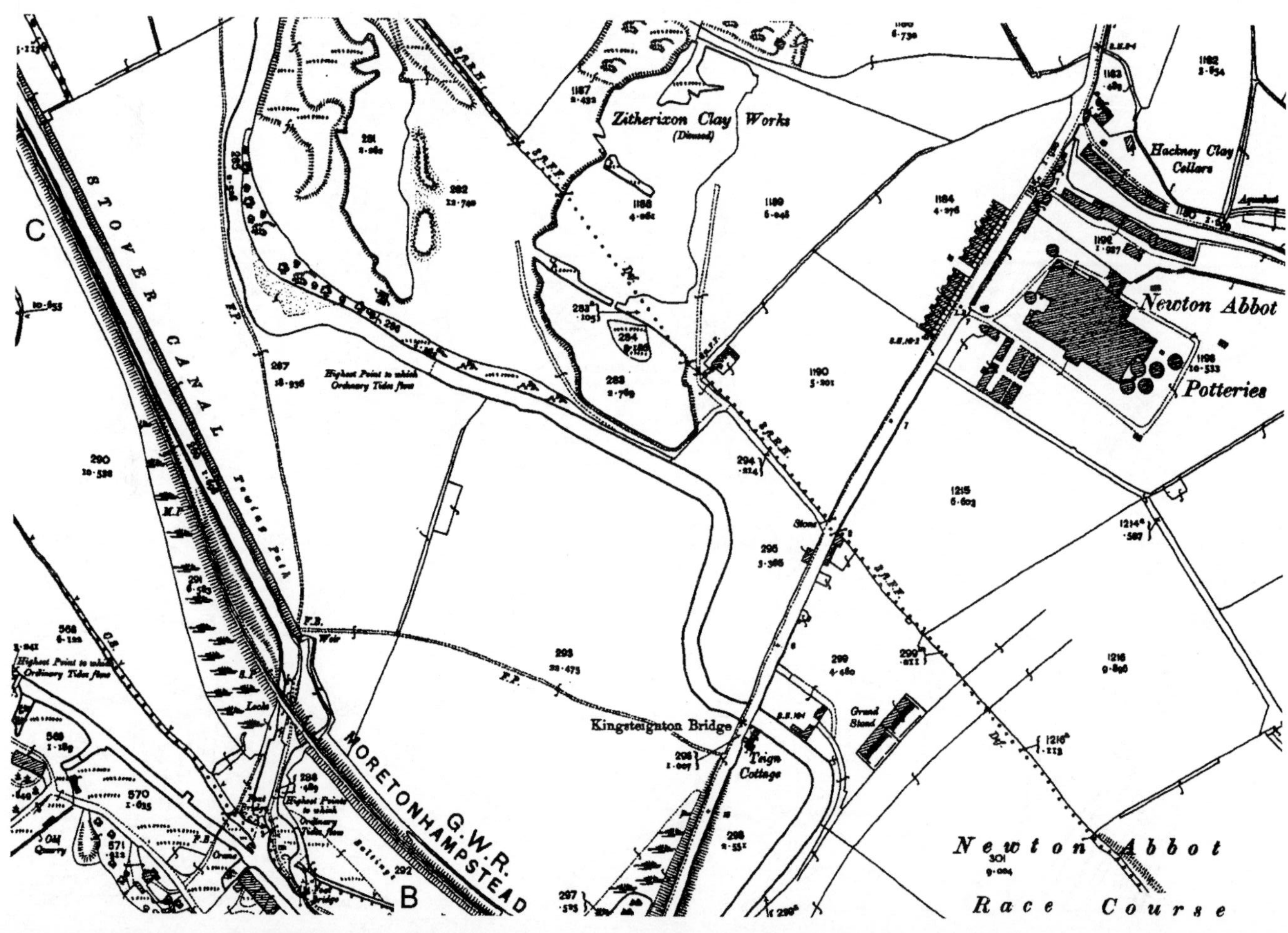
STOVER CANAL
Towing Path
Zitherixon Clay Works
(Disused)
Hackney Clay
Cellars
Newton Abbot
Potteries
Highest Point to which
Ordinary Tides flow
Kingsteignton Bridge
Teign
Cottage
Grand
Stand
Old
Quarry
MORETONHAMPSTEAD
G.W.R.
Newton Abbot
Race Course

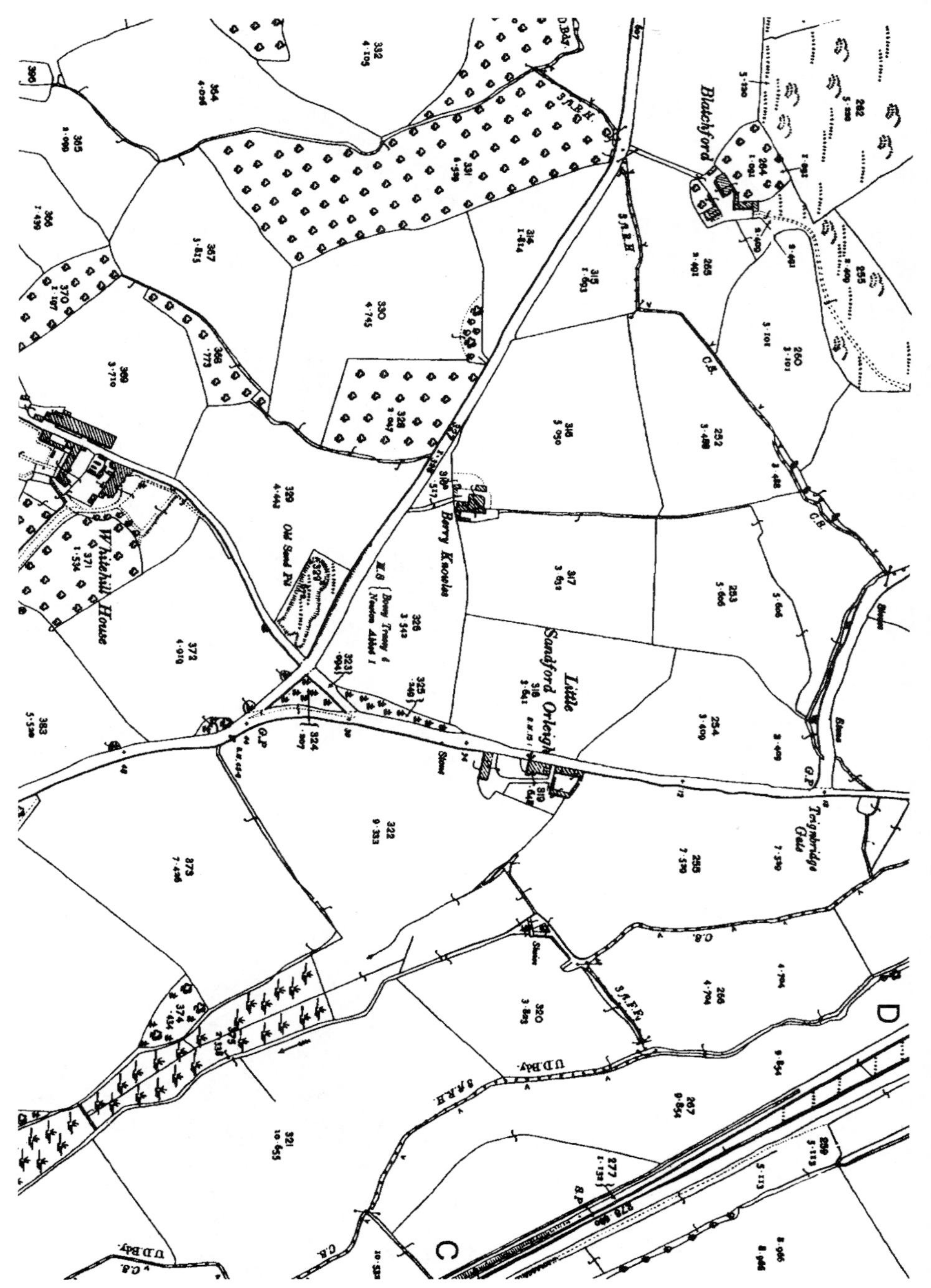

Blatchford
Whitehill House
Berry Knowles
Little Sandford Orleigh
Teignbridge Gate
Old Sand Pit
C
D

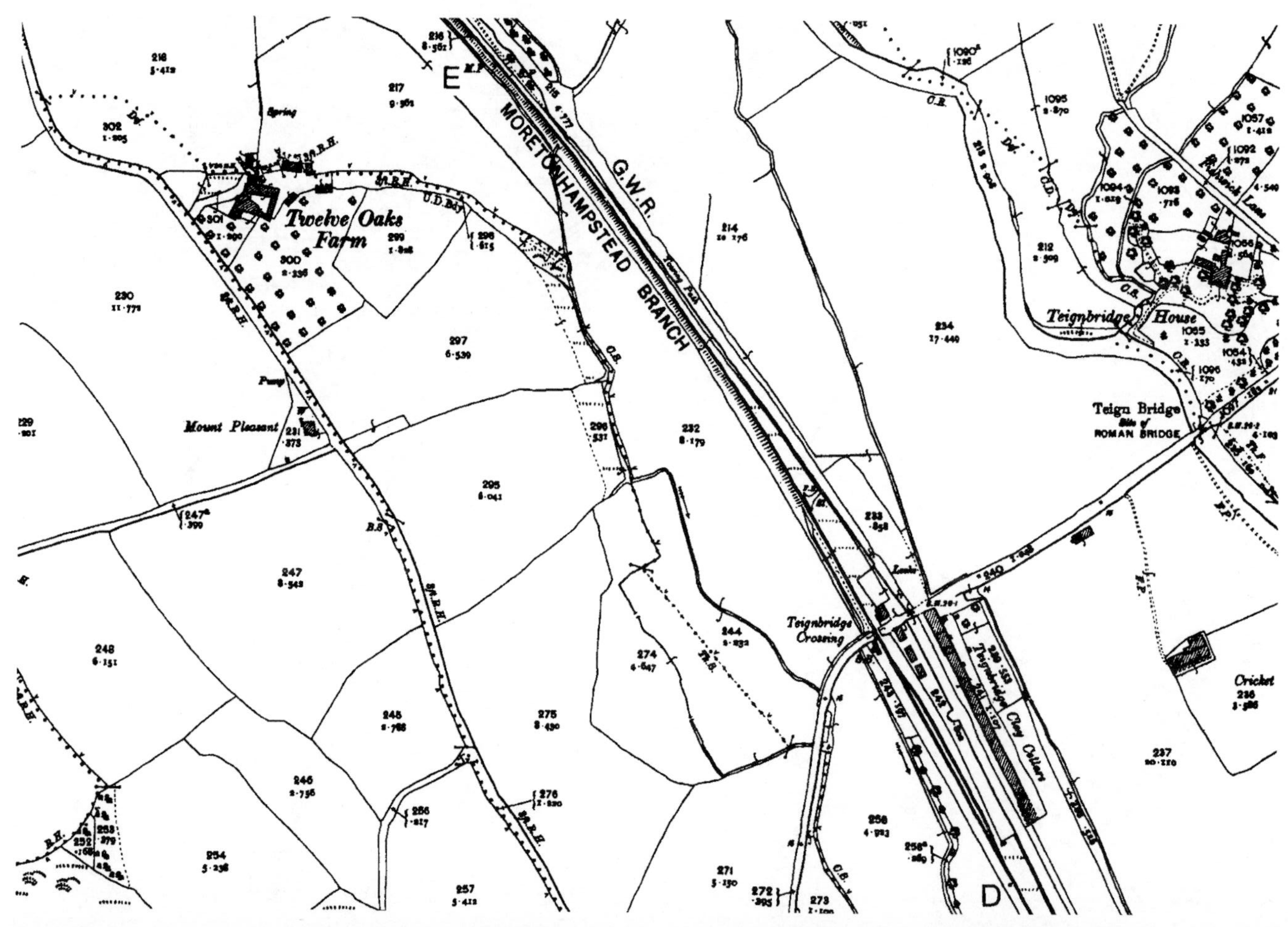

MORETONHAMPSTEAD BRANCH
G.W.R.
Twelve Oaks Farm
Spring
Pump
Mount Pleasant
Teignbridge Crossing
Clay Cellars
Teignbridge
Teignbridge House
Teign Bridge
Site of ROMAN BRIDGE
Cricket
E
D

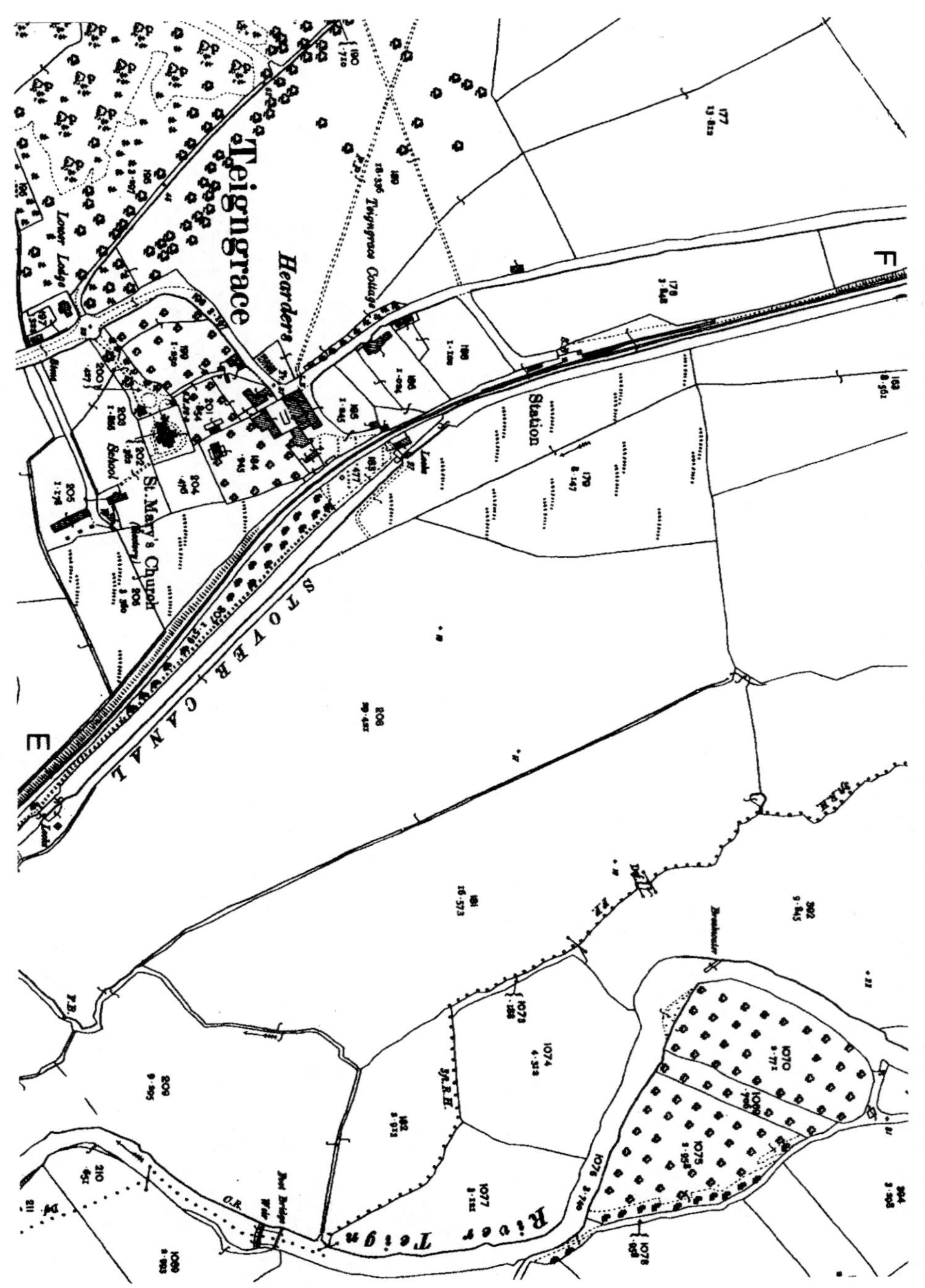

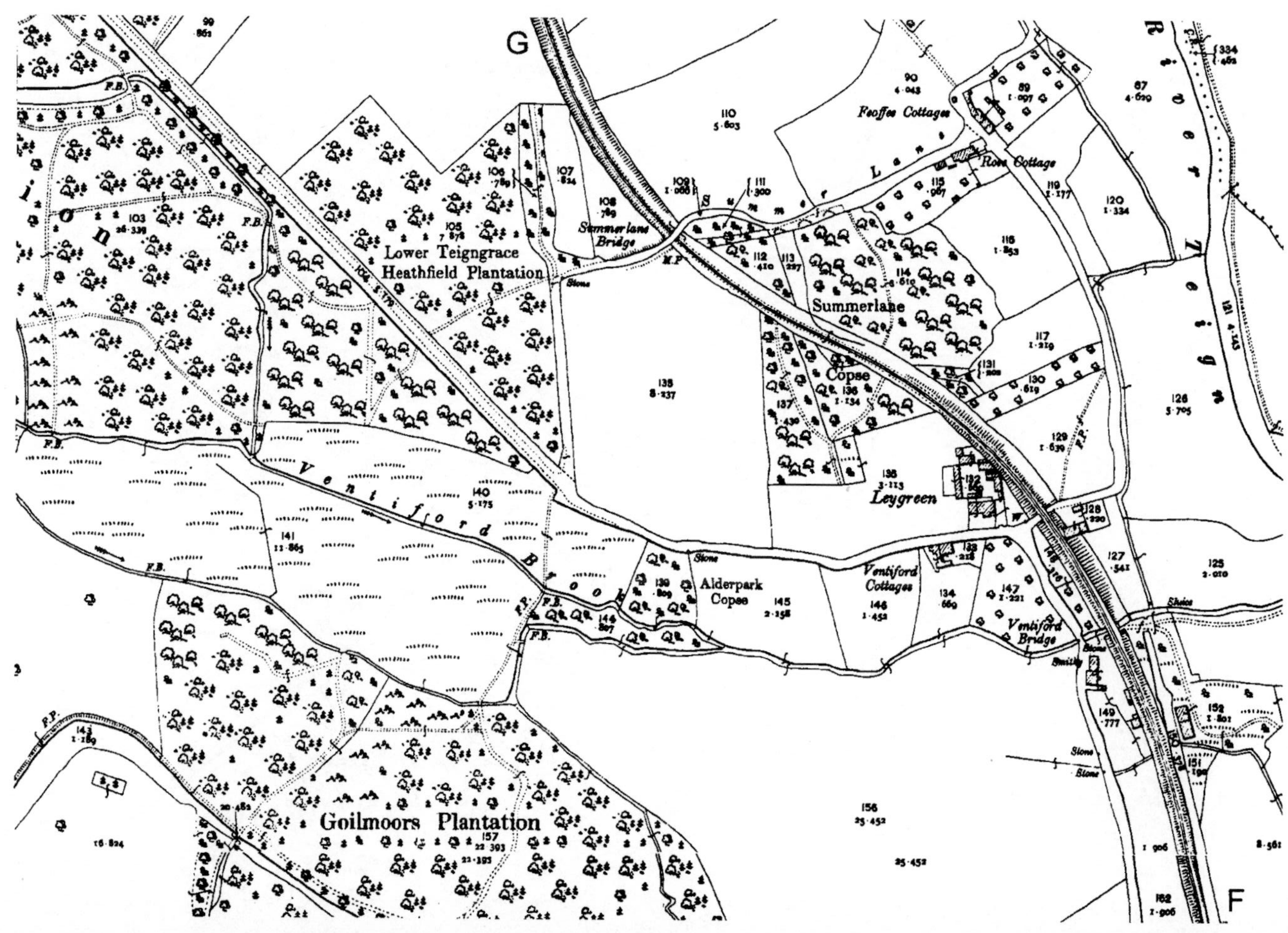
G
Lower Teigngrace
Heathfield Plantation
Summerlane Bridge
Summer Lane
Feoffee Cottages
Rose Cottage
Summerlane
Copse
Leygreen
Ventiford Brook
Alderpark
Copse
Ventiford
Cottages
Ventiford
Bridge
Goilmoors Plantation
F

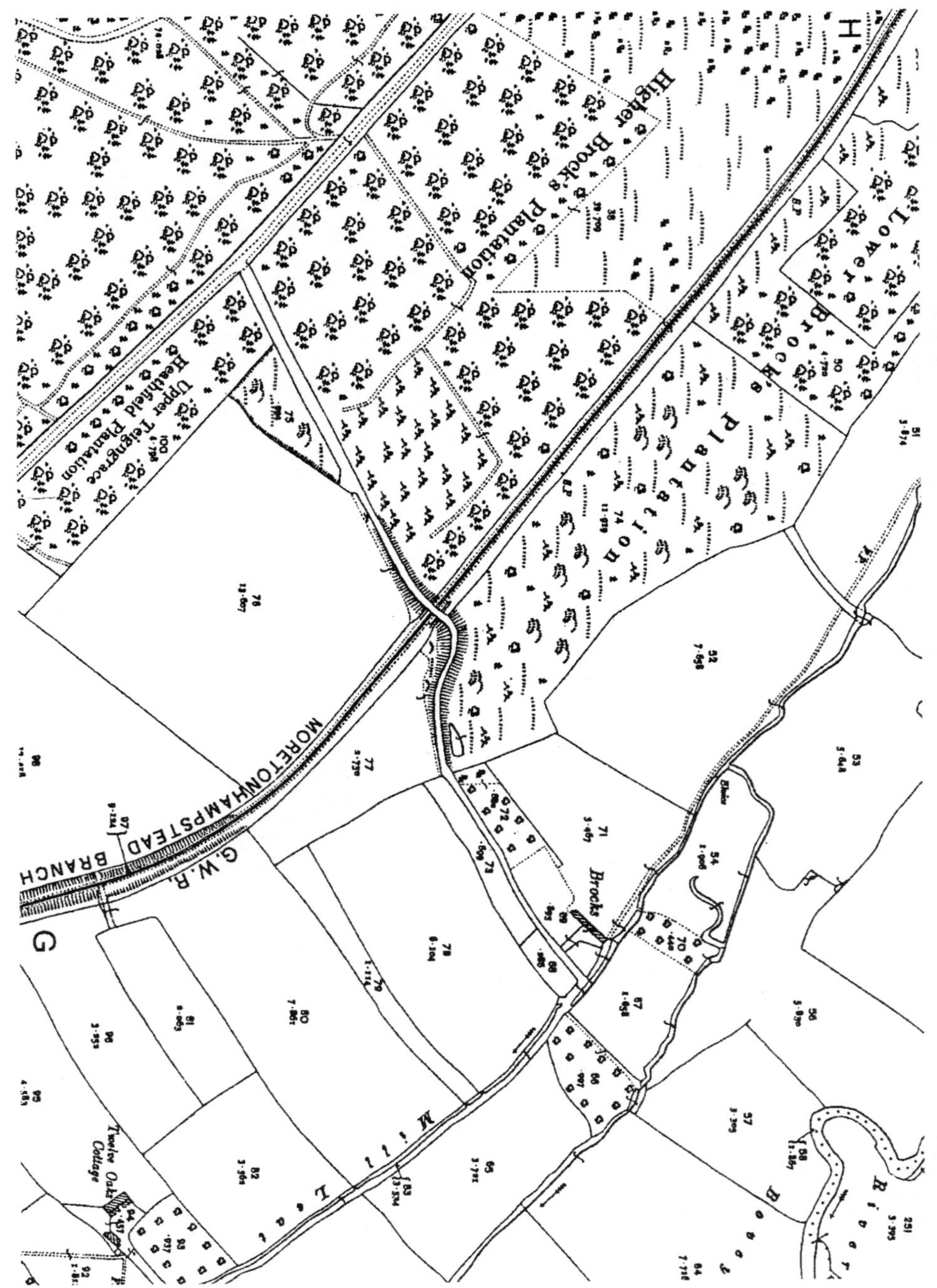

Higher Brock's Plantation
Lower Brock's Plantation
Upper Teigngrace Heathfield Plantation
MORETONHAMPSTEAD BRANCH
G.W.R.
Brocks
Twelve Oaks Cottage
Mill Leat

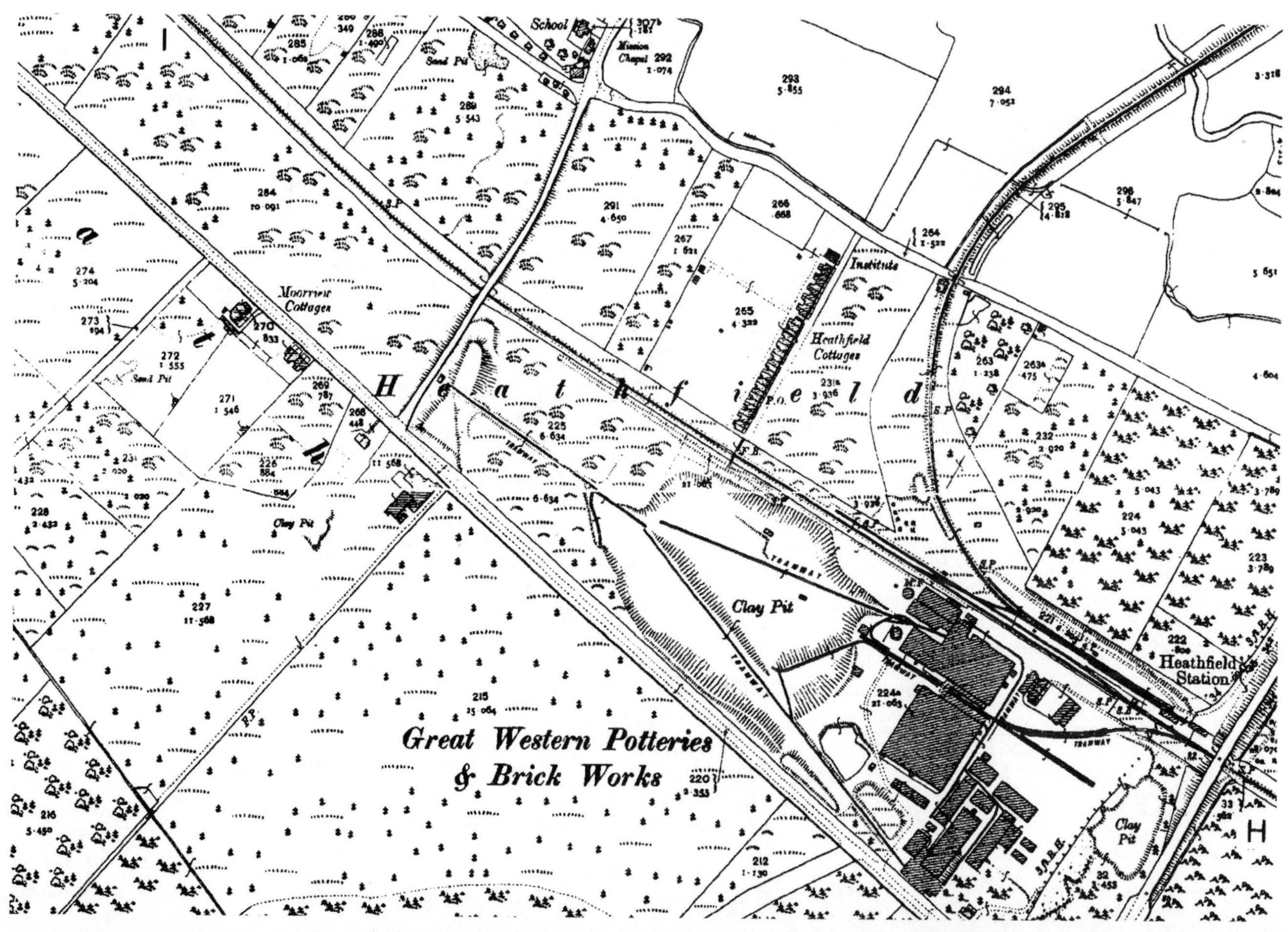

Great Western Potteries
& Brick Works
Heathfield
Clay Pit
Heathfield Cottages
Heathfield Station
Moorview Cottages
Institute
School
Mission Chapel
Sand Pit
Tramway

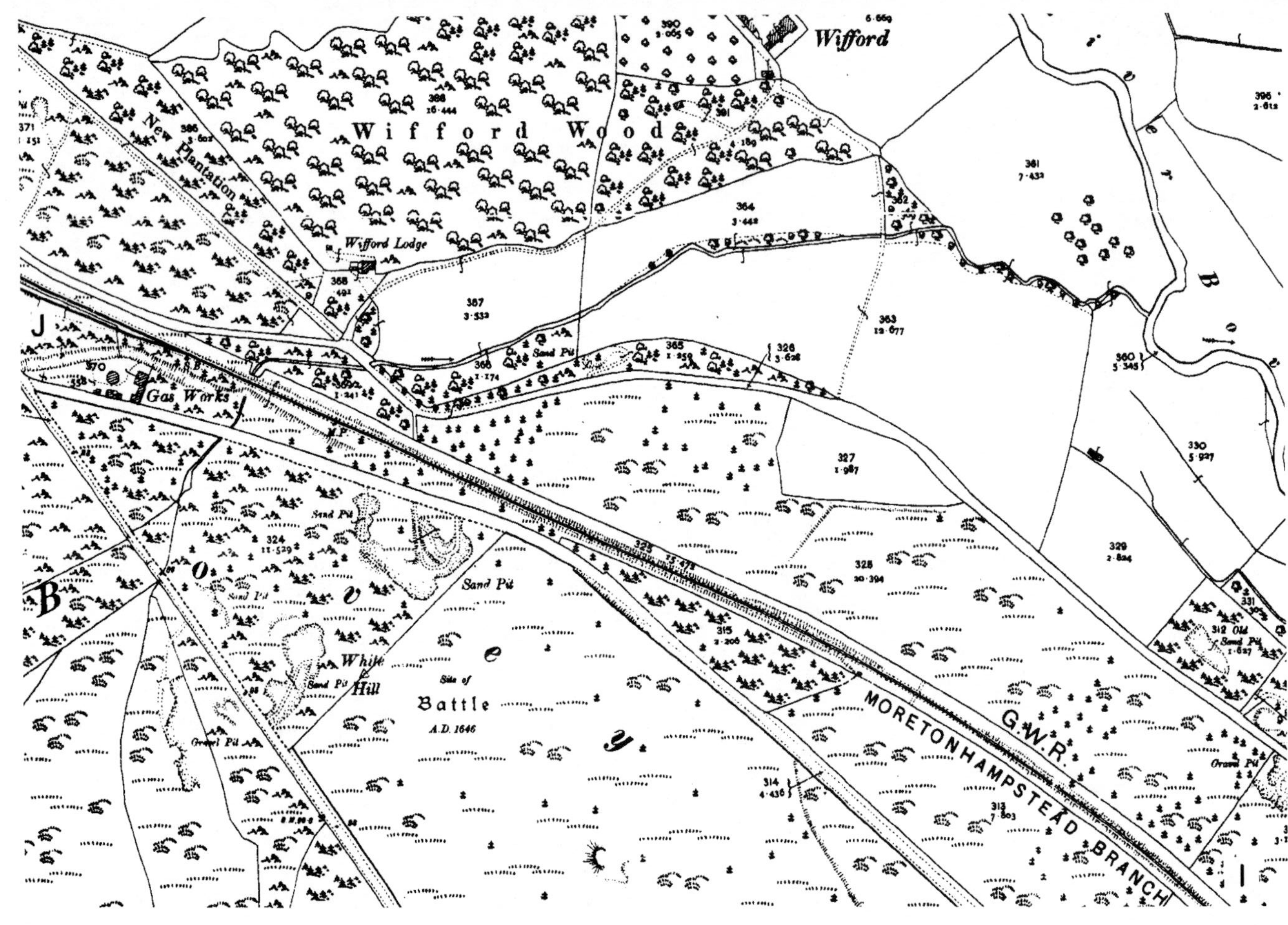
Wifford Wood
New Plantation
Wifford Lodge
Wifford
Gas Works
Sand Pit
White Hill
Site of Battle A.D. 1646
Gravel Pit
MORETONHAMPSTEAD BRANCH
G.W.R.

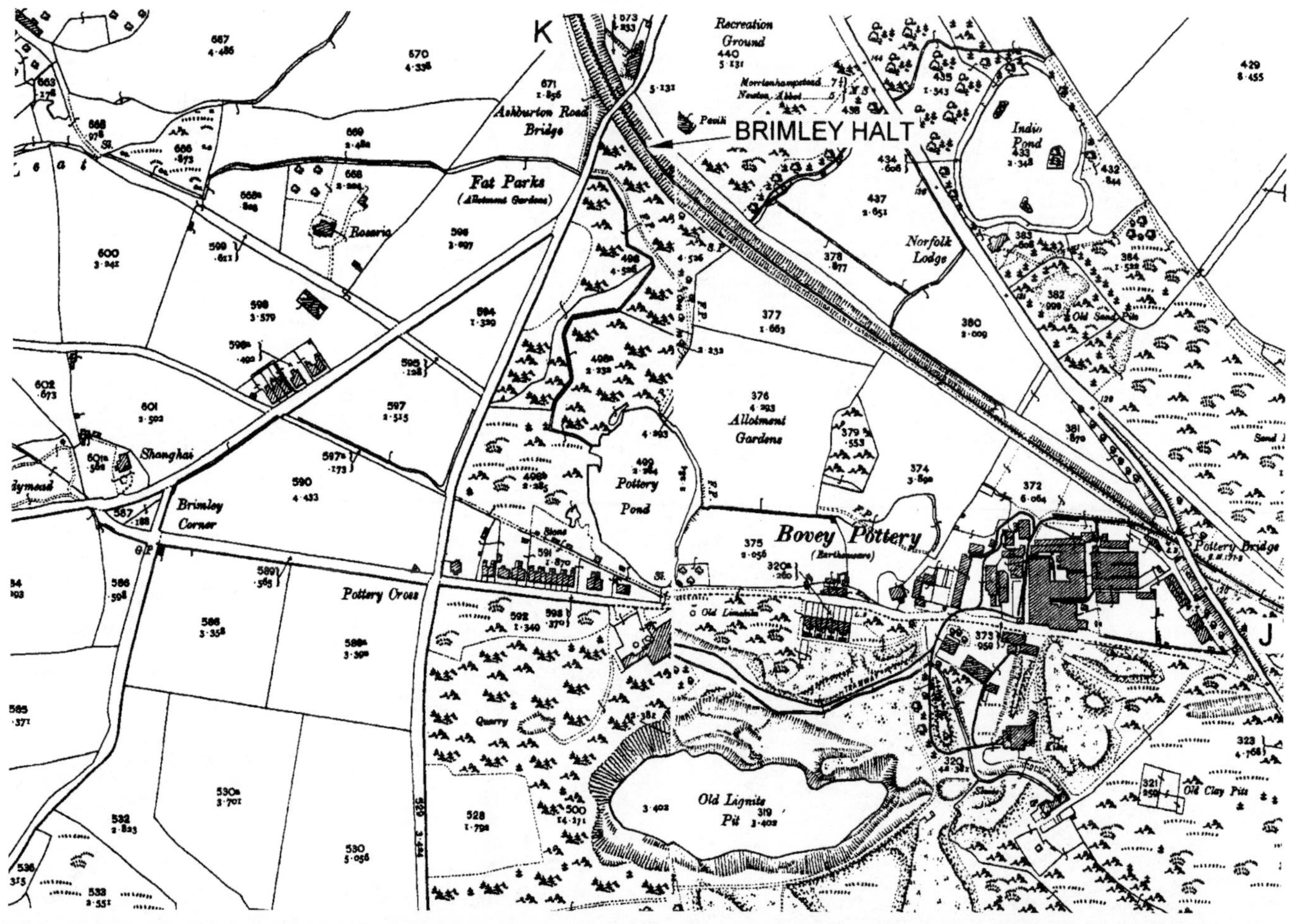

K
Recreation Ground
BRIMLEY HALT
Ashburton Road Bridge
Fat Parks
(Allotment Gardens)
Rosaria
Indio Pond
Norfolk Lodge
Shanghai
Brimley Corner
Pottery Cross
Pottery Pond
Allotment Gardens
Bovey Pottery
(Earthenware)
Pottery Bridge
Old Limekiln
Quarry
Old Lignite Pit
Old Sand Pit
Old Clay Pits
J

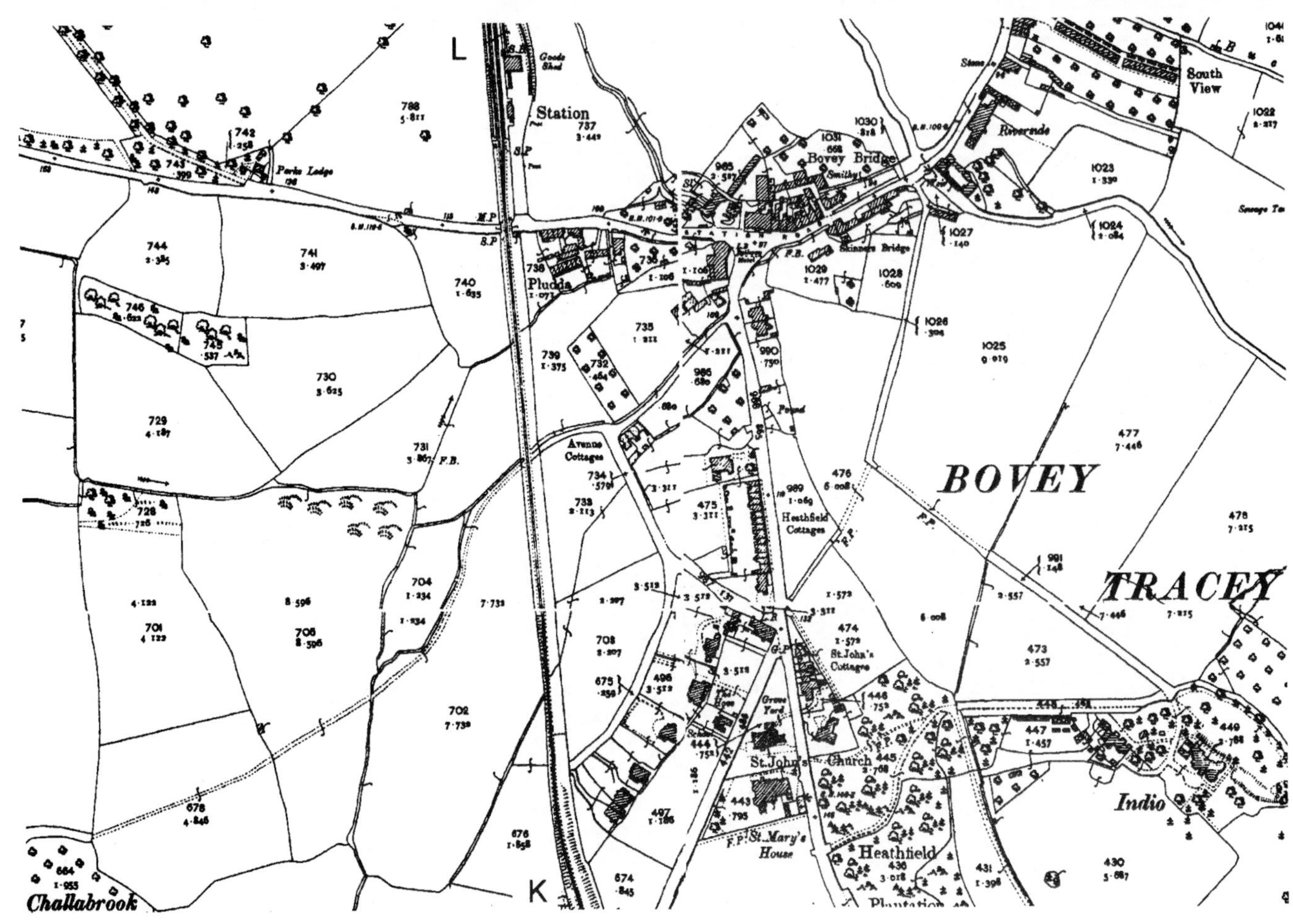

Challabrook
Station
Parke Lodge
Pludda
Avenue Cottages
Bovey Bridge
Riverside
South View
Heathfield Cottages
St. John's Cottages
St. John's Church
St. Mary's House
Heathfield
Indio
BOVEY
TRACEY

Old Quarries
Aqueduct
Southbrook
Southbrook Bridge
Southbrook Lane
Parke Bridge
MORETONHAMPSTEAD BRANCH
G.W.R.
Bovey River Bridge
Mill Leat
Fish Pond
Parke

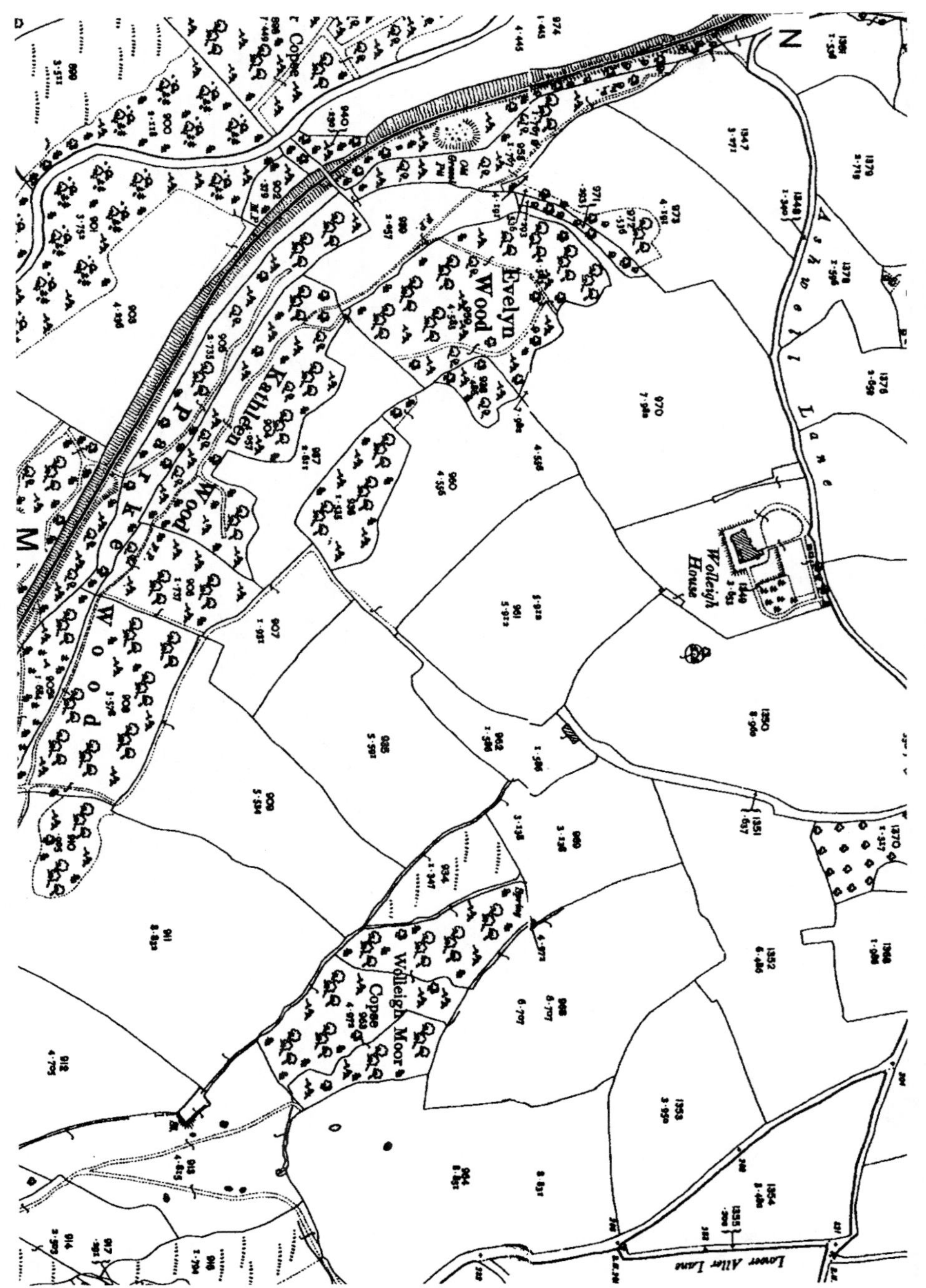
Evelyn Wood
Kathleen Wood
Park Wood
Wolleigh House
Wolleigh Moor Copse

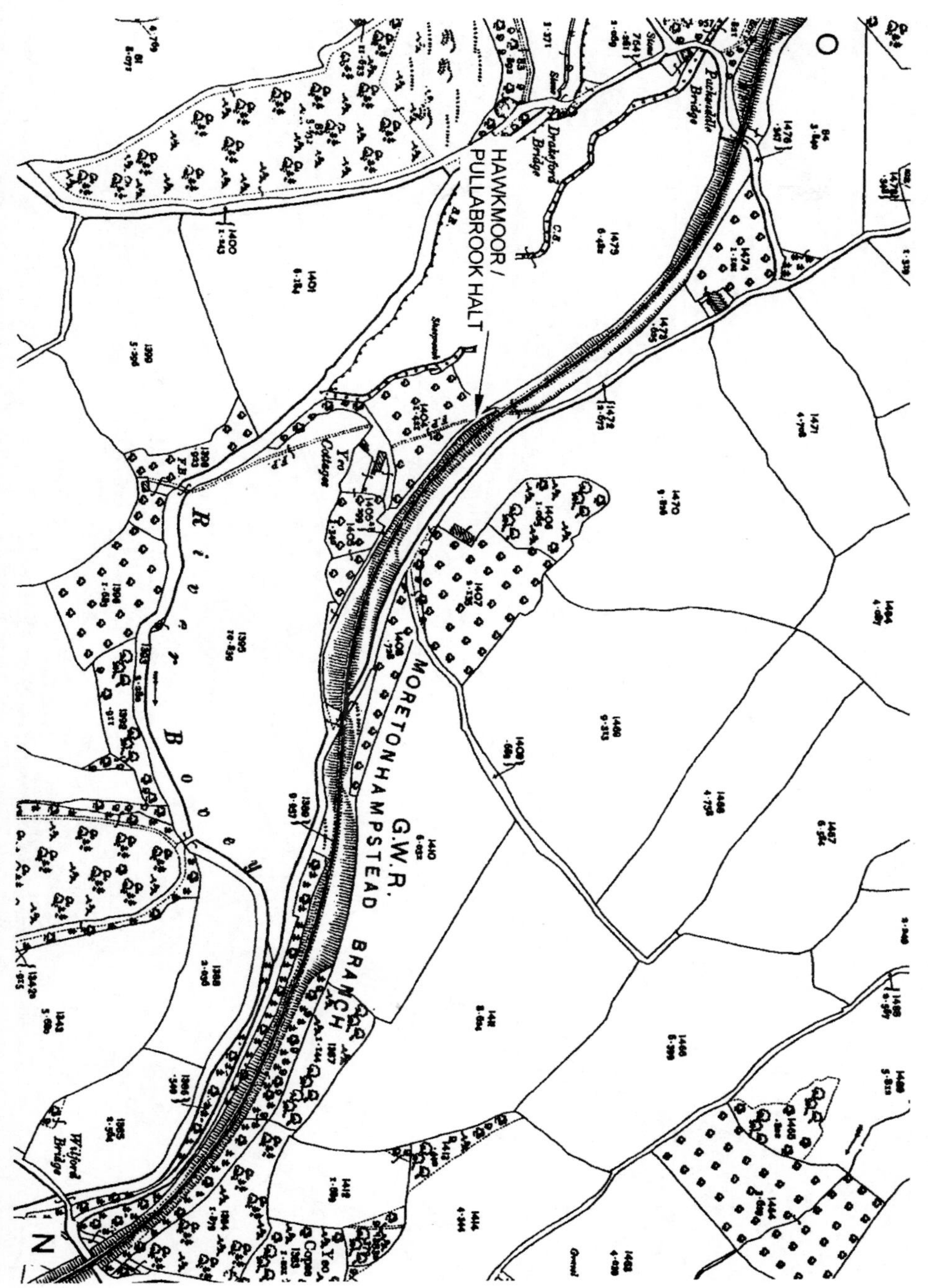
HAWKMOOR / PULLABROOK HALT
G.W.R.
MORETONHAMPSTEAD BRANCH
River Bovey
Yeo Cottage
Drakeford Bridge

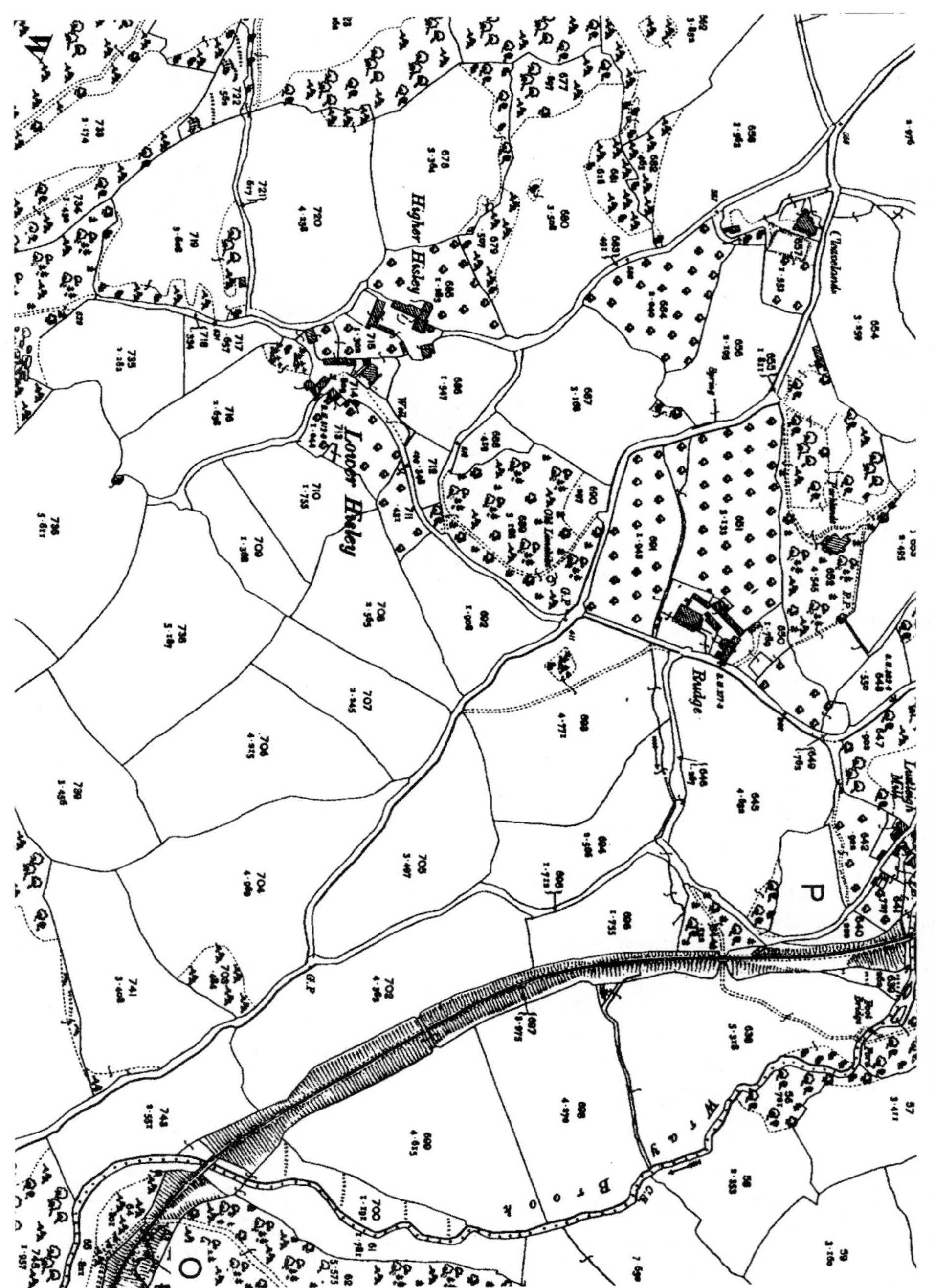
Higher Hisley
Lower Hisley
Bridge

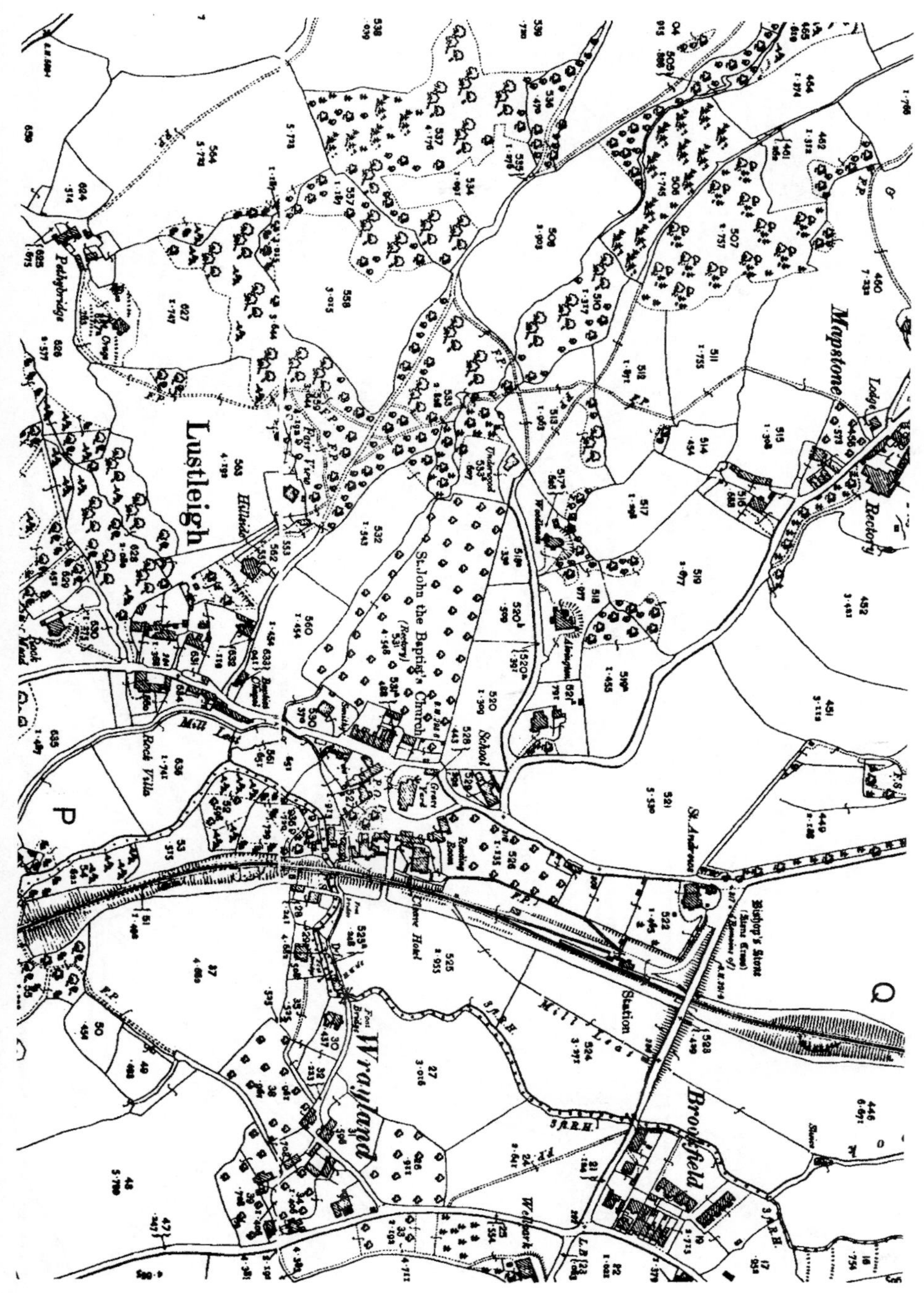
Lustleigh
Wrayland
Brookfield
Mapstone
Lodge
Rectory
St. John the Baptist's Church
School
Station
Mill Leat
Rock Villa
Hillside
Cleave Hotel
Bishop's Stone
Grave Yard
Reading Room
Wellpark
P
Q

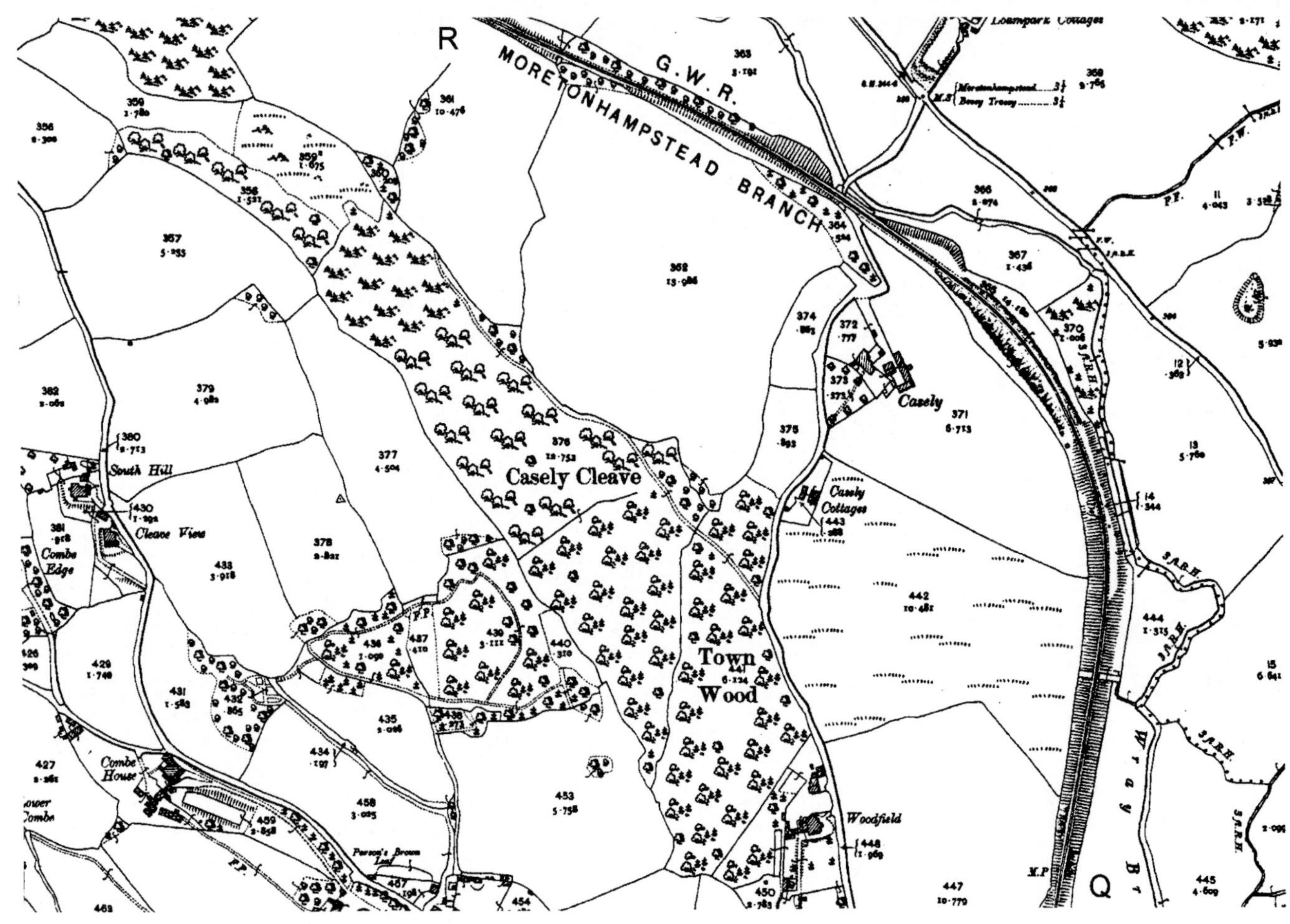
R
Q
MORETONHAMPSTEAD BRANCH
G. W. R.
Casely Cleave
Town Wood
Casely Cottages
Casely
Woodfield
Combe House
Combe Edge
South Hill
Cleave View
Loampark Cottages
Wray Br

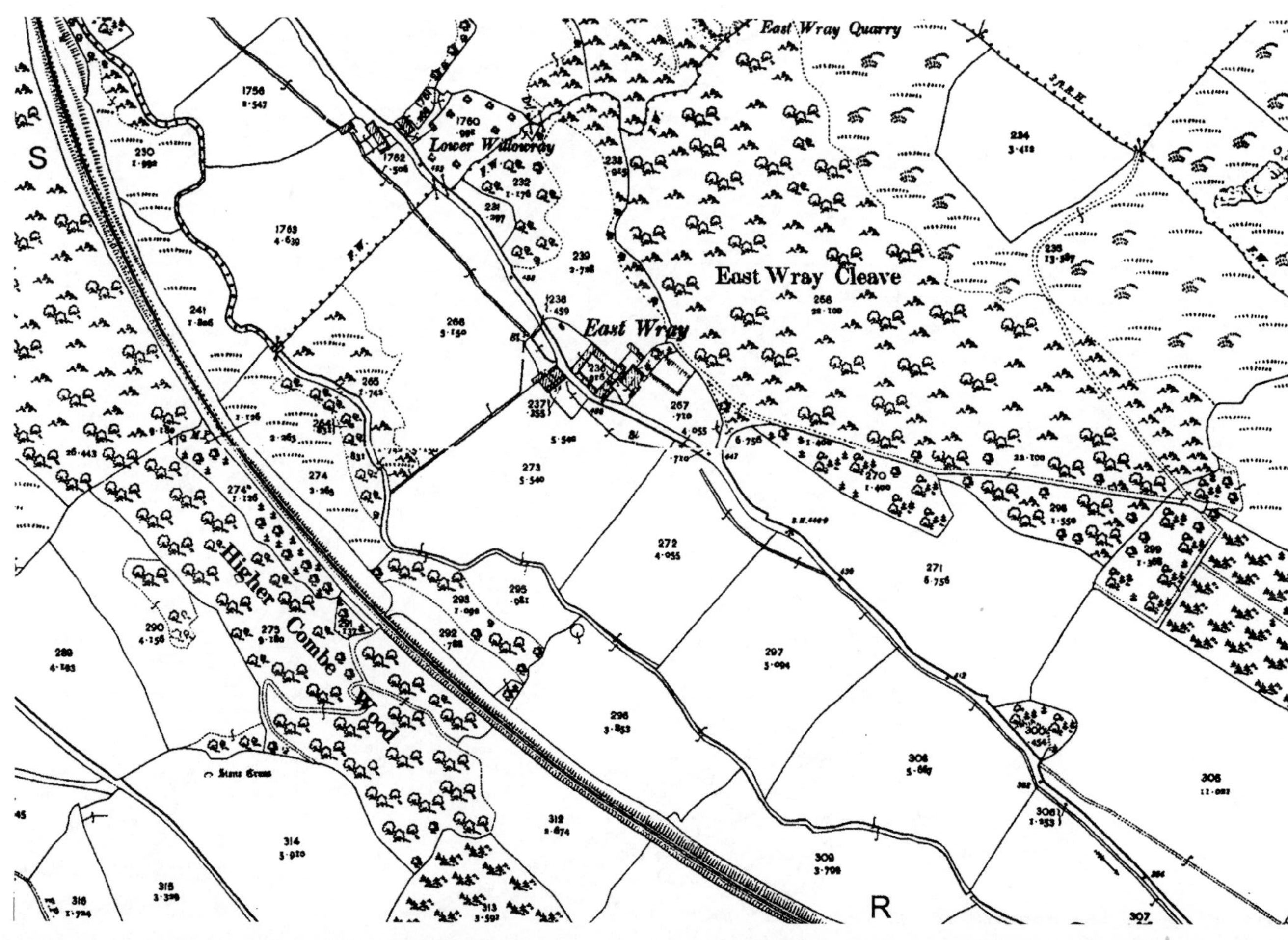
East Wray Quarry
Lower Willowray
East Wray Cleave
East Wray
Higher Combe Wood
Stone Cross

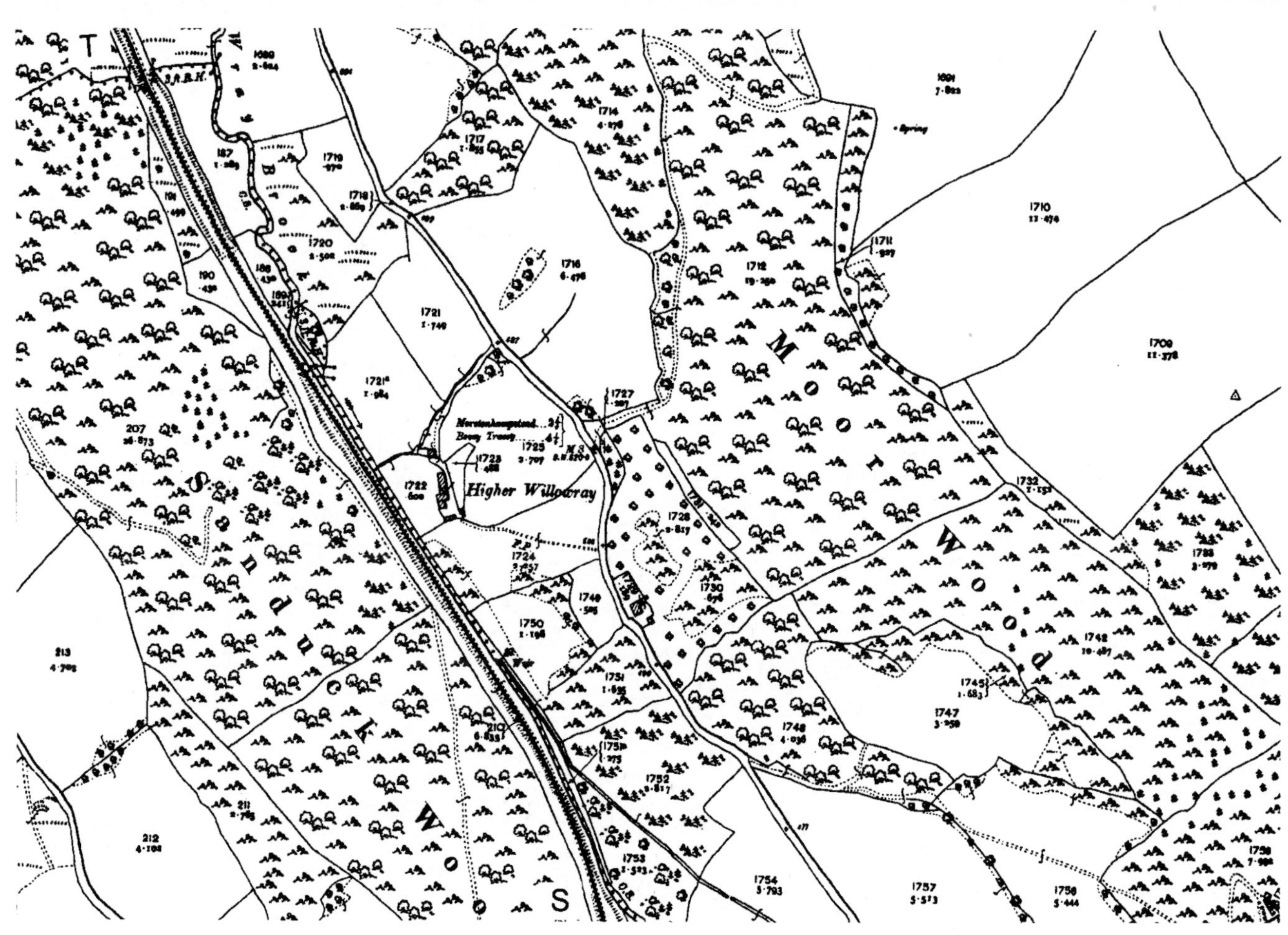
Moor Wood
Higher Willowray
Moretonhampstead
Bovey Tracey
Spring

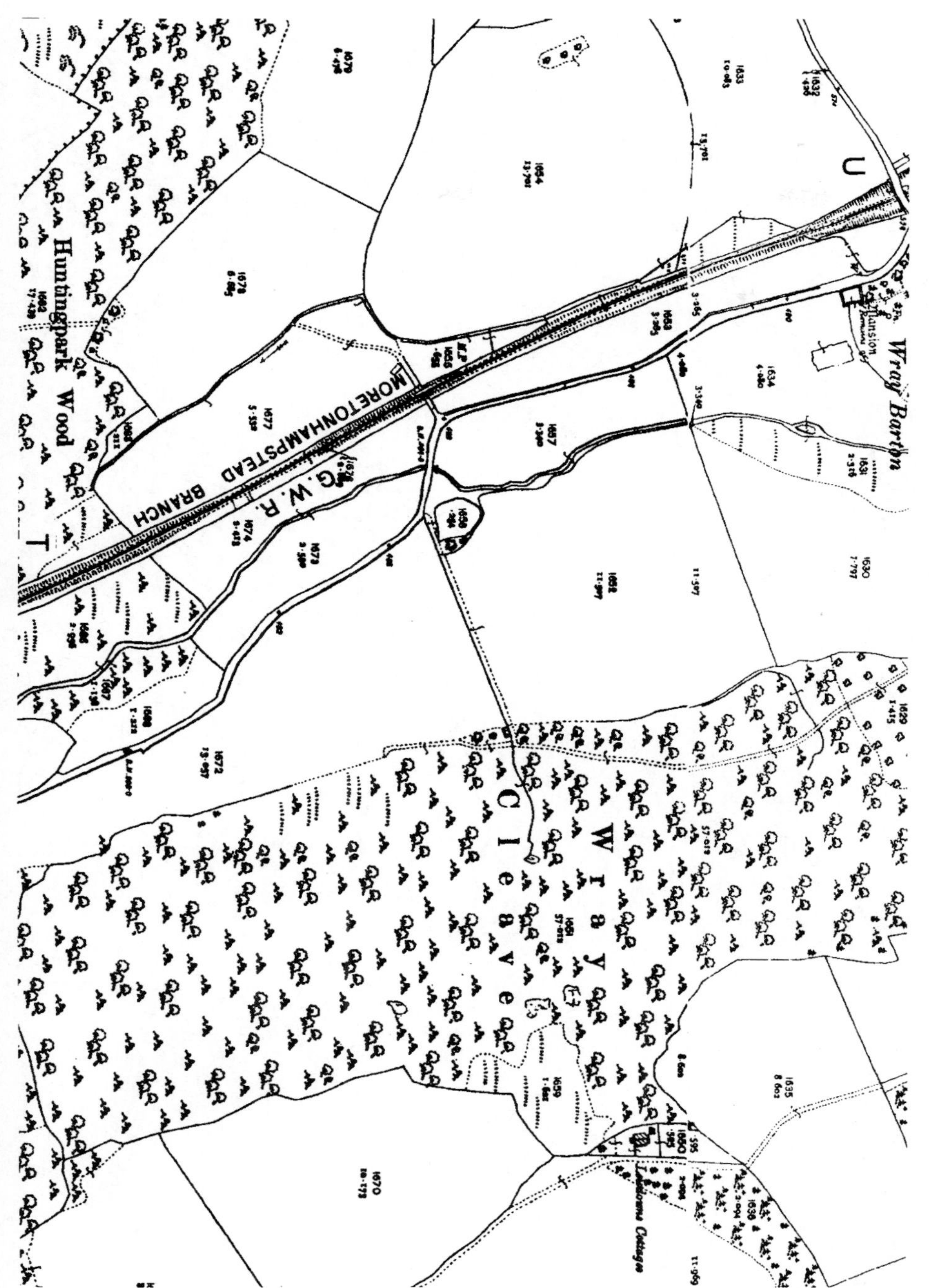
Wray Barton
Mansion
Huntingpark Wood
MORETONHAMPSTEAD BRANCH
G. W. R.
Wray Cleave

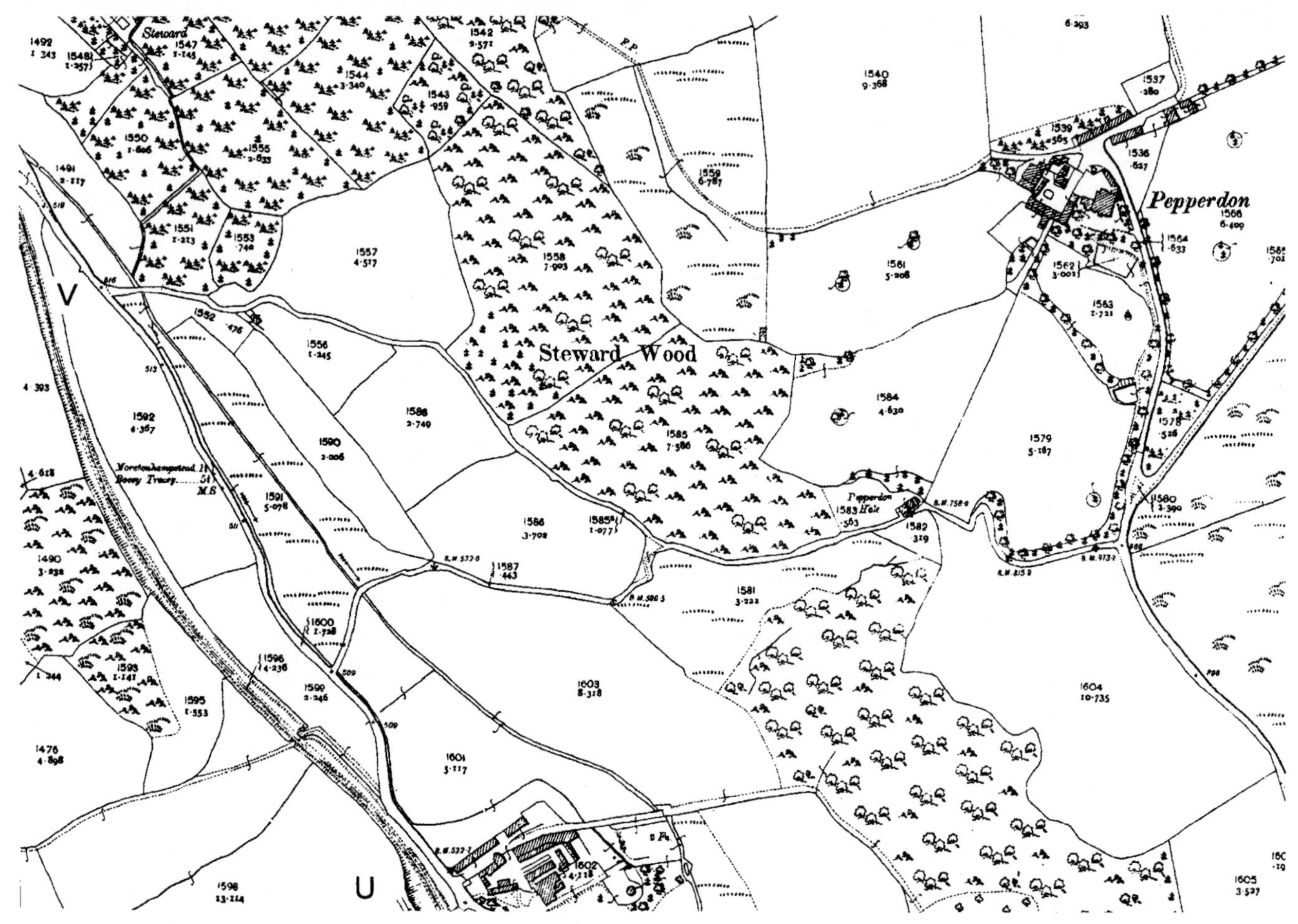
V
U
Steward
Steward Wood
Pepperdon
Pepperdon
Moretonhampstead
Bovey Tracey

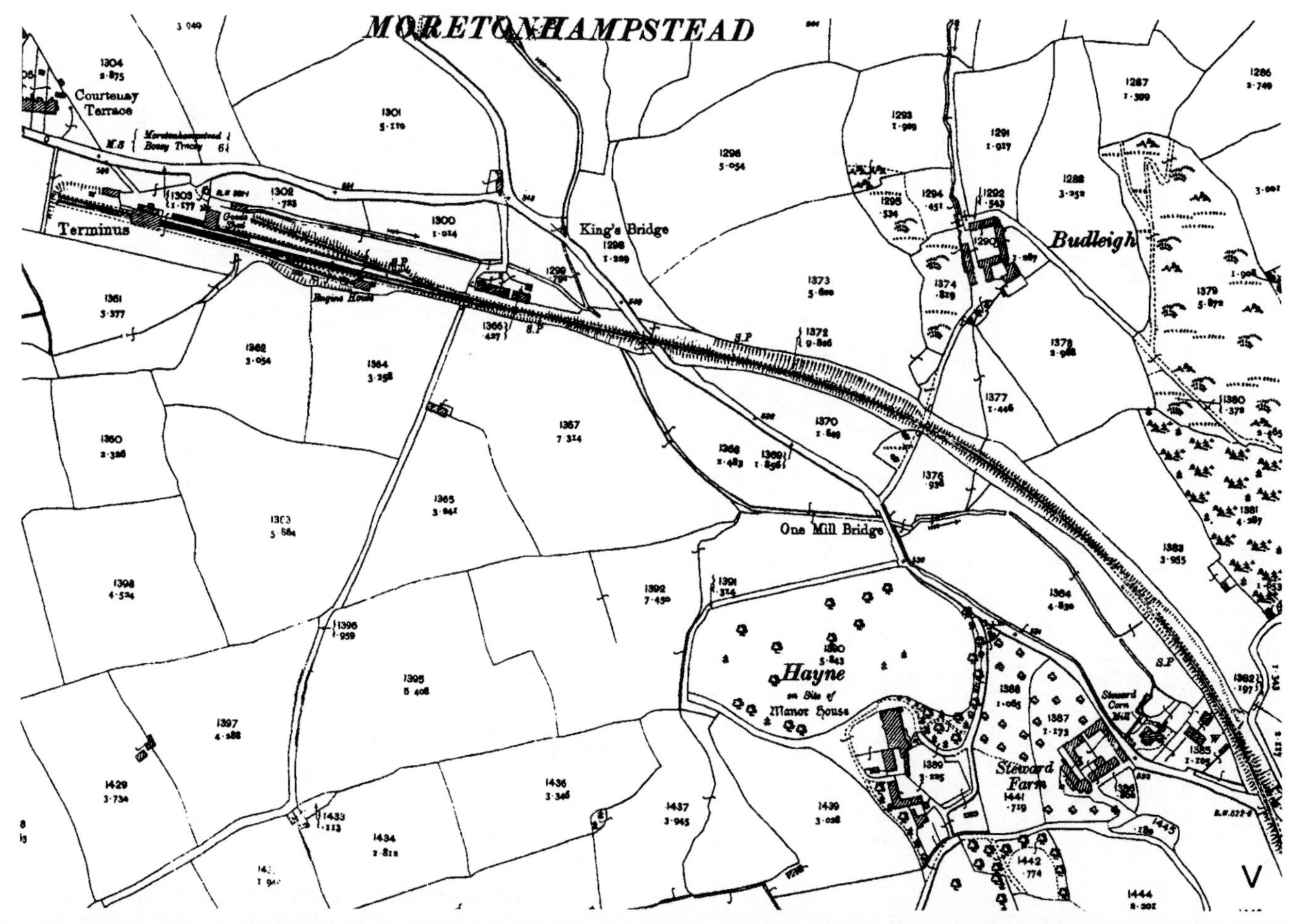

MORETONHAMPSTEAD
Courtenay Terrace
Terminus
Engine House
King's Bridge
Budleigh
One Mill Bridge
Hayne
on Site of Manor House
Steward Corn Mill
Steward Farm

HISTORY

Prelude:–

(a) The arrival of railways in Devon.

The origin of railways, for the exclusive use of vehicles with flanged wheels, can be traced back to mining practice in medieval Germany, but the development of railways, as a public means of transport, took place entirely in Great Britain.

The first railway of any significance opened in Devon on 16th September 1820, and was built by George Templer as a means of transporting granite from quarries owned by him on Haytor Down to other parts of the country, most notably to London for use in the construction of London Bridge. Known as the Haytor Granite Tramway, it was constructed of granite setts, cut with a flange to prevent the flat iron wheels of open, flat-topped, horse-drawn wagons from leaving the track, and had a gauge of 4 feet 3 inches. It covered a distance of about 8 miles and had to negotiate a descent of some 1,300 feet before linking up with the upper terminus of the Stover Canal at Ventiford. There, the granite blocks were off-loaded onto barges and taken down the two-mile long canal and thence down the Teign estuary to the port of Teignmouth, ready for shipment in sea-going vessels. The canal itself had been completed in 1792 by James Templer II (George Templer's father), principally to improve the means by which local ball clay bound for the Staffordshire potteries could be transported to the quays of Newton Abbot.

After 1820, a further 24 years were to pass before the first steam train reached Devon. At 12.30 p.m., on 1st May 1844, vast crowds at Exeter welcomed the engine *Actaeon* drawing the six carriages which comprised the train. After a great lunch in the goods shed at St David's, the return journey to Paddington commenced at 5.20 p.m. Among the passengers on the train was Sir Thomas Ackland, MP; at 10.30 that evening he rose in the House of Commons to say that he had been in Exeter little more than five hours earlier! The Bristol & Exeter Railway had arrived. It had been authorized by Parliament in May 1836, at the instigation of a group of Bristol merchants. In the meantime, no sooner had the Act of 1836 been passed than a group of enterprising Plymouth men proposed another railway, to link up at Exeter. Nothing became of this proposal, however, due to lack of support by the Devonshire people to subscribe the necessary capital, and, similarly, several other schemes brought before the public over the next six years met with the same fate. By then Isambard Kingdom Brunel had long since surveyed the countryside, and the Haldon range of hills, south-west of Exeter, had compelled him to plan for a line from Exeter to Starcross and along the coast to Dawlish and Teignmouth. Initially, it would then have continued over the River Teign to the neighbourhood of Torquay, thence over the Dart and into the South Hams. But, when the locomotive had shown its capabilities for hill climbing, he had abandoned the idea for a direct run from Teignmouth to Torquay, which would have involved many expensive works, in favour of a line running alongside the Teign estuary to Newton Abbot, and thence over the southern spurs of Dartmoor to Totnes, Ivybridge, Plympton and Plymouth.

Finally, in 1843, the Bristol & Exeter and Great Western Railway companies, together with the Bristol & Gloucester Railway, took up the matter and agreed to subscribe liberally to Brunel's project. This set the project on its feet; in October the prospectus of the Plymouth, Devonport & Exeter Railway – soon to become the South Devon Railway – was issued and the construction of the broad-gauge line was authorized the following July. Furthermore, in less than two years, on 30th May 1846, the line was open for traffic as far as Teignmouth and, by the end of that year, it had reached Newton Abbot. Work proceeded, and Plymouth (Laira Green) was reached on 5th May 1848, but this was not its terminus. Mutley Tunnel had to be completed before it reached Millbay, in April of the following year.

(b) Some other early projects in Devon.

In the wake of the railway reaching Devon many other schemes were brought before the public, for by then it was already evident that a rapid means of communication was essential in the interests of commercial well-being. Indeed, such was the excitement and interest that many writers have referred to the mid-1840s as a period of railway 'mania'. A large number of these schemes, however, were destined for failure for one reason or another, and one of the earliest to fall into this category was a proposed railway from Torquay Harbour to Aller Barn (Newton Abbot) on the South Devon Railway – under the auspices of the Torquay and Newton Abbot Railway Company. In this instance, following the issue of a prospectus in 1844 and plans being deposited, the scheme was killed off by objectors, who felt that a station at Aller was close enough for Torquay.

Following hard on the heels of this proposed line from Torquay Harbour came another proposal, from a group of local gentlemen, for a broad-gauge line from Dartmouth to Aller (and a branch to Ashburton, which was later deleted). It was proposed to work this line on the atmospheric method, and the engineer was to be W. R. Neale (an assistant to the London & South Western Railway's engineer, Joseph Locke). In July 1845, however, this proposal, and a separate plan for a South & North Devon Junction Railway from Newton (Abbot) to Crediton, were swept into the 'narrow-gauge' camp by Joseph Locke, with a promise of support from London. The Dartmouth, Torbay & Exeter Railway began with separate branches from Dartmouth and Brixham, which combined at Galmpton and continued via Torbay, Newton Abbot and Moretonhampstead. At Exeter it would have joined up with intended 'narrow-gauge' lines via Yeovil and Salisbury to London.

At last disturbed by these attempts at competition, the South Devon Railway presented a Bill to the 1846 Session of Parliament. This proposed a branch from the South Devon Railway at Aller to Kingswear routed through Torquay, Paignton, Churston and Brixham Quay. Some £45,750 was paid into the Court of Chancery in support of the Bill on 3rd February 1846. On the following day the competing 'narrow-gauge' Dartmouth, Brixham, Torbay, Exeter and North Devon Junction Railway (to quote its full title) deposited £24,500 in the same Court on account of its Bill. However, the 'narrow-gauge' interest was defeated on technical objections; the Bill had been completed with too much haste. The South Devon Railway (Amendments and Branches) Act, on the other hand, received the Royal Assent on 28th August 1846, but strong opposition from Paignton and Goodrington residents (who feared loss of access to the beach) had foreshortened the line and the Act showed it to terminate in field No. 23 in the parish of Tormohan (Torquay). The station was to be under Chapel Hill, at 'St Michaels' (Torre), but was named Torquay: this was to remain its name after the line was opened, on 18th December 1848, until 1st August 1859. It was then, because of a new station being opened at Livermead in conjunction with the Dartmouth and Torbay Railway's line to Kingswear, which, on that date, became operational to as far as Paignton, that the original station was renamed Torre. This latter company, incidentally, had been set up in 1856 under the direction of Charles Seale Hayne and received the Royal Assent to its Act on 27th July 1857.

Returning now to 1846, one of the consequences of the failure on the part of the Dartmouth, Brixham, Torbay, Exeter and North Devon Junction Railway Company in obtaining Parliamentary approval of its Bill was that any hopes that the local populace in and around the Moretonhampstead area may have had of having a railway connection nearby were dashed. Whether or not this led to another scheme being proposed at about this time is pure conjecture but, in his book *Small Talk at Wreyland*, Cecil Torr states that there was a project for a railway here (Wreyland, Lustleigh) as soon as the main line had reached Newton. He then quotes from a letter written to his father by his grandfather on 25th April 1847, as follows:–

> The surveyors have been from Newton to Okehampton, marking out a new line. They seem to be guided by the stream, and (if it takes place) they will go right up the meadows under here … I cannot fancy it will take place, for people are a little cooled down, and not so mad for speculation. Had it been projected some little time ago, no doubt it would have taken.

Unfortunately, apart from stating that the project came to nothing, Cecil Torr makes no further comment about this particular scheme, and, despite extensive research, no documentary evidence of it has come to light. This, in itself, seems to suggest that it was an entirely local promotion arising from discussions within the trading community, something that would have been in common with many other short-lived schemes of this period.

(The authors wish to express their sincere thanks to C. R. Potts (and The Oakwood Press) for permission to reproduce extracts from his book *The Newton Abbot to Kingswear Railway (1844 – 1988)* in compiling part of the above sub chapter.)

Phase 1 – 1858 to 1861: The preamble and conception by the Newton & Moretonhampstead Railway Committee.

Towards the end of the 1840s the country entered a period of sustained economic recession and, locally, the South Devon Railway Company fell into dire financial straits due to the amount of money spent on its ill-fated atmospheric system of propulsion on the main line between Exeter and Newton Abbot. As a result, the next ten years or so saw only a very limited number of railway schemes being proposed and only two of them in Devon reaching fruition – the Plymouth to Tavistock line and the Torquay to Paignton line (as part of the Dartmouth and Torbay Railway's line to Kingswear, already mentioned above). However, during the latter part of the 1850s, one of the schemes under consideration was for a railway to link Moretonhampstead to Newton Abbot. In this instance the promoters were a small group of individuals who owned land between these two locations and who were keen to improve the means by which their produce could be taken to the markets of Newton Abbot and Torquay. One of them was the Rector of Stokeinteignhead, the Reverend John Nutcombe Gould, and on 18th August 1858 he addressed an inaugural public meeting about the proposal at the Globe Hotel in Newton Abbot, a meeting presided over by Samuel Trehawke Kekewich – the Lord of the Manor of Stokeinteignhead and one of South Devon's newly-elected MPs.

Eight days later a full account of the meeting appeared in the columns of the *Exeter Flying Post*, and it was reported that during his address the rector had stated that he "did not believe there was another line in England that could be made so cheaply" and "that the engineering difficulties were comparatively trifling". It was also reported that he had not hesitated to assert that the first week the railway was opened the traffic that would go upon it would pay every expense and give every shareholder a fair and profitable return. From this it can be gleaned that the rector had been carried away somewhat by his enthusiasm, but at least it had achieved the desired effect: a resolution had been passed at the meeting "approving of a Line of Railway from Newton Abbot to Moretonhampstead through the Bovey Valley". At the same meeting another resolution had also been passed whereby a committee was appointed, "with power to add to their number", under the chairmanship of the Reverend J. N. Gould. Among the persons named were George Bragg (a Moretonhampstead solicitor), the Reverend William Charles Clack (Rector of St Andrew's Church, Moretonhampstead), Elias Cuming (of Linscott), John Rowell (a farmer at Teigngrace) and George and Thomas Wills (farmers at Kelly and East Wray respectively). The others were Messrs John Courtier (of Wray), John Drew (of Peamore, near Exeter), William Harris (of Plumley), Thomas Hatch (of Newton Abbot), Charles Langley (of Chudleigh), Alfred Puddicombe (of Moretonhampstead) and another member of the Wills family at Kelly.

Records of subsequent committee meetings include the following extracts:–

Meeting of the Committee held on 25th August 1858

It was resolved unanimously that Josiah Harris Esq. & William Sarl Esq. be added to the original Committee.
Resolved that the Gentlemen present – the Revd. J. N. Gould, Messrs. Wm. Harris, Puddicombe, Courtier, Drew, Thomas Wills, George Bragg, C. Langley, Josiah Harris, J. W. Rowell, John Vicary and the Revd. Clack be appointed the Acting Committee to make the preliminary arrangements for carrying out the objects of the Meetings of the 18th Instant in promoting a Railway from Newton to Moretonhampstead with power to add to their number.
That the following members of the Committee be requested to Canvas the Landowners and others in the neighbourhood of the intended Line for subscriptions in aid of the preliminary expences (which are estimated at £100) viz Messrs. Wm. Harris, Thomas Wills, John Harris, Hatch, Rowell, John Vicary, Puddicombe, George Bragg and that they be requested to report the result of their operations to an adjourned Meeting to be held this *day week.
Mr Josiah Harris consented to act as Honorary Secretary.

*The next meeting was held on 8th September 1858.

Meeting of the Committee held on 8th September 1858

The Gentlemen appointed at the last Meeting to collect subscriptions handed in their lists by which it appeared that £61. 14. 0 had been subscribed.
Mr [Thomas] Whitaker [of Exeter] gave his opinion as to the best means to be adopted to make a Survey of the Line and offered to prepare plans and Sections and to obtain estimates of the Cost of construction etc. for £50 upon which it was Resolved that Mr Whitaker be requested to make a preliminary survey of the proposed Line with plans of the Lands required and a detailed estimate of the Cost forthwith at a Cost not exceeding Fifty pounds, to be paid out of the Subscriptions and to make his report and furnish tracings of the Lands required with a detailed estimate to this Committee on the 29th Instant.
Resolved that a Sub-committee to consult with Mr Whitaker from time to time be the Revd. J. N. Gould, Thomas Wills, George Bragg, A. Courtier and Josiah Harris.

Meeting of the Committee held on 29th September 1858

It was Resolved that George Wills Esq. of Narracombe be added to the Committee.
Mr Whitaker having produced his Survey with Gradients of the intended Line and estimates of the Cost and submitted them to the Committee, It was Resolved that Mr Thomas Wills and Mr Courtier be appointed a Sub-committee to wait upon such Landowners or their Agents as they may desire necessary with Mr Whitaker in order to submit the plans to them and to ascertain their views on the subject and report the result of their operations to the next Meeting.

Meeting of the Committee held on 13th October 1858
(Chaired by Mr John Courtier in the absence of the Revd. J. N. Gould)

It was Resolved that *Lord Courtenay and Mr Kekewich be added to the Committee.
Messrs. Courtier, Bragg, Wills and others of the Committee reported that the proposed Line was favourably looked upon by most of the influential Landowners.
Resolved that £50 be paid to Mr Whitaker as per Agreement for preparing Plans and Sections and for estimating the Cost of the proposed Line, and that the balance of the Subscriptions [£1. 12. 0d] be placed in the hands of Mr Harris the Honorary Secretary for the payment of Printing and Current expences.

*Lord Courtenay was the son of the 10th Earl of Devon and, consequently, a very influential person to have on the Committee.

Meeting of the Committee held on 3rd November 1858
(Chaired by Mr George Bragg in the absence of the Revd. J. N. Gould)

It was Resolved that the Secretary be requested to write [to] Lord Courtenay & Mr Kekewich to solicit their attendances with the Committee appointed to wait upon his Grace the Duke of Somerset and to make an appointment for such purposes.

Meeting of the Committee held on 29th December 1858

It was resolved that the Secretary be requested to wait on Lord Courtenay with the Plans and Estimates and that he be authorized to State to Lord Courtenay that the Committee will be quite prepared to entertain the question of compensating the Duke of Somerset for the value of his Canal – either by absolute purchase or by way of annual Rent Charge in the event of his Grace assenting to the formation of the intended Railway through his Lands.

(Apart from the Stover Estate, the Duke of Somerset now also owned the Stover Canal and the Haytor Granite Tramway.)

Meeting of the Committee held on 26th January 1859

The Secretary laid before the Committee 2 Letters from Lord Courtenay under date 11th January giving an account of a very satisfactory interview with the Duke of Somerset and also under the date of the 14th January suggesting an alteration in the intended Line near the Pottery at Bovey Tracey and – It appearing to this Committee that the Landowners on the Line are favourable to the Scheme – It was resolved that Messrs. Courtier, Bragg, Langley and the Secretary be appointed a Sub-committee to wait upon the several Landowners on the intended Line in furtherance of the undertaking and to obtain all the necessary information as to traffic and other matters for bringing the Scheme fully before the Public.
That Mr Bragg be requested to write [to] Mr Bidder the Engineer on the subject

to know if he be disposed to render any assistance and report thereon to the next Meeting.

The Secretary having read a letter from Mr James Wills declining any further attendance on the Committee, Resolved that his resignation be accepted.

Meeting adjourned to Wednesday the 23 February next.

The meeting referred to directly above was never held. Instead, after a promising start, the project was abandoned – for the time being, at least. The reason for this was not any lack of enthusiasm, but almost certainly the poor level of response to requests for subscriptions. Indeed, apart from the sum of £61 14s. 0d. mentioned at the meeting held on 8th September 1858, no money at all appears to have been forthcoming and the balance in hand was just £1 12s. 0d.

It was not until 31st October 1860 that anything further was heard on the matter. Then, at long last, another meeting of the Committee did take place, although the only persons present, apart from the Revd. J. N. Gould, who took the chair, were Messrs Drew, Langley and J. Harris. Furthermore, the only resolution passed was "that the Hon. Secretary be requested to watch the progress of Mr Toogood's Scheme for a Line down the Teign, to call a special meeting of the Committee when necessary and at present to let all proceedings in opposition to the proposed line stand over till further information be obtained".

'Mr Toogood's Scheme' was, in fact, part of the Devon Central Railways Company's plan, of which so much has been written elsewhere – including a whole chapter on the subject in Peter Kay's excellent book *The Teign Valley Line* – that to repeat it here in detail is unnecessary. However, in simplistic terms it was connected with the arrival, in Exeter, of the London & South Western Railway Company's 'narrow-gauge' line from Salisbury, in July 1860, and the desire on the part of Sir Lawrence Palk of Haldon House to have a railway link to his estates in the Teign Valley and Torquay, in the interests of commercial gain.

In order to try and achieve these aims, Palk had secured the services of William Toogood (a parliamentary agent with interests in railway promotion generally) and persuaded a number of other local notables to join him, including Lord Courtenay – now the 11th Earl of Devon, following the death of his father in 1859. On the face of it the new earl's involvement was a surprise, as he had once been a director of the South Devon Railway Company and, more recently of course, had joined the Newton & Moretonhampstead Railway Committee. However, as part of its overall scheme, the Devon Central Railways Company was proposing to build several other lines, one of which would commence from a junction with the proposed Teign Valley line at Leigh Cross (near Dunsford), pass near Moretonhampstead and continue to Chagford. It was this, in fact, that had persuaded the earl to join the 'narrow-gauge' camp: he owned estates in the Moretonhampstead/Chagford area and had become frustrated by the failure on the part of the South Devon Railway Company, still hard-pressed financially, to promote a railway link to his property from Newton Abbot, or to support the Newton & Moretonhampstead Railway Committee's project.

Suffice to say, the plans of the Devon Central Railways Company were to end in failure. Petitions against the scheme were lodged by both the South Devon Railway Company and the Bristol & Exeter Railway Company, and after the Devon Central had presented its Bill to Parliament – with the London & South Western Railway Company also in opposition – it was eventually rejected in its entirety by a House of Commons Committee on 28th May 1861. This, of course, threw everything back into the 'melting pot'. However, the chairman of the South Devon Railway Company, Thomas Woollcombe, responded immediately by entering into a series of discussions with his consultant engineer, John Fowler, and others to determine the best way forward as regards pre-empting any further opposition from within the 'narrow-gauge' camp. At this time the company was still in no position financially to promote any new lines, although it was agreed that it could at least offer favourable working agreements for any promoted by nominally independent companies and that efforts should be made to secure the promotion of two lines in particular. One would be from Tavistock to Launceston via Lydford, and the other would be either from Newton Abbot to Dunsford via the Teign Valley or from Newton Abbot to Moretonhampstead: eventually, on the recommendation of John Fowler, it was agreed that it should be the latter.

Quite apart from anything else, this proposal to support a line from Newton Abbot to Moretonhampstead fulfilled the aims and ambitions of the Earl of Devon. As a result, he was now enticed back into the broad-gauge camp, where many thought that he rightfully belonged, and on 11th September 1861 took the chair at the next meeting of the Newton & Moretonhampstead Railway Committee. Held once again at the Globe Hotel in Newton Abbot, the committee members on this occasion consisted of the Revd. J. N. Gould, Thomas Wills, John Rowell, John Drew Jnr., Elias Cuming, William Harris and Charles Langley. Of even greater significance, however, were some of the persons who had been invited "to meet the Committee", for these included Thomas Woollcombe, representatives of two influential landowners (the Duke of Somerset and William Hole of the Parke Estate in Bovey), John Divett (the owner of Bovey Pottery), John Hayman Whiteway (a local clay trader) and John Wills (a farmer of Higher Hisley, Lustleigh).

It is recorded that during this important meeting, when the Earl of Devon called upon him as the representative of the South Devon Railway Company to state the assistance that might be expected from that company to the proposed line, Mr Woollcombe responded with a speech. This included the following comments:–

> Subject to proper co-operation on the part of the Landowners for the purpose of forming an Independent Company the Directors of the South Devon Railway Company would be prepared to recommend their Shareholders to agree that the South Devon Railway Company should work the line for 50 per cent of its

gross receipts, and also to give a rebate of 25 per cent upon Passenger traffic passing from the new line over the South Devon line and vice versa. That the cost at which the Goods traffic could be worked and any rebate to be granted in respect thereof would require further consideration.

The South Devon Railway Company would not subscribe any of the Capital, but [he] would not object as an individual to subscribe £500 provided that the Landowners acted in a liberal spirit in giving their lands on easy terms, and taking their proper share in raising the Capital. [He also thought that] if £1000 a mile was raised locally there ought to be no difficulty in carrying the matter out.

Other extracts from the minutes of this same meeting include the following:–

The Revd. J. N. Gould consented to give the Land required.

Mr Thos. Wills consented to have his Land valued by Mr Hooper of Chagford at an Agricultural Value and to take it out in paid up Shares. He was also authorised to state that Mr George Wills of Kelly would do the same.

Mr Wm. Harris consented to sell such Land as required at an Agricultural Value and to take payment in Shares.

[It was then resolved] that a Sub-committee be appointed consisting of Messrs. Thos. Wills, Mr Courtier, Wm. Harris and John Drew Junr. for the purpose of ascertaining,

1st. From the Landowners on the Line on what terms they are disposed to part with their Land for the purposes of the intended Railway.

2nd. From the Public generally what amount of Shares [are] likely to be taken.

3rd. What amount each Subscriber is prepared to give towards the necessary preliminary expenses, the amount Subscribed to be allowed in Shares, – such Sub-committee to report at the earliest practicable period.

It was now over three years since the first meeting of the Newton & Moretonhampstead Railway Committee had taken place, but, at long last, it seemed that real progress was being made as regards achieving its aims. A fortnight later, at the next meeting of the Committee (and various landowners, or their agents), this was confirmed still further when it was reported by the Sub-committee that fourteen "Gentlemen" had, between them, already consented to take shares to a total value of £1,675, and that two more landowners, George Wills of Narracombe and John Nosworthy of Steward Wood, would consent to sell their land at an agricultural value; the former "to be paid in a Rent Charge on Condition of a Station being at Lustleigh"! Moreover, during the meeting, the Committee also obtained the consent of Messrs Divett, Amery, White and Stevens "to part with their Lands upon an Agricultural Valuation and to accept payment by a Rent Charge". Finally, before the meeting ended, it was agreed to take up a written offer received from a Newton Abbot surveyor, Mr John Adams, to prepare maps and plans of the railway, and a recommendation was made "that Public Meetings be held at Chagford, Moreton Hampstead, Bovey and Newton Abbot and that a Prospectus be issued giving full particulars of Capital, Cost of Construction, terms with the South Devon Railway Company etc.".

MORETONHAMPSTEAD AND SOUTH DEVON RAILWAY.

At a meeting of the Inhabitants of Newton Abbot, and Landowners in the vicinity, held at the Globe Hotel, on Tuesday, the 8th October, 1861, WILLIAM JOHN WATTS, Esq., in the Chair—

Proposed by Mr. E. KENT, and seconded by Dr. GAY, and resolved unanimously—

"That this meeting, having heard with great satisfaction the explanation of the Provisional Committee of the Moretonhampstead and South Devon Railway Company, and viewing the undertaking as opening a rich and important agricultural district to the markets of this increasing town, consider it entitled to their warmest support."

W. J. WATTS, Chairman.

MORETONHAMPSTEAD AND SOUTH DEVON RAILWAY.

Capital: £100,000, in 4,000 shares of £25 each. Deposit: £1 per share.

CHAIRMAN:
The Right Honourable the Earl of Devon.

VICE-CHAIRMAN:
Thomas Woollcombe, Esq., Chairman of the South Devon Railway.

ENGINEERS:
John Fowler, Esq., 2, Queen Square-place, Westminster.
Peter John Margary, Esq., Dawlish.

SOLICITORS:
Messrs. Whiteford and Bennett, Plymouth.

BANKERS:
Messrs. Watts, Whidborne, and Moir, Newton Abbot.
The Devon and Cornwall Banking Company.

A detailed prospectus will be shortly published, with a complete list of Provisional Directors and other particulars.

JOSIAH HARRIS, Secretary.

Newton Abbot, 7th October, 1861.

At a public meeting held at the Three Crowns Inn, Chagford, on Monday, the 7th October, 1861, the Right Honourable the Earl of DEVON in the chair.

Proposed by JOHN HOOPER, Esq., seconded by Dr. BISHOP, and unanimously:—

Resolved—"That the formation of the proposed Moreton and South Devon Railway, which will afford to Chagford and the adjoining district an easy communication with Torquay and the other places connected with the South Devon Line, is deserving the cordial support of this meeting and of the other landowners and inhabitants of the district."

DEVON, Chairman.

MORETONHAMPSTEAD AND SOUTH DEVON RAILWAY.

At a numerous and influential Meeting of the Landowners and Inhabitants of Moreton, held at the White Hart, on Monday, the 7th October, 1861, the Right Honourable the Earl of DEVON in the Chair—

Moved by ELIAS CUMMING, Esq., seconded by MOSES HARVEY, Esq., supported by WM. FROUDE, Esq., Director of the Dartmouth and Torbay Railway, and unanimously:—

Resolved—"That the projected Moreton and South Devon Railway is calculated to produce the greatest advantage to the town and neighbourhood in developing their abundant natural resources, and placing them in immediate connection with the South Devon Railway system;—and that the undertaking is deserving the best support of this meeting, and of the landowners and inhabitants of the district."

DEVON, Chairman.

MORETONHAMPSTEAD AND SOUTH DEVON RAILWAY.

At a meeting of the Landowners and Inhabitants of Bovey Tracey, held in the Union Hotel, in Bovey, on Wednesday, the 7th October, 1861, JOHN DIVETT, Esq., in the Chair—

Proposed by W. R. HOLE, Esq., of Park, seconded by CHARLES LANGLEY, Esq., of Chudleigh, and resolved unanimously—

"That this meeting has read with great satisfaction the announcement of the projected Moreton and South Devon Railway, as calculated materially to advance the manufacturing and general interests of this district, and pledge themselves to give the undertaking their united and cordial support."

JOHN DIVETT, Chairman.

The advertisement that appeared in the local press after the four public meetings at Chagford, Moretonhampstead, Bovey Tracey and Newton Abbot.

These meetings, of course, were necessary to try and encourage the public to subscribe for shares and subsequently took place in Chagford (at noon), Moretonhampstead (in the afternoon) and Bovey (in the evening) on 7th October 1861, and in Newton Abbot on the following afternoon. All four were well attended, particularly those held on the first day, and followed essentially the same format whereby the chairman gave an opening address outlining the anticipated commercial and other benefits of the proposed railway, Thomas Woollcombe explained the amount of assistance that would be given by the SDR Company, and Peter Margary (the SDR's engineer) gave details of the proposed route and the anticipated cost. At each meeting resolutions were also passed in support of the scheme, which then promptly appeared in the form of an advertisement in the local press, as shown.

As can be seen, the advertisement also carried other, significant, information which, it needs to be explained, arose from a separate meeting held at Chagford earlier on the same day as the public meeting. Those recorded as being present at this meeting were the Earl of Devon (chairman) and Messrs John Drew, Thomas Wills, Elias Cuming, Thomas Woollcombe, C. C. Whiteford, W. Carr, G. Pridham, J. Belfield, P. J. Margary & Lloyd, and during the course of it the following resolutions were passed:–

> That the undertaking commenced in 1858 under the title of the Newton and Moreton Hampstead Railway up the Bovey Valley be henceforth designated the Moreton Hampstead and South Devon Railway and a Company be formed to carry the same into effect.
> That the Capital of the Company be £100,000 in 4,000 Shares of £25 each and a deposit not exceeding £1 per Share be paid.
> That John Fowler and P. J. Margary be the Engineers of the Company.
> That Messrs. Whiteford & Co. be the Solicitors of the Company.
> That Messrs. Watts, Whidborne and Moir and the Devon and Cornwall Bank be the Bankers.
> That Mr Josiah Harris be the Hon. Secretary.
> That a Committee Meeting be called for at an Early Day to appoint Provisional Directors.

(For reasons unknown the original promoter of the scheme, the Revd. J. N. Gould, did not attend this meeting and appears not to have had any further involvement in the matter. Another absentee was John Adams, the Newton Abbot surveyor appointed to prepare maps and plans of the railway. However, according to Thomas Woollcombe doubts had arisen over whether he could complete the survey and sections in time to comply with the Standing Orders of the House of Commons and, as a result, "an arrangement had been made with Mr Margary that he would complete all Engineering and Surveying including Lithographing Plans and every other expense for £375 a mile, payment to be made one third in Cash, one third in Debentures and one third in Shares".)

Phase 2 – 1862 to 1866: The Moretonhampstead & South Devon Railway Company.

(a) Events leading up to obtaining the Act of Incorporation.

The first 'proper' meeting of the Moretonhampstead & South Devon Railway Committee, which was really no more than a continuation of the former Newton & Moretonhampstead Railway Committee, took place at the Globe Hotel in Newton Abbot on 30th October 1861. It was attended by the Earl of Devon (chairman), Thomas Woollcombe, John Drew, Thomas Wills, William Harris, John Rowell, John Fowler and Peter Margary – by now, all familiar names – and the main business to be conducted concerned the appointment of provisional directors of the proposed company. In the event this was dealt with by three separate resolutions. The first was that there should be five provisional directors, "with power to add two to their number"; the second was a requirement that each director should hold shares in the company to the value of £500; and the third was that the Earl of Devon, Thomas Woollcombe, John Divett and Thomas Wills should be the provisional directors of the company, "with power to add three to their number". Three of the newly-appointed provisional directors (John Divett was not present) then held a separate meeting immediately afterwards to confirm the appointments made by the Committee at the earlier meeting held at Chagford on the morning of 7th October.

The next important development came on 14th November, when a working agreement was drawn up in the form of a 'Heads of Arrangement for Working the Line by the South Devon Railway Company, and for Rebates to be allowed to the Moreton Hampstead and South Devon Railway Company'. This, it stated, was "between the Moreton Hampstead and South Devon Railway Company (hereinafter called "The Moreton Company") of the first part; the South Devon Railway Company (hereinafter called "The South Devon Company") of the second part; and each of the Great Western Railway Company, the Bristol and Exeter Railway Company, and the Cornwall Railway Company (hereinafter called the "Three Companies") ... of the third part", and amongst its many clauses (or 'Heads') were the following:–

1. – These Heads to be subject to the Sanction of Parliament.
2. – The Moreton Company, at their own expense, to make and complete the intended Moreton and South Devon Railway from Moreton Hampstead to Newton (hereinafter called the "New Line"), according to their Act, as a Single Line, but with Land and Overbridges for a Double Line, with Double Line where requisite, and all proper and sufficient Works and conveniences, including a Junction at Newton with the South Devon Railway; and all to the reasonable satisfaction of the South Devon Company's Engineer.
3. – All Contracts affecting the working of the Line, or involving conditions or engagements to be carried out either directly or indirectly by the South Devon Company, are to be made subject to approval by them.
4. – The New Line and Works to be maintained by the Contractor for making the railway, for Twelve Months after completion, to the satisfaction of the South Devon Company's Engineer.
5. – After the New Line is authorized to be opened for Public Traffic, the South Devon Company at all times, at their own expense, to maintain (without prejudice to the fourth head), stock, work, and use the New Line so as properly to develope and accommodate the local and general Traffic of the District.
6. – If, and whenever after the opening of the New Line, it shall be required, in consequence of increased Traffic or for the Public safety, to make additions to the Stations or Works, such additions as shall be reasonably required by the South Devon Company's Engineer shall be made at the expense of the Moreton Company, who shall provide Capital for the purpose, not exceeding the amount authorized by their Act.

This somewhat lengthy document also made provision for "Fifty per cent of the gross traffic receipts for all traffic conveyed over the New Line to be paid to the South Devon Company for their expenses of maintaining, managing and working the line and traffic, and the other fifty per cent to be paid to the Moreton Company" and contained numerous other clauses, several of which related to the granting of rebates by the 'South Devon Company' and the 'Three Companies' in respect of any through traffic to, or from, any of the stations on the new line.

As recorded in the minutes, the document was read during a meeting of the provisional directors of the Moretonhampstead & South Devon Railway Company held at the Globe Hotel in Newton Abbot on 12th December 1861 and duly approved: by then it had already been signed by the Earl of Devon and Thomas Woollcombe (on behalf of the Moretonhampstead & South Devon Railway Company and the South Devon Railway Company respectively) and also by the chairmen of the 'Three Companies'. The minutes of this same meeting also include the following other items of note:–

> The Chairman [the Earl of Devon] reported that he had communicated with Mr [William] Hole and Mr Hames [the Reverend Hayter George Hames, Rector of Chagford] with reference to their becoming Provisional Directors, and that Mr Hole in reply had consented to join the Board but Mr Hames had declined.
>
> Read – Letter from Mr Josiah Harris of the 26th Nov. last tendering his resignation as Secretary. Resolved that Mr Harris's resignation be accepted & that the best thanks of the Board be conveyed to him for the zeal and energy which he has displayed in promoting the interests of the Company. It was proposed by Mr Woollcombe, seconded by Mr Divett and Resolved that Mr [Alexander E.] Lhoyd be, and he is hereby, appointed Secretary of the Company.
>
> Mr Whiteford submitted a print of the Bill for the Incorporation of the Company and the Board proceeded to discuss the amount of Capital to be raised, the nominal value of the Shares & the qualification of Directors – Mr Woollcombe stated that although he believed the line could be constructed for less than £10,000 a mile it would be desirable to provide a larger sum which would be available at a future time for the construction of sidings or other general purposes. Resolved that the Share Capital of the Company shall be £105,000 in 10,500 Shares of £10 each with power to borrow £35,000 and that the qualification of a Director be the holding of thirty Shares.
>
> The Petition for the Bill was then signed by the Directors present, and the Secretary was instructed to arrange with the Devon and Cornwall Bank or Messrs. Watts & Co. [bankers of Newton Abbot] for a loan of Stock to meet the required Parliamentary deposit.
>
> Mr Woollcombe referred to the necessity of appointing a Surveyor to negotiate for the purchase of the land. Resolved that Mr Hooper [of Chagford] be requested to act as the Surveyor of the Company and to proceed as far as possible to arrange the necessary purchases.

Within just a few weeks of this meeting the Bill referred to above (with the Heads of Arrangement annexed to it) had been deposited and was first read in the House of Commons on 10th February 1862. After two further – unopposed – readings it was then referred to the House of Lords, where, apart from one or two minor amendments being found necessary by a Lords Committee, it again had a smooth passage and the resulting Act received the Royal Assent on 7th July 1862. It authorised "the making of a Railway from the South Devon Railway, near to the Newton Station thereof, in the Parish of Wolborough in the County of Devon to Moretonhampstead in the same County" and was cited as "The Moretonhampstead and South Devon Railway Act, 1862". It also authorised a share capital of £105,000 in £10 shares, with borrowing power to the extent of £35,000, and contained a number of stipulations. These included a figure of £300 being quoted as a qualification for directorship; the number of directors being six; the named directors – The Right Honourable the Earl of Devon, Elias Cuming, John Divett, William Robert Hole, Thomas Wills and Thomas Woollcombe – being obliged to remain in office until "the first ordinary meeting" of the company; the various categories of traffic that could be carried over the line and the tolls relating to each of them; and the maximum tolls to be charged for passengers conveyed in first, second and third class carriages (3d., 2d. and 1½d. per mile respectively).

(b) The construction of the line.

Having obtained their Act, the promoters now arranged for the circulation of a new prospectus and for the "first ordinary meeting" of the newly-incorporated company to be held at the Union Hotel in Bovey Tracey on 4th August 1862. During this meeting, which was chaired by Thomas Woollcombe, the six directors named in the Act were formally elected as the first directors of the company, speeches were made outlining the benefits of the proposed railway and the amount of progress made to date, and a resolution passed that "local Committees be formed at Moretonhampstead, North Bovey, Chagford, Lustleigh and Bovey Tracey for the purpose of canvassing additional shares". Afterwards, at the Commercial Hotel in Bovey Tracey, the 'new' directors also held their first meeting, at which the main business to be conducted was the appointment of Alexander E. Lhoyd as the company secretary.

As can be seen from the prospectus (reproduced in Appendix I), the promoters had, by now, also secured the services of one of the best known railway contractors in the country at that time, Thomas Brassey of Messrs Brassey & Ogilvie, who had agreed to construct the line for £88,500 (payable in cash, debentures and shares in three equal proportions). In addition, they had entered into tentative arrangements with a number of landowners to acquire the land needed for the railway at an agricultural value and, after protracted negotiations, agreed to purchase outright such land belonging to the Duke of Somerset as was required: this included the lower section of the Haytor Granite Tramway and, at the duke's insistence, the whole of the Stover Canal. Although not mentioned in the prospectus, the total purchase price was to be £8,000 and the agreement had been made on the understanding that a siding would be installed at the junction of the duke's tramway near Bovey Pottery so that granite quarried on Haytor Down could still be transported out of the area, using the surviving section of the tramway for the initial stage of the journey.

At this point in time, apart from what had already been achieved by the promoters, it was clear that, locally, enthusiasm for the proposed railway had reached an all-time high. Indeed, the townspeople of Bovey Tracey had already indicated this fact by setting aside an entire day (Tuesday, 1st July) on which to celebrate the then imminent passing of the Act; celebrations which had included the flying of flags, music being provided by the town's brass band, bellringing and an open-air tea for around 500 people. However, over the ensuing weeks it soon became apparent that this enthusiasm meant very little when it came to the more serious business of subscribing for shares. Instead, in November, when the interest became payable on a loan of £8,500 taken out to pay the parliamentary deposit, the company's finances were in such a parlous state that the directors had to dig into their own pockets and negotiate a temporary loan from the South Devon Railway Company! The second half-yearly meeting of the shareholders, which was held at the Union Hotel in Bovey Tracey on Saturday, 28th February 1863, was also notable for its lack of support. In fact, with only two of the directors, the company secretary, the company's engineer and one shareholder in attendance, there was an insufficient number to constitute a quorum. Consequently, the meeting had to be adjourned until the following Monday, but, once again, there was an insufficient number present to constitute a quorum and the meeting, as such, had to be abandoned.

In a contemporary newspaper report it was stated that "the smallness of the attendance [at the meeting] arose entirely from the fact that there was scarcely any business to be disposed of; the meeting being a formal one held in conformity with the Act of Parliament". Even so, the lack of interest could hardly have instilled confidence amongst the promoters, who were now (and had been for some while) working in collaboration with the South Devon Railway Company to try and devise a means of raising a sum of £25,000, the amount still needed before work could commence on the construction of the line. This behind-the-scenes activity was, therefore, of considerable importance – if not crucial – as regards the future of the proposed railway, and continued with a conference being held in London on 23rd March. By that time consultations had also taken place with John Fowler and Thomas Brassey, and during the conference supplementary Heads of Arrangement were agreed upon between the Moretonhampstead & South Devon Railway and the South Devon Railway companies, which were recorded in the form of a memorandum, as follows:–

Memorandum of Conference on the affairs of the Moretonhampstead and South Devon Railway – 23rd March 1863.

Present for the Company
The Earl of Devon and the Secretary
For the South Devon Railway Company
Messrs Woollcombe, Pridham and Brown

1. Proposed that with consent of the Ordinary Moreton Shareholders the South Devon shall guarantee that in addition to the dividends on the Ordinary shares any deficiency not exceeding 5 per cent per annum upon an amount of £25,000 shall be paid by the South Devon Company, the South Devon taking the whole of the rebates.

2. That it be proposed to Mr. Brassey that £3,000 be added to his original Tender of £88,500 in consideration of his surrender of the rebates on his ordinary shares and agreeing to accept payment as follows.

In Ordinary Shares	36,500
In Cash to be raised on the guaranteed Shares	25,000
In debentures	30,000
	£91,500

3. That in modification of the original Agreement with the Engineers and in consideration of their giving up the rebates they be paid as follows.

In Ordinary Shares	4,000
Debentures	1,500
Cash	1,000
	£6,500

4. The following is the Estimate for the cost of the line exclusive of Stations under the foregoing arrangement.

	To be paid			
	In shares	Debentures	Cash	Total
Cost of Act and Law Expenses	660	500	2,500	3,660
Land	6,100		11,155	17,255
Guaranteed Contract	36,500	30,000	25,000	91,500
Engineering	4,000	1,500	1,000	6,500
Office Expenses			585	585
	£47,260	£32,000	£40,240	£119,500

5. The above is to be provided for as follows.

By allotment of Paid up Shares To Solicitors, Landowners, Contractors and Engineers as above		47,260
By proceeds of Debentures To Solicitors, Contractors and Engineers as above		32,000
By proceeds of Subscriptions		
General List	8,000	
Conditional List	1,720	
Further to be raised	5,000	14,720
By proceeds of guaranteed Shares		25,000
By proceeds of further Debentures		520
		£119,500

6. In consideration of an Engagement by the South Devon Board to recommend to their Shareholders, and use their best endeavours to carry out as must be advised by Counsel the proposed arrangements for guaranteeing the £25,000, Lord Devon and the other Local Gentlemen promoters of the Moretonhampstead Line will guarantee the income of £5,000 to the Local subscription before referred to. This Guarantee however to be conditional on the sanction by the South Devon Shareholders of the Guarantee by the South Devon as to the £25,000.

7. The foregoing arrangement will leave reserve for Stations etc. as follows.

Unissued Shares	18,020
Unissued Debentures	2,480
	£20,500

The next task, of course, was to obtain the views of the shareholders on the proposed arrangement, and in order to do this specially convened meetings took place in Newton Abbot and Moretonhampstead shortly after the Earl of Devon had returned from London. At the next meeting of the directors, held at the company offices in Newton Abbot on 15th April, he was then able to report that "the same had been generally approved and £3,700 had been already subscribed towards making up the further amount required to be raised in the District". Bearing in mind the lack of support that they had received over the preceding six months or so, the directors must have been decidedly encouraged by this response and, during the meeting, resolved "that Lord Devon and Mr. Woollcombe be requested to appoint the days for holding the Special Meetings of their respective companies as soon as the draft [of the supplementary Heads of Arrangement] had been settled by Counsel".

As already indicated in paragraphs 1 and 6 of the Memorandum above, these 'Special Meetings' were necessary to obtain the shareholders' formal approval to the proposed arrangement, and the first – that of the Moretonhampstead & South Devon Railway Company – took place at the White Hart Hotel in Moretonhampstead on 28th May. Well attended and chaired by the Earl of Devon, this included a report of the directors (setting out the proposals in detail) being read by the company secretary; the earl making a speech, during which he explained why the modifications had been found to be necessary and that without them " it was not at all possible that the required capital could be raised under any circumstances"; and, finally, a motion giving the required approval being proposed by John Divett and subsequently being carried unanimously.

On the following day the shareholders of the South Devon Railway Company, at its extraordinary general meeting, also gave their approval to the proposed arrangement. Consequently, the promoters could now concentrate their efforts on making final arrangements for work to be started on the construction of the line, and extracts from the minutes of another meeting of the directors held a few weeks later, on 5th August, clearly indicate that this was being done:–

> Mr. Margary reported that he had finally settled the Sections of the line with Mr. Ogilvie, on the part of the Contractors, and that the works could be commenced as soon as the Board thought fit to give the necessary directions.
> Resolved – That the Engineers be instructed to proceed with the works forthwith and to furnish Mr. Hooper with the land plans, to enable him to make arrangements with the landowners.
> The Secretary submitted the draft Contract for the Execution of works, and read [a] letter received from Mr. Whiteford calling the Board's attention to one or two of the clauses as to which a difference of opinion existed between himself and the Contractors' Solicitors.
> Resolved – That Mr. Margary be requested to compare the draft with the original Specification, and to return it to Mr. Whiteford with any observations that he might have to make in support of the Company's interests – and that subject to such revision, the draft, as now submitted, be approved.
> The necessity of making a call on the Shareholders, and the amount of such call having been discussed.
> It was resolved – That a call of £2 per Share payable on the 5th day of September next, and the same is hereby made, and that credit be given to the several shareholders for all sums which may have been paid on account of deposit, or by subscriptions towards the preliminary Expenses.
> The Board proceeded to consider the financial arrangements which it would be necessary to make to enable them to meet the payments to the Contractors, and to complete the several land purchases, more particularly that of the Duke of Somerset's Canal.
> Resolved – That the Secretary be instructed to communicate with Messrs. Sanders & Co., and Messrs. Watts & Co., and to ascertain on what terms they will be prepared to negotiate a loan of £10,000 or £12,000, either on security of calls, or on the deposit of guaranteed Shares – and that Mr. Woollcombe be also requested to apply to the Devon & Cornwall Bank with the same object.

Moreover, it was only five days later that the first sod was cut, a ceremony performed on Bovey Heath by William Crosley in his official capacity as the engineer and manager for Messrs Brassey & Ogilvie, the contractors. According to a contemporary report "the works were [then] vigorously commenced", and would, in the opinion of the directors, be completed in about 18 months. In the event, this timescale was somewhat over-optimistic for reasons partly revealed in some of the Engineers' Reports submitted at the next six half-yearly general meetings of the shareholders, as follows:–

Third Half-Yearly General Meeting, August 26th, 1863.

The working survey is almost completed, and, in order to expedite the works, many of the landed proprietors and tenants have kindly given us permission to enter on their lands in anticipation of formal possession being obtained in the ordinary course.
The Contractors have nearly completed the diversion of the road on the Bovey Heath, which we were required to make by our agreement with the Enclosure Commissioners.
As soon as your orders to proceed with the works were received, the contractors commenced some of the cuttings, and they are now making all necessary arrangements for the vigorous continuation of the works.

Fourth Half-Yearly General Meeting, February 18th, 1864.

The Contractor has made fair progress with the prosecution of the Works since he received the order to commence.
The long diversion of the Road on the Bovey Heath which, as stated in our last Report, had to be made by our agreement with the Enclosure Commissioners, is completed, and the traffic has been turned on to it.
The Railway Cutting which the old Road retarded is now completed, and the Work near the Bovey Pottery is being satisfactorily proceeded with.
The Contractor has concentrated his men between the Bovey Heath and Moretonhampstead, on which length of the Line several of the Cuttings are in a forward state, and some of them will shortly be completed.

Fifth Half-Yearly General Meeting, August 24th, 1864.

The Contractors have hitherto chiefly concentrated their men on the works between Bovey Tracey and Moretonhampstead, in consequence of the delay experienced in obtaining the land between the Bovey Heathfield and Newton. That has been settled [following difficulties in establishing the Duke of Somerset's legal title to the land required from him] and the Contractors are now in possession of the land for nearly the whole length of the line.
Between Jews Bridge, on the Southern borders of the Bovey Heathfield, and Moretonhampstead, the Contractors have made fair progress with the works. Some of the cuttings and embankments are completed, and the masonry of the piers and abutments of several of the bridges have been built, and the arches are being turned.
The Works are now in full progress between Jews Bridge and Newton.

Sixth Half-Yearly General Meeting, February 22nd, 1865.

We regret our inability to announce as much progress having been made with the works since our last report as we could have desired, the Contractors having considerably reduced the number of their men, but we hope that shortly they will be enabled to push the work on again with vigour.
The works have been in progress and are generally in an advanced state throughout the whole length of the line, excepting at Ponsford Yeo, where difficulties [over legal title] have occurred in obtaining the land, but the arrangements are now completed, and the Contractors have been put into possession.

Seventh Half-Yearly General Meeting, August 25th, 1865.

Since our last Report the Contractors have proceeded with renewed energy, and they have made considerable further progress with the Earthworks and Masonry.
The wrought iron girders for the bridges in the Newton Marshes, and elsewhere, have been ordered, and the ballasting has been commenced.
Several tons of the Permanent Rails have been delivered on to the ground, and the arrival of the timber for the Longitudinals of the Permanent Way is daily expected.

Eighth Half-Yearly General Meeting, February 21st, 1866.

The continuous rains of the last several months, have considerably retarded the whole of the works, but they have had the beneficial effect of consolidating the embankments.
The late flood, which we are informed has been the highest known for the last thirty years, only damaged the Line at the Teign Bridge road, where from being ponded back by the heaps of Potters' Clay deposited by the side of the Canal and the hedges of the Turnpike road, it washed across the Line and scoured away about eighteen chains of the low gravel embankment.
The violence of the flood was increased by the water of the Canal breaking the bank close to the Railway by the Teign Bridge road.
It has been arranged to restore the embankment at once, making larger flood openings, and to raise a bank to keep the floods from in future washing over the embankment.
The Permanent Way is being laid; it will soon be completed from Newton to Bovey, and the Contractors have given orders for it to be pushed forward as quickly as possible.
The Iron Girders for the river Lemon and Whitelake Bridges are in a forward state and we trust will soon be in place.
The earthwork and the Masonry of the Platform Walls and Station Foundations are in progress.

Another reason why the work did not progress as quickly as originally anticipated (which is directly linked to the comments made in the opening paragraph of the Engineers' Report submitted to the half-yearly meeting held on 22nd February 1865) is that in the autumn of 1864 it actually

After aquiring land for the building of their line, the Moretonhampstead & South Devon Railway Company laid a number of inscribed granite blocks to serve as boundary markers. The example shown above was photographed on 4th August 1958 at the side of the post and wire-fenced footpath leading from the station at Lustleigh to the village.

E. R. Shepherd

stopped for a short while – because of "the inability of the Company to meet their engagements with the Contractors". In other words the company had run into serious financial trouble. This was in spite of the fact that a banker's loan of £10,000 had been obtained earlier in the year, along with an overdraft and a somewhat smaller loan from two other banking institutions, and cash had been received from four calls of £2 each made on the ordinary shares between August 1863 and September 1864. However, during a conference held at John Fowler's office in London on 7th December, which was attended by the Earl of Devon, Thomas Woollcombe, Mr Brassey and Mr Ogilvie, new Heads of Arrangement were agreed upon " for the disposition of the Special Shares [the 'guaranteed' shares referred to in the memorandum dated 23rd March 1863, reproduced on pages 109/110] and the general settlement of the Company's affairs". Under this new arrangement, the contractors were to receive 500 of the special shares, debentures, which were "to be sealed and issued forthwith according to Certificates [for work done on the line]", and, when payment became due, the proceeds from the sale of a further 1,200 special shares. In consideration of this, the contractors were to "engage that the Works shall be resumed and pressed forward with every possible expedition". The company, meanwhile, was to take the residue of the special shares (800) at its own risk with a view to raising £8,000.

Ten days later, during a special meeting of the directors held at the White Hart Hotel, in Moretonhampstead, the terms of the new arrangement were formally approved by the passing of a resolution. At the same time the company secretary was "instructed to address a circular to all the Shareholders offering the Special Shares pro rata according to their original subscriptions, the Shareholders being requested to signify their option to receive an allotment or not, on or before 5th January next". It was also stated "that allotters be informed in the circular that payments will have to be made in moieties of £5 each, the first payable on the 1st day of February and the second on the 1st day of April 1865". Unfortunately, though, the subsequent response from the shareholders was disappointing to the extreme: only 22 of the special shares were taken up! Consequently the company's financial situation, eased only marginally by cash received from a final call of £2 each on the ordinary shares being made on 8th February 1865, remained in a critical state. Moreover, had it not been for the contractors agreeing to take a further 1,200 special shares later in the year in lieu of the cash of £12,000 included under the new Heads of Arrangement, and also the bankers extending their loan of £10,000 for a further six months, it seems almost certain that the work on building the line would have ground to a halt again.

In the event, the work progressed reasonably smoothly during 1865, despite an extremely wet winter, but behind the scenes there was soon another major problem looming for the company's directors – the question of "the mode in which the Capital could be raised for completing the line and constructing the Stations, and also for meeting the loan of £10,000 [from the bankers]". In order to address this matter, another conference was eventually held at John Fowler's office in London on 26th October of that year, with those in attendance on this occasion being the Earl of Devon, Thomas Woollcombe, Alexander Lhoyd, Peter Margary and Mr Whiteford (the company's solicitor). During the conference Peter Margary expressed the opinion "that sufficient Station accommodation might be provided for opening the Line by a cash outlay of about £6,000, but that it was most desirable that £10,000 should be provided". In response, it was proposed to raise a loan of £5,000 to be secured by deposit of the unissued ordinary shares, representing £17,165, and that an application should be made to the South Devon Railway Company for an advance of £5,000 on the security of the future traffic receipts. As regards the discharge of the banker's loan, it was proposed that the sum of £2,220 should be applied from the proceeds of sales of surplus lands and unissued debentures of the company; a further sum of £2,780 should be raised by the directors and officials of the company by taking up 278 of the unallotted special shares; and that "Mr Brassey should be applied to, to take the remaining 500 [unallotted special] shares". However, it is clear from the Directors' Minutes Book that these proposals were not fully implemented. Instead, included in the minutes of a meeting of the directors held on 14th April 1866, it is stated "that the Secretary reported that the South Devon Company had consented to guarantee an advance of £5,000 by the Devon & Cornwall Bank on the understanding that the amount be applied solely to Station purposes". In addition, included in the minutes of another meeting of the directors held on 2nd June 1866, concerning the banker's loan of £10,000, is mention of a proposal "that £5,000 should be paid off by the first of August and the balance on the 31st December, interest to be charged at the Bank of England rate".

(c) The opening of the line.

Despite the various difficulties described above, and the weather during the winter of 1865/66 being even wetter, and stormier, than the previous year – causing particular problems at Teignbridge (as outlined in the Engineers' Report submitted to the half-yearly meeting held on 21st February 1866) – the engineering work and the laying of the permanent way was almost complete by the early spring of 1866. In addition, having obtained the plans from Peter Margary, the contractors had commenced work on the construction of the platform walls and station foundations at Bovey, Lustleigh and Moretonhampstead, and were now reported to be making good progress. The directors, meanwhile, had accepted a tender from Messrs Call & Pethick of Plymouth for erecting the station buildings above the level of the platforms at a cost of £3,136. Earlier in the year the directors had also made arrangements for other matters to receive attention, such as the installation of the telegraph wires and signals, and were now hoping that the line could be opened to passenger traffic towards the end of May. Indeed, with this in mind, it was not long before they instructed the company secretary to send a preliminary notice to the railway department of the Board of Trade, stating that it was the company's intention "to open for the public conveyance of Passengers after the expiration of one Calendar month from this date [26th April 1866] their Railway …".

It soon became apparent, however, that the proposed opening date could not be met, due to the work on completing the line taking a little longer than at first anticipated. As a result, the required Board of Trade inspection had to be deferred, and it was not until 20th June that the matter arose again. Then the company secretary was instructed to send another letter, giving notice "that in the opinion of the Moretonhampstead and South Devon Railway Company their Railway … will on the Second day of July next be sufficiently completed for the safe conveyance of Passengers, and is now ready for inspection". In the meantime, at least two trains were reported to have passed over the entire length of the line, for testing purposes and for the benefit of the local press, and the directors, rather than await the outcome of the Board of Trade inspection, had publicly announced their intention to hold an official opening ceremony on 26th June. Although it is no more than pure conjecture, the reason for this apparent lack of patience appears to have been that the directors, no doubt eagerly awaiting the first traffic receipts in order to ease the company's financial position, wanted to dispense with the formalities as soon as possible. In this way a public service could then be instigated immediately after the line had passed its inspection. Whatever, both the company and the inhabitants of Moretonhampstead were now busy making preparations for the event, which was to be celebrated with a local public holiday.

The opening day celebrations were subsequently reported in the local press, and the following extracts are from a detailed account that appeared in *The Weekly Express* on 27th June:–

OPENING OF THE

Moretonhampstead & South Devon Railway.

… The route was originally projected by P. J. Margary, Esq., of Dawlish, one of the principal engineers of the line, who had the Parliamentary plans and sections prepared, and succeeded in getting them adopted by Parliament. The masonry bridges were designed and the working levels taken, and all the earth and other works carried out by William Crosley, Esq., the representative of Messrs. Brassey and Ogilvie, the eminent railway contractors, who undertook the contract for making the line; and the amount of skill and forethought which he has displayed throughout the entire construction of the line, supported by the powerful influence, wealth and energy of his principals, now yields to the inhabitants of the neighbourhood a railway, which but a few years ago, from the tortuitous hilly and rocky character of the country, would have been deemed an impossibility. To them therefore praise is due for the spirited manner with which they have carried on and brought to a successful conclusion these works. To A. E. Lhoyd, Esq., the secretary, much praise is also due for his exertions in at all times promoting the interests of the Company with an urbanity of manner which has won for him many friends. Mr. Fowler, of London, is joint engineer of the line along with Mr. Margary — and Mr. Little, of Bovey Tracey, is the resident or assistant-engineer to the last named gentleman …

THE OPENING

The importance attaching to the opening of the railway naturally created great enthusiasm in the hearts of the inhabitants of Moretonhampstead, Bovey Tracey, Lustleigh, and throughout the district, and to give a hearty reception to the directors on their arrival the Moretonians speedily set to work to provide the requisite funds for celebrating the event. On the 26th of May a public meeting was held at the White Hart Hotel to take the matter into consideration, when the following gentlemen were appointed a committee, with power to add to their number, to make the necessary arrangements:— Rev. W. C. Clack (rector), Capt. Adair, Dr. Collins, Mr. H. Harvey, Dr. Hunt, Mr. W. Harvey, Mr. N. Neck, and Mr. George Marwood. The committee were very active in fulfilling their duties, and considerably over £100 were collected for the demonstration. At a subsequent meeting the committee considered in what manner it would be best for them to appropriate the funds, and after mature deliberation it was determined that a luncheon should be provided for the directors and others, tickets for which were issued at 3s. 6d. each, or 6s. for a lady and gentleman. A public tea for women and children was also decided upon, for which £30 were allowed from the funds. The committee appointed to undertake the management of this portion of the proceedings were:- Mrs. Clack, Mrs. Isaacs, Mrs. Bragg, Mrs. Brewer, Mrs. Collins, Mrs. Hill, Miss White, Miss Wills, Miss Germon, and Mrs. Harvey. Various sums were apportioned to the sub-committees for carrying out the other features of the demonstration, namely:— £5 towards decorating the town, in addition to the tasteful operations of the townspeople, who were desirous of beautifying their own establishments in honour of the occasion; £15 for the providing of rural sports; and £22 for refreshments to be given to the men. The band of the Newton Rifle Corps was also engaged for the day. In addition to these amounts there were extras to be provided for, which the committee rightly took into consideration.

THE DAY

A more glorious morning than Tuesday it is not easy to think of — the misty dawn of early morn was chased away by a bright rising sun whose effulgence tinged the hills and valleys with dazzling splendour. Nature seemed vocal, and hearts full of enthusiasm on this particular occasion harmonized with the self-speaking influences around. In fact all was joyous, and the opening of the Moretonhampstead and South Devon Railway could not have been celebrated with more apparent manifestations of gaiety than those which were observable. At an early hour the bells of St. Andrew's church sent forth merry peals as a prelude to the day's proceedings; the inhabitants of Moreton were early astir, and the decorative genius of each individual was displayed in adorning the streets of the town with devices of exquisite taste. Throughout the morning hundreds of visitors flocked into the town from the neighbouring parishes and perambulated the streets until about twelve o'clock, at which time the opening train was expected to arrive. The station, which is about a quarter of a mile distant, then became a scene of bustle and confusion; the hundreds which had assembled at Moreton were there centred, and their numbers were turned into thousands by the immense body of people brought by the train. Of course every one was eager to obtain a view of it and the accidental crushing of any lady's crinoline was good humouredly considered to be mishap which could not well be prevented. The train consisted of 13 carriages drawn by two engines, viz:— the Lion and the Lance, each being beautifully decorated with wreaths of flowers and evergreens. The train started from the Newton Railway Station at 11.15 a.m., and on its arrival at the Bovey Station it halted for some time to receive an addition to its living freight. Proceeding onwards the train passed through the Lustleigh Station without stopping, an arrangement which had been previously intimated by the directors. At 11.55 the long-looked for locomotive entered the Moreton Station amidst the enthusiastic cheering of the crowd. On coming to the halt the directors alighted on the platform, where they were received by the Rev. W. C. Clack, W. Harvey, Esq., J. Little, Esq., and other gentlemen. The following address was then read:—

To the Right Honourable the Earl of Devon, Chairman, and Directors of the Moretonhampstead and South Devon Railway,

As representing the inhabitants of Moretonhampstead and the surrounding district, allow us in their names and as expressing their feelings generally, to heartily congratulate you on your safe arrival here on this eventful occasion, by that steam-horse and iron road now so essential and necessary for the progress and advancement of every neighbourhood: and to say that we feel assured none ever have been or ever can be more welcome visitors to our little town than you are this day. Of course we know that you have had no ordinary difficulties to surmount, and it would indeed be ungrateful on our parts if we did not in some way or other show that we know how to appreciate the value of your services and the strenuous exertions you have used, as well as the anxiety and trouble which we feel sure you must have endured to enable you to contend with the difficulties that you have met with at every turn, but which only the perseverance and industry you have displayed could have enabled you to overcome. Allow us also to express our earnest wish that you may have passed as safely through all the opposition you have met with, and may nothing be now left to mar or damp the pleasure which you must feel in having conferred this boon upon us, and to you alone must be due the honour of having acquired and handed down to posterity such a complete and much to be desired means of communication, not only with other parts of our tight little island, but also with the whole commercial world, and which will bring the iron and granite into a closer alliance than ever.

We sincerely trust that so important an event may be crowned with the success it deserves, even beyond the wishes and expectations of its most sanguine and ardent admirers, and that not only in a business point of view, but in giving such opportunities to the tourist with his knapsack, the artist with his pencil, or the geologist with his hammer, to visit us, and who, whilst roaming at pleasure amidst our lovely valleys and lofty tors, must feel grateful to the authors of the picturesque road, which has so quickly and easily brought them among such beautiful scenery and invigorating breezes.

Were we to write a more lengthy address, even to volumes, we could not more earnestly express our feelings of gratitude to you on this occasion; but we cannot conclude without through you tendering our thanks to Messrs. Brassey and Ogilvie, the contractors, for the very substantial way in which they appear to have carried out their work. To Mr. Crosley, who has in their behalf, superintended the works, to Mr. Lhoyd, the secretary, to Messrs. Fowler, Margary, and Little, the engineers, for the great courtesy and kind attention they have always shewn to every one with whom they have been brought into contact. And lastly we wish that the same success will attend your future undertakings, and that all and each of you may be rewarded by witnessing the increasing benefits resulting from your labours.

Per multos et felices annos.

Hearty cheers were given for the Earl of Devon and for the officials of the company. Among the visitors in the train were the Rt. Hon. the Earl of Devon, W. R. Hole, Esq., J. Divett, Esq., E. Cuming, Esq., T. Wills, Esq., (directors); T. Woollcombe, Esq. (chairman of the South Devon Company), — Sergeant Esq. (traffic superintendent of the South Devon Railway), Wm.

Crosley, Esq., P. J. Margary, Esq., A. Lhoyd, Esq. (secretary to the Moretonhampstead and South Devon Railway Company), &c., &c.

THE LUNCHEON

At about one o'clock the company proceeded to the Smythurst School-room, which was kindly lent by the trustees for the luncheon. The room was large and convenient, and 213 tickets were issued for its space. In addition to this luncheon was also provided at the hotels and inns in the town. The appearance at the luncheon in the school-room was very animated, for the presence of ladies added a lustre to the aspect. The Earl, accompanied by the directors and officials, entered at the head of the room, and shortly afterwards the Rev. W. C. Clack, rector of Moreton, was elected to preside. The interior of the building was decorated with engravings, and over the chairman hung a faithful likeness of the noble lord.

The following is the bill of fare:— Pickled salmon, roast and boiled, spiced beef, quarters and legs of lamb, veal pies, chicken pies, ducks, chicken, hams, tongues, loin of veal, sausage rolls, lobster salads, salads and cucumbers, potatoes, cheese. Wines:— Port, Sherry, Champagne, Claret, Hock.

The luncheon was provided by Mr. Gray, of the White Horse Hotel, and Mr. Pollard, of the White Hart Hotel. The satisfactory manner in which the arrangements were carried out are worthy of particular mention, as they reflected great credit to the proprietors of the above establishments.

On grace being said by the rector [loyal and patriotic toasts were drunk, and these were followed by further toasts, including the toast of the day – "Success to the Moretonhampstead and South Devon Railway" – with appropriate responses from the likes of the Earl of Devon, Thomas Woollcombe, Thomas Wills, Elias Cuming, Peter Margary and William Crosley].

THE TEA

During the afternoon a public tea took place on Greenhill and in the vicinity of the market. The provision made comprised 25lbs. of tea, 100lbs sugar, and from 5 to 6 hundred weight of cake. The following ladies presided at the tables, and great praise is due to them for the admirable manner in which they conducted the arrangements:— Miss Clack, Miss Harvey, Mrs. Harvey, Miss Wills, Mrs. Cann, the Misses Cuming, Miss White, Mrs. Hill, Miss Germon, Miss Mary Germon, Mrs. Germon, Mrs. and Miss Isaacs, Mrs. Brewer, Miss Tremlett, Mrs. Neck, Mrs. Satterly, Miss Heyward (Hele), Miss Heyward, Mrs. George Bragg, Mrs. Collyns, Miss Nosworthy, Miss Harvey (Thorn), Miss Hunt, Miss Steer, Miss Peters, Mrs. Hewett, Mrs. G. Cann, Mrs. Thornton (North Bovey), Miss Harvey (Budleigh), Mrs. Passmore, Mrs. Peters, Mrs. Dibble, and Mrs. Heyward.

A variety of rural sports took place in the evening, and afforded considerable amusement to the numerous spectators.

In every respect the holiday passed off well and the inhabitants of Moreton will for many years to come regard the 26th of June, 1866, as a red-letter day in their existence.

Almost before the last cheers from the opening day celebrations had subsided Colonel N. Yolland arrived to carry out the official inspection of the line on behalf of the Board of Trade. This actually commenced on the following day, and both the inspection and the subsequent opening of the line to passenger traffic, on 4th July, were once again reported in the local press. The following is an account that appeared in *The Torquay and South Devon Journal* on Wednesday, 11th July:–

MORETONHAMPSTEAD AND SOUTH DEVON RAILWAY

The opening of the Moretonhampstead and South Devon Railway for public traffic took place on Wednesday, but was not attended with any sort of demonstration on any point of its route, although a large number of persons availed themselves of the benefit of the increased communication between these places in the district through which the railway passes. Colonel Yolland, Government Inspector of Railways attached to the railway department of the Board of Trade, inspected the line on Wednesday and Thursday of last week, the two days succeeding the directors' opening. The gallant gentleman in these two days thoroughly inspected and tested the whole of the line and its works. Two of the heaviest goods engines that were at hand, with carriages coupled together, were placed at his disposal for testing the line. On Wednesday morning the gallant colonel commenced the work of his inspection, being taken up the line in a carriage which stopped at every kind of work for inspection. The whole of the bridges were most severely tested. The train of two engines were drawn across them slowly, then at a high speed, and ultimately brought to a standstill on the bridges. Two goods engines were the best means of testing the strength of the bridges, as in them are concentrated the greatest weight that it would be possible in any train to bring to bear upon it at one time. As these tests were made, and these immense weights were brought to bear, the deflection in the iron girder bridges was notified, but in the majority of cases it was hardly appreciable. The whole of the bridges stood the test admirably, and the same remark will

SOUTH DEVON RAILWAY

OPENING OF THE

MORETONHAMPSTEAD LINE.

THE RAILWAY BETWEEN
NEWTON AND MORETONHAMPSTEAD WILL BE
OPENED FOR PASSENGER TRAFFIC
ON WEDNESDAY, 4TH JULY.

The Trains will run as under:

Down.	Week Days. a.m.	p.m.	p.m.	Sundays. a.m.	p.m.
Moretonhampstead dep.	9.50	2.20	6.40	7.30	7.15
Lustleigh	10. 2	2 32	6.52	7.42	7.27
Bovey	10.11	2.41	7. 1	7.51	7.36
Newton arr.	10.25	2.55	7.15	8. 5	7.50

Up.	Week Days. a.m.	p.m.	p.m.	Sundays. a.m.	p.m.
Newton dep.	11. 0	3.35	8.55	8.35	8.55
Bovey	11.15	3.50	9.10	8 50	9.10
Lustleigh	11.25	4. 0	9.20	9. 0	9.20
Moretonhampstead arr.	11.40	4.15	9.35	9.15	9.35

For times at which the Main Line and Torquay Branch Trains leave Newton see the published Train Tables of the Company.

By order of the Directors.

L. J. SEARGEANT, Secretary.

An advertisement that appeared in the local press on the day before the opening of the line to passenger traffic.

Above: This would appear to be the earliest known photograph of the station at Moretonhampstead and was taken in the latter part of the 19th century. It was owned by the late G. P. Brook, who kept the White Hart Hotel in the 1890s and who was contracted by the railway company (by then the GWR) to provide a link for passengers between Moretonhampstead and Chagford using his four-in-hand coaches.

Reproduced by kind permission of his grandson, David Ellis

Below: Another early photograph of the station taken from a slightly different viewpoint.

Dartington Rural Archive

equally apply with regard to the curves and other works of the line. The accommodation works — the diversion of roads and carrying over of roads and the approaches — were found to have been completed in perfect accordance with the regulations laid down by the Acts of Parliament and the Poor Law Board. Colonel Yolland openly expressed himself as to the creditable manner in which the contractors by their agent (Mr. W. Crosley), had carried out the whole of the works, and at the completion of his inspection on Thursday he expressed himself satisfied with the safety of the line, and said that the line could be opened as soon as the company could make it convenient after the completion of a turn table for engines had been made at the Moreton end of the line. This was fully completed by Saturday night, and on Sunday morning the official report of the Railway Department of the Board of Trade, consequent upon the report of Col. Yolland [see Appendix III], authorizing opening the line for public traffic, was received, so that, save the fact that the public opening could not be advertised before the reception of the report, there was nothing in the way to prevent the public opening of the line on Monday last, July 2nd, as originally contemplated. Wednesday being market day at Newton, the traffic from Moreton and Bovey Tracey was great. The public traffic commenced at Moreton by a train leaving there at 9.50 a.m., and the whole of its carriages were full, whilst at every station large wondering crowds were gathered to witness the arrival of the trains. At Newton accommodation was found for the trains on the same platforms at which trains arrive from and depart for Exeter. It is arranged that three trains shall run each way of the line so far, and in conjunction with South Devon trains, which cross at Newton. Wednesday Mr. Crosley, agent of Brassey and Ogilvie, accompanied the enginemen on the engine every journey that was made, so as to instruct the drivers as to the curves and the gradients, which is much required on the first day of the opening of a line. The drivers soon became acquainted with their work, and no inconvenience was felt either from the curves or the gradients. No line could ever be in a more complete state for opening, and throughout its length it worked remarkably smooth, and not the slightest casualty of any kind occurred. By tests on Wednesday, it was found that the time fixed for the journey — 35 minutes from Moreton to Newton, and 40 from Newton to Moreton, admirably suited the character of the line. It was expected that at Bovey there would have been demonstrations of an extensive character, but from various causes this was prevented. It was intended to have had one grand demonstration in honour of the opening of the railway for the public, and the opening of the Town Hall just built in the town; but in consequence of the Town Hall not being finished, and several gentlemen being out of the town, the demonstration could not be held. The opening of the Town Hall is fixed for the 29th of the present month, and it seems hard to conceive how the Bovey people will assimilate the two events, and honour both by one demonstration.

[The opening of the railway was, however, celebrated at Lustleigh – although not until 31st July. Then, after having been arranged by Thomas Wills and several other local farmers and landowners, two fields adjoining the station were "set apart for rural sports of all kinds, which were indulged in by a large number of persons of both sexes", a specially-prepared luncheon was held in two marquees for the villagers and, later, a tea was provided for "all-comers". These included visitors arriving in trains from Moretonhampstead and Bovey Tracey, "who prolonged the festivities until a late hour".]

Phase 3 – 1866 to 1876: Life of the line as the Moretonhampstead & South Devon Railway.

Although the line was now open to passenger traffic, there was still much to be done. For a start, there was a need to attend to additional requirements being demanded by some of the landowners from whom land had been purchased for the railway, such as extra accommodation works, and even to arrange for the completion of legal formalities in one or two instances. However, the main priority of the directors at this time was, undoubtedly, arranging for the station buildings to be completed, which, at Bovey and Moretonhampstead, included substantial goods sheds so that goods services could be introduced. As this work continued over the ensuing weeks, ultimately leading to the introduction of goods services on 8th October, the single junction with the main line of the South Devon Railway at Newton Abbot (mentioned in Col. Yolland's report) was replaced by the recommended double junction, and arrangements were also put in hand for the provision of a siding near the Bovey Pottery. According to the Duke of Somerset, "Haytor Granite Quarry was now being worked" and, in consequence, he had demanded that the company should fulfil its obligations by constructing and maintaining a siding and crane near the point at which the tramway diverged away from the railway: it was needed, supposedly, in order that the quarried stone could be transported out of the area. This requirement, in fact, had formed part of the agreement when the duke had sold the lower section of the tramway to the company, and was duly carried out to completion either towards the end of the year or in the early part of 1867. When completed, the siding became known as Bovey Granite Siding or, in its shortened version, as Granite Siding.

SOUTH DEVON RAILWAY.

ON AND AFTER MONDAY, 8TH OCTOBER,

GENERAL MERCHANDISE TRAFFIC

WILL BE CONVEYED TO AND FROM

BOVEY AND MORETONHAMPSTEAD.

Information of the arrangements, and the rates to be charged, may be obtained on application at the several Stations of the Company, or of Mr. W. H. AVERY, the Goods Manager, Plymouth.

By Order of the Directors,

L. J. SEARGEANT, Secretary.

Plymouth, 26th September, 1866.

An advertisement that appeared in the *Western Morning News* announcing the introduction of goods services on 8th October 1866.

Almost concurrently with the duke's demand, a request for another siding was made by John Divett, of the Bovey Pottery. In this instance, he advised the company that he "was desirous of having a siding into the Potteries", so that completed earthenware products could be despatched direct by rail. During the discussions that followed, including working arrangements being agreed with the South Devon Railway Company, John Divett also managed to persuade his fellow directors to make a contribution of £175 out of company funds towards the installation costs of the siding. It was then opened a few months later than its nearby counterpart and was known as Bovey Pottery Siding – more often referred to as simply Pottery Siding.

Two studies of Bovey Pottery c.1910:–
Above: Looking southwards from just beyond Pottery Bridge and showing, in the foreground, the loading sheds and a pair of private owner wagons parked in the siding.

Courtesy of Dave Lewis

Below: Looking eastwards across part of the pottery's extensive narrow-gauge (2 feet) railway network, on which wooden-bodied wagons were manhandled around the site.

Courtesy of Mrs M. Tregoning

During the summer of 1867 the company received another approach from the Duke of Somerset, requesting that a station should be built at Teigngrace. Once again discussions followed, and it was agreed that the construction costs, estimated at £200, "would be paid for out of Special Shares to be subscribed for by the Duke of Somerset and others in the neighbourhood". The work then commenced shortly afterwards and was completed in time for the station to be opened on 16th December of the same year. By then the company had already received a request for another station to be erected. On this occasion it had come from a representative of the inhabitants of Chudleigh, who wanted a station at Jews Bridge (the name of a bridge over the River Bovey on the turnpike road between Plymouth and Exeter, situated just to the north of the railway line in the vicinity of what would later become known as Heathfield). However, after leaving the matter in abeyance for around six months, until being pressed for a decision, the directors resolved to instruct the company secretary to inform the representative of the Chudleigh inhabitants "that the Board had given the matter careful consideration but were not prepared at present to undertake the cost".

A photograph taken at Teigngrace (then a station) at around the end of the 19th century showing what is almost certainly a '517' class 0–4–2T arriving with a train from Newton Abbot. Note the ornate glass lanterns on the platform containing oil lamps.

Carrett Collection

Amalgamation with the South Devon Railway Company (1872).

The negative response from the directors to the request for a station to be erected at Jews Bridge, which emanated from a meeting held on 16th April 1868, was, without doubt, attributable to the company's ongoing financial problems. These, in fact, were highlighted during the same meeting when the company's solicitor, Mr Whitehead, submitted a 'rough estimate' showing that the outstanding liabilities of the company amounted to £26,980 4s. 10d. and the assets to £10,930. Moreover, the estimate also revealed that there was a deficiency of income to meet the annual charges of £627, so from this it was clear that the railway was not proving to be the financial success that the directors had originally anticipated. In part, at least, this was due to outside influences and their effect on traffic receipts, as explained in the following extract from the Directors' Report that had been submitted to the twelfth half-yearly general meeting of the shareholders held on 28th February 1868:–

> A slight decrease is shewn in the amount of receipts [£2,167 10s. 11d.], as compared with the corresponding period of the previous year, but this reduction is not more than may be accounted for by the falling off of Tourist and pleasure Traffic occasioned by the Paris Exhibition, and the continued Commercial depression by which the Railway Interest generally has been so much affected.

Interestingly, though, a report of the meeting that had appeared in the *Western Morning News* on the following day revealed that some of the shareholders held other views on why the traffic receipts had decreased. First a Mr Mugford had interrupted the proceedings by stating that he "thought there were certain disadvantages of which they [the shareholders] had a right to complain, and he had a memorial which would point out alterations that might be made in the train arrangements which would be alike advantageous to the public and the shareholders". Then, after the Earl of Devon (as chairman) had asked whether it bore on any matter connected with the Directors' Report, another shareholder, a Dr Haydon, had responded with a far longer speech. In it was included a description of the manner in which the railway operated at that time and, for this reason alone, it is considered well worthwhile reproducing the speech, as reported, in its entirety:–

> The resolution which was going to be moved did [in answer to the earl's question], inasmuch as they [the shareholders] believed that other causes than those stated by the directors had interfered with the full development of the traffic upon their line. They considered that if more accommodation was given to the public a larger number of people would travel. In the first half-year there were four trains up and down every day, and they carried 2,963 first-class, 11,041 second-class, and 35,349 third-class passengers. In the corresponding half just terminated they had carried 2,451 first-class, which was a falling off of upwards of 500; 7,255 second-class, which was a falling

off of 4,000; and 38,254 third-class passengers, which was an increase of about 3,000. They knew from inquiries which they had made that a large proportion of their traffic came from the morning trains, as parties, particularly on a Monday, would return from the country where they had gone on the Saturday night to spend the Sunday with their friends, to their different places of labour. He had ascertained from the booking clerks that they were in the habit of receiving from the morning trains, especially on a Monday, a larger sum of money than they received from all the other trains throughout the day. He knew that many strangers in the neighbourhood of Bovey during last summer were compelled to hire or take their own carriages to go to Newton if they wanted to catch the 8 a.m. train to Plymouth, who would have gone over their line if an opportunity had been afforded. Just at the starting of the line the mid-day third-class was taken off; it was found to be a failure. Afterwards it was put on again, but within the last few months the mid-day third-class had been again removed, and to his knowledge a large number of persons in the place where he lived who could not afford a second-class return had walked to Newton, and then gone back by train. Had there been a third-class they would have ridden both ways. A luggage train left Newton every night for Bovey at nine o'clock. Attached to that train was a passenger carriage which operated as a brake-van, and in it he was informed some individuals were allowed to ride. Many persons were desirous of going by that train, and he did not see why arrangements could not be made for conveying them at a fair remuneration. Another matter he would allude to was the falling off in the goods traffic. They only ran one-half of the first half-year, and then they conveyed 5,917 tons of goods; in the next half-year ending June, 1867, 8,649 tons, and in the last half-year ending December only 7,176 tons, shewing a falling off of 1,500 tons in the last half-year.

At the end of the speech no resolution had been moved. Instead, after the Directors' Report had finally been passed and adopted – notwithstanding the comments – the memorial referred to by Mr Mugford had been presented to the Earl of Devon with the request that he lay it before the directors of the South Devon Railway Company. The memorial itself expanded on the issues that had been mentioned by Dr Haydon and contained further examples of why the train services were considered inadequate and poorly scheduled. However, in essence, it failed to achieve the desired effect except that during the following year the South Devon Railway Company finally adopted one of the suggestions by providing an early morning train on all weekdays rather than just on Tuesdays and Wednesdays. In the meantime, the traffic receipts were still showing little sign of improvement, remaining at around the rate of £4,000 per annum, of which sum, of course, 50 per cent was retained by the South Devon Railway Company for working the line. Furthermore, this was to remain the pattern until eventually, with the company's financial position still deteriorating, albeit only marginally, the Earl of Devon entered into negotiations with the chairman and secretary of the South Devon Railway Company on the subject of amalgamating the two companies. This was at the beginning of 1871, and by the end of the summer a tentative agreement had been made, which was then included in the Directors' Report submitted to the nineteenth half-yearly general meeting of the shareholders held on 15th September of that year, as follows:–

> The gross Traffic Receipts for the half year ending on the 30th June last amounted to £2,123 18s. 4d., as against £2,120 in the corresponding half of 1870, and after deducting 50 per cent. for working expenses, the amount to be placed to the credit of Revenue account is £1,061 19s. 2d.
>
> There has been no improvement in the Goods traffic, which has been partly owing to the suspension of the lime works at Brixham, and partly to the fact that the Directors have not thought it advisable, in the present condition of the Company, to undertake the execution of new works, although the same are unquestionably required for the better accommodation of the district and the proper development of the traffic.
>
> The Directors, having disposed of portions of their superfluous lands, have determined to apply the proceeds towards the construction of a siding at Teigngrace in accordance with their obligation to the Duke of Somerset, who has hitherto very kindly forborne to press his claim. [This subject had first been discussed at a meeting of the directors held on 28th February 1868 after a letter had been received from the Duke of Somerset's land agent requesting the construction of the siding in return for the duke accepting payment in special shares (£362 17s. 6d.) for additional land required from him near Jews Bridge. The cost of the siding had subsequently been estimated by Peter Margary at £260, and the directors of the South Devon Railway Company had later consented to work it, if constructed: the task was, in fact, eventually carried out and the siding brought into use on 14th June 1872 for the transfer to rail of minerals from the nearby Stover Estate and, possibly, iron ore from Smallacombe Mine in the adjoining parish of Ilsington.]
>
> Negotiations have recently taken place with the South Devon Company with a view to the amalgamation of the two undertakings, and an agreement has been come to, subject to the approval of the Proprietors, for such amalgamation, on the basis of an exchange of the Company's Ordinary Shares for 50 per cent. of their nominal amount in South Devon Ordinary Stock, provision being also made for meeting the Debenture debt and other charges of this Company.
>
> The Directors believe that these terms will be found to be fair and equitable to both parties, and, when the details have been adjusted, and the formal agreement for giving effect to them has been settled, it will be submitted to the Shareholders for their approval at a Special Meeting.
>
> Under these circumstances the Shareholders will perceive that, with the exception of the Teigngrace siding above referred to, it would be impolitic to incur any further expenditure on Capital account [currently £155,010 14s. 3d.] even for the purpose of meeting the demands which continue to be made for additional accommodation on the line.

During the meeting the chairman, the Earl of Devon, explained that "the financial position of the company was such that they had been obliged to trust to the forbearance of their creditors, but as this could not long continue the directors had thought it best to enter into negotiations with the

South Devon Company, and they had effected an agreement, ... He considered the arrangement satisfactory, and if carried into effect the shareholders will have conferred considerable benefit on the district". According to a contemporary newspaper report, the Directors' Report had then been passed and adopted at the meeting without opposition.

Over the weeks that followed, the negotiations continued behind the scenes until 'Heads of arrangement' between the two companies were prepared and agreed upon. Out of necessity, these were then submitted for approval at the next half-yearly general meetings of the shareholders of both the South Devon Railway Company and the Moretonhampstead & South Devon Railway Company held on 22nd February 1872 and on 8th March 1872 respectively. In both instances, apart from a few concerns being voiced, no opposition was raised to the proposed amalgamation and the terms were duly adopted. They were quoted as being as follows:–

> The South Devon Company to pay to the Moretonhampstead Company in cash, such a sum as shall be sufficient to discharge their debts and liabilities (except their debenture debt), owing on the 1st of January, 1872, not exceeding on the whole £19,500. The amount so payable to be applied in discharge of those debts and liabilities, under the supervision of the South Devon Company. All interest accruing after the 1st of January 1872, on the debts, to be provided for by the South Devon Company under this head to be paid by the Company. The Moretonhampstead Company to incur no further liability on capital account after the date of these heads, except in the construction of a siding at Teigngrace, at a cost not exceeding £200, without the consent of the South Devon Company. The South Devon Company also take upon themselves the debenture debt of the Moreton Company amounting to £25,000. The special shares in the Moreton line, amounting to £25,000 to be converted into 5 per cent rent charge stock, on the terms of each holder of those shares receiving in exchange for his shares such an amount of stock as will produce a like income with the shares standing in his name. The ordinary shares in the Moreton Co. now existing, £77,550, to be converted into consolidated ordinary stock of the South Devon Co. on the terms of every holder of those shares receiving in exchange for his shares such a nominal amount of the said stock as shall be equal to one-half the nominal amount of the shares held by him.

By now, in anticipation of the terms of arrangement being adopted by the shareholders, the 'Heads' had already been annexed to a Bill which the South Devon Railway Company was promoting in the current session of Parliament, with a view to their being confirmed. Then, on 1st July 1872 – almost exactly 10 years after the promoters of the Moretonhampstead & South Devon Railway had obtained their Act of Incorporation – the two companies were formally amalgamated, with the result that the Moretonhampstead line became part of the South Devon Railway system. However, this was to prove a somewhat short-lived situation, as less than four years later, on 1st February 1876, the South Devon Railway Company was itself absorbed by the Great Western Railway Company, prior to the two companies being formally amalgamated on 1st August 1878; each £100 of South Devon Railway ordinary stock being exchanged for £65 of Great Western Railway ordinary stock and each £100 of South Devon Railway debenture stock for £100 of Great Western Railway 5% debenture stock. During this relatively brief period there were few noticeable changes, certainly from an operating point of view, but one significant development was the construction of the long-awaited station near Jews Bridge: this was opened as Chudleigh Road Station on 1st July 1874 and consisted of one, 200-feet long, platform (built on the eastern side of the single-line track) plus a short goods siding, the latter lying parallel to the running line and extending northwards from the base of the platform.

A magic lantern slide of Heathfield Station as it was at around 1900. The locomotive standing at the platform is a '1076' class 0–6–0ST.

Carrett Collection

96 **S.D.R.**

Passenger Luggage.

Lustleigh to

BodminRd.

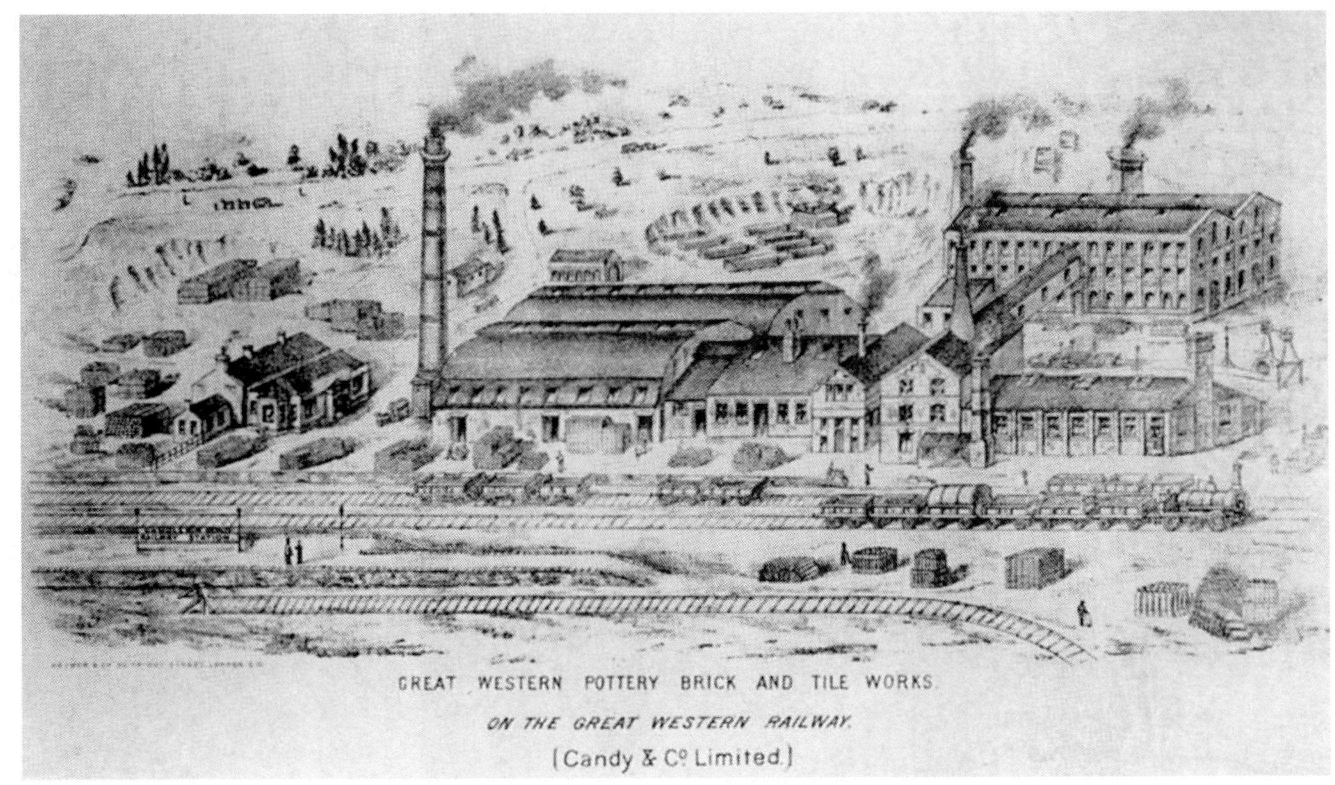

An engraving of the Great Western Pottery Brick and Tile Works owned by Candy & Co. Limited at Heathfield, c.1880.

Phase 4 – 1876 to 1947: Life as a Great Western Railway branch line.

Initially, in what effectively was the beginning of a new era for the line, no major changes were made, and the train service continued to consist of just four trains in each direction on weekdays and two on Sundays. As before, no separate goods trains were provided beyond Bovey – all goods traffic between there and Moretonhampstead was attached to the aforementioned services as and when required – and the locomotives employed to haul the familiar six-wheeled coaches of the day were almost certainly confined exclusively to the same Daniel Gooch-designed 4-4-0 saddle tanks that the South Devon Railway Company had probably been relying on ever since the line opened.

Over the course of the next five years or so there is little to record except that the GWR gradually began introducing different types of locomotives to the branch (see 'Time Tables and Branch Working') and some attempt was made to improve the level of service by an extra afternoon working being added to the summer timetable, an arrangement that took effect in 1877. However, in 1882, the year during which the daily goods train eventually started covering the entire length of the line, came the first major event of historical importance for the branch under GWR ownership – the opening, on 9th October, of the independently-owned Teign Valley Railway. Of standard gauge, this new line had been an 'on-off' affair for almost 20 years, but had now finally been completed. It ran from the eastern side of Chudleigh Road Station (renamed Heathfield eight days earlier in order to avoid any confusion with the newly-built station situated on the outskirts of Chudleigh) to Ashton, a distance of 6¼ miles, before continuing, as a goods siding, for a further 1½ miles to Teign House (Christow). At Heathfield, the initial layout for the Teign Valley trains comprised a 270-feet long bay platform built adjacent to its original counterpart, run-round facilities and a transhipment siding alongside the earlier, but by now slightly extended, broad-gauge siding. Here, there were no new buildings as such because it had previously been agreed with the GWR that the station could be shared. A condition of this arrangement, though, was that the Teign Valley Railway Company had to meet the cost of having the original goods shed enlarged and also provide a 25-lever frame signal box; this had a brick base and a hipped slate roof, and was sited just beyond the goods shed.

Apart from the installation of Candy & Co.'s private siding on the western side of the line at Heathfield in April 1888 – to serve the rather grandiosely-named Great Western Pottery Brick and Tile Works (opened in 1874) – the only change of any significance to occur over the next ten years was when all the remaining broad-gauge lines west of Exeter were converted to standard gauge over the momentous weekend of 21st/22nd May 1892. Up until then the broad-gauge Moretonhampstead line and the standard-gauge Teign Valley Railway merely existed side by side with no physical connection between them, and goods had to be laboriously transhipped from wagon to wagon. However, the standardisation of the gauge now presented an opportunity for the two lines to be connected, and during the following year the transhipment siding was removed and a connection, facing towards Moretonhampstead, put in. This revised layout, which involved reversal and was initially used only for goods shunting, also resulted in the original goods siding on the Moretonhampstead side becoming a 360-feet long loop with a short northern spur; it could not, however, be used to cross passing trains because it was not signalled as a running loop.

Elsewhere along the Moretonhampstead branch the gauge conversion produced no appreciable changes, both as regards the layout at each of the other four stations and the train service on offer. It did, however, lead to the introduction of an increasing variety of locomotives and rolling stock over the ensuing years, although initially the typical motive power for passenger and goods workings alike was provided by 0-6-0 saddle tanks.

By now, of course, the branch had become well established and not only were the levels of passenger traffic improving, but also the amount of freight being carried over the line. Coal formed the bulk of the incoming goods traffic, while outward goods traffic included frequent consignments of timber from the surrounding woodlands, cattle (particularly from Moretonhampstead), large hampers of rabbits and farm produce as well as general merchandise of widely varying type from such sources as the Bovey Pottery and the Great Western Pottery Brick and Tile Works at Heathfield. Increasing amounts of ball clay were now also being transported out of the area by rail

A pre-1927 view of Candy's Siding, occupied by private owner wagons, and the factory beyond as seen from the platform at Heathfield.

Courtesy of Dave Lewis

and, in 1893, the loading facilities that already existed at Heathfield and Teigngrace for this commodity were supplemented by the opening of a purpose-built siding at Teignbridge; the result of an Agreement made between the GWR and Mr William Herbert Whiteway-Wilkinson of Whiteway & Co.

The opening of the clay siding at Teignbridge was to be the last item of note in this opening phase of the history of the line under GWR ownership. Nevertheless, brief mention must be made here of a proposed Brent, Ashburton & Heathfield Railway. It emanated from interests connected with the Exeter, Teign Valley and Chagford Railway Company, which had been incorporated in 1883 "for the purpose of connecting the city and port of Exeter with the existing Teign Valley line", and led to plans being deposited in November 1897. These, which are now residing at the Devon Record Office in Exeter, show that two lines were to be constructed. The first was to run from a junction with the Teign Valley line, crossing the Moretonhampstead branch to Ashburton, a total length of 7 miles 3 furlongs and 7 chains: the second was to run from Ashburton via Buckfastleigh to join the main line at a point east of Marley tunnel, Brent, a total length of 7 miles 6 furlongs 19 chains. However, the GWR was in opposition to the Bill, and in January 1898 the promoters withdrew it.

A magic lantern slide, dating from around 1900, showing what would appear to be a '517' class 0–4–2T about to leave Bovey Station with a Newton Abbot-bound train. The letter 'S' appearing on the ground frame cabin to the right of the picture indicates that a signal engineer is required to call at the signal box.

Carrett Collection

Two early 20th century studies of Bovey Station viewed from the west, showing *(above)* the goods shed, signal box and open-fronted waiting shelter/gents' toilet on the 'down' platform, and *(below)* the main station building.

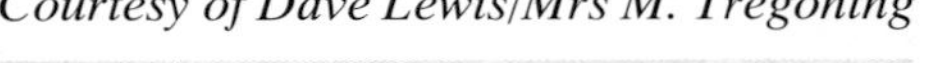
Courtesy of Dave Lewis/Mrs M. Tregoning

An early 20th century view of the village of Lustleigh and a Newton Abbot-bound train, hauled by what appears to be a '2161' class 2–6–2T, soon after departing from the nearby station.

Dartington Rural Archive

By the turn of the century the attractions of Dartmoor and its many picturesque villages were becoming more and more widely known through the publication of various books on the subject, several of them written by the much-respected Dartmoor author William Crossing. As well as writing books under his own name, Crossing wrote numerous articles appertaining to Dartmoor for local newspapers and contributed to other books, including one entitled *Dartmoor with its Surroundings*. Subtitled 'A Handbook for Visitors', this was just one of an extremely popular series of guidebooks known as 'The Homeland Handbooks'.

The opening chapter of this particular publication is entitled 'Attempts to introduce the traveller to the moor' and, whilst the book's impact in that respect is, of course, immeasurable, it almost certainly played a part in encouraging people to start exploring the moor for themselves. Whatever, it soon became clearly evident that ever-increasing numbers of visitors were now starting to travel over the branch, particularly during the summer months, and that many of them were daytrippers from the growing coastal resorts of Torbay. Of these, a large proportion were disembarking at Bovey and climbing aboard horse-drawn carriages, which met the trains and took them off to Haytor Rocks or other beauty spots in the locality. The remainder, on the other hand, were either continuing their train journey to Lustleigh, perhaps with the aim of strolling out to the nearby Lustleigh Cleave, or completing it to Moretonhampstead, from where a locally-operated horse-bus provided a connection with Chagford until being

Two crowded scenes at Bovey in Edwardian times showing *(above)* the station forecourt with a horse-drawn carriage about to take daytrippers off to Haytor Rocks (or other beauty spots in the locality) and *(below)* members of Bovey Tracey Baptist Church Sunday School about to embark on their anniversary outing to the seaside in 1910.

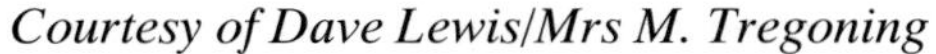

Courtesy of Dave Lewis/Mrs M. Tregoning

A view of Bovey Station at around the beginning of the 20th century showing the arrival of a train from Newton Abbot hauled by a '1076' class 0–6–0ST.

Lens of Sutton

supplanted by the GWR's own motor bus in 1906. Meanwhile, so far as the GWR was concerned, these visitors provided a welcome source of revenue and resulted in the level of service being gradually increased until, by the summer of 1911, there were as many as nine passenger trains in each direction on Wednesdays/Saturdays and eight on other weekdays – one of which included a newly-instigated (June 1911) through coach from Paddington! In addition, there was an extra train on the fourth Tuesday of each month in connection with the cattle market at Moretonhampstead (a service that had first been provided in the late 1890s) and a Sunday service, although this still consisted of just two trains in each direction.

During this opening ten-year period of the new century the infrastructure of the branch remained essentially the same except for the introduction of the electric train staff system of signalling in November 1901. However, in 1913 further, minor, changes were brought about at Heathfield by the installation of another private (loop) siding on the western side of the Moretonhampstead line. Situated on the Newton Abbot side of the A38 road bridge, it was needed for the transportation of sawn timber from the nearby Stover Estate and was known, initially, as Stover Siding, before becoming more widely known as Timber Siding. Of far greater significance, though, was the further remodelling of the station that took place some three years later and came into effect on 2nd October 1916. Then, at long last, a direct connection facing towards Newton Abbot was put in between the Moretonhampstead and Teign Valley lines, after it had been decided by the GWR that the latter (extended to Exeter in 1903)

A fine view of Heathfield Station and the factory of Candy & Co. as a train arrives from Moretonhampstead hauled by an unidentified '2161' class 2–6–2T running bunker first, c.1906.

Chapman & Son

should be made available as a diversionary route. This was in the event of problems arising along the coastal section of the main line between Exeter and Newton Abbot. At the same time both the run-round loop on the Teign Valley side and the original goods siding on the Moretonhampstead side were extended and the original signal box replaced by a much larger structure, which was sited adjacent to the new junction. Appropriately, it was built of the buff-coloured bricks produced at the adjoining factory of Candy & Co., had a hipped slate roof and contained 42 levers. At this point it is also interesting to note that now, for the first time, it was permissible for two goods trains, or a passenger and goods train, to cross at Heathfield – but only if 'absolutely necessary'.

In the meantime, further improvements had also been carried out at Teignbridge by the opening of a second 'clay' siding on 22nd January 1914, but, as elsewhere, the branch was now feeling the full effect of the war with Germany. Already this had led to a marked reduction in the number of trains, and by the end of 1916 the Sunday service – not for the first time – had been withdrawn completely. Moreover, because of the ongoing wartime economies, further cuts were soon destined to follow. These, in turn, led to the station at Teigngrace becoming a casualty at the beginning of the following year, when it was temporarily closed, and to the train service continuing to dwindle until, during the final year of hostilities in 1918, there were just four trains running in each direction, weekdays only.

A train of assorted passenger stock arriving at Moretonhampstead in 1909 headed by an unidentified '2161' class 2–6–2T.

Chapman & Son

Lustleigh Station as seen in 1912, with '2161' class 2–6–2T No. 2179 in charge of a train of assorted passenger stock bound for Moretonhampstead. Note the tidy and well-maintained station garden.

Chapman & Son

A view of Bovey in 1925 as the staff pose for the camera in front of the main station building.

Courtesy of Mrs M. Tregoning

After the end of the war the rate of recovery, both locally and throughout the country as a whole, was painfully slow due to a variety of reasons, of which one of the most obvious (and tragic) was a severe shortage of manpower. As time went by, though, the overall situation gradually started to improve until, by the summer of 1922, the train service on the Moretonhampstead branch was more or less back to its immediate pre-war level. No doubt influenced by a steady resurgence in tourist traffic, the GWR had, nevertheless, now brought into effect a number of operational changes which included Bovey receiving two terminating services for the first time. In addition, whilst the through coach from Paddington had become a thing of the past due to the onset of war, the timetable now included recently-introduced through workings from Paignton and Kingswear, one of them, the 10.15 a.m. from Paignton, running non-stop to Bovey after calling at Torquay and Torre. On arriving at Bovey, the visitors could then board one of a number of charabancs lined up in the station forecourt, which the GWR had started providing from its own fleet of motorised road vehicles, and enjoy a moorland tour to Haytor Rocks or to Tavistock, via Moretonhampstead and Princetown. Indeed, these moorland bus tours were to become so popular that within another three years they had been extended to include Becky Falls and Manaton, and, later, Widecombe.

Above: A trio of AEC charabancs lined up in the station forecourt at Bovey ready to take would-be passengers to Haytor Rocks in the early 1920s.
Below: A slightly later photograph taken at Bovey showing, in the foregound to the left, another AEC bound for Haytor Rocks and, on the right, a Burford ready for a trip to Becky Falls and Manaton.

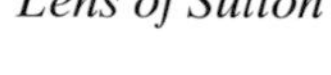
Lens of Sutton

As the 1920s progressed, support for the train and road motor services continued to gain momentum, which was encouraged by an increasing number of through workings being added to the timetable, including even one from Plymouth. Other changes came about mainly because of stations beginning to take on different appearances. This was particularly so at Newton Abbot, where, in September 1923, preliminary work commenced on a major rebuilding/expansion programme of the old South Devon Railway station. Carried out in stages, and including a separate bay

Two studies of the former main station building and forecourt at Newton Abbot before work on the rebuilding/expansion programme began in earnest in November 1924:–

Above: Looking from a north-westerly direction towards the entrance.

Lens of Sutton

Below: Looking from a south-westerly direction, again towards the entrance.

National Railway Museum

A view from underneath the overall roof at Newton Abbot Station looking northwards in October 1924. This shows the 'up' main line (left) and the line (centre) from which the Moretonhampstead branch and Teign Valley line trains departed, but the 'down' main line is out of the picture, just beyond the easternmost of the two island platforms.

National Railway Museum

platform being provided for the Moretonhampstead and Teign Valley trains, this task took more than three years until being completed in time for an official opening ceremony of the new station to be held on 11th April 1927. By then, further alterations were also being carried out at Heathfield, which, in June of that same year, led to a 'proper' crossing loop – to give an operational length of 1,040 feet for crossing trains – being provided for the Moretonhampstead side of the station, together with a second platform. This new 'down' platform was 320 feet long and 12 feet wide, and, like most of its 'up' counterpart, had a finished surface of tarmac chippings edged with concrete slabs with rounded shoulders on the lineside. The only facilities provided for passengers using it, however, were a small, round-topped, waiting shelter of corrugated iron, which was situated at about the midway point, and a timber foot crossing just beyond the signal box for access to and from the 'up' platform. In order to facilitate the improvements, which also included the earlier oil lamps being replaced by electric lighting, the original platform was cut back, the goods shed was substantially reduced in size and re-erected close to the station building, and the signal box was equipped with a new, 58-lever, frame to cope with the extra signalling needed. In addition, the original platform was extended northwards to a length of 413 feet so that it now terminated at the same point as the Teign Valley bay platform.

Following hard on the heels of these important developments came two more. First, on 21st May 1928, the GWR opened a halt on the southern outskirts of Bovey Tracey at Brimley, which was done, like many others throughout the GWR system, in a bid to stem increasing road competition and on the basis that there would be sufficient passengers to make it viable. Then, on 1st March 1929, the company purchased the Manor House at North Bovey from Lord Hambleden (a director of the GWR and grandson of the founder of W. H. Smith & Son) and converted it into a luxury hotel. The reason for this, together with some interesting details about the property, is explained in the following extracts from a contemporary brochure published soon after the hotel opened:–

> THE MANOR HOUSE, near MORETONHAMPSTEAD, was purchased and converted into a very comfortable country Hotel by the Great Western Railway to assist in providing accommodation for the increasing number of persons desiring to visit the West of England. The hotel is ideally situated on Dartmoor, 700 feet above sea level, and has its own grounds of 200 acres of park and pleasure lands.
>
> It presents the amenities of a country house in the heart of some of the finest scenery in "Glorious Devon," and will at once appeal to a great number of visitors in search of rest and recuperation in health-giving Moorland air.
>
> In every direction are beautiful views, across pleasure grounds and rock gardens falling gently to a lake and to the River Bovey, which flows through the property, winding through woods and meadowlands.
>
> In the distance are vistas of the incomparable moors. Easdon Tor (1439 feet) is within two miles of the house.
>
> The building was completed in 1907 and is a Jacobean replica in stone with stone mullions, oak window frames, and stone-tiled roof, built on broad South and West terraces.
>
> The interior accommodation and fittings include many interesting features, of which a few may be mentioned.
>
> An oak-panelled entrance hall gives communication through a carved screen, with oak doors to inner and staircase halls.
>
> Throughout the house are wide corridors with oak-panelled walls and stone arches and ceilings, all carved out in Jacobean style.
>
> One of the finest rooms is the oak-panelled lounge, an apartment measuring 43 by 33 feet, and the open fireplace and Jacobean carved stone chimney piece combine to produce a magnificent setting.
>
> The public rooms are very spacious and comfortably furnished in harmony with the interior decoration of the hotel. The bedrooms are lofty, light, and airy and command splendid views of the surrounding country.
>
> Central heating and electric lighting are installed throughout the building and the drainage and the water supply are of modern type.
>
> A new wing has been added, and various internal alterations to the existing

Two photographs of the Manor House at North Bovey after being converted into a luxury hotel:–
Above: An aerial view of the hotel and part of its extensive grounds.
Below: The hotel viewed from the south.

Courtesy of Valerie Huish

Building completed, including hot and cold running water in every room.
The Cellars contain complete stocks of choice wines.
The new full size Squash Rackets Court, a large Recreation Room and Badminton Court adjoining, and the latest conception of Ladies' and Gentlemen's changing and drying Rooms provide the guests with a variety of sporting entertainments and amenities.
The hotel also own the trout fishing rights on the south bank of the River Teign for upwards of five miles, and hotel resident visitors can fish this water at a charge of 5/- a day. On this stretch of the river is the famous beauty spot Fingle Bridge.
Other sports catered for are tennis on hard courts and grass courts, croquet, and there is a bathing pool in the lake.
Devotees of the game of Golf will find that their enjoyment has been catered for by the eighteen-hole golf course within the private grounds of the Hotel which was completed in June, 1930.
The nearest railway station is Moretonhampstead (2 miles) and there is a good train service (via Newton Abbot) from all parts. An hotel omnibus will meet the principal trains, but if arrangements have not been made for intending visitors to be met on arrival the Newton Abbot Station Master will, on request, send a message, free of charge, to the hotel.
Good class private motor cars of various capacities can be requisitioned through the Hotel management to convey visitors from and to the station, or they can, of course, be conveyed from or to Newton Abbot, Exeter, or other adjacent stations.

It was just two months before this latest acquisition by the GWR that the company's road motor services were taken over by the National Omnibus & Transport Co. Ltd which, in Devon and Cornwall, became the Western National Omnibus Co. Ltd with effect from 28th February 1929. Under this arrangement the GWR took a 50 per cent shareholding in the new company and nominated half the directors, and the road services were to be co-ordinated with those of the railway rather than be in competition with them. As a result, the two existing bus services from Bovey Station – to Becky Falls and Manaton, and to Haytor and Widecombe – and that between Moretonhampstead and Chagford now came under the control of Western National.

These revised arrangements, however, were to be relatively short-lived.

Opposite: On various occasions down through the years the branch suffered from the effect of adverse weather, as these three photographs appearing on the facing page of Bovey during the winter of 1929/30 clearly indicate, although the train service was seldom seriously disrupted:–
Top and centre: Floodwater, after the nearby River Bovey had burst its banks, lapping against the side of the 'up' platform.

Roy Wills/Courtesy of Mrs M. Tregoning

Bottom: A view of the level-crossing gates and entrance to the station forecourt after a fairly heavy snowfall.

Courtesy of Dave Lewis

1930

G

All three routes were detached from the main operating area of Western National and the cost of maintaining an outstation at the Dolphin Hotel in Bovey Tracey (where the buses were garaged), combined with only modest numbers of passengers during the winter months, meant that the buses were soon proving to be not very remunerative. To exacerbate matters the Devon General Omnibus & Touring Co. Ltd, in which the GWR had acquired a 30 per cent interest on 1st July 1929, were now also running buses between Moretonhampstead and Chagford (from Newton Abbot). The seemingly inevitable outcome was that eventually, in 1934, arrangements were made for Western National to pull out of the operations at Bovey Tracey and Moretonhampstead, for Devon General to assume a monopoly of the Moretonhampstead to Chagford route, and for a local private operator – J. Potter & Sons of Haytor – to take over the two moorland routes from Bovey Station, as part of their 'Tor Bus' service, with effect from 1st January 1935.

During this sequence of events affecting the road services the GWR continued to encourage even more passenger traffic on the branch by steadily increasing the number of daily workings and, as elsewhere throughout the network in the Westcountry, by conducting sophisticated advertising campaigns. Other means were also employed. These included the opening of another halt on 1st June 1931 – provided partly for the benefit of moorland walkers and for visitors to patients at Hawkmoor Hospital (after which it was named) – and also the provision of summer holiday accommodation when, in 1934, Lustleigh became one of a number of rural stations in the Westcountry to be allocated a camping coach. By that stage the number of weekday trains between Newton Abbot and Moretonhampstead had already grown to ten in each direction (seven on summer Sundays), but in the following year this improved still further to eleven. Of these, no less than seven were through workings – three each from Kingswear and Paignton plus an early morning train from Totnes – and, in addition, Bovey was now receiving seven terminating services, all operated by push-pull auto trains from Newton Abbot. In contrast, one goods train in each direction was still sufficient to cope with the branch freight.

Over the course of the next three or four years life on the branch remained fairly stable, although, as elsewhere, road competition and increasing private car ownership started to have an adverse effect on passenger and goods returns alike. Before the full impact of this could be felt, however, there was soon a much larger shadow looming on the horizon – the outbreak of World War II on 3rd September 1939. Once again, as in 1914, this quickly brought about an end to the tourist traffic on the branch and also led to a significant reduction in the train service, which included the removal from the timetable of two of the through workings from both Kingswear and Paignton. Other cutbacks soon followed until, during the early months of 1940, the typical wartime service became six or seven trains in each direction on weekdays and none at all on Sundays. The

In 1937 the branch received what is believed to have been its first royal visitor when King George VI spent the night of 30th November/1st December on the royal train just to the north of the road overbridge at Wray Barton and disembarked at Moretonhampstead Station on the following morning:–

Above: The scene shortly after the arrival of the train at Moretonhampstead as crowds gather around it trying to get a glimpse of their king.

Dartington Rural Archive

Below: The scene a few minutes later with the king meeting local dignitaries prior to setting off, by car, to Princetown and a tour of Duchy of Cornwall property.

Courtesy of Mrs Glyn-Jones

services terminating at Bovey were also withdrawn and those run within the confines of the branch, together with the early morning through working from Totnes, all became auto train-operated.

Apart from a daring air raid on the station at Newton Abbot during the evening of 20th August 1940, which resulted in considerable damage being done and 75 people being injured, 14 of them fatally, the war was to have no significant effect on the day-to-day running of the branch in the physical sense. It did, however, lead to a noticeable increase in the amount of passenger traffic in the early 1940s as more and more military personnel started arriving in the area, including a large number of Americans billeted in towns such as Moretonhampstead or based at military encampments set up on Knighton Heath (Heathfield) and on Mardon Down (Moretonhampstead). In addition, the ancestral home of the Hole family in Bovey Tracey, Parke, became occupied by the army as an Infantry Brigade headquarters and a number of other large properties in the area were taken over for military purposes. Among them were The Manor House Hotel, which became a hospital for British, American and Canadian officers, and Stover House, where a large American military hospital was established nearby.

It was during these dark days, in May 1943 and in conjunction with the government's programme for increasing the capacity of diversionary routes during World War II, that the final stage in the development of Heathfield Station occurred. Principally, this involved the extension of the crossing loop in the Newton Abbot direction to give an operational length of 1,100 feet for crossing Teign Valley trains (1,520 feet for Moretonhampstead trains) and the provision of a double junction connecting the Teign Valley line to both 'up' and 'down' Moretonhampstead lines. Other work carried out at this time included the installation of an intermediate crossover in the extended crossing loop (immediately on the Newton Abbot side of the A38 road bridge), the engine release crossover in the Teign Valley bay being removed, which resulted in the bay siding becoming a purely goods siding, and further modifications being made to the original goods siding. In this latter instance these involved the removal of the loop connection at the northern end of the siding, and to the siding itself being extended by a further 242 yards. At around the same time it was also equipped with a metal weighbridge, with an adjoining corrugated iron cabin, and a loading gauge.

When hostilities finally ended in Europe on 8th May 1945 the overall situation was very similar to that of 1918 in many respects, except that the country was now also in the grip of a fuel shortage. As a result, the post-war recovery proved to be slow in the extreme, and this was particularly so as regards the train service on the Moretonhampstead branch: some two years later, at the end of one of the worst winters in living memory (which helped turn the fuel shortage into a crisis), there were just seven return workings, plus an extra one from Moretonhampstead on Saturday evenings. There was no Sunday service at all and only two through workings – the 7.25 a.m. service from Totnes and the 10.5 a.m. service from Paignton, the last remaining through working from Kingswear having been withdrawn during the war.

This, then, was the scenario in what was to be the final year of GWR ownership, for at midnight on 31st December 1947 – just over a month after the engine shed at Moretonhampstead was officially closed – the railways were nationalised by the Labour government then in power and the branch became part of British Railways (Western Region).

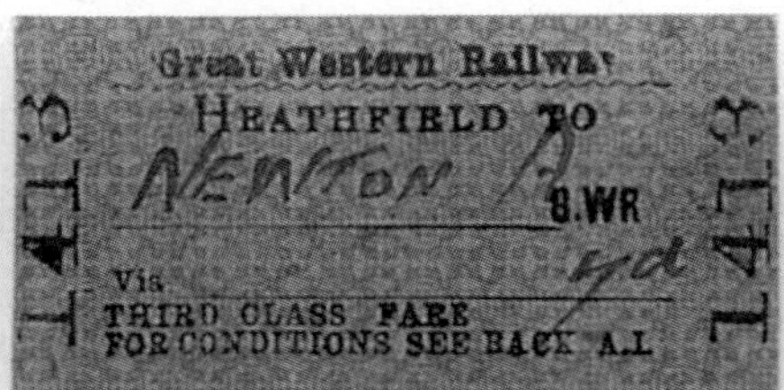

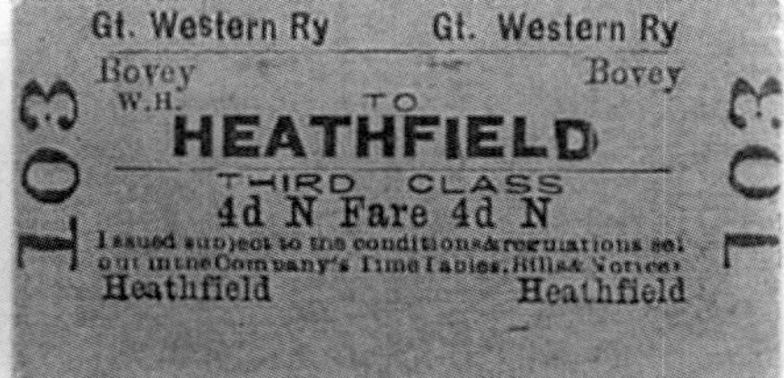

The changing face of Heathfield Station during GWR days:–

The very restricted pre-1916 layout at Heathfield is clearly evident in this 1900s view from the A38 overbridge, as a Moretonhampstead to Newton Abbot train stands at the platform. The siding connection which the Teign Valley goods trains and excursions had to use up until 1916 is just visible under the rear coaches. Note how the signal box faced away from the Moretonhampstead line, having been designed in the anticipation that it would only control Teign Valley Railway trains.

Lens of Sutton

Another 1900s view of Heathfield Station, with shunting in progress.
Courtesy of Dave Lewis

A 1930s view of Heathfield Station, again with shunting in progress but now in a somewhat less cramped environment following the major alterations carried out in June 1927.
G. N. Southerden (Courtesy of Wild Swan Publications)

Two later photographs taken at Heathfield showing the layout at the southern end of the station following the alterations made in 1943:–
Above: The 'new' intermediate crossover in the crossing loop, which can just be seen behind the rear coach of the train standing at the 'up' platform on 3rd April 1948.

Courtesy of Peter W. Gray

Below: The crossing loop, which had previously terminated at a point almost directly opposite the gate by the entrance to Timber Siding, as viewed from the A38 overbridge on 15th June 1950.

E. R. Shepherd

Phase 5 – 1948 to 1959: Life of the line after nationalisation.

A passenger travelling on the Moretonhampstead branch during the weeks that followed nationalisation would not have been aware of any obvious differences. The locomotives and rolling stock remained unchanged from the days of the Great Western Railway and, similarly, the timetable was left unaltered. Even when BR did eventually issue a new timetable, to take effect from 31st May 1948, there were no radical changes made, for it included just one additional return working on weekdays only, making eight in all. This, in turn, meant that there was still no Sunday service, although in the following year, and in line with the GWR's policy ever since before World War I, it was finally reinstated for the summer months only. Apart from that, little serious effort was forthcoming to build up business on the line, or to try and counter the combined effect of mounting road competition and ever-increasing private car ownership. As a result, it soon became only too evident that the branch was steadily losing traffic, and led to the first ominous sign that the passenger service to Moretonhampstead was being considered for withdrawal coming as early as July 1952. At that time stationmasters received a notice from the Railway Executive (Western Region) requesting details of their staffing requirements in the event of the passenger train service being discontinued. In addition, information concerning the number of passenger tickets issued annually and the amount of parcels forwarded had to be given.

These requests were duly complied with, and it was also pointed out that milk traffic had ceased in 1950, the rate for carriage of parcels had increased in 1951, and one bus company had started using double-deckers to cater for the increasing numbers of passengers. However, after the completion of these returns, there were no immediate developments or suggestions from the Western Region headquarters, so the passenger trains continued as before, often consisting of an 0–4–2 tank locomotive and a single autocoach. Interestingly, there was also no apparent attempt made to reduce costs, the daily service still being operated in such a way that two train sets were necessary.

Almost coincidental with the above-mentioned notice being issued by Western Region headquarters, and also in July 1952, the branch enjoyed a brief period of intensive working in connection with the holding of the Royal Show at Stover Park, near Teigngrace. For four days, from the first to the fourth of the month, a service of twelve return workings operated over the entire branch, with all trains calling at Teigngrace Halt. There was also an additional afternoon train from Heathfield to Newton Abbot and return, this being the Teign Valley line service. Bank holidays, too, were still busy occasions for the branch in the early to mid-1950s, and on Easter Monday in 1954, for example, one of the branch trains – composed of auto saloons 224 and 234 in the charge of 0–4–2T No. 1439 – was quite literally packed to the doors. Such days, however, did not compensate for the loss of regular local users of the branch trains, which were steadily becoming ever fewer in number.

In 1956 articles began to appear in the local press describing the personalities of the line, the possible consequences of its closure, and a warning to "use it or lose it". It seemed unlikely, however, that local residents would do this, for as far back as 1951 the total number of tickets issued at one of the stations (Bovey) had been around only 7,500 for the whole year. In the face of this decline, the British Transport Commission took no action to increase the use of the line by retiming some trains to suit local needs, or effecting economies such as issuing tickets on the trains, as is done on many surviving branches today. Indeed, the railway authorities seemed to regard the majority of branch lines as an encumbrance rather than an asset. Goods traffic also continued to decline, one example being the Bovey Pottery, which had been a regular user of the line for many years but ceased to despatch its products via its private siding in 1956.

In July 1958 the period of uncertainty came to an abrupt end when the British Transport Commission gave official notice that, subject to the approval of the South Western Area Transport Users Consultative

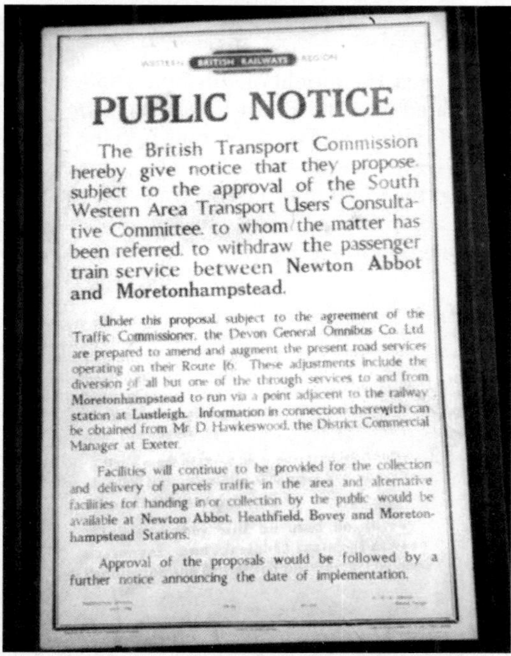

The British Transport Commission's notice of its proposal to withdraw the passenger service between Newton Abbot and Moretonhampstead, photographed outside Lustleigh Station on 4th August 1958.

E. R. Shepherd

Two photographs taken at Heathfield on 7th June 1958, the last day on which passenger trains operated over the Teign Valley line, showing:–
Above: The scene as Prairie tank No. 5536 runs into the bay platform with the 4.35 p.m. train from Exeter and 0–4–2T No. 1427 stands ready to propel the autocoaches forming the 5.10 p.m. train from Moretonhampstead on to Newton Abbot, after any passengers have made their connection.
Below: The view in the opposite direction a few minutes later.

Peter W. Gray

Committee, it proposed to withdraw the passenger service between Newton Abbot and Moretonhampstead. The announcement caused great concern in the towns and villages along the line, and was discussed as a matter of urgency by the town council at Bovey Tracey, the parish councils at Lustleigh and Moretonhampstead, and both the urban and rural district councils at Newton Abbot. It was decided to oppose the proposed withdrawal of the trains, the feeling being that considerable economies could be made by such measures as introducing diesel 'railcars', retiming some trains and simplifying the signalling system. In addition, there were doubts regarding the authenticity of the passenger figures quoted in regard to when a week's 'sample' count was taken, as there could be a great difference between a summer bank holiday week and a wet week in midwinter.

In the opinion of the British Transport Commission the railway was losing £17,000 annually, and this was a loss which could not be perpetuated. Parish councils prepared questionnaires for local residents, a typical example enquiring how often the individual rode on the railway, which stations and trains were used, and the reason for travelling by rail. A final query concerned what arrangements could be made for travel if the trains were withdrawn. Public petitions against the closure were prepared in local communities, including the village shop at Lustleigh, and were signed by a great number of people. However, these had no effect on the British Transport Commission, and evoked no support from the TUCC, which, significantly, was legally not permitted to have railway employees in its membership. The only small positive note was a recommendation that the position be reviewed when diesel railcars were introduced in the area. As this was not to be implemented until at least 1961, the suggestion was, to say the least, not very helpful or practical.

Another factor which did not bode well for the future was the permanent withdrawal of passenger trains on the adjoining Teign Valley line on 7th June 1958, and the complete closure of the section of that line between Christow and Alphington. This withdrawal would, of course, reduce the number of passengers using the junction station at Heathfield. To make matters still worse, it was only another three weeks or so before the last remaining daily through service from Paignton, together with the entire summer Sunday service (which included morning and afternoon through workings from Goodrington Sands Halt and Kingswear respectively), fell victim to BR (Western Region) service cuts that took effect on 30th June 1958.

The hope of any reprieve for the passenger service on the Moretonhampstead branch was ended when a notice from the British Transport Commission was posted at the line's stations, announcing that the passenger trains would be withdrawn as from Monday, 2nd March 1959. As there was no Sunday service, this meant that the final trains would be operated on Saturday, 28th February. The notice also gave the names of local omnibus operators who would amend or increase their services in place of the trains, together with information regarding the continuance of parcels and general merchandise traffic.

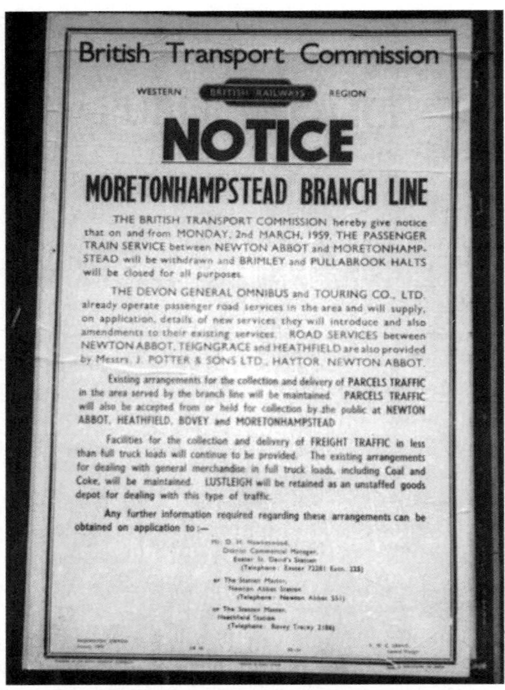

British Transport Commission

WESTERN BRITISH RAILWAYS REGION

NOTICE

MORETONHAMPSTEAD BRANCH LINE

THE BRITISH TRANSPORT COMMISSION hereby give notice that on and from MONDAY, 2nd MARCH, 1959, THE PASSENGER TRAIN SERVICE between NEWTON ABBOT and MORETONHAMPSTEAD will be withdrawn and BRIMLEY and PULLABROOK HALTS will be closed for all purposes.

THE DEVON GENERAL OMNIBUS and TOURING CO., LTD. already operate passenger road services in the area and will supply, on application, details of new services they will introduce and also amendments to their existing services. ROAD SERVICES between NEWTON ABBOT, TEIGNGRACE and HEATHFIELD are also provided by Messrs. J. POTTER & SONS LTD., HAYTOR, NEWTON ABBOT.

Existing arrangements for the collection and delivery of PARCELS TRAFFIC in the area served by the branch line will be maintained. PARCELS TRAFFIC will also be accepted from or held for collection by the public at NEWTON ABBOT, HEATHFIELD, BOVEY and MORETONHAMPSTEAD.

Facilities for the collection and delivery of FREIGHT TRAFFIC in less than full truck loads will continue to be provided. The existing arrangements for dealing with general merchandise in full truck loads, including Coal and Coke, will be maintained. LUSTLEIGH will be retained as an unstaffed goods depot for dealing with this type of traffic.

Any further information required regarding these arrangements can be obtained on application to:—

The British Transport Commission's closure notice, photographed outside Moretonhampstead Station on 31st January 1959.
E. R. Shepherd

In the face of this news, a last-minute deputation to the Minister of Transport was organised, but to no avail, and it was accepted that no further action could be taken to save the trains.

There was, however, a group of people who felt that perhaps a society could be formed which would take over the running of the trains, as had been done some years before on the narrow-gauge Talyllyn Railway in mid-Wales. Indeed, the first action to achieve this was taken on the very day that the last BR-operated passenger trains ran to Moretonhampstead!

Up until the BR (Western Region) service cuts that took effect on 30th June 1958, and with the exception of Sundays and summer Saturdays, the daily through working between Moretonhampstead and Paignton was a regular feature for many years. The photographs *opposite* and those that appear on *the following two pages* were taken at various locations along the Kingswear branch, and are included because of their historical interest. *All are reproduced courtesy of Peter W. Gray.*

Prairie tank No. 5551 about to depart from Paignton with the 10.5 a.m. train to Moretonhampstead on 10th September 1946.

Taken almost ten years later than the previous photograph, on 19th May 1956, 0–4–2T No. 1466 is seen in charge of the 10.5 a.m. service from Paignton to Moretonhampstead on this occasion and is captured at Hollacombe, between Paignton and Torquay.

Travelling in the opposite direction to that shown in the photograph at the foot of the previous page, because it is in charge of the 8.40 a.m. working from Moretonhampstead to Paignton, No. 1466 is seen here propelling its two autocoaches out of Torquay.

0–4–2T No. 1427 seen leaving Torre Station with its Moretonhampstead-bound train on the morning of 10th May 1958, shortly after having taken water from the tank mounted between the 'up' and 'down' tracks. On this particular occasion a cafeteria car, which is being taken to Newton Abbot to be included in a later main line working, has been attached to the rear of the train.

Hard at work on the 1 in 55 gradient out of Torquay, 0–4–2T No. 1439 is depicted approaching Shiphay Bridge with the morning through service to Moretonhampstead on 5th May 1951.

'Last Day' events

As was usual on such occasions, the number of regular travellers on the Moretonhampstead line on that final day of 28th February 1959 was expected to be greatly exceeded by people (many of whom had probably never used the trains regularly, if at all) wishing to make a 'last chance' journey over the line. In anticipation of this, all the trains on the day were strengthened with additional coaches, the first being the simultaneous departures from either end of the line at 7.50 a.m. From Newton Abbot, 0–4–2T No. 1466 hauled three non-corridor coaches, whilst from Moretonhampstead a similar three-coach train was in the charge of 2–6–2T No. 5196, the two trains crossing at Bovey Station. No. 1466 returned from Moretonhampstead with the 8.40 a.m. working, following which No. 5196 operated the 9.20 a.m. train to Moretonhampstead, running back to Newton Abbot with the 10.15 a.m. return working. All was quiet then for nearly two hours, until 0–4–2T No. 1466 was rostered to head the 12.50 p.m. departure to Moretonhampstead, which was made up to four non-corridor coaches, all well loaded with would-be passengers. The driver, however, insisted that his locomotive would be unable to surmount the steep gradients at the upper end of the line, and the fourth coach was eventually removed and its occupants crammed into the three remaining coaches. In the event, the train reached the terminus only about five minutes late, and after running around its train and visiting the water column, the little 0–4–2T departed again, still a few minutes behind time.

The remaining workings of the day were all headed by another 2–6–2T, No. 4117, in very clean condition and looking extremely smart in full lined green livery. The 2.15 p.m. departure from Newton Abbot, with four non-corridor coaches, reached Lustleigh some 20 minutes late at 2.58 p.m., returning from Moretonhampstead with the departure timetabled for 3.15 p.m.

Whilst these journeys were taking place, an inaugural meeting of the people endeavouring to take over the running of the branch passenger trains was being held at the Queens Hotel in Newton Abbot. The meeting agreed to set up an organisation to be called the South Devon Railway Preservation Society and to ascertain if an arrangement could be made with the British Transport Commission to achieve this aim by the purchase or lease of the railway.

The next train out of Newton Abbot, at 4.25 p.m., was strengthened by the addition of a fifth coach which had been chartered by the newly-formed preservation society, whilst the locomotive carried a wreath on the front of its smokebox. Departure was made from one of the main line platforms. The next return working, leaving at 6.5 p.m., was reduced to the original four coaches, both trains being very well loaded.

The weather, which had stayed fine all through the day, remained dry into the evening as people (a large proportion of them being railway enthusiasts) began to assemble on platform 9 at Newton Abbot to witness the 'last rites' of the final train along the branch. The coach which earlier in the day had been chartered by the fledgling preservation society now stood empty nearby as the crowd waited for the arrival of the penultimate train. This was due at 7.34 p.m., but it was 7.40 p.m. before it appeared around the curve and came to rest at the platform.

A good number of passengers alighted, after which the locomotive reversed her coaches, ran around, took water and rejoined the coaches before returning to the platform.

Intending passengers then boarded the train which was headed by 2–6–2T No. 4117 and consisted of the four coaches used earlier. The wreath was no longer on the locomotive, but various slogans had appeared on some coach windows, such as "Sack our Brian Robertson" (the head of British Railways at that time) etc, etc. Departure time was at 8.18 p.m., only three minutes late, and the train drew out to the accompaniment of escaping steam, whistling and a fusillade of eight detonators, leaving only a handful of people on the platform to watch it leave.

It was soon apparent that one passenger had brought his trumpet, but the locomotive was also making its presence felt, and both whistles were sounding as the well-filled train drew into Teigngrace Halt. No spectators or would-be passengers were waiting on the platform, but the guard alighted here and collected the hurricane lamp which had been hanging from the halt's nameboard. Someone yelled into the gloom "Change here for Crewe" and then the journey was resumed to Heathfield. Quite a few people awaited the train here, some of whom boarded the coaches, whilst at the next stop, Brimley Halt, more people were standing on the platform and the approach path; again some boarded the train. Down at Bovey, where the 'up' platform was entered, yet more people were waiting, and after the necessary pause the locomotive announced the train's departure with both whistles.

After passing through the woods around Parke, it was not long before Pullabrook Halt was reached, where the train stopped twice, presumably to allow a passenger or passengers to alight from a coach which had not reached the short platform. At Lustleigh, more people were standing on the platform to greet their last train, and then began the final climb up the Wray valley to Moretonhampstead, until, eventually, No. 4117 brought her train in alongside a crowded platform at the terminus at 9.2 p.m.; when many of the passengers had alighted, the station must have been busier than for many years but, unfortunately, it was now all too late.

It was noticeable, both here and at Lustleigh and Bovey, that there was no form of civic farewell by the local councils. They had, in fact, decided to ignore the occasion as a protest, believing that it was not justified, and also hoping that diesel trains might bring a revival at some future date.

The locomotive ran around, took water and coupled back onto its train as the passengers retook their seats. The last passenger train from Moretonhampstead then pulled out of the station at 9.17 p.m., with much use of both whistles and a cannonade of at least 22 detonators. This final journey was, of course, an extra working not shown in the normal timetable and therefore the train did not have to stop at all stations. Lustleigh was passed non-stop, although a few hardy souls had waited to wave the train through, and, similarly, there was no stop at Pullabrook Halt, only a farewell salute with both whistles. However, the train announced its arrival at Bovey at 9.30 p.m. with the explosion of seven detonators which no doubt startled some of the crowd on the platform; after a wait of three minutes four more explosions marked its departure.

Brimley Halt was passed with double whistles acknowledging the waves of a small group of people, then a stop was made at Heathfield at 9.37 p.m., where many passengers alighted. Restarting at 9.45 p.m., it took only four minutes to reach and pass the empty platform at Teigngrace before running beside the overgrown course of the Stover Canal, across the level crossing at Teignbridge and so to the outskirts of Newton Abbot. Adverse signals here kept the train waiting for several minutes on the curve approaching the station, but after receiving the 'green' the locomotive drew its train into the main line platform 1 at 9.59 p.m. The passengers alighted, the driver signed autographs, and, following the Teign Valley line some eight months earlier, the regular passenger trains of the Moretonhampstead branch passed into history.

The day had been a mixture of regret, even sadness for some, and for others an occasion for trying to create a carnival atmosphere with loud laughter and noise. One thing was certain, however, that as the local roads grew ever more crowded, the area was the poorer for the loss, after 93 years, of its faithful little branch line trains.

A selection of 'last day' views along the branch:–

0–4–2T No. 1466 arrives at the 'down' platform at Bovey with the first train of the day, the 7.50 a.m. departure from Newton Abbot.

Peter W. Gray

From the opposite direction, 2–6–2T No. 5196 approaching Bovey with the day's first working from Moretonhampstead, also a 7.50 a.m. departure, whilst No. 1466 waits to resume its journey.

Peter W. Gray

With the same two trains as in the previous photograph now having crossed – the last such occurrence at Bovey – No. 5196 can be seen in the distance pulling away towards Newton Abbot, whilst No. 1466 heads off towards Moretonhampstead.

Peter W. Gray

2–6–2T No. 5196 running around her train at Moretonhampstead prior to departure for Newton Abbot at 10.15 a.m.

R. G. W. Margetts

No. 1466, in charge of the 12.50 p.m. service from Newton Abbot, about to cross the three-arched Knowle viaduct between Pullabrook Halt and Lustleigh.

Peter W. Gray

The same train as above, only now nearing the end of its journey to Moretonhampstead as the photographer attracts the attention of the fireman just beyond Steward Bridge.

Peter F. Bowles

No. 1466, having run around her train, now about to begin the return journey from Moretonhampstead with the 1.35 p.m. service to Newton Abbot.

E. R. Shepherd

Following the early afternoon working from Moretonhampstead to Newton Abbot, 2–6–2T No. 4117 was brought into service for the remaining 'last day' trips. Here, she is seen crossing the three-arched Knowle viaduct with the 2.15 p.m. train from Newton Abbot.

Authors' Collection

Two more views of No. 4117 and her four-coach train seen pulling away from Lustleigh *(above)* and approaching Wray Barton *(below)*.

Peter W. Gray/Peter F. Bowles

For the next working, and the last in daylight as it was the 4.25 p.m. departure from Newton Abbot, the train was strengthened to five coaches and No. 4117 now had a wreath on her smokebox. These final two photographs show her leaving Bovey *(above)* and approaching Letford Bridge, just beyond Pullabrook Halt *(below)*.

Peter W. Gray/R. G. W. Margetts

Phase 6 – 1959 to 2004: Life of the line after partial closure.

In the days following the withdrawal of the passenger service the daily goods train continued to be operated as before, but was later reduced to a thrice weekly trip, running on Mondays, Wednesdays and Fridays. This was augmented by a 'runs when required' extension of the Teign Valley line goods train from Heathfield as far as Bovey on Tuesdays and Thursdays.

On 18th August 1959 a passenger train (limited to a speed of 15 mph) reappeared on the branch when a Sunday School Special was operated from Moretonhampstead to Goodrington Sands Halt and return. The train, formed of five non-corridor coaches hauled by 2–6–2T No. 5164, was worked up from Newton Abbot as 'E.C.S.' (empty carriage stock) and left Moretonhampstead with its load of youthful passengers at 8.50 a.m., reaching Goodrington at 10.7 a.m. The return from Goodrington was at 7.10 p.m., giving a long day on the beach, and final arrival at Moretonhampstead was at 8.26 p.m.

Also in August of 1959, the South Devon Railway Preservation Society issued a prospectus outlining its intention to approach the British Transport Commission regarding the acquisition or lease of the line and its suggestion, if successful, to run a service of 'GWR railcars'. An invitation was also made to join the society (annual membership 21/- (105p)) and to offer volunteer support. Prominent members of the society were Canon O. M. Jones of Teigngrace (chairman), Mr R. J. Cottrell of Wellington and Mr E. G. Parrott of Torquay. Public meetings were held at several towns around the district, and for a time hopes were high that there could be a successful outcome. The society featured prominently in the local press when, on 6th June 1960, a special passenger train was chartered to make a return trip from Paignton to Moretonhampstead. Headed by 2–6–2T No. 4174 and made up of six corridor coaches, the 'Heart of Devon Rambler' departed from Paignton at 12.25 p.m.

Some of the passengers had been concerned by the less-than-clean condition of No. 4174 and were permitted to clean the platform side of the locomotive prior to departure, but the other side remained untouched! During the journey, members of the society distributed itineraries of the trip, which included stops at Torquay and Torre stations to allow more passengers to join the train, and after a brief stop at Kingskerswell the 'Rambler' drew into platform 6 at Newton Abbot at 12.50 p.m., where the civic heads of the Newton Abbot councils boarded. Leaving again at 1.15 p.m., the crew collected the single line token for the branch and the train proceeded sedately at the regulation 15 mph to Teigngrace Halt. People had collected on the weedgrown platform here and flags were displayed on the station building and nameboard. Canon Jones joined the train and the journey was resumed to Heathfield, where there was a wait of six minutes before leaving again at 1.26 p.m. A further stop ensued at Brimley Halt before Bovey was reached at 1.37 p.m., the train running in alongside the 'up' platform. A number of people were present here, some of whom joined the train during a lengthy 14-minute wait, after which No. 4174 took her train through the woods and on to

Two photographs of the South Devon Railway Society's 'Heart of Devon Rambler', which ran from Paignton to Moretonhampstead and back on 6th June 1960, showing 2–6–2T No. 4174 hauling the six-coach train towards Pottery Bridge on the outskirts of Bovey Tracey *(above)* and taking a pause at Brimley Halt *(below).*

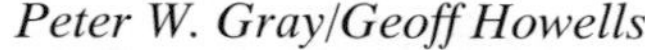

Peter W. Gray/Geoff Howells

Two further views of the 'Heart of Devon Rambler' as it crosses the three-arched Knowle viaduct between Pullabrook Halt and Lustleigh *(above)* and pulls out of Lustleigh on the return journey to Paignton *(below)*.

Peter W. Gray

Pullabrook Halt, which sported a large Union Jack. Here again, one or two more passengers entrained.

The climb onwards to Lustleigh was taken fairly easily, and on arriving there at 2.4 p.m. the train was greeted by a sizeable crowd on the flag-bedecked platform as well as on the road bridge. Restarting at 2.15 p.m. to rousing cheers, the locomotive raised its voice for the final climb to Moretonhampstead which was reached at 2.29 p.m., one minute ahead of the very generous scheduled arrival time. A small crowd awaited the train's arrival, the passengers alighting to examine the station area, take photographs and watch a presentation being made to Canon Jones. A telegram from the Bluebell Railway was also read, and the grubby side of the locomotive received a clean, completing the task commenced at Paignton. A point of interest was noted during an inspection of the cattle dock siding, which was found to contain a chair reading 'S.D.R. 1875'.

The passengers presently rejoined the train, which commenced the return journey at 3.40 p.m. to the accompaniment of four detonators and much whistling. Stops were made at all the stations and halts; a wait at Heathfield allowed some passengers to alight and walk around the station.

Canon Jones alighted at Teigngrace and thanked everyone for supporting the trip, after which the 'Rambler' ran through to Newton Abbot, arriving at platform 2 at 4.45 p.m. After a short wait the train then began the final part of the journey, stopping at all stations to allow passengers to detrain, and reaching Paignton some 18 minutes early, at 5.12 p.m. The whole of the day had been very pleasant, with a cheerful atmosphere throughout, for at this time there were still high hopes for the achievement of the society's aims.

The annual Sunday School Special continued to run to Goodrington in August 1960, again a five-coach train, but hauled by 2–6–2T No. 5573, whilst a further excursion was planned by the S.D.R.P.S. in the October, this time taking the form of a brake van trip from Newton Abbot to Heathfield and up the surviving portion of the Teign Valley line to Christow. However, prior to the date intended for the event, very severe flooding forced a large breach in the railway just by the bridge over the Stover Canal on the outskirts of Newton Abbot, on 1st October, the damage being so severe that the line was not reinstated and reopened until 4th November.

Throughout this period of disruption the locomotive which had been working the local goods, 0–6–0PT No. 3659, was cut off from the main system, and remained 'dead' in the Teign Valley bay at Heathfield.

The South Devon Railway Society (as it had now become known) had established a base at Teigngrace Halt by 1961, taking a lease on the station building and commencing some restoration work there. The society also continued to press for the restoration of the passenger trains and was in communication with the general manager of British Railways (Western Region), but with no definite outcome. A positive development concerning goods traffic, however, was the opening of a rail-served warehouse for distribution of bananas at Heathfield in February 1961, owned by Geest Industries Ltd.

The banana warehouse of Geest Industries Ltd at Heathfield, which opened in February 1961 and was served by a purpose-built siding installed on the north-eastern side of the station site.

Rev. H. Stephens (Courtesy of L. W. Pomroy)

During the following month, on 4th March, the postponed brake van trip of the S.D.R.S. was run, and consisted of eight brake vans headed by 2–6–2T No. 4174. About 50 people were on the train, which ran from platform 9 at Newton Abbot at 2.0 p.m., crossing the embankment which had been rebuilt after the flood, and running non-stop through Teignbridge level crossing, the gates of which had already been opened for the train. A brief stop at Teigngrace Halt allowed Canon Jones and his lady to board one of the vans before the train continued to Heathfield, where a leisurely stop of 17 minutes allowed the passengers to walk around the station. Leaving again at 2.28 p.m., the train crossed to the Teign Valley line for the remainder of the journey, which was again affected by flood damage, in this case resulting in track being washed out between Ashton and Christow. This meant the train had to be terminated at Trusham Station.

The return trip commenced at 3.42 p.m., and Newton Abbot (again at platform 9) was reached at 4.35 p.m.

One other train carrying passengers ran on the Moretonhampstead branch in 1961, this being another annual Sunday School Special on 10th August, the destination again being Goodrington Sands Halt.

In the following year, in a further attempt to attract support for its aims, the S.D.R.S. chartered a second train to Moretonhampstead, on 11th June 1962, again starting from Paignton. The six-coach train, headed by 2–6–2T

The second of the two trains chartered by the S.D.R.S., the 'South Devon Phoenix', seen approaching Teignbridge Crossing *(above)* and travelling over the mainly gorse-covered expanse of Bovey Heath *(below)*, 11th June 1962.

Peter W. Gray

Two more photographs of the 'South Devon Phoenix' after arriving at Lustleigh *(above)* and Moretonhampstead *(below)*.

Geoff Howells

No. 5153, was named the 'South Devon Phoenix' and carried a passenger complement of about 200, a number similar to that carried by the earlier 'Rambler' train of 1960.

In the absence of a headboard, the locomotive carried the title of its train chalked on the front of its smokebox. Calls were made at all stations along the line, Lustleigh in particular welcoming the train with flags and bunting.

The 'Phoenix' had been a success it itself, but there was still no sign from officialdom that consideration was being given to the reinstatement of regular passenger services, and the three-year period wait for diesel units mentioned in the TUCC statement in 1959 was well past. This was in spite of the fact that diesel multiple unit trains had come to the area, an example being the Plymouth to Saltash local service, which had received such units as early as June 1960.

In the face of this indifference the S.D.R.S. members decided that their cause was a lost one, relinquished their tenancy of Teigngrace Halt and turned their aspirations to the Ashburton branch, which had lost its passenger trains in November 1958 and was in imminent danger of complete closure, which, in fact, came in September 1962.

Apart from the unlikely event of any type of resumed passenger trains to Moretonhampstead making a financial profit for the railway authorities, the line was still carrying considerable amounts of ball clay and some local merchandise. Therefore it was considered impracticable (or inconvenient) for a preservation society to use the branch at the same time, and this attitude remained unchanged.

A short freight working in the charge of 2–6–2T No. 4555 at Lustleigh in the early 1960s, prior to the complete closure of the section of line from the northern side of Bovey Station to Moretonhampstead on 6th April 1964.

J. R. Besley (Courtesy of Ian Allan Publishing)

The driver of 0–6–0PT No. 3796 relinquishes the token for the Newton Abbot to Heathfield section of the Moretonhampstead branch after arriving at Newton Abbot East Box with a goods train on 1st August 1962. The banana vans would be part of regular consignments to and from the Geest ripening warehouse at Heathfield.

J. R. Besley (Courtesy of Ian Allan Publishing)

One final Sunday School Special was run on 16th August 1962 from Moretonhampstead, this time the destination being Teignmouth, and in the event this proved to be the last occasion on which a passenger train traversed the full length of the branch.

The year 1963 passed without further reductions on the line, but a tragic incident occurred outside Bovey Station on 26th September, when the sole rail employee stationed there was opening the level-crossing gates to allow the passage of a goods train. After the gates were opened, the train began to move forward, but at the same time one gate, apparently unsecured, started to swing back across the line. The gateman attempted to run across in front of the diesel locomotive, but fell and was pinned beneath it, receiving injuries which proved fatal. The subsequent inquest found that full safety measures had not been carried out, and a recommendation was made that such procedures must be put into practice at all times.

The following year of 1964 brought the first reduction in the length of the branch when goods facilities were withdrawn from Lustleigh and Moretonhampstead stations and the section from Bovey (exclusive) to Moretonhampstead was closed to all traffic as from 6th April; however, the goods shed at the former terminus continued to deal with small goods sent by lorry from Bovey until the end of the year.

The rundown of the line continued in 1965 with the lifting and removal of the closed section of track, the task being completed by 21st June. The signal box at Heathfield was another casualty, being closed in October of the same year.

The task of lifting and removing the closed section of track from Moretonhampstead to the northern side of Bovey Station nearing completion in June 1965.
Courtesy of Mrs M. Tregoning

While these events were taking place, a Goods Concentration Scheme came into force at Newton Abbot, resulting in the withdrawal of parcels and general merchandise facilities from Bovey Station, leaving only such commodities as coal and grain to be delivered there 'as required', in full loads. The surviving branch goods trains at this period were being operated by the North British-built class 22 diesel-hydraulic locomotives.

As a respite from this depressing picture a significant development took place early in 1966 when an oil distribution depot owned by Gulf Oil (Great Britain) Ltd near Heathfield was connected to the branch by means of a 'trailing' connection at 4 miles 36 chains, which led to two sidings inside the depot. The first oil deliveries, carried in bogie tank wagons, commenced in January, the trains originating from Milford Haven in South Wales. This oil traffic, of course, brought increased use of part of the line, but also at this time Bovey Station was closed and the line beyond the oil depot was used

North British-built class 22 diesel-hydraulic No. 6329 on freight duties at Bovey in 1966, shortly after the demise of steam.

Authors' Collection

only for intermittent deliveries of coal or grain to the station area there. The decline continued in 1967, when Candy's Siding at Heathfield, which became disused some time before, was closed on 10th March and subsequently lifted. In the following September Granite Siding, which had seen little or no activity for at least ten years, was also taken out of use. Three months later, on 4th December, traffic on the remaining portion of the Teign Valley line to Chudleigh and Trusham finally ceased and the line was officially closed in July of the following year.

Although having no direct bearing on the use of the Moretonhampstead branch, platform 9 at Newton Abbot Station was given a new lease of life during the year when Motorail trains were introduced on the main line and the cars were loaded at the former branch platform.

Finally, in December, a Coal Concentration Depot was brought into use at Exmouth Junction in Exeter, whereby all coal deliveries in Devon were made from that site by road, thus ending any coal trains which might have been operated to Bovey.

For the next two years the line continued to operate without significant change, although two events deserve mention. Firstly, in November 1968 the main station building at Moretonhampstead was demolished, but fortunately the goods shed and engine shed were allowed to remain. Secondly, on 27th July 1969 the Queen reviewed the Fleet in Torbay, and following the event the royal train travelled along the branch to Heathfield and was stabled there overnight.

Two photographs of the diesel multiple unit used for the four special 'farewell' trips from Newton Abbot to Bovey and return on 5th July 1970 taken from the Shilston Lane Bridge looking towards Heathfield *(above)* and from the rather overgrown 'down' platform at Bovey *(below)*.

Peter W. Gray/R. A. Lumber

Further curtailment of the line took place in 1970, when the grain traffic to Bovey transferred to road haulage in May of that year.

Complete closure beyond Heathfield now seemed inevitable and formal notice of this soon followed, the date being announced as 5th July. Prior to this occurring, however, a series of special 'farewell' passenger trains was operated from Newton Abbot to Bovey on 5th July. Four return trips were made on that day, starting from platform 9 at Newton Abbot and ironically using diesel multiple units which were never permitted to be tried in regular service on the line. The train was made up with a three-car set and two single cars, running as a five-car set. The fare was ten shillings (50p) return and the venture attracted a total of some 500 passengers during the day.

These were the last trains to reach Bovey and the track was lifted soon afterwards, the work being completed by 8th September, leaving the extremity of the line at a point 4¾ miles from Newton Abbot. Further track removal followed in 1971, when the siding at Teigngrace was lifted after being out of use for several years.

By the end of the year there was a change in the motive power on the branch freight trains when the class 22 diesel-hydraulic locomotives were replaced on most workings by the larger class 31 diesel-electric locomotives.

Ball clay wagons assembled in the easternmost of the two sidings at Teignbridge c.1970. Later, when they have all been filled, these wagons will be taken to Newton Abbot and attached to a 'Clayliner' train operating between Cornwall and the Staffordshire potteries.

Watts Blake Bearne & Company Plc

Two views from inside the oil distribution depot at Heathfield from around the 1970s, showing:–

Above: Rail tank cars (RTCs), purpose-built for Gulf Oil (Great Britain) Ltd, on the two sidings and the discharging pumps in the foregound.

Heltor Ltd

Below: A Newton Abbot-based diesel shunter No. 08281 pulling out the empties (45-ton RTCs) under the watchful eye of terminal manager John Tapp, who is wearing a safety helmet.

Vosper Arthur (Courtesy of L. W. Pomroy)

An aerial view of the Heathfield Industrial Estate clearly showing the two sidings serving the oil depot and the stop blocks at the end of the truncated Moretonhampstead branch c.1980.

Vosper Arthur (Courtesy of L. W. Pomroy)

Part of a 22-car train of 45-ton RTCs arriving at the oil depot in the early 1980s.
Vosper Arthur (Courtesy of L. W. Pomroy)

Another step in the downgrading of the line was taken in 1972, when Heathfield Station became unstaffed on 5th June. Meanwhile, the trains continued to carry the fuel oil and ball clay traffic, and also to serve the banana distribution depot at Heathfield. This last-named traffic, however, did not continue for many more years and ceased in 1975.

A further short reduction was made in the length of the line in 1974, when the rails were lifted back to a headshunt 4 miles 46 chains from Newton Abbot, which allowed the oil trains to reverse into the fuel depot.

Railway lines which have no regular passenger services have a fascination for railway enthusiasts and from time to time special trains are chartered by railtour organisations which include such lines as part of their itinerary. The remaining portion of the Moretonhampstead line has featured in quite a number of such excursions, and possibly the first of these trains ran on 20th April 1974. Named the 'Devon Rambler' and organised by the Railway Correspondence and Travel Society (RCTS), the three-car diesel multiple unit started its journey from Bristol and visited the Torrington and Meldon goods-only lines before coming to Newton Abbot and making a return trip to Heathfield. A second railtour, organised by F. & W. Railtours, visited Heathfield as part of its journey to Cornwall around 1980, but details of the exact date and train formation are unknown.

Returning to the abandoned portion of the line, the former station site at Moretonhampstead was taken over by the road haulage firm of B. Thompson & Sons (Transport) Ltd in 1976. The goods shed and engine shed, however, were left 'in situ', the latter being used as a vehicle repair building; it was, in fact, declared a Grade II listed building in 2002.

A distinguished visitor came to the line in 1983 when the royal train, with the Prince and Princess of Wales on board, was stabled overnight on 8th/9th

The royal train, with the Princess of Wales on board, approaching Heathfield Station on the morning of 9th March 1983.
E. R. Shepherd

March at a point between Teignbridge Crossing and Teigngrace. The train was made up of eight bogie coaches, hauled by class 47 diesel-electric locomotive No. 47500 *Great Western*. On the morning of the 9th, the train drew forward into Teigngrace Halt, which had been cleared of encroaching greenery, and had fresh gravel laid across the platform at the alighting point. The prince alighted at 9.35 a.m. and walked to a waiting car which took him up the tree-lined station approach and away to a meeting at Parke, in Bovey Tracey. Meanwhile, a class 31 diesel-electric locomotive arrived, running 'light engine' from Newton Abbot, and coupled onto the rear of the train, which presently departed for Heathfield, arriving there at 10.25 a.m. The princess alighted onto the semi-derelict former 'up' platform, from which all buildings had been removed sometime in the 1970s, and was taken by car to a separate engagement at Bovey Tracey. The royal train then returned to Newton Abbot without delay at 10.30 a.m., with the '31xxx' leading and providing traction, but with No. 47500 still coupled at the rear of the train.

Closely following the royal train, on 30th April 1983, another enthusiasts' railtour visited Heathfield, again organised by the RCTS, and named 'Devonian Railtour'. The train, consisting of diesel-electric multiple unit set 1014, ran from Waterloo to Paignton and return, with a trip along the branch en route.

In the years that followed, a number of railtours included a return trip to Heathfield in their itinerary and it is, perhaps, appropriate to mention at this point in the story that details of these are included in the next chapter.

During the years in which these special passenger trains were visiting the line a number of developments took place, both on the remaining and abandoned portions of the line. By the end of 1984 the sidings at Teignbridge had been out of use for some time and were becoming overgrown, but ball clay was still being dispatched from the clay siding near the Kingsteignton Road Bridge as well as from Timber Siding at Heathfield, and this continued up to the early 1990s.

In 1986 work began on the construction of a much-needed bypass road for Bovey Tracey laid on the route of the branch from a point to the south-east of Pottery Bridge to just beyond Bovey Station, a distance of some 1½ miles.The trackbed was widened and the bridge over the route by the site of Brimley Halt was demolished and replaced by a new structure in November 1986.

A number of local residents petitioned Bovey Tracey Town Council against the demolition of the two-arched Pottery Bridge, but without success, and had to be content with the hope that a photographic record would be made of this 'superb piece of architecture' prior to its demolition.

Down at Bovey Station, the 'up' side station building and goods shed were retained, but both platforms and the canopy over the 'up' platform were removed. The new road was officially opened to traffic on 16th October 1987.

Overleaf: A map showing the route of the former railway line from the south-eastern outskirts of Bovey to the northern side of where the station was sited, superimposed by the route of the bypass opened in 1987.

Reproduced courtesy of Roy Wills

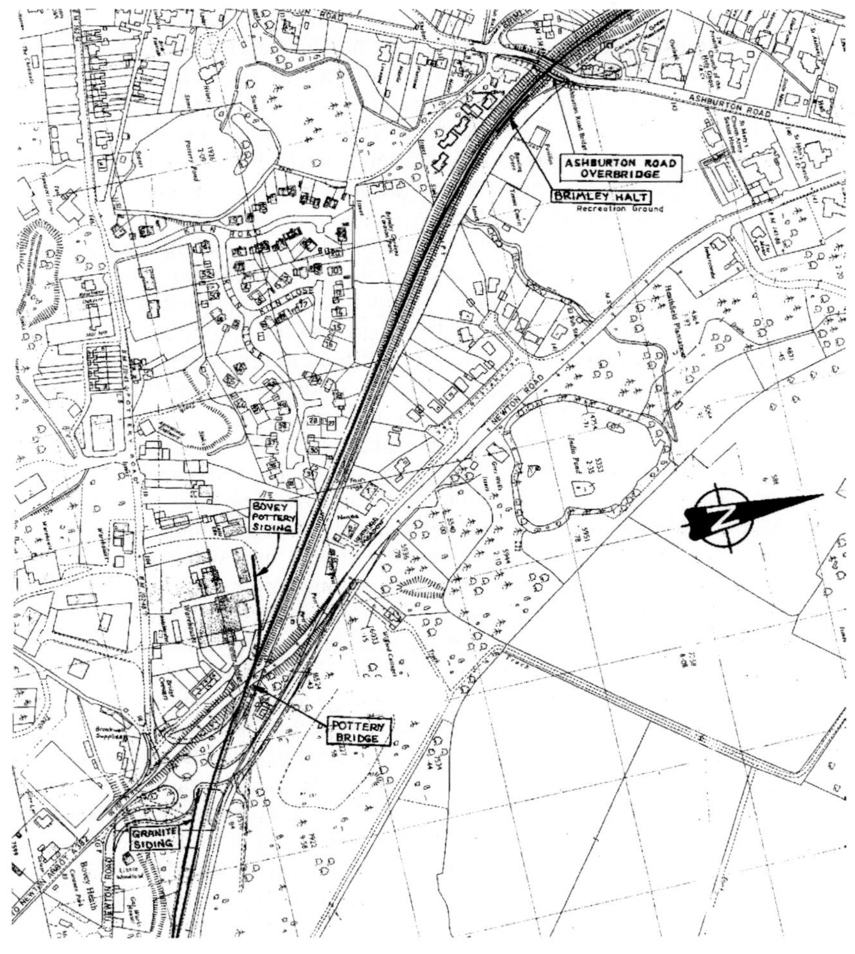

As indicated by the map, the whole of the trackbed of the former railway line from a point immediately adjacent to the western end of Granite Siding to just beyond the site of Bovey Station was used for the bypass. The trackbed then veers off north-westwards towards Moretonhampstead and, in parts, is now well used by walkers.

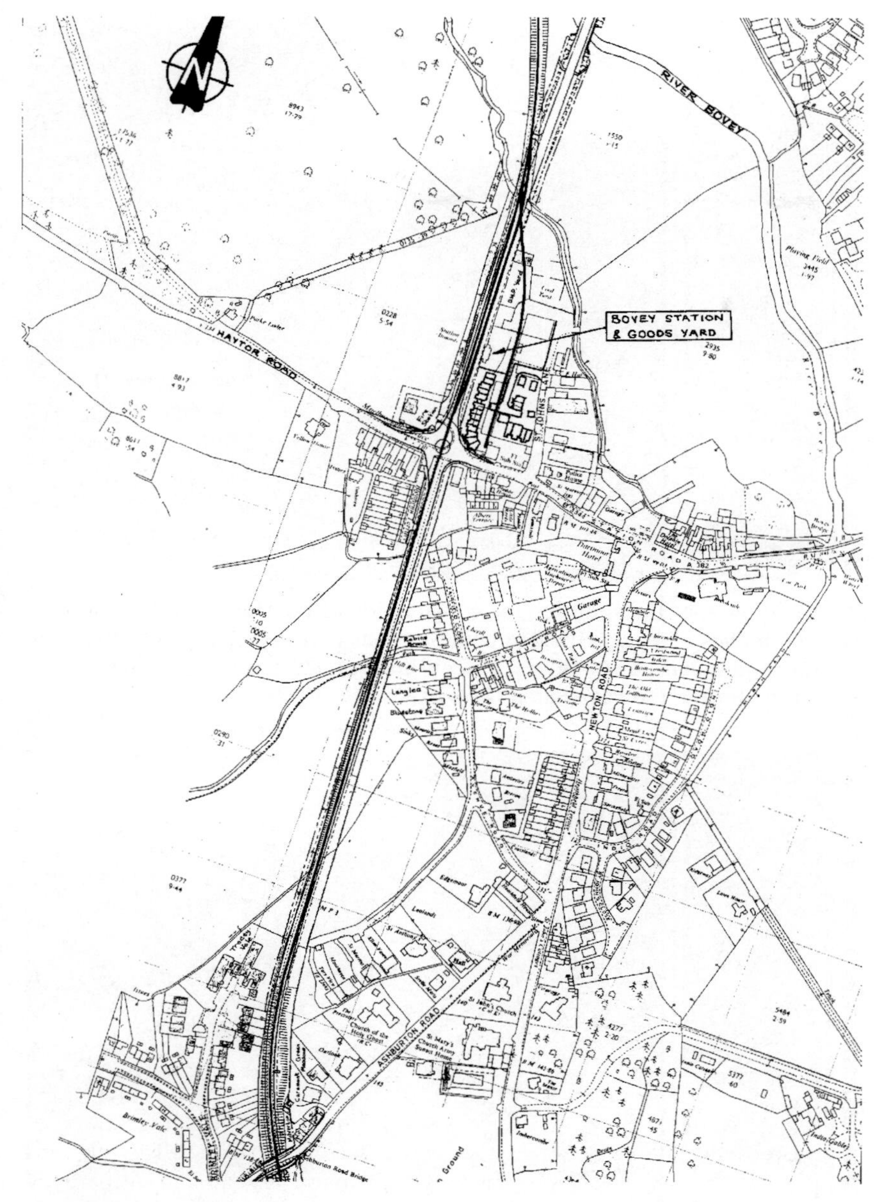

BOVEY STATION
& GOODS YARD
RIVER BOVEY
HAYTOR ROAD
STATION ROAD
NEWTON ROAD
ASHBURTON ROAD
Playing Field
Dartmoor Hotel
Garage
Longlea
Bluestone
Edgemoor
Leonards
St John's Church
Brimley Vale
Ashburton Road Bridge

Two photographs taken during the construction of the Bovey bypass showing the two arches of Pottery Bridge being used as part of a temporary diversion of traffic into and out of Bovey Tracey *(above)* and work in progress at the site of the former railway station *(below)*.

Roy Wills

Developments also took place concerning the ball clay traffic in 1987, when the open wagons used were withdrawn and replaced by bogie wagons classified as PBA, together with Ferry vans and PGA four-wheeled hopper wagons.

The provision of these modern vehicles, although allowing simplified carriage of the clay, unfortunately was not sufficient to ensure the viability of the operation, and by the early 1990s the clay trains had ceased to run. The exact date of the last train is not clear, but local newspaper reports place it between 1990 and 1994.

Class 50 diesel-electric No. 50149 (in Railfreight livery) waits for the level-crossing gates to be closed behind its train of two loaded PBA clay wagons at Teignbridge before continuing with the 10.45 a.m. working from Heathfield to St Blazey during a very wet morning on 28th July 1988.

Hugh Ballantyne

At this period the branch was being worked with diesel-electric locomotives of classes 37, 47 and 50; as an example, a fuel tanker train recorded on 25th February 1992 consisted of class 37 locomotives Nos. 37215 and 37072 (working in multiple) with twelve large bogie wagons.

By 1995, however, fuel trains were using the line only once a week, and soon after a decision was taken by Heltor Ltd (which had taken over ownership of the Heathfield depot from Gulf Oil (Great Britain) Ltd in the 1980s) to abandon the use of rail transport and replace it with seaborne deliveries to a distribution depot in Plymouth, with final deliveries by road.

Two views from the early 1990s, showing:–
Above: Class 37 diesel-electric No. 37254 arriving at the Heathfield oil depot with a consignment of sugar beet pulp, another commodity distributed by Heltor Ltd at this time.
Below: Class 50 diesel-electric No. 50037 withdrawing the empties from the two sidings at the oil depot.

Geoff Myers

The last working by rail took place on 17th January 1996, when class 37 locomotive No. 37141 arrived at the depot from Newport at 10.50 a.m. to collect the final batch of empty RTCs (rail tank cars). There were thirteen of these altogether, which had to be hauled from the sidings and propelled back to Heathfield Station prior to the locomotive running around the train and coupling onto the leading tanker. Watched by a small group of railway enthusiasts, the long train finally departed at 11.40 a.m., passing Teigngrace at 11.47 a.m., Teignbridge Crossing at 11.54 a.m., and arriving at Newton Abbot at 12.10 p.m., from where it then set off for the remainder of the return journey to Newport.

A somewhat sombre moment, matched by the weather, as class 37 diesel-electric No. 37141 prepares to leave Heathfield Station for Newport with the final batch of empty RTCs (rail tank cars) from the nearby oil depot on the morning of 17th January 1996.

Karen Lang

At the time many people felt that this was the final chapter in the story of the Moretonhampstead line, but there remained a feeling that efforts should be made to revive the branch for clay and freight traffic, possibly to a new road/rail interchange at Heathfield. Suggestions were also made to provide a commuter passenger service from a park and ride facility at the end of the line.

Teignbridge District Council undertook research into the possible revival of the railway and the Teignbridge Local Plan (1996) Policy supported the principle of a road/rail interchange at Heathfield. Approaches to Railtrack, Freightliner and English Welsh & Scottish Railways also produced agreement in principle, subject to a site of at least 0.5 hectares being made available at Heathfield for such an interchange, and that a viable level of commercial interest could be generated.

A subsequent survey of 81 local businesses was made, of which only 15 expressed an interest in possibly making use of any revived freight operation. Suggestions were also made regarding the resumption of rail transport of the ball clay to Teignmouth Docks, but the excessive costs of installing the necessary signalling and reconnection of the docks to the main line made the scheme impracticable. Railtrack also indicated that to restore the Heathfield line to regular passenger-carrying standards would require substantial works which would be very costly and could interfere with the operation of freight traffic.

During the period of these discussions, the line was virtually disused, seeing only the very occasional passenger charter train, but on 28th May 1998, after an interval of over two years, goods trains began to run once more. On that day a regular once-weekly service was reintroduced between Newton Abbot and Timber Siding (Heathfield) for the carriage of powdered clay, and this has continued to the present time.

In February 1999 Candy's Tile Works at Heathfield was taken over and modernised by the British Ceramic Tile Co., and it was hoped that its products might have been dispatched by rail, but up to the present day this has not been the case.

In September 1999 the disused sidings at Teignbridge were the subject of an application to Teignbridge District Council by Railtrack and the M&W Plant Hire firm, to reinstate the sidings and create a goods yard for the import and export of goods by rail. Objections were raised concerning the unsuitability of adjacent roads to carry the extra traffic which would be generated and the application was subsequently withdrawn 'due to a technicality' in January 2000. Later in 2000 a similar application was submitted by Teigngrace Freight Ltd; this plan was supported by English Welsh & Scottish Railways who were prepared to operate trains to a restored siding and goods yard.

In spite of these encouraging signs, this second attempt to bring further revenue back to the line was also unsuccessful, and the ball clay treatment plant at Timber Siding remained the only source of traffic.

TIME TABLES AND BRANCH WORKING

Branch Workings

SDR Broad Gauge

(SDR branch line code – Black board with two white diamonds)

Opening Ceremony (26th June 1866):–

4–4–0STs *Lion* and *Lance*

1866 to 1876

– 4–4–0ST *Meteor* (Allocated to Moretonhampstead – one of its drivers, Charles Marsh, was killed at Torquay Station in 1868 whilst in charge of a goods train which ran into empty coaching stock after the porter on duty there had failed to change the points).

– 0–6–0STs *Dido* and *Tarus* (Both goods engines – driver Mark West).

– 4–4–0ST *Magpie* (Fired by *Castor's* former driver, Joe Rowland, during the 1870s: he returned to the Launceston branch during 1874/5).

– 4–4–0ST *Aurora* (Allocated to Moretonhampstead during the mid-1870s – driver George Little and fireman Nicholas Way).

4–4–0ST *Aurora.*

J. B. N. Ashford

GWR Broad Gauge

1876 to 1892 – 4–4–0ST *Melling* (Converted from 'Hawk' class).

– 2–4–0ST *Penn, *Hedley* and **Pollux.*

– 0–6–0ST *Rosa* (Goods engine, which had been built in1862 for the Llynvi Railway in Wales and later transferred to the West Cornwall Railway before being allocated to Moretonhampstead. It had also been derailed, with its goods train, at Brent in 1868).

GWR Standard Gauge

Early 1900s – 0–4–2Ts of '517' class, *viz* *530, 571, *1443, 1487, *1488, 1496 and 1499.

– 2–6–2Ts of '2161' class, *viz* 2168, 2169, 2171, 2173, 2174, 2176, 2178, 2179, 2182 and 2188.

(Later Nos. 4507, 4508, 4510, 4512, 4513, 4515, 4517, 4518, 4521 and 4527).

– 0–6–0STs of '1076' class, *viz* *731, 737, 1650 and 1658.

– 0–6–0ST of '2721' class, *viz* *2780.

– 2–4–0Ts of 'Metro' class, *viz* 3590 and 3593.

– 2–6–2Ts of 45xx class, *viz* 4504, 4510, 4513, 4514, 4538 and 4544.

1920s/1930s – 0–4–2Ts of '517' class (Residue running from the 1900s).

– 2–4–0Ts of 'Metro' class (Residue running from the 1900s, plus 470).

– 2–6–2Ts of 45xx class, *viz* 4516, 4522, 4524, 4529, 4530, 4535, 4536, *4537, 4538, 4540, 4547, 4550, 4555, 4557, 4560, 4565, 4576, 4582, 4583, 4585, 4591, 5550, 5505 and 5557.

– GWR Steam Railcars, *viz* 71, 76, 80, 81, 96 and 97.

An 0–4–2T of the '517' class, No. 1487, seen here at Newton Abbot in 1934 whilst in charge of a 'Clifton Down' two-coach auto set with eight-compartment non-corridor coach 3275 coupled to five-compartment coach 3331, the latter fitted with a guard luggage compartment and a driving compartment. First constructed as normal non-corridor coaches in 1898, these vehicles had been converted for auto working (originally in the Bristol area) in 1913, and this particular set was used extensively on the Moretonhampstead branch during World War II.

E. R. Shepherd

An unidentified steam railcar, strengthened by a four-wheel Van Third, seen passing Newton Abbot East Box in the spring of 1935. At that time there was a 3 p.m. service (Wednesdays and Saturdays only) from Newton Abbot to Heathfield, and from around the late 1920s up until the previous year Exeter-based steam railcars such as this one had also been employed on a shuttle service between Heathfield and Bovey during the middle of the day.

G. N. Southerden (Courtesy of Wild Swan Publications Ltd)

'Metro' class 2–4–0T No. 3590 at Heathfield with a Moretonhampstead train on 22nd July 1939.

G. N. Southerden (Courtesy of Wild Swan Publications Ltd)

A member of the 48xx (later 14xx) class, No. 4827, at Moretonhampstead, c.1940.

Courtesy of Peter W. Gray

1939 to 1945 (WWII)

1945 to 1959

- 2–4–0Ts of 'Metro' class, *viz* 3581, 3582, 3587 and 3590.

- 0–4–2Ts of 48xx class, *viz* 4827, *4832, 4839, 4866, 4868 and 4870.

  (Renumbered 14xx class in 1946).

- 0–4–2Ts of 14xx class, *viz* *1414, 1427, 1429, 1433, 1439, 1450, 1451, 1452, 1466, 1468, 1469, 1470 and 1472.

  (NB No. 1439 was withdrawn in August 1957 following an accident at Newton Abbot and replaced by No. 1452).

- 2–6–2Ts of 44xx class, *viz* *4400, *4405 and 4406.

- 2–6–2Ts of 45xx class, *viz* 4516, 4518, 4526, 4532, 4547, 4555, 4558, 4568, 4582, 4587, 5516, 5530, 5533, 5539, 5551, 5552, *5553, 5557, 5567, 5570, 5571, 5572 and 5573.

2–6–2T No. 5533, a 45xx class locomotive, shown awaiting departure from Moretonhampstead with a Newton Abbot-bound train in the summer of 1957.
Geoff Howells

- 2–6–2Ts of '5101' class, *viz* 4105, 4117, 4145, 4150, 4174, 4176, 4178, 4179, 5108, *5150, 5153, 5154, *5158, 5164 5168, 5174, *5178, 5183, *5195 and 5196.

A 57xx class 0–6–0PT, No. 3796, depicted above taking water at Moretonhampstead during the summer of 1957.

Geoff Howells

BR standard class 3 2–6–2T No. 82032 about to leave Moretonhampstead with the 11.35 a.m. service to Newton Abbot on 21st December 1955, the first year in which this type of locomotive appeared on the Moretonhampstead branch.

Hugh Ballantyne

1939 to 1945 (WWII)

1945 to 1959 *(Continued)*

– 0–6–0PTs of 57xx class, *viz* 3600, 3606, 3609, 3659, 3677, 3794, 3796, 5786, 5796, *5798, 7716, 7761, *8709, *8717, *9623, 9633, 9668 and 9678.

– 0–6–0PTs of 64xx class, *viz* 6407 and 7427 (non-auto fitted).

– 2–6–2Ts of BR standard class 3, *viz* 82001, 82002, 82009, 82032, 82033, 82034 and 82039.

1959 to 2004

Goods only traffic – 2–6–2T of 45xx class, *viz* 4555.

– 2–6–2Ts of '5101' class, *viz* 4148 and 4174.

– 0–6–0PTs of 57xx class, *viz* 3659, 3796 and 9671.

– Diesel-hydraulic locomotives of class 22, *viz* D6310, D6329 and D6354.

– Diesel shunters, *viz* 08238 and 08281.

– Diesel-electric locomotive of class 31, *viz* 31273.

– Diesel-electric locomotives of class 37, *viz* 37072, 37141, 37215, 37254, 37673 and 37674.

– Diesel-electric locomotives of class 47, *viz* 47079 and 47197.

– Diesel-electric locomotives of class 50, *viz* 50037 and 50149.

– Diesel-electric locomotives of class 66, *viz* 66002, 66016, 66049, 66119, 66162 and 66194.

Specials

1959 (18th August) – Sunday School Special ran from Moretonhampstead to Goodrington Sands Halt and return – 2–6–2T No. 5164 with five coaches.

1960 (6th June) – South Devon Railway Society's 'Heart of Devon Rambler' ran from Paignton to Moretonhampstead and return – 2–6–2T No. 4174 with six coaches (5903 – 9106 – 1114 – 8052 – 587 – 2172).

BR Engine Restrictions, 16th September 1957.

Selected extract from the BR (Western Region) Working Time Table of passenger trains, Exeter District, for the period 16th September 1957 to 8th June 1958 (or until further notice).

C76

ENGINE RESTRICTIONS—continued.

Branch Lines—continued.

Section of Line	Route Colour	Engines Authorised	Prohibitions
City Basin Junction : Heathfield.	Uncoloured	All Uncoloured types. Yellow types specially authorised. 2-6-2T. 0-6-0T.	
		Blue types : 2-8-0, B.R. Standard 9F. ..	To be used only for shunting Alphington Road Loop and Cattle Pens Sidings. Not to pass Down Teign Valley Branch Advanced Starting Signal. Speed not to exceed 10 miles per hour.
		2-6-2T., 4-6-0 (78XX), 2-6-0 (43XX)	Maximum speed 25 m.p.h.
			Note—During emergency working over this Branch, see Notice No. 464.
Newton Abbot Station : Over Moretonhampstead Branch (East End).	—	—	**Electricity Sidings**—All engines other than 0-6-0T (except 84XX and 94XX Class) and 2-6-2T (45XX and 55XX Classes). No engine to pass Stopboard. **Goods Yard Cattle Pens**—All outside cylinder engines except 45XX and 55XX. **Beyond second river bridge** .. / **Mileage Sidings** .... / **Store Line** .... } 60XX.
Newton Abbot : Moretonhampstead	Blue ..	All Uncoloured, Yellow and Blue types.	**Heathfield (Candy and Co's Siding)**—No engines to pass Stopboard except Uncoloured, Yellow and Blue Tank engines and B.R. Standard 3 (2-6-2T). **Pottery Siding**—No engine to pass Stopboard. **Granite Siding**—No engine to pass Stopboard. **Note**—For emergency working between Newton Abbot and Heathfield, see Notice No. 464.

Specials *(Continued)*

1960 (August) – Sunday School Special ran from Moretonhampstead to Goodrington Sands Halt and return – 2–6–2T No. 5573 with five coaches.

1961 (4th March) – South Devon Railway Society's brake van trip ran from Newton Abbot to Trusham and return – 2–6–2T No. 4174 with eight brake vans.

1961 (10th August) – Sunday School Special ran from Moretonhampstead to Goodrington Sands Halt and return – details of train formation are unknown.

1962 (11th June) – South Devon Railway Society's 'South Devon Phoenix' ran from Paignton to Moretonhampstead and return – 2–6–2T No. 5153 with six coaches.

1962 (16th August) – Sunday School Special ran from Moretonhampstead to Teignmouth and return – details of train formation are unknown.

1970 (5th July) – 'Farewell' passenger trains ran from Newton Abbot to Bovey and return (four trips) – diesel multiple unit consisting of a three-car set comprising vehicles W55016 – 51327 – 51312 and two single cars (vehicles W59481 and W51329) running as a five-car set (organised by BR – fare 10/-).

Specials *(Continued)*

1974 (20th April) – 'The Devon Rambler', organised by the Railway Correspondence & Travel Society and consisting of a three-car diesel multiple unit comprising vehicles W 51580 – 59586 – 51589, ran from Bristol, visiting Torrington and Meldon goods-only lines before going to Newton Abbot and making a return trip to Heathfield.

c.1980 – A railtour, organised by F. & W. Railtours, visited Heathfield en route to Cornwall, but details of the exact date and train formation are unknown.

1983 (8/9th March) – The royal train, hauled by class 47 diesel-electric locomotive No. 47500 *Great Western* and consisting of eight bogie coaches, was stabled overnight at a point between Teignbridge Crossing and Teigngrace with the Prince and Princess of Wales on board. On the following morning, with a class 31 diesel-electric locomotive coupled onto the rear of the train, the prince disembarked at Teigngrace Halt and the princess (on a separate engagement) at Heathfield.

1983 (30th April) – 'The Devonian Railtour', again organised by the RCTS and consisting of diesel-electric multiple unit set 1014, ran from Waterloo to Paignton, with a trip along the branch to Heathfield en route.

1984 (28th May) – 'The Devonian', organised by the Lancashire Locomotive Society and T. and N. Railtours, ran from Preston to Paignton with class 40 locomotives as motive power. The train divided at Exeter, one portion, hauled by class 31 locomotives Nos. 31180 and 31259, visiting Meldon Quarry and Heathfield.

1986 (21st Sept.) – 'The Dartmoor Skipper', again organised by the RCTS, and consisting of class 142 units Nos. 142020 and 142026, ran from Exeter to Goodrington, returning via Heathfield and Meldon Quarry.

1987 (16th May) – 'The Torbay Express' railtour, comprising eleven coaches hauled by class 47 locomotive No. 47583 *County of Hertfordshire*, included a visit to Heathfield.

'The Dartmoor Skipper' at Heathfield on 21st September 1986.
Peter Kay

'The Taw Tor Tourer' at Teignbridge Crossing on 16th September 1990.
Geoff Howells

The Pathfinder Tours' train from Wolverhampton returning from the stop blocks at Heathfield on 7th January 1995.

Geoff Myers

The first of the three workings from Newton Abbot to Heathfield in connection with the 'Newton Abbot 150' celebrations, seen here at Teigngrace on New Year's Eve 1996.

Karen Lang

Specials *(Continued)*

1987 (31st May) – 'The Dartmoor Boundaryman', organised by the Plymouth Railway Circle and consisting of class 142 units Nos. 142015 and 142016, ran from Plymouth to Meldon Quarry and return, visiting Buckfastleigh and Heathfield en route.

1988 (4th Sept.) – 'The Devon Rambler' comprised a DMU set with vehicles 51939 and 52057 chartered by the Cornwall Railway Society, which ran from Penzance to Meldon, Heathfield and Paignton.

1990 (16th Sept.) – 'The Taw Tor Tourer' was organised by Pathfinder Tours and included a visit to Heathfield, the train hauled by class 50 locomotives No. 50032 *Courageous* and No. 50031 *Hood.*

1993 (20th Feb.) – 'The Par Snip', organised by Hertfordshire Rail Tours, ran from Paddington to Par and Parkandillack on the Cornish clay lines, with a visit to Heathfield en route, using class 47 locomotive No. 47833 and class 37 locomotive No. 37670.

1995 (7th Jan.) – Pathfinder Tours ran a trip from Wolverhampton to Buckfastleigh, visiting Heathfield on the return trip, using class 31 locomotive No. 31417 and class 37 locomotive No. 37695.

1996 (31st Dec.) – A series of three workings composed of four coaches ran to Heathfield with class 37 locomotives Nos. 37668 and 37416. This train was part of the 'Newton Abbot 150' celebrations.

1997 (26th April) – An Intercity 125 HST set, chartered by the South Devon Railway Association as part of the celebrations marking the 125th anniversary of the opening of the Ashburton branch line, ran from Buckfastleigh to Heathfield and return.

1997 (13th Dec.) – A Christmas Special Intercity 125 HST set, with power cars 43004 and 43192, ran from Plymouth to Okehampton and return, with a visit to Heathfield en route.

The Intercity 125 HST set about to leave Heathfield for the return journey to Buckfastleigh on 26th April 1997.

Karen Lang

0–6–0PT No. 9600 and its train approaching Summer Lane Bridge, Teigngrace, on the final trip to Heathfield during the second day of the 'Newton Abbot Festival of Transport 2000', 14th May 2000.

Karen Lang

Specials *(Continued)*

1999 (5th April) – 'The Heathfield Mule', chartered by Past Time Rail, ran from Exeter to Heathfield and return, using steam locomotive 2–6–4T No. 80079 and diesel-electric locomotive No. 37412.

2000 (13/14th May) – As part of a two-day 'Newton Abbot Festival of Transport 2000', a series of five return trips (three on the 13th and two on the 14th) was run from Paignton or Newton Abbot to Heathfield. These trains were named 'The Newton Antelope' (reputed to commemorate the name of the locomotive which headed the first public train to arrive at Newton Abbot), the steam locomotive used being 0–6–0PT No. 9600, looking very smart in lined black livery. A journey on 13th May in one of these trains which started from Paignton was notable for the inhabitants of lineside houses there and in Torquay waving at the train as it passed and also for a very spirited climb of the bank up from Torquay and Torre stations by the little locomotive with her well-filled five-coach train. The part of the trip along the branch was much more restrained, and the arrival at Heathfield was somewhat of an anti-climax as passengers were not permitted to alight onto the bare expanse of the neglected former 'up' platform, much to the dismay of the organisers of the trip.

Some delay then ensued whilst permission was sought to allow the locomotive to proceed farther up the line in order to run around her train. This was eventually sorted out and the train commenced its return journey. A notable visitor to platform 9 on that day was the ex-LNER Pacific locomotive No. 4472 *Flying Scotsman,* which had arrived with a special train from London's Victoria Station.

2002 (25th May) – 'The Clayliner', organised by Hertfordshire Rail Tours, ran from Paddington to Plymouth (Friary) and Fowey Docks, with a visit to Heathfield en route. The locomotives were class 66 Nos. 66040 and 66168.

Coaches and other rolling stock witnessed between 1940 and 1959

Two-coach auto-fitted 'Clifton Down' set	–	3275 and 3331.
Saloons	–	104, 122, 132, 146, 147, 148, 149, 155, 157, 158, 215, 222, 224, 234, 240 and 241.
GWR coaches	–	809, 821, 1486, 2369, 2642, 2806, 3536, 4289, 4379, 4481, 4510, 4735, 5007, 5186, 6837, 7087, 7103, 7571, 7926, 7960 and 7991.
LMS coaches	–	1972, 2710, 2939 and 27289.

Authors' notes

The information given above relating to the period from 1866 to 1959 has been verified from the personal records of the late J. B. N. Ashford (SDR/GWR locomotive inspector based at Newton Abbot and Laira during the late 19th century and early 20th century), the late P. J. T. Reed (and his books on 'Locos of the GWR', published for the RCTS) and Mr E. R. Shepherd (covering the years from 1940 to 1959). Other information has been gleaned from various sources. However, where this has not been verified, an asterisk has been inserted.

Locomotives used for Teign Valley line workings, insofar as they included the section between Newton Abbot and Heathfield, have also been included. One deliberate omission, however, is 4–6–0 No. 7806 *Cockington Manor*, for which an undated photograph exists of this locomotive at Christow in charge of a goods train thought to have originated from Newton Abbot.

One final comment concerns the inordinate number of locomotives used over the branch as compared to others. This is probably accounted for by the fact that Newton Abbot was a divisional headquarters with an extensive motive power depot which carried out major repairs to most of the small engines in the division as well as being responsible for upwards of 80 engines of its own. There would, therefore, have been a continuous turnover of locomotives and at least some of these would have been available for use on the branch, if only on a short-term basis, before being returned to their 'normal' locations.

Time Tables

A representative selection of public and working timetables from the opening of the branch, including:-

1866	– The first timetable (see page 121).
1871	– PTT for the last winter period before the Moretonhampstead & South Devon Railway Company was formally amalgamated with the South Devon Railway Company in July of the following year.
1879	– The earliest PTT available following the formal amalgamation of the South Devon Railway and Great Western Railway companies on 1st August 1878.
1892	– The last WTT prior to the narrowing of the gauge over the weekend of 21st/22nd May 1892.
1913	– PTT for the last full summer period of peacetime before the outbreak of World War I in the following August, and also the road motor service timetable for the same period.
1924	– WTT, including the through workings from Plymouth, Kingswear and Paignton, which were still a comparatively new innovation.
1928	– PTTs from the last 'GWR Road Motor Services for Devon' timetable.
1930s	– PTT (1934), Western National Timetable (1934), WTT (1935), Tor Bus Timetable (1935), PTT (1936) and Motor Omnibus Services Timetable (1936), showing the level of service during the peak years of the branch.
1948	– The first WTT issued by British Railways.
1958/59	– WTT for the last winter of the passenger service on the branch, which was not completed due to withdrawal effectively taking place on 28th February 1959. Freight timetable for the same period.
1964	– Freight timetable shortly after the section of line beyond Bovey had been closed.

NB Throughout the broad-gauge era trains running along the branch towards Moretonhampstead from Newton Abbot were referred to as 'up' trains and those running in the opposite direction were referred to as 'down' trains. However, in July 1893 this was changed by the GWR so that from thereon 'up' trains to Moretonhampstead became 'down' trains and vice versa. In this book the terms 'up' and 'down' are used in the post-1893 sense.

September 1871.

TABLE No.32 from the Great Western Railway Public Timetable dated September 1871.

MORETONHAMPSTEAD BRANCH

DOWN TRAINS.		WEEK DAYS.					SUNDAYS.	
		1 2 3	1 2 3	1 2 3	1 2 3		1 2 3	1 2 3
		a.m.	a.m.	p.m.	p.m.		a.m.	p.m.
Newton	dep	8 30	10 55	4 15	8 5		8 35	9 5
Teigngrace	"	8 37	11 2	4 22	8 12		8 42	9 12
Bovey	"	8 45	11 10	4 30	8 20		8 50	9 20
Lustleigh	"	8 55	11 20	4 40	8 30		9 0	9 30
Moretonhampstead	arr	9 10	11 35	4 55	8 45		9 15	9 45

UP TRAINS.		WEEK DAYS.					SUNDAYS.	
		1 2 3	1 2 3	1 2 3	1 2 3		1 2 3	1 2 3
		a.m.	a.m.	p.m.	p.m.		a.m.	p.m.
Moretonhampstead	dep	7 25	10 0	1 25	7 10		7 30	7 15
Lustleigh	"	7 37	10 12	1 37	7 22		7 42	7 27
Bovey	"	7 46	10 21	1 46	7 31		7 51	7 36
Teigngrace	"	7 53	10 28	1 53	7 38		7 58	7 43
Newton	arr	8 0	10 35	2 0	7 45		8 5	7 50

NB The numbers 1, 2 and 3 refer to the classes of accommodation.

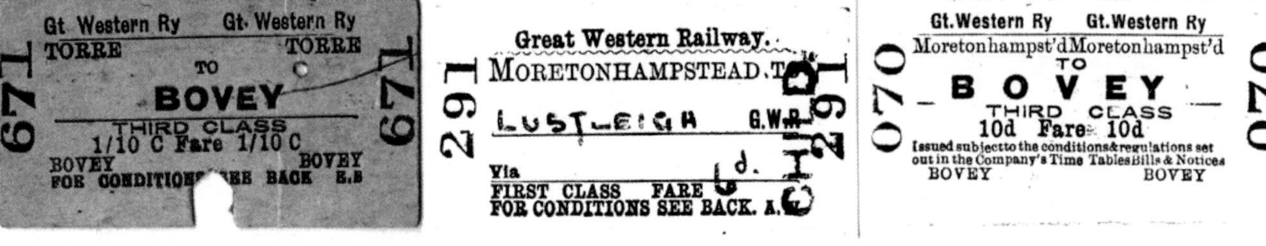

June 1879 until further notice.

Moretonhampstead Branch Trains.

UP TRAINS.

Distances.	STATIONS.		Week Days 1 Passenger.	2 Passenger.	3 Passenger.	4 GOODS.	5 Passenger.	6 Passenger.		Sundays 1 Passenger.	2 Passenger.
			a.m.	a.m.	p.m.	p.m.	p.m.	p.m.		a.m.	p.m.
	Newton Abbot ...	dep.	8 27	11 53	1 50	4 45	5 30	8 25	...	8 30	8 5
2¼	Teigngrace ...	..	8 34	12 0	1 57	4/55	5 37	8 32	...	8 37	8 12
3¾	Chudleigh Road ...	...	8 39	12 5	2 2	5/0	5 42	8 37	...	8 42	8 18
6	Bovey	...	8 45	12 11	2 8	5 5	5 48	8 43	...	8 48	8 23
8¾	Lustleigh	...	8 55	12 21	2 18		5 58	8 53	...	8 58	8 33
12¼	Moretonhampstead	arr.	9 9	12 35	2 33	...	6 13	9 8	...	9 13	8 48

DOWN TRAINS.

Distances.	STATIONS.		Week Days 1 Passenger.	2 Passenger.	3 Passenger.	4 Passenger.	5 GOODS.	6 Passenger.		Sundays 1 Passenger.	2 Passenger.
			a.m.	a.m.	p.m.	p.m.	p.m	p m		a.m.	p.m.
	Moretonhampstead	dep.	7 15	10 50	12 50	4 5	...	7 15	...	7 35	7 5
3½	Lustleigh	...	7 26	11 1	1 1	4 16	...	7 27	...	7 47	7 17
6¼	Bovey	...	7 34	11 9	1 13	4 28	5 50	7 36	...	7 56	7 26
8½	Chudleigh Road	...	7 40	11 15	1 19	4 34	6 35	7 42	...	8 2	7 32
10	Teigngrace ...	...	7 45	11 20	1 24	4 39	C.R.	7 47	...	8 7	7 37
12¼	Newton Abbot ...	arr.	7 53	11 28	1 30	4 45	7 5	7 55	...	8 15	7 45

96 **S.D.R.**

Passenger Luggage.

Lustleigh to

BRIDGEWATER

April 1892 until further notice.

MORETONHAMPSTEAD BRANCH.

Single Line, Broad Gauge, worked by Block Telegraph and Train Staff. Crossing Place, Bovey.

Form of Staff.	Colour of Ticket.	Working Between
Square	Red	Moretonhampstead Junction and Bovey.
Round	Blue	Bovey and Moretonhampstead.

Down Trains.—Week Days. / SUNDAYS.

Dist. from Moreton-hampstead.		STATIONS.	1		2		3		4		5		6		7		8		Sundays 1		2		3	
			Passenger. A		Passenger. A		Passenger. A		Passenger. A		Passenger. A		Goods. D		Passenger. A				Passenger. A		Passenger. A			
M.	C.		arr.	dep.	arr.	dep.	arr.	dep.	arr.	dep.	arr.	dep.	arr.	dep.	arr.	dep.	arr.	dep.	arr.	dep.	arr.	dep.	arr.	dep.
			A.M.	A.M.	A.M.	A.M.	A.M.	A.M.	P.M.	P.M.	P.M.	P.M.	P.M.	P.M.	P.M.	P.M.			A.M.	A.M.	P.M.	P.M.		
				Staff		Staff		Staff		Staff		Ticket		Staff		Staff				Staff		Staff		
—	—	Moretonhampstead	—	7 15	W	9 45	—	10 45	—	1 55	W	4 10	—	4 30	—	7 30	......	......	—	7 40	—	6 47	......	......
3	44	Lustleigh	7 23	7 24	9 54	9 55	10 53	10 54	2 3	2 4	4 18	4 19	C	R	7 38	7 39	...	...	7 48	7 49	6 55	6 56	...	...
				Staff		Ticket		Staff		Staff		Staff		Ticket		Staff				Staff		Staff		
6	24	Bovey	7 30	7 32	10 3	X10 5	11 0	11 2	2 10	X2 12	4 25	4 27	4 55	X6 5	7 45	7 47	......	......	7 55	7 56	7 2	7 4	......	......
8	42	Heathfield	7 37	7 39	10 10	10 12	11 7	11 9	2 17	2 19	4 32	4 34	6 20	7 0	7 52	7 54	...	...	8 1	8 2	7 9	7 10	...	...
10	1	Teigngrace	7 43	7 44	10 16	10 17	11 13	11 14	2 23	2 24	4 38	4 39	C	R	7 58	7 59	......	......	8 6	8 7	7 14	7 15	......	......
10	59	Teign Bridge L. Crsg	—	—	—	—	—	—	—	—	—	—	—	—	—	—	...	...	—	—	—	—	...	...
12	9	Moretonhmstd Junc.	—	—	—	—	—	—	—	—	—	—	—	—	—	—	......	......	—	—	—	—	......	......
12	30	Newton Abbot arr.	7 50	—	10 23	—	11 20	—	2 30	—	4 45	—	7 20	—	8 5	—	...	...	8 13	—	7 21	—	...	...

Up Trains.—Week Days. / SUNDAYS.

Dist. from Newton Abbot.		STATIONS.	1		2		3		4		5		6		7		8		Sundays 1		2		3	
			Passenger. A		Passenger. A		Passenger. A		Goods. D		Passenger. A		Passenger. A		Passenger. A				Passenger. A		Passenger. A			
M.	C.		arr.	dep.	arr.	dep.	arr.	dep.	arr.	dep.	arr.	dep.	arr.	dep.	arr.	dep.	arr.	dep.	arr.	dep.	arr.	dep.	arr.	dep.
			A.M.	A.M.	A.M.	A.M.	P.M.	NOON.	P.M.	P.M.	P.M.	P.M.	P.M.	P.M.	P.M.	P.M.			A.M.	A.M.	P.M.	P.M.		
—	—	Newton Abbot dep.	—	8 27	—	9 47	—	12 0	—	1 20	—	3 18	—	5 46	—	8 33	......	......	—	8 30	—	7 46	......	......
				Ticket	W	Staff		Ticket		Staff	W	Staff		Staff		Staff				Staff		Staff		
0	21	Moretonhmstd Junc.	—	—	—	—	—	—	—	—	—	—	—	—	—	—	...	...	—	—	—	—	...	...
1	51	Teign Bridge L. Crsg		—	—	—	—	—	—	—	—	—	—	—	—	—	......	......	—	—	—	—	......	......
2	29	Teigngrace	8 32	8 33	9 52	9 53	12 5	12 6	C	R	3 23	3 24	5 50	5 51	8 38	8 39	...	...	8 35	8 36	7 51	7 52	...	...
3	68	Heathfield	8 37	8 39	9 57	9 59	12 10	12 12	1 32	2 0	3 28	3 29	5 55	5 57	8 43	8 45	......	......	8 40	8 41	7 56	7 57	......	......
				Staff		Staff		Staff		Ticket		Staff		Staff		Staff				Staff		Staff		
6	6	Bovey	8 44	8 46	10 4	X10 6	12 17	12 19	2 8	X2 45	3 34	3 36	6 2	X6 4	8 50	8 52	...	...	8 46	8 47	8 2	8 3	...	...
8	66	Lustleigh	8 55	8 56	10 10	10 15	12 28	12 29	C	R	3 44	3 45	6 13	6 14	9 1	9 2	......	......	8 56	8 57	8 12	8 13	...	......
12	30	Moretonhampstead	9 9	—	10 27	—	12 42	—	3 10	—	3 57	—	6 27	—	9 15	—	...	...	9 10	—	8 26	—	...	...

CROSSING.—X The 9.45 a.m. Down Passenger Train and the 9.47 a.m. Up Passenger Train will cross at Bovey.
X The 1.55 p.m. Down Passenger Train and the 1.20 p.m. Goods at Bovey.
X The 4.30 p.m. Down Goods and 5.46 p.m. Up Passenger Train at Bovey.
W Wednesdays only and third Tuesday in each month.

12th July to 30th September 1913.

NEWTON ABBOT AND MORETONHAMPSTEAD. 85

		Week Days.									Sundays.		
		a.m.	a.m.	a.m.	p.m.	p.m.	p.m.	p.m.	p.m.	p.m.	a.m.	p.m.	p.m.
Newton Abbot	dep	7X10	8 10	9 52	12 3	3 0	3 45	5R 0	5 52	9 8	11 0	1 30	7 55
Teigngrace	,,	.	8 15	9 58	12 9	3 6	3 55	5R 6	5 58	.	.	.	.
Heathfield	,,	7X19	8 20	10 4	12 15	3 12	4 2	5R11	6 4	9 18	11 9	1 39	8 5
Bovey	,,	7X28	8 29	10 11	12 22	3 19	4 12	5R18	6 11	9 25	11 15	1 45	8 11
Lustleigh	,,	7X38	8 40	10 21	12 32	3 29	4 22	5R28	6 21	9 35	11 25	1 55	8 21
Moretonhampstead	arr	7X51	8 53	10 34	12 45	3 42	4 35	5R41	6 35	9 50	11 40	2 10	8 35

		a.m.	a.m.	a.m.	a.m.	p.m.	p.m.	p.m.	p.m.	p.m.	a.m.	p.m.	p.m.
Moretonhampstead	dep	7 10	8X 7	9 52	10 45	1 50	3 56	5 55	7 0	8R 0	8 45	7 0	7 50
Lustleigh	,,	7 19	8X16	10 1	10 54	1 59	4 5	6 4	7 9	8R 9	8 54	7 9	7 59
Bovey	,,	7 27	8X26	10 10	11 2	2 7	4 13	6 12	7 18	8R16	9 1	7 16	8 6
Heathfield	,,	7 34	8X31	10 17	11 9	2 15	4 20	6 18	7 24	8R22	9 7	7 22	8 12
Teigngrace	,,	7 39	8X38	10 22	11 14	2 20	4 25	6 23	7 29	...	...	...	...
Newton Abbot	arr	7 45	8X46	10 28	11 20	2 26	4 31	6 29	7 35	8R33	9 17	7 32	8 22

R—Not after September 13th. **X**—Wednesdays only.

Road Motor Services.

MORETONHAMPSTEAD AND CHAGFORD. (Week Days only.)

		a.m	a.m.	p.m.	p.m	p.m	p.m.	p.m
Moretonhampstead (Station)	dep.	9 0	10 40	12 55	3 50	4 40	5N50	6 40
Half Way House	,,	9 17	10 57	1 12	4 7	4 57	6N 7	6 57
Easton Cross (For Fingle Bridge)	,,	9 23	11 3	1 18	4 13	5 3	6N13	7 3
Chagford { Moor Park Hotel	,,	9 35	11 15	1 30	4 25	5 15	6N25	7 15
Chagford { G.W. Office, Rock House	arr.	9 37	11 17	1 32	4 27	5 17	6N27	7 17

		a.m	a.m.	p.m.	p.m	p.m	p.m	p.m.
Chagford { G.W. Office, Rock House,	dep.	9 0	9 50	12 10	3 5	5 5	6 0	7N10
Chagford { Moor Park Hotel	,,	9 2	9 52	12 12	3 7	5 7	6 2	7N12
Easton Cross (For Fingle Bridge)	,,	9 12	10 2	12 22	3 17	5 17	6 12	7N22
Half Way House	,,	9 18	10 8	12 28	3 23	5 23	6 18	7N28
Moretonhampstead (Station)	arr.	9 40	10 30	12 50	3 45	5 45	6 35	7N50

N—Will not run after September 13th.

MORETONHAMPSTEAD AND PRINCETOWN. (Week Days only).

			a.m.	
Moretonhampstead (Station)	dep	...	10 40	...
Warren Inn	arr. abt.	.	10 45	.
Post Bridge	,, ,,	...	11 55	...
Two Bridges	,, ,,	.	12 20	.
Princetown (Station)	arr	...	12 40	...

		p.m.	p.m.	
Princetown (Station)	dep.	3H 0	4N30	...
Two Bridges	dep. abt.	3H10	4N40	.
Post Bridge	,, ,,	3H40	5N10	...
Warren Inn	,, ,,	4H 0	5N30	.
Moretonhampstead (Station)	arr.	5H 0	6N30	...

H—September 15th to 30th inclusive. **N**—Will not run after September 13th.

MORETONHAMPSTEAD BRANCH.

Single Line, worked by **Electric Train Staff** during time **Newton Abbot Goods Yard Box** open, when shut worked by **Electric Tablet** between **Moretonhampstead Junction** and **Heathfield**, and **Electric Train Staff** between **Heathfield** and **Moretonhampstead**. **The Crossing Stations are Moretonhampstead Junction**, and **Bovey**. **The Staff Stations are Moretonhampstead Junction, Newton Abbot Goods Yard, Heathfield, Bovey and Moretonhampstead.**
When absolutely necessary two Goods Trains, or a Passenger and a Goods Train may cross at Heathfield on the understanding that the Passenger Train is always kept on the Running Line, and that if the Passenger Train has to stop at Heathfield it must stop at the Platform.

Down Trains. — Week Days.

Dist. from Newton Abbot. M.	C.	STATIONS.	Station No.	Ruling Gradient.	Time Allowances for ordinary Freight Trains, see page 2. Point to Point Times.	Allow for Stop.	Allow for Start.	1 K Exeter Goods. arr.	dep.	2 arr.	dep.	3 B Passenger. arr.	dep.	4 arr.	dep.	5 B Plymouth Passenger. arr.	dep.	6 arr.	dep.	7 B Kingswear Passenger. arr.	dep.	8 arr.	dep.	9 K Goods. arr.	dep.
					Mins.	Mins.	Mins.	A.M.	A.M.			A.M.	A.M.			A.M.	A.M.			A.M.	A.M.			A.M.	A.M.
—	—	**Newton Abbot** ..	1566	—	—	—	1	—	6 30	..	..	—	**7 55**	..	..	**8 42**	**8 55**	..	..	**10 19**	**10 25**	..	..	—	11 5
—	21	Moretonhampstead J	1637	—	—	—	—	C	S	....	....	C	S	....	....	C	S	....	....	C	S	....	....	C	S
—	48	Goods Yard ..	—	132 F.	1	1	1	—	—	..	..	—	—	..	..	—	—	..	..	—	—	..	..	—	—
—	—	Teign Bdg. Level C.	1638	—	—	—	—	—	—	....	....	—	—	....	....	—	—	....	....	—	—	....	....	—	—
1	43	Teign Bridge Siding	1639	100 R.	3	1	1	6 36	6 55	..	..	—	—	..	..	—	—	..	..	—	—	..	..	C	R
2	28	Teigngrace	1640	100 R.	—	—	—	—	—	....	....	7 59	8 0	....	....	8 59	9 0	....	....	10 29	10 30	....	....	—	—
3	70	**Heathfield** ..	1641	70 R.	5	1	1	7 2	8 40	..	..	**8 4**	**8 6**	..	..	**9 4**	**9 6**	..	..	**10 34**	**10 36**	..	..	11 20	11 35
5	6	Granite Siding	1642	69 R.	—	—	—			....	....	—	—	....	....	—	—	....	....	—	—	....	....	C	R
5	19	Pottery Siding ..	1643	53 R.	—	—	—	..	..	..	..	—	—	..	..	—	—	..	..	—	—	..	..	C	R
6	6	Bovey	1644	66 F.	5	2	2	....	....	....	....	8 11	X8 14	....	....	9 11	X 9 14	....	....	10 41	X10 43	....	....	11 43	X12 22
8	66	Lustleigh ..	1645	50 R.	11	1	2	..	..	..	..	8 22	8 25	..	..	9 22	9 25	..	..	10 51	10 54	..	..	CR	ST
12	28	**Moretonhampst'd**	1647	49 R.	14	1	—			....	....	**8 37**	—	....	....	**9 37**	—	....	....	**11 6**	—	....	....	12 51	—

Down Trains. — Week Days. — Sundays.

STATIONS.	10 B Paignton Passenger. arr.	dep.	11 arr.	dep.	12 B Passenger. arr.	dep.	13 arr.	dep.	14 K Goods. RR arr.	dep.	15 B Passenger. arr.	dep.	16 B Kingswear Passenger. arr.	dep.	17 B Passenger. Q arr.	dep.	Sundays 1 B Passenger. Y arr.	dep.	2 arr.	dep.	3 B Passenger Y arr.	dep.
	P.M.	P.M.			P.M.	P.M.			P.M.	P.M.	P.M.	P.M.	P.M.	P.M.	P.M.	P.M.	A.M.	A.M.			P.M.	P.M.
Newton Abbot	**12 32**	**12 46**	..	..	—	**3 10**	..	..	—	*5 0*	—	**5 25**	**7 10**	**7 25**	—	*9 40*	—	*10 40*	..	..	—	*7 15*
Moretonhampstead J	C	S	....	....	C	S	....	....	C	S	C	S	C	S	C	S	C	S	..	..	C	S
Goods Yard	—	—	..	..	—	—	..	..	—	—	—	—	—	—	—	—	—	—	....	....	—	—
Teign Bdg. Level C.	—	—	....	....	—	—	....	....	—	—	—	—	—	—	—	—	—	—	..	..	—	—
Teign Bridge Siding	—	—	..	..	—	—	..	..	—	—	—	—	—	—	—	—	—	—	....	....	—	—
Teigngrace	12 50	12 51	....	....	3 14	3 15	....	....	*5 10*	—	5 29	5 30	7 29	7 30	—	—	—	—	....	....	—	—
Heathfield	**12 55**	X**12 56**	..	..	**3 19**	**3 21**	..	..			**5 34**	X**5 36**	**7 34**	X**7 36**	*9 47*	*9 48*	*10 47*	*10 48*	..	..	*7 22*	*7 23*
Granite Siding	—	—	....	....	—	—	....	....	....	....	—	—	—	—	—	—	—	—	....	....	—	—
Pottery Siding	—	—	..	..	—	—	..	..	..	..	—	—	—	—	—	—	—	—	..	..	—	—
Bovey	1 1	1 2	....	....	3 26	X 3 29	....	....	....	....	5 41	5 44	7 41	7 43	*9 53*	*9 55*	*10 53*	*10 55*	....	....	*7 28*	*7 30*
Lustleigh	1 10	1 13	..	..	3 37	3 40	..	..	..	..	5 52	5 55	7 51	7 54	*10 3*	*10 5*	*10 3*	*11 6*	..	..	*7 38*	*7 41*
Moretonhampstead	**1 25**	—	....	....	**3 52**	—	....	....	....	....	**6 7**	—	**8 6**	—	*10 17*	—	*11 18*	—	....	....	*7 52*	—

Q—Saturdays only until May 2nd. Daily commencing May 4th. **Y**—September 28th, during October, and commencing May 3rd.

22nd September 1924 (Continued).

Moretonhampstead Branch—*continued.*

Up Trains. — Week Days.

STATIONS.	Ruling Gradient	Time Allowances for ordinary Freight Trains, see page 2. Point to Point times.	Allow for Stop.	Allow for Start.	1 B Passenger. arr.	1 B dep.	2	2	3 B Plymouth Passenger. arr.	3 B dep.	4	4	5 B Paignton Passenger. arr.	5 B dep.	6	6	7 B Plymouth Passenger. arr.	7 B dep.	8 K Exeter Goods. arr.	8 K dep.	9	9	10 B Passenger. arr.	10 B dep.
		Mins.	Mins.	Mins.	A.M.	A.M.			A.M.	A.M.			A.M.	A.M.			A.M.	A.M.	P.M.	P.M.			P.M.	P.M.
Moretonhampst'd	—	—	—	1	—	**7 55**	..	..	—	**8 55**	..	..	—	**10 25**	..	..	—	**11 35**	....	....	..	..	—	**1 35**
Stop Board 12mp.	L.	—	1	1	—	—	..	..	—	—	..	..	—	—	..	..	—	—	..	..	..	..	—	—
Lustleigh ..	49 F.	10	1	1	8 3	8 4	..	..	9 3	9 4	..	..	10 33	10 34	..	..	11 43	11 44	....	....	..	..	1 43	1 44
Stop Board 6m.15½c.	50 F.	—	—	—	—	—	..	..	—	—	..	..	—	—	..	..	—	—	..	..	..	..	—	—
Bovey	50 F.	8	2	2	8 10	X 8 13	..	..	9 10	X 9 13	..	..	10 40	X10 43	..	..	11 50	X11 53	....	....	..	..	1 50	1 52
Pottery Siding ..	66 R.	2	2	2	—	—	..	..	—	—	..	..	—	—	..	..	—	—	..	..	..	..	—	—
Granite Siding	53 F.	1	1	1	—	—	..	..	—	—	..	..	—	—	..	..	—	—	....	....	..	..	—	—
Heathfield ..	69 F.	3	1	1	**8 18**	**8 20**	..	..	**9 18**	**9 20**	..	..	**10 48**	**10 50**	..	..	**11 58**	**11 59**	12 30	X1 40	..	..	**1 57**	**1 58**
Teigngrace	70 F.	—	—	—	8 24	8 25	..	..	9 24	9 25	..	..	10 54	10 55	..	..	12 4	12 5	—	—	..	..	2 2	2 3
Teign Bridge Siding	100 F.	6	1	1	—	—	..	..	—	—	..	..	—	—	..	..	—	—	C	R	..	..	—	—
Teign Bdg. Level C.	—	—	—	—	—	—	..	..	—	—	..	..	—	—	..	..	—	—	—	—	..	..	—	—
Goods Yard	100 F.	3	1	1	—	—	..	..	—	—	..	..	—	—	..	..	—	—	—	—	..	..	—	—
Moretonhampst'd J.	—	—	—	—	C	S	..	..	C	S	..	..	C	S	..	..	C	S	C	S	..	..	C	S
Newton Abbot ...	132 R.	1	1	—	**8 30**	—	..	..	**9 30**	**9 36**	..	..	**11 0**	**11 5**	..	..	**12 12**	**12 21**	1 55	—	..	..	**2 8**	—

Up Trains. — Week Days. / Sundays.

STATIONS.	11	11	12 K Goods. N arr.	12 K dep.	13	13	14 B Passenger. arr.	14 B dep.	15	15	16 K Goods. RR arr.	16 K dep.	17 B Plymouth Passenger. arr.	17 B dep.	18 B Passenger. Q arr.	18 B dep.	19	19	Sundays 1 B Passenger. Y arr.	1 B dep.	2	2	3 B Passenger Y arr.	3 B dep.
			P.M.	P.M.			P.M.	P.M.			P.M.	P.M.	P.M.	P.M.	P.M.	P.M.			A.M.	A.M.			P.M.	P.M.
Moretonhampst'd	..	..	—	2 15	..	..	—	**4 20**	..	..	..	..	—	**6 35**	—	8 20	..	..	—	11 50	..	..	—	8 [illegible]
Stop Board 12mp.	..	..	2 16	P2 18	..	..	—	—	..	..	..	..	—	—	—	—	..	..	—	—	..	..	—	—
Lustleigh ..	..	..	2 27	2 40	..	..	4 28	4 29	..	..	..	..	6 43	6 44	8 28	8 29	..	..	11 58	11 59	..	..	8 23	8 24
Stop Board 6m.15½c.	..	..	2 48	P2 50	..	..	—	—	..	..	..	..	—	—	—	—	..	..	—	—	..	..	—	—
Bovey	..	..	2 51	3 40	..	..	4 35	4 38	..	..	..	..	6 50	6 52	8 35	8 36	..	..	12 5	12 6	..	..	8 30	8 32
Pottery Siding	..	..	C	R	..	..	—	—	..	..	..	..	—	—	—	—	..	..	—	—	..	..	—	—
Granite Siding ..	..	..	C	R	..	..	—	—	..	..	..	..	—	—	—	—	..	..	—	—	..	..	—	—
Heathfield	..	..	4 15	X•6 5	..	..	**4 43**	**4 45**	..	..	—	X 5 40	**6 57**	**6 59**	8 41	8 42	..	..	12 11	12 13	..	..	8 37	8 38
Teigngrace	..	..	—	—	..	..	4 49	4 50	..	..	—	—	7 3	7 4	—	—	..	..	—	—	..	..	—	—
Teign Bridge Siding	..	..	6 11	6 30	..	..	—	—	..	..	5 46	6 0	—	—	—	—	..	..	—	—	..	..	—	—
Teign Bdg. Level C.	..	..	—	—	..	..	—	—	..	..	—	—	—	—	—	—	..	..	—	—	..	..	—	—
Goods Yard	..	..	—	—	..	..	—	—	..	..	—	—	—	—	—	—	..	..	—	—	..	..	—	—
Moretonhampst'd J.	..	..	C	S	..	..	C	S	..	..	C	S	C	S	C	S	..	..	C	S	..	..	C	S
Newton Abbot ..	..	..	6 35	—	..	..	**4 55**	—	..	..	6 5	—	**7 10**	**7 20**	8 50	—	..	..	12 21	—	..	..	8 46	—

N Trucks taken on at Lustleigh and Bovey to be marshalled at Heathfield. **Q** Saturdays only until May 2nd. Daily commencing May 4th.
Y September 28th, during October, and commencing May 3rd.

24th September 1928 until further notice.

MORETONHAMPSTEAD AND NEWTON ABBOT TRAIN SERVICE.

(RAIL MOTOR CAR, ONE CLASS ONLY.)

		WEEK DAYS.										SUNDAYS.			
		a.m.	a.m.	a.m.	a.m.	p.m.	p.m.	p.m.	p.m.	p.m.	p.m.	a.m.	p.m.	p.m.	p.m.
MORETONHAMPSTEAD	dep.	7 55	8 45	10 30	11 35	1 35	..	4 20	6 50	8J20	..	11K50	4K25	6K20	8K30
LUSTLEIGH	„	8 4	8 54	10 39	11 44	1 44	..	4 29	6 59	8J29	..	11K59	4K34	6K29	8K39
BOVEY	„	8 13	9 1	10 46	11 52	1 52	2 30	4 37	7 7	8J36	..	12K 6	4K41	6K36	8K46
BRIMLEY HALT ..	„	8 16	9 4	10 49	11 55	1 55	2 32	4 39	7 10	8J39	..	12K 9	4K44	6K39	8K49
HEATHFIELD	„	8 21	9 10	10 56	12 0	2 0	2 37	4 45	7 15	8J44	10V44	12K14	4K49	6K44	8K54
TEIGNGRACE	„	8 26	9 15	11 1	12 5	2 5	2 41	4 50	7 20	..	..	..	..	..	..
NEWTON ABBOT ..	arr.	8 31	9 20	11 6	12 10	2 10	2 46	4 55	7 25	8J51	10V51	12K22	4K57	6K52	9K 2

		WEEK DAYS.										SUNDAYS.			
		a.m.	a.m.	a.m.	p.m.	p.m.	p.m.	p.m.	p.m.	p.m.	p.m.	a.m.	p.m.	p.m.	p.m.
NEWTON ABBOT ..	dep.	7 55	8 55	10 45	12 46	..	3 0	3 15	6 0	7 30	9J45	10K20	3K30	5K20	7K23
TEIGNGRACE	„	8 0	9 0	10 50	12 51	..	3 5	3 20	6 5	7 35	..	..	..	..	..
HEATHFIELD	„	8 4	9 9	10 56	12 55	2 10	3 8	3 24	6 9	7 39	9J53	10K28	3K38	5K28	7K31
BRIMLEY HALT ..	„	8 9	9 14	11 1	1 0	2 15		3 29	6 14	7 44	9J58	10K33	3K43	5K33	7K36
BOVEY	„	8 14	9 16	11 3	1 4	2 16	..	3 33	6 18	7 48	10J 0	10K35	3K45	5K35	7K38
LUSTLEIGH	„	8 23	9 29	11 14	1 15		..	3 44	6 29	7 59	10J11	10K46	3K56	5K46	7K49
MORETONHAMPSTEAD	arr.	8 34	9 38	11 25	1 26	..	..	3 55	6 40	8 10	10J22	10K57	4K 7	5K57	8K 0

J—Saturdays only until April 27th, 1929. Daily commencing April 29th, 1929. **K**—Runs from September 30th to October 28th, 1928, inclusive, and from May 5th, 1929.

V—Runs daily to Oct. 27th, 1928, and from April 1st, 1929; runs Sats only, Nov. 3rd, 1928, to March 30th, 1929.

24th September 1928 until further notice.

Road Motor Services.

MORETONHAMPSTEAD AND CHAGFORD.

	Early Closing.
MORETONHAMPSTEAD.	Thursday.
CHAGFORD	Wednesday.

WEEK DAYS ONLY.

		a.m.	a.m.	a.m.	p.m.	p.m.	p.m.		
MORETONHAMPSTEAD (Station)	dep.	8W50	10 15	11 35	1 35	4 10	8 15	..	..
CHAGFORD CROSS	,,	8W55	10 20	11 40	1 40	4 15	8 20	..	..
SLONCOMBE LANE	,,	8W57	10 22	11 42	1 42	4 17	8 22	..	..
HALF WAY HOUSE	,,	9W 2	10 27	11 47	1 47	4 22	8 27	..	..
†EASTON CROSS (for Fingle Bridge)	,,	9W 7	10 32	11 52	1 52	4 27	8 32	..	..
WESTCOTT LANE	,,	9W12	10 37	11 57	1 57	4 32	8 37	..	..
CHAGFORD (G.W. Office)	arr.	9W15	10 40	12 0	2 0	4 35	8 40	..	..
		a.m.	a.m.	a.m.	p.m.	p.m.	p.m.		
CHAGFORD (G.W. Office)	dep.	8W10	9 40	10 55	1 0	3 30	6 15	..	..
WESTCOTT LANE	,,	8W13	9 43	10 58	1 3	3 33	6 18	..	..
†EASTON CROSS (for Fingle Bridge)	,,	8W18	9 48	11 3	1 8	3 38	6 23	..	..
HALF WAY HOUSE	,,	8W23	9 53	11 8	1 13	3 43	6 28	..	..
SLONCOMBE LANE	,,	8W27	9 57	11 12	1 17	3 47	6 32	..	..
CHAGFORD CROSS	,,	8W30	10 0	11 15	1 20	3 50	6 35	..	..
MORETONHAMPSTEAD (Station)	arr.	8W35	10 5	11 20	1 25	3 55	6 40	..	..

† For Fingle Bridge follow road to Sandy Park Bridge and after passing through the White Gate, proceed along left bank of river for 1½ miles. W—Wednesdays only.

For Train Service see Page 34.

BOVEY AND HAYTOR (MOORLAND HOTEL).

	Market Day.	Early Closing.
BOVEY	—	Wednesday.

From November 5th, 1928, to March 23rd, 1929, this service will operate on Tuesdays, Thursdays and Saturdays only.

WEEK DAYS ONLY.

		a.m.		p.m.		p.m.		p.m.	
BOVEY (Station)	dep	11 5	..	1 5	..	3 35	..	6 20	..
ULLACOMBE	,,	11 20	..	1 20	..	3 50	..	6 35	..
HAYTOR (Moorland Hotel)	arr.	11 29	..	1 29	..	4 0	..	6 44	..
		a.m.		p.m.		p.m.		p.m.	
HAYTOR (Moorland Hotel)	dep.	11 30	..	1 30	..	4 10	..	6 45	..
ULLACOMBE	,,	11 40	..	1 40	..	4 20	..	6 55	..
BOVEY (Station)	arr.	11 50	..	1 50	..	4 30	..	7 5	..

BOVEY, BECKY FALLS AND MANATON.

From November 5th, 1928, to March 23rd, 1929, this Service will operate on Mondays, Wednesdays and Fridays only.

WEEK DAYS ONLY

		a.m.		a.m.		p.m.		p.m.	p.m.
BOVEY (Station)	dep.	8W 0	..	11 5	..	1 5	..	3 35	6 20
BECKY FALLS	,,	8W15	..	11 20	..	1 20	..	3 50	6 35
MANATON	arr.	8W25	..	11 29	..	1 29	..	4 0	6 44
		a.m.		a.m.		p.m.		p.m.	p.m.
MANATON	dep.	8W30		11 30	..	1 30	..	4 5	6 45
BECKY FALLS	,,	8W35	..	11 35	..	1 35	..	4 10	6 50
BOVEY (Station)	arr.	8W55	..	11 50	..	1 50	..	4 30	7 5

W—Wednesdays only.

9th July to 30th September 1934.

NEWTON ABBOT AND MORETONHAMPSTEAD (for Chagford).

WEEK-DAYS.

				M	M		M		M		M				M	M		M		
	a.m.	a.m.	a.m.	a.m.	p.m.	p.m.	p.m.	p.m.	p.m.		p.m.	p.m.	p.m.		p.m.	p.m.	p.m.	p.m.		p.m.
NEWTON ABBOT .. dep.	7 55	8 55	10 24	11 0	12 20	12 50	2 10	2 50	3 5	..	4 10	5 0	6 8	..	6 35	7 30	7 50	9 10	..	9 45
Teigngrace .. ,,	8 0	9 0	..	11 4	12 24	..	2 14	..	3 9	..	4 14	5 5	..	..	6 39	7 35	..	9 14	..	..
Heathfield .. ,,	8 4	9 9	10 30	11 8	12 31	12 56	2 18	2 59	3 13	..	4 20	5 9	6 17	..	6 43	7 41	7 57	9 19	..	9 53
Brimley Halt .. ,,	8 9	9 13	10 35	11 13	12 36	1 1	2 23	3 4	3 18	..	4 25	5 14	6 21	..	6 48	7 45	8 1	9 23	..	9 58
Bovey .. ,,	8 14	9 16	10 38	11 15	12 38	1 4	2 25	3 7	3 20	..	4 28	5 16	6 24	..	6 50	7 48	8 5	9 25	..	10 0
Hawkmoor Halt .. ,,	8 18	9 20	10 42	—	—	1 8	—	3 12	—	..	4 33	5 21	6 28	..	—	—	8 9	—	..	10 5
Lustleigh .. ,,	8 23	9 26	10 48	..	..	1 14	..	3 18	..	..	4 36	5 26	6 33	..	..	..	8 14	..	..	10 12
MORETONHAMPSTEAD arr.	8 34	9 37	11 0	..	..	1 26	..	3 30	..	..	4 50	5 38	6 45	..	..	..	8 26	..	..	10 23
Chagford (Road Motor) arr.	9 10	10 25	11 25	..	..	1 55	..	4 5	..	..	..	6 5	7 10	..	..	..	8 50	..	..	10W45
	a.m.	a.m.	a.m.	a.m.	a.m.		p.m.		p.m.	p.m.	p.m.	p.m.	M p.m.	p.m.	p.m.	p.m.	p.m.	p.m.	p.m.	
Chagford (Road Motor) dep.	..	8 10	9 35	..	11 30	..	..	..	1 0	..	..	3 15	..	5 15	..	6 15	..	8 0	..	..
MORETONHAMPSTEAD dep.	7 55	8 45	10 5	..	12 5	..	..	..	1 35	..	..	3 55	5 0	5 50	..	7 0	..	8 35	..	..
Lustleigh .. ,,	8 4	8 54	10 14	..	12 14	..	..	..	1 44	..	..	4 4	5 9	5 59	..	7 9	..	8 44	..	..
Hawkmoor Halt .. ,,	8 6	8 56	10 16	M	12 16	..	M	..	1 46	M	M	4 6	5 11	6 1	M	7 11	M	8 46	M	..
Bovey .. ,,	8 13	9 1	10 21	11 35	12 20	..	12 48	..	1 51	2 30	3 30	4 11	5 18	6 6	6 55	7 17	8 5	8 50	9 45	..
Brimley Halt .. ,,	8 16	9 4	10 24	11 37	12 23	..	12 50	..	1 54	2 32	3 32	4 14	5 21	6 8	6 57	7 20	8 7	8 53	9 47	..
Heathfield .. ,,	8 21	9 10	10 30	11 43	12 30	..	12 57	..	1 59	2 38	3 38	4 19	5 26	6 15	7 2	7 25	8 12	8 58	9 54	..
Teigngrace .. ,,	8 25	9 14	..	11 46	..	..	1 1	..	..	2 41	3 41	4 23	5 30	..	7 6	..	8 16	..	..	..
NEWTON ABBOT .. arr.	8 30	9 19	10 38	11 52	12 38	..	1 7	..	2 6	2 47	3 47	4 29	5 35	6 23	7 12	7 32	8 22	9 6	10 2	..

SUNDAYS.

	M	M	M	M	M	M
	a.m.	a.m.	p.m.	p.m.	p.m.	p.m.
NEWTON ABBOT .. dep.	8 30	10 20	2 5	3 0	5 10	7 23
Teigngrace .. ,,	..	..	..	..	..	..
Heathfield .. ,,	8 38	10 28	2 12	3 8	5 18	7 31
Brimley Halt .. ,,	8 43	10 33	2 17	3 13	5 23	7 36
Bovey .. ,,	8 45	10 35	2 19	3 15	5 25	7 38
Hawkmoor Halt .. ,,	8 49	10 39	—	3 19	5 29	7 42
Lustleigh .. ,,	8 55	10 46	..	3 26	5 35	7 49
MORETONHAMPSTEAD .. arr.	9 6	10 57	..	3 37	5 46	8 0
Chagford (Road Motor) .. arr.	9 45	11 45	..	..	6 30	8 40

	M	M	M	M	M	M
	a.m.	a.m.	p.m.	p.m.	p.m.	p.m.
Chagford (Road Motor) .. dep.	8 55	11 0	..	..	5 45	7 50
MORETONHAMPSTEAD .. dep.	9 25	11 50	..	4 20	6 10	8 25
Lustleigh .. ,,	9 34	11 59	..	4 29	6 19	8 34
Hawkmoor Halt .. ,,	9 36	12 1	..	4 31	6 21	8 36
Bovey .. ,,	9 41	12 5	2 30	4 36	6 26	8 41
Brimley Halt .. ,,	9 44	12 8	2 33	4 39	6 29	8 44
Heathfield .. ,,	9 49	12 14	2 38	4 44	6 34	8 49
Teigngrace .. ,,	..	..	..	..	..	..
NEWTON ABBOT .. arr.	9 57	12 22	2 46	4 52	6 42	8 57

M Rail Motor Car (one class only). **W** Wednesdays only.

SERVICE No. 122.

BOVEY TRACEY AND HAYTOR

OCTOBER 1st, 1934

and until further notice.

WEDNESDAYS AND SATURDAYS ONLY.

		pm	pm
Bovey Tracey (Station)	dep	1 0	5 20
Ullacombe	,,	1 15	5 35
Haytor	arr	1 25	5 45

		pm	pm
Haytor	dep	1 26	5 45
Ullacombe	,,	1 36	5 55
Bovey Tracey (Station)	arr	1 46	6 5

SERVICE No. 123.

BOVEY TRACEY AND MANATON

OCTOBER 1st, 1934

and until further notice.

WEDNESDAYS AND SATURDAYS ONLY.

		WO am	am	pm	WO pm
Bovey Tracey (Station) ...	dep	8 0	11 0	3 35	6 25
Becky Falls	,,	8 20	11 15	3 55	6 40
Manaton	arr	8 29	11 19	3 59	6 44

		WO am	am	pm	WO pm
Manaton	dep	8 30	11 20	4 0	6 45
Becky Falls	,,	8 35	11 25	4 5	6 50
Bovey Tracey (Station) ...	arr	9 0	11 50	4 30	7 10

W.O.—Wednesdays only.

The above Services are operated subject to the Conditions and Regulations published in the Company's Official Timetable.

Local Office—
G.W.R. Station,
Bovey Tracey

Head Office—
48/50 Queen Street,
Exeter.

28/9/34

8th July to 29th September 1935.

MORETONHAMPSTEAD BRANCH.

Single Line, worked by Electric Train Staff. Heathfield and Bovey are Crossing Stations. The Staff Stations are Newton Abbot, Heathfield, Bovey, and Moretonhampstead.

DOWN TRAINS. WEEK DAYS.

M.P. Mileage		STATIONS.	Ruling Gradient.	Time Allowances for Ordinary Freight Trains, see page 2.			K		B		B		B		B		B		K		B		B	
				Point-to-Point Times.	Allow for Stop.	Allow for Start.	Trusham Goods.		7.25 a.m. Totnes Passenger.		8.10 a.m. Paignton Passenger.		Auto.		9.55 a.m. Kingswear Passenger. ‡		Auto.		Goods.		Motor.		Auto.	
							arr.	dep.	arr.	dep.	arr.	dep.	arr.	dep.	arr.	dep.	arr.	dep.	arr.	dep.	arr.	dep.	arr.	dep.
M.	C.			Mins.	Mins.	Mins.	a.m.	a.m.	a.m.	a.m.	a.m.	a.m.	a.m.	a.m.	a.m.	a.m.	a.m.	a.m.	a.m.	a.m.	p.m.	p.m.	p.m.	p.m.
—	—	**NEWTON ABBOT**	—	—	—	1	—	7 0	**7 40**	**7 55**	**8 32**	**8 55**	—	**9 52**	**10‡35**	**X1040**	—	**11 30**	—	10 48	..	..	—	**12 20**
1	43	Teign Bridge Siding	100 R.	4	1	1	7 6	7 25	—	—	—	—	—	—	— •	—	—	—	C	R	SUS	S-	—	—
1	51	Teign Bridge Level C.	—	—	—	—	—	—	—	—	—	—	—	—	—	—	—	—	—	—	PEN	DED	—	—
2	28	Teigngrace	100 R.	—	—	—	—	—	7 59	8 0	8 59	9 0	9 56	9 56½	—	—	11 34	1134½	—	—	....	....	12 24	1224½
3	70	**HEATHFIELD**	70 R.	5	1	1	**7 32**	**8 40**	**8 3½**	**8 4½**	**9 3½**	**X9 9**	**10 0**	**10 1**	**10 46**	**10 47**	**11 38**	**11 39**	**11 0**	**X11 15**	—	**X12 0**	**12 28**	**X1232**
5	6	Granite Siding	69 R.	—	—	—			—	—	—	—	—	—	—	—	—	—	C	R	—	—	—	—
5	19	Pottery Siding	53 R.	—	—	—	Goods Brake		—	—	—	—	—	—	—	—	—	—	C	R	—	—	—	—
5	46	Brimley Halt	53 R.	—	—	—	Van to be		8 8	8 9	9 12½	9 13½	10 4½	10 5½	1050½	1051½	11 42	1143½	—	—	12 4½	12 5	1235½	1236½
6	6	Bovey	66 F.	5	2	2	sent Heath-		8 10½	X8 14	9 15	9 16	10 7	X10 8	10 53	X1054	11 45	—	**11 23•**	**X12 25**	12 7	—	12 38	—
7	61	Hawkmoor Halt	—	—	—	—	field on this		—	8 19	—	9 21	—	—	—	10 59			—	—				
8	66	Lustleigh	50 R.	11	1	2	train daily.		8 22	8 23	9 24	9 26	10 15	10 17	11 2	11 5	..	..	**CR**	**ST**	..	..	..	..
12	28	**MORETONHAMPSTEAD**	49 R.	14	1	—			**8 34**	—	**9 37**	—	**10 28**	—	**11 16**	—	....	....	**12 52**	—	....	....	....	....

DOWN TRAINS. WEEK DAYS—continued.

STATIONS.	B		B		B		B		B		B		G		B		B		B		B		B	
	12.20 p.m. Paignton Passenger.		Auto.		Passenger.		2.0 p.m. Kingswear Passenger. ‡		Auto.		Auto.		Engine		Auto.		3.45 p.m. Kingswear Passenger.‡		5.35 p.m. Paignton Passenger.		Auto.		Motor.	
	arr.	dep.	arr.	dep.	arr.	dep.	arr.	dep.	arr.	dep.	arr.	dep.	arr.	dep.	arr.	dep.	arr.	dep.	arr.	dep.	arr.	dep.	arr.	dep.
	p.m.	p.m.	p.m.	p.m.	p.m.	p.m.	p.m.	p.m.	p.m.	p.m.	p.m.	p.m.	p.m.	p.m.	p.m.	p.m.	p.m.	p.m.	p.m.	p.m.	p.m.	p.m.	p.m.	p.m.
NEWTON ABBOT	**12 43**	**12 50**	—	**2 15**	—	**2 15**	**2‡47**	**X2 53**	—	**3 5**	—	**3 14**	—	X 3 50	—	**4 10**	**4‡35**	**5 2**	**5 57**	**X6 8**	—	**6 35**	....	....
Teign Bridge Siding	—	—	—	—	SUS	S-	—	—	—	—	SUS	S-	—	—	—	—	—	—	—	—	—	—	SUS	S-
Teign Bridge Level C.	—	—	—	—	PEN	DED	—	—	—	—	PEN	DED	—	—	—	—	—	—	—	—	—	—	PEN	DED
Teigngrace	—	—	2 19	2 19½	—	—	—	—	3 9	3 9½	3 18	3 19	—	—	4 14	4 14½	5 6	5 7	—	—	6 39	6 39½	..	..
HEATHFIELD	**1256X**	**12 57**	**2 23**	**2 24**	**2 21½**	**2 22½**	**2 59**	**3 0**	**3 13**	**3 14**	**3 22½**	**3X23½**	**4‖ 0**	—	**4 18**	**X4 21**	**5 10½**	**5 11½**	**6 14**	**X6 17**	**6 43**	**6 44**	-- X	**7 26**
Granite Siding	—	—	—	—	—	—	—	—	—	—	—	—			—	—	—	—	—	—	—	—	—	—
Pottery Siding	—	—	—	—	—	—	—	—	—	—	—	—	..	..	—	—	—	—	—	—	—	—	—	—
Brimley Halt	1 0½	1 1½	2 27½	2 28½	2 26	2 27	3 3½	3 4½	3 17½	3 18½	3 27	3 28	....	....	4 24½	4 25½	5 15	5 16	6 20½	6 21½	6 47½	6 48½	7 29½	7 30
Bovey	1 3	1 4	2 30	—	2 28½	X2 30	3 6	X3 7	3 20	—	3 29½	X3 32	..	..	4 27	4 28	5 17½	X5 19	6 23	6 24	6 50	—	7 32	—
Hawkmoor Halt	—	1 9			—	2 35	—	3 12			—	3 37	....	....	—	4 33	—	5 24	—	6 29				
Lustleigh	1 12	1 15	..	..	2 38	2 40	3 15	3 18	..	..	3 40	3 42	..	..	4 36	4 38	5 27	5 29	6 32	6 34	..	..	..	..
MORETONHAMPSTEAD	**1 26**	—	....	....	**2 51**	—	**3 29**	—	....	....	**3 53**	—	....	....	**4 49**	—	**5 40**	—	**6 45**	—	....	....	....	....

‡ Starts from Newton Abbot on Saturdays.

8th July to 29th September 1935 (Continued).

Moretonhampstead Branch—*continued.*

UP TRAINS. WEEK DAYS—continued.

STATIONS.	Ruling Gradient.	Time Allowances for Ordinary Freight Trains, see page 2.			B		B		B		B		B		B		B		B		K		B	
		Point-to-Point Times.	Allow for Stop.	Allow for Start.	Passenger.		Passenger		Passenger.		Auto.		Auto.		Auto.		Passenger.		Motor.		Trusham Goods.		Auto.	
					arr.	dep.	arr.	dep.	arr.	dep.	arr.	dep.	arr.	dep.	arr.	dep.	arr.	dep.	arr.	dep.	arr.	dep.	arr.	dep.
		Mins.	Mins.	Mins.	a.m.	a.m.	a.m.	a.m.	a.m.	a.m.	a.m.	a.m.	a.m.	a.m.	a.m.	a.m.	p.m.	p.m.	p.m.	p.m.	p.m.	p.m.	p.m.	p.m.
MORETONHAMPSTEAD	—	—	—	1	—	**7 55**	—	**8 45**	—	**9 51**	—	**10 37**	....	....	—	**11 35**	—	**12 5**	....	....	....	....	....	....
Stop Board 12mp.	L.	—	1	1	—	—	—	—	—	—	—	—	..	..	—	—	—	—	..	..	..	..	..	..
Lustleigh	49 F.	10	1	1	8 3	8 4	8 53	8 54	9 59	10 0	10 45	10 46	...	...	11 43	11 44	12 13	12 14	**SU**	**S-**	....	....	....	....
Hawkmoor Halt	—	—	—	—	—	8 6	—	8 56	—	10 2	—	10 48	..	..	—	11 46	—	12 16	**PEN**	**DED**	..	..	..	..
Stop Board 6m. 15½c.	50 F.	—	—	—	—	—	—	—	—	—	—	—	....	....	—	—	—	—	....	....	....	....	....	....
Bovey	50 F.	8	2	2	8 10	X8 13	9 0	9 1	10 6	X1014	10 52	X10 55	—	11 50	11 50	X11 52	12 20	X1221	—	12 40	..	..	—	12 48
Brimley Halt	66 R.	—	—	—	8 15	8 16	9 3	9 4	10 16	10 17	10 57	10 58	11 52	11 53	11 54	11 55	12 23	12 24	12 42	12 43	....	....	12 50	12 51
Pottery Siding	53 F.	2	2	2	—	—	—	—	—	—	—	—	—	—	—	—	—	—	—	—	..	..	—	—
Granite Siding	53 F.	1	1	1	—	—	—	—	—	—	—	—	—	—	—	—	—	—	—	—	....	....	—	—
HEATHFIELD	69 F.	3	1	1	**8 20**	**8 21**	**9 8**	**X9 10**	**10 21**	**10 22**	**11 2X**	**11 3**	**11 57**	**11 58**	**11 59**	**X12 0**	**12 28½**	**X12 31**	**12 47**	X —	**12 3**	**1 10**	**12 55**	**X1258**
Teigngrace	70 F.	—	—	—	8 24	8 25	9 13	9 14	10 25	10 26	—	—	12 1	12 2	12 3	12 4	—	—			—	—	1 1	1 2
Teign Bridge Level C.	—	—	—	—	—	—	—	—	—	—	—	—	—	—	**SU**	**S-**	—	—	....	....	—	—	—	—
Teign Bridge Siding	100 F.	6	1	1	—	—	—	—	—	—	—	—	—	—	**PEN**	**DED**	—	—	..	..	**C**	**R**	—	—
NEWTON ABBOT	132 R.	4	1	—	**8 30**	—	**9 19**	—	**10 31**	X —	**11 10**	—	**12 7**	—	**12 9**	—	**12 38**	‡	....	....	**1 20**	—	**1 7**	—

UP TRAINS. WEEK DAYS—continued.

STATIONS.	B		B		B		B		B		K		B		B		K		B		B		B	
	Passenger.		Auto.		Motor. **WSO**		Auto.		Passenger.		**Goods.**		Passenger.		Auto.		**Goods.**		Passenger.		Auto.		Passenger.	
	arr.	dep.	arr.	dep.	arr.	dep.	arr.	dep.	arr.	dep.	arr.	dep.	arr.	dep.	arr.	dep.	arr.	dep.	arr.	dep.	arr.	dep.	arr.	dep.
	p.m.	p.m.	p.m.	p.m.	p.m.	p.m.	p.m.	p.m.	p.m.	p.m.	p.m.	p.m.	p.m.	p.m.	p.m.	p.m.	p.m.	p.m.	p.m.	p.m.	p.m.	p.m.	p.m.	p.m.
MORETONHAMPSTEAD	—	**1 35**	....	....	....	....	....	....	—	**3 15**	—	**2 5**	—	**3 55**	—	**5 0**	....	....	—	**5 50**	....	....	—	**7 0**
Stop Board 12mp.	—	—	..	..	**SU**	**S-**	..	..	—	—	**2 6**	**P2 8**	—	—	—	—	..	..	—	—	..	..	—	—
Lustleigh	1 43	1 44	....	....	**PEN**	**DED**	....	....	3 23	3 24	**2 17**	**2 25**	4 3	4 4	5 8	5 9	....	....	5 58	5 59	....	....	7 8	7 9
Hawkmoor Halt	—	1 46	..	..	..	..	..	..	—	3 26	—	—	—	4 6	—	5 11	..	..	—	6 1	..	..	—	7 11
Stop Board 6m. 15½c.	—	—	....	....	....	....	....	....	—	—	**2 33**	**P2 35**	—	—	—	—	....	....	—	—	....	....	—	—
Bovey	1 50	1 51	—	2 35	..	..	—	3 30	3 30	X3 34	**2 36●**	**X 3 40**	4 10	4 12	5 15	X5 20	..	..	6 5	6 6	—	6 55	7 15	7 17
Brimley Halt	1 53	1 54	2 37	2 38	....	....	3 32	3 33	3 36	3 37	—	—	4 14	4 15	5 22	5 23	....	....	6 8	6 9	6 57	6 58	7 19	7 20
Pottery Siding	—	—	—	—	..	..	—	—	**SU**	**S-**	**C**	**R**	—	—	—	—	..	..	—	—	—	—	—	—
Granite Siding	—	—	—	—	....	....	—	—	**PEN**	**DED**	**C**	**R**	—	—	—	—	....	....	—	—	—	—	—	—
HEATHFIELD	**1 58**	**1 59**	**2 42**	**2 43**	—	*2 40*	**3 37**	**3 38**	**3 41**	**3 43**	**4 10**	**●X4 30**	**4 19**	**X4 20**	**5 27**	**5 28**	—	**5 38**	**6 13X**	**6 16**	**7 2**	**7 3**	**7 24**	**7 25**
Teigngrace	2 2	2 3	—	—	—	—	3 41	3 42	3 46	3 47	—	—	4 23	4 24	5 31	5 32	—	—	—	—	7 6	7 7	—	—
Teign Bridge Level C.	—	—	—	—	—	—	—	—	—	—	—	—	—	—	—	—	—	—	—	—	—	—	—	—
Teign Bridge Siding	—	—	—	—	—	—	—	—	—	—	—	—	—	—	—	—	**5 44**	**6 0**	—	—	—	—	—	—
NEWTON ABBOT	**2 8**	—	**2 50**	X —	*2 47*	—	**3 47**	X —	**3 52**	X —	**4 40**	—	**4 29**	—	**5 37**	—	**6 5**	X —	**6 23**	—	**7 12**	—	**7 32**	X —

‡—Forms 12.45 p.m. to Kingswear, Saturdays excepted

8th July to 29th September 1935 (Continued).

Moretonhampstead Branch—*continued.*

DOWN TRAINS. WEEK DAYS—continued. | SUNDAYS.

STATIONS.	B		B		B		B		B		B		B		B		B		B		B		B	
	Auto.		Passenger.		Auto.		Passenger.		Passenger.		Passenger.		Passenger.		Passenger.		Passenger.		Passenger.		Passenger.		Passenger	
	arr.	dep.	arr.	dep.	arr.	dep.	arr.	dep.	arr.	dep.	arr.	dep.	arr.	dep.	arr.	dep.	arr.	dep.	arr.	dep.	arr.	dep.	arr.	dep.
	p.m.	p.m.	p.m.	p.m.	p.m.	p.m.	p.m.	p.m.	a.m.	a.m.	a.m.	a.m.	p.m.	p.m.	p.m.	p.m.	p.m.	p.m.	p.m.	p.m.	p.m.	p.m.	p.m.	p.m.
NEWTON ABBOT	—	X7 33	—	7 53	—	X9 10	—	9 47	—	9 30	— X	10 50	—	2 19	—	3 26	—	4 15	—	6 2	—	7 40	—	9 10
Teign Bridge Siding	—	—	—	—	—	—	—	—	—	—	—	—	—	—	—	—	—	—	—	—	—	—	—	—
Teign Bridge Level C.	—	—	—	—	—	—	—	—	—	—	—	—	—	—	—	—	—	—	—	—	—	—	—	—
Teigngrace	7 37	7 37½	—	—	9 14	9 14½	—	—	—	—	—	—	—	—	—	—	—	—	—	—	—	—	—	—
HEATHFIELD	7 41	7 42	7 59	8 0	9 18	9 19	9 53	X9 54	9 37	9 38	10 57	10 58	2 26	2 27	3 33	3 34	4 22	4 23	6 9	6 10	7 47	7 48	9 17	9 18
Granite Siding	—	—	—	—	—	—	—	—	—	—	—	—	—	—	—	—	—	—	—	—	—	—	—	—
Pottery Siding	—	—	—	—	—	—	—	—	—	—	—	—	—	—	—	—	—	—	—	—	—	—	—	—
Brimley Halt	7 45½	7 46½	8 3½	8 4½	9 22½	9 23½	9 57½	9 58½	9 41½	9 42½	11 1½	11 2½	2 30½	2 31½	3 37½	2 38½	4 26½	4 27½	6 13½	6 14½	7 51½	7 52½	9 21½	9 22½
Bovey	7 48	—	8 6	X8 7	9 25	—	10 0	10 1	9 44	9 45	11 4	11 5	2 33X	2 36	3 40	—	4 29	X4 32	6 16	6 17	7 54	7 55	9 24	9 25
Hawkmoor Halt	━━	━━	—	8 12	━━	━━	10 5	10 7	—	9 50	—	11 10	—	2 41	━━	━━	—	4 37	—	6 22	—	8 0	—	9 30
Lustleigh	....	....	8 15	8 17	..	..	10 10	10 12	9 53	9 55	11 13	11 15	2 44	2 46	..	..	4 39	4 42	6 25	6 27	8 3	8 5	9 33	9 35
MORETONHAMPSTEAD	....	....	8 28	—	....	....	10 23	—	10 6	—	11 26	—	2 57	—	....	....	4 53	—	6 38	—	8 16	—	9 46	—

UP TRAINS. WEEK DAYS—*continued.* | SUNDAYS.

STATIONS.	B		B		B		B		B		B		B		B		B		B		B		B	
	Motor.		Auto.		Paignton Passenger.		Auto.		Passenger.		Passenger.		Passenger.		Passenger.		Passenger.		Passenger.		Passenger.		Passenger.	
	arr.	dep.	arr.	dep.	arr.	dep.	arr.	dep.	arr.	dep.	arr.	dep.	arr.	dep.	arr.	dep.	arr.	dep.	arr.	dep.	arr.	dep.	arr.	dep.
	p.m.	p.m.	p.m.	p.m.	p.m.	p.m.	p.m.	p.m.	a.m.	a.m.	a.m.	a.m.	p.m.	p.m.	p.m.	p.m.	p.m.	p.m.	p.m.	p.m.	p.m.	p.m.	p.m.	p.m.
MORETONHAMPSTEAD	....	....	....	....	—	8 36	....	....	—	10 15	—	11 38	—	2 20	....	....	—	4 15	—	5 22	—	6 50	—	8 25
Stop Board 12mp.	SUS	S-	..	..	—	—	..	..	—	—	—	—	—	—	..	..	—	—	—	—	—	—	—	—
Lustleigh	PEN	DED	....	....	8 44	8 45	....	....	10 23	10 24	11 46	11 47	2 28	2 29	....	....	4 23	4 24	5 30	5 31	6 58	6 59	8 33	8 34
Hawkmoor Halt	..	..	..	..	—	8 47	..	..	—	10 26	—	11 49	—	—	..	..	—	4 26	—	5 33	—	7 1	—	8 36
Stop Board 6m. 15½c.	....	....	....	....	—	—	....	....	—	—	—	—	—	—	....	....	—	—	—	—	—	—	—	—
Bovey	—	7 45	—	X8 10	8 51	8 52	—	9 45	10 30	10 31	11 53	11 54	2 34	X2 35	—	3 45	4 30	X4 31	5 37	5 38	7 5	7 6	8 40	8 41
Brimley Halt	7 47	7 48	8 12	8 13	8 54	8 55	9 47	9 48	10 33	10 34	11 56	11 57	2 37	2 38	3 47	3 48	4 33	4 34	5 40	5 41	7 8	7 9	8 43	8 44
Pottery Siding	—	—	—	—	—	—	—	—	—	—	—	—	—	—	—	—	—	—	—	—	—	—	—	—
Granite Siding	—	—	—	—	—	—	—	—	—	—	—	—	—	—	—	—	—	—	—	—	—	—	—	—
HEATHFIELD	7 52	X —	8 17	8 18	8 59	9 0	9 52	X9 55	10 38	10 39	12 1	12 2	2 42	2 43	3 52	3 53	4 38	4 39	5 45	5 46	7 13	7 14	8 48	8 49
Teigngrace	━━	━━	8 21	8 22	—	—	—	—	—	—	—	—	—	—	—	—	—	—	—	—	—	—	—	—
Teign Bridge Level C.	..	..	—	—	—	—	—	—	—	—	—	—	—	—	—	—	—	—	—	—	—	—	—	—
Teign Bridge Siding	....	....	—	—	—	—	—	—	—	—	—	—	—	—	—	—	—	—	—	—	—	—	—	—
NEWTON ABBOT	..	..	8 27	—	9 7	X9 10	10 2	—	10 47	X —	12 9	—	2 50	—	4 0	—	4 47	—	5 54	—	7 22	—	8 57	—

TOR BUS SERVICE

SUMMER TIME TABLE (July 8th to September 29th, 1935)

BOVEY TRACEY MANATON

Depart.	WEEK DAYS a.m.	p.m.	p.m.	p.m.	p.m.	SUNDAYS a.m.	p.m.	p.m.
BOVEY	11. 0	1.10	3.10	4.30	6.25	11. 5	2.40	4.35
BECKY FALLS	11.20	1.30	3.30	4.50	6.40	11.20	3. 0	4.55
MANATON arrive	11.25	1.35	3.35	4.55	6.50	11.25	3. 5	5. 0

MANATON BOVEY TRACEY

Depart.	a.m.	p.m.	p.m.	p.m.	p.m.	a.m.	p.m.	p.m.
MANATON	11.45	2. 0	3.40	5.30	6.50	11.25	3.15	5. 5
BECKY FALLS	11.50	2. 5	3.45	5.35	6.55	11.30	3.20	5.10
BOVEY arrive	12.10	2.25	4. 5	5.55	7.15	11.45	3.40	5.30

WIDECOMBE HAYTOR BOVEY TRACEY

Depart.	WEEK DAYS a.m.	a.m.	a.m.	a.m.	p.m.	p.m.	p.m.	p.m.	p.m.	p.m.	SUNDAYS a.m.	p.m.	p.m.	p.m.	p.m.
WIDECOMBE			10.50	11.40		1.15	1.55	4.45	5.10			1.15	3.50	5. 0	
HAYTOR	9.50	10.35	11.30	12. 0	12.30	1.30	2.15	5. 0	5.30	6.50	10.10	2.15	4.10	5.20	6.40
BOVEY arrive	10. 5	10.50	11.45	12.15	12.45	1.45	2.30	5.15	5.50	7.10	10.25	2.30	4.25	5.35	7. 0

BOVEY TRACEY HAYTOR WIDECOMBE

Depart.	a.m.	a.m.	a.m.	p.m.	p.m.	p.m.	p.m.	p.m.	p.m.	p.m.	p.m.	a.m.	p.m.	p.m.	p.m.	p.m.
BOVEY	10.10	11. 0	11.50	12.45	1.10	2.35	3.10	5.20	6.30	7.20	7.50	11.10	2.40	3.45	5.40	7.55
HAYTOR	10.30	11.20	12.10	1. 5	1.30	2.55	3.30	5.40	6.50	7.40	8. 5	11.30	3. 0	4.15	6. 0	8.15
WIDECOMBE arrive	10.50	11.37			1.50		3.45						3.15	4.30		

WIDECOMBE HAYTOR NEWTON ABBOT

WEEK DAYS

Depart.	a.m.	a.m.	p.m.	p.m.	p.m.	p.m.	p.m.
WIDECOMBE		10.50	1.15		4.45	6. 5	7.45
HAYTOR	9.30	11.10	1.30	4. 0	5. 5	6.20	8. 5
ILSINGTON	9.40	11.20	1.40	4.10	5.15	6.30	8.15
LIVERTON	9.53	11.33	1.53	4.23	5.28	6.43	8.28
HEATHFIELD CROSS	10. 0	11.40	2. 0	4.30	5.35	6.50	8.35
TEIGNGRACE	10. 5	11.45	2. 5	4.35	5.40	6.55	8.40
NEWTON arrive	10.20	11.55	2.20	4.50	5.55	7.10	8.55

NEWTON ABBOT HAYTOR WIDECOMBE

Depart.	a.m.	p.m.	p.m.	p.m.	p.m.	p.m.	p.m.	p.m. S	p.m. S
NEWTON	10.30	12. 0	2.35	5. 0	6.20	7.20	9.15	10.15	11.15*
TEIGNGRACE	10.40	12.10	2.45	5.10	6.30	7.30	9.25	10.25	
HEATHFIELD CROSS	10.45	12.15	2.50	5.15	6.35	7.35	9.30	10.30	
LIVERTON	10.55	12.25	3. 0	5.25	6.45	7.45	9.40	10.40	
ILSINGTON	11. 5	12.35	3.10	5.35	6.55	7.53	9.48		
HAYTOR	11.20	12.50	3.20	5.45	7.5	8. 5	10. 0		
WIDECOMBE arrive	11.37	1.10	3.40	6. 0[illegible]	7.25				

WIDECOMBE HAYTOR NEWTON ABBOT

SUNDAYS

Depart.	a.m.	a.m.	p.m.	p.m.	p.m.	p.m.	p.m.
WIDECOMBE	12.10‡		1.15		5. 0	7.45	
HAYTOR MOORLAND HOTEL	12.30	10.40‖	1.30	2.30	5.25	8. 5	9.10
ILSINGTON		10.50	1.40	2.40	5.35	8.15	9.20
LIVERTON		11. 3	1.53	2.48	5.48	8.28	9.30
HEATHFIELD		11.10	2. 0	2.55	5.55	8.35	9.38
TEIGNGRACE		11.15	2. 5	3. 0	6. 0	8.40	9.45
NEWTON arrive		11.28	2.20	3.15	6.15	8.55	9.58

NEWTON ABBOT HAYTOR WIDECOMBE

Depart.	a.m.	a.m.	p.m.	p.m.	p.m.	p.m.	p.m.
NEWTON		11.30	2.35	3.30	6.20	9.15	10. 0
TEIGNGRACE		11.40	2.45	3.40	6.30	9.25	10.10
HEATHFIELD		11.45	2.50	3.45	6.35	9.30	10.15
LIVERTON		11.55	3. 0	3.55	6.45	9.40	10.25
ILSINGTON		12. 3‖	3.10	4. 3	6.55	9.50	10.33
HAYTOR	10.35‡	12.20	3.20	4.15	7. 5	10. 0	10.45
WIDECOMBE arrive	10.55	12.40	3.40	4.30	7.25		

(S) Saturdays only.

(*) Special Theatre Bus. All Stages to Haytor.

MARKET BUS. LEAVES WIDECOMBE 9-15 AM. WEDS ONLY

‡ Special Church Bus to Widecombe. Leave Widecombe at conclusion of Church Service.

‖ **10.40** a.m. To Ilsington Church. Return **12.3** p.m. from Ilsington.

J. POTTER & SONS, Tor Garage, Haytor. **Phone, Haytor 33**

1st April to 5th July 1936.

12

NEWTON ABBOT, BOVEY, and MORETONHAMPSTEAD.

WEEK DAYS.

		M	T	T	MT			M	M		T		MT					
		a.m.	a.m.	a.m.	a.m.	p.m.	p.m.	p.m.	p.m.	p.m.	p.m.		p.m.		p.m.		p.m.	
Paignton	dep.	7 22	8 10	9 25	10 20	12 10	1 53	2W20	2 40	3 34	4 30	...	5 40	...	7 4	...	9V 15	...
Torquay	,,	7 29	8 16	9 31	10 26	12 16	1 59	2W27	2 46	3 40	4 37	.	5 46	.	7 12	.	9V 24	.
Torre	,,	7 32	8 21	9 35	10 29	12 21	2 3	2W32	2 50	3 44	4 42	...	5 51	...	7 20	...	9V 29	...
Newton Abbot	dep.	7 55	8 55	9 52	10 50	12 40	2 25	3W 0	3 14	4 12	5 4	.	6 5	.	7 45	.	9V 45	.
Teigngrace	,,	8 0	9 0	9 56	10 54	12 44	...	3W 4	3 19	4 16	5 8	...	6 10	...	7 50	...	...	...
Heathfield	,,	8 4	9 9	10 0	11 0	12 49	2 32	3W 8	3 23	4 20	5 13	.	6 17	.	7 54	.	9V 53	.
Brimley Halt	,,	8 9	9 13	10 4	11 4	12 53	2 36	—	3 27	4 25	5 17	...	6 21	...	7 59	...	9V 58	...
Bovey	,,	8 14	9 16	10 7	11 7	12 56	2 39	.	3 32	4 29	5 20	.	6 24	.	8 1	.	10V 0	.
Hawkmoor Halt	,,	8 18	9 20	...	11 12	1 1	2 44	...	3 37	4 34	5 25	...	6 28	...	8 6	...	10V 5	...
Lustleigh	,,	8 23	9 26	10 16	11 17	1 7	2 49	.	3 41	4 39	5 30	.	6 33	.	8 11	.	10V 12	.
Moretonhampstead	arr.	8 34	9 37	10 28	11 30	1 18	3 0	...	3 53	4 50	5 42	...	6 45	...	8 23	...	10V 23	...

			M	T	T	M		M	M			M				M		
		a.m.	a.m.	a.m.	a.m.	a.m.		p.m.	p.m.	p.m.		p.m.	p.m.		p.m.	p.m.	p.m.	
Moretonhampstead	dep.	7 55	8 45	9 50	10 35	11 40	...	1 30	...	3 15	...	4 12	5 0	...	5 50	7 0	8V 35	...
Lustleigh	,,	8 4	8 54	9 59	10 44	11 48	.	1 39	.	3 24	.	4 20	5 8	.	5 59	7 9	8V 44	.
Hawkmoor Halt	,,	8 6	8 56	10 1	10 46	11 50	.	1 41	...	3 26	.	4 22	5 10	...	6 1	7 11	8V 46	...
Bovey	,,	8 13	9 1	10†13	10 51	11 56	...	1 47	.	3 33	...	4 30	5 20	...	6 6	7 17	8V 50	...
Brimley Halt	,,	8 16	9 4	10 16	10 54	11 59	.	1 50	...	3 36	.	4 33	5 23	...	6 8	7 20	8V 53	.
Heathfield	,,	8 21	9 10	10 21	11 0	12 4	...	1 55	2W40	3 42	...	4 40	5 28	.	6 15	7 25	8V 58	...
Teigngrace	,,	8 25	9 14	10 25	11 4	12 8	...	1 59	...	3 46	...	4 44	5 32	...	6 19	7 29	.	...
Newton Abbot	arr.	8 30	9 19	10 31	11 9	12 14	.	2 7	2W47	3 52	.	4 51	5 38	.	6 25	7 34	9V 7	.
Torre	arr.	8 52	9 38	11 3	11 27	12 33	...	2 35	3W16	4 15	...	5 14	6 2	...	6 41	8 7	9V 23	...
Torquay	,,	8 56	9 43	11 6	11 31	12 35	.	2 38	3W19	4 18	.	5 18	6 5	.	6 44	8 10	9V 26	.
Paignton	,,	9 2	9 50	11 14	11 37	12 42	...	2 46	3W27	4 26	...	5 25	6 13	...	6 51	8 18	9V 32	...

SUNDAYS. (Commencing May 10th.)

		a.m.	a.m.	p.m.	p.m.	p.m.	p.m.	p.m.
Paignton	dep.	7 35	10 20	2 50	4 50	6 20	6P 55	8 28
Torquay	,,	7 55	10 27	3 0	4 57	6 26	7P 1	8 36
Torre	,,	8 2	10 32	3 5	5 2	6 31	7P 6	8 41
Newton Abbot	dep.	9 30	10 50	3 20	5 20	7 23		9 0
Teigngrace	,,	.	.	.	.	.		.
Heathfield	,,	9 37	10 57	3 28	5 28	7 31		9 7
Brimley Halt	,,	9 42	11 2	3 33	5 33	7 36		9 12
Bovey	,,	9 44	11 4	3 35	5 35	7 38		9 14
Hawkmoor Halt	,,	9 49	11 9	3 39	5 39	7 42		9 19
Lustleigh	,,	9 54	11 14	3 46	5 45	7 49		9 24
M'hampstead	arr.	10 6	11 26	3 57	5 56	8 0		9 36

								T
		a.m.	a.m.	p.m.	p.m.		p.m.	p.m.
M'hampstead	dep.	10 15	11 50	2 35	4 25	...	6 10	8 25
Lustleigh	,,	10 23	11 59	2 44	4 34	.	6 19	8 34
Hawkmoor Halt	,,	10 25	12 1	2 46	4 36	...	6 21	8 36
Bovey	,,	10 30	12 5	2 51	4 41	.	6 26	8 41
Brimley Halt	,,	10 33	12 8	2 54	4 44	...	6 29	8 44
Heathfield	,,	10 38	12 14	2 59	4 49	.	6 34	8 49
Teigngrace	,,	...	...	...	...	...	...	...
Newton Abbot	arr.	10 47	12 22	3 7	4 57	.	6 42	8 57
Torre	arr.	11 7	12 43	3 54	5 18	...	7 8	9 18
Torquay	,,	11 11	12 46	3 57	5 20	.	7 11	9 21
Paignton	,,	11 23	12 53	4 6	5 26	...	7 18	9 27

G—Saturdays excepted. **M**—One Class only. **P**—Commences June 7th. **S**—Saturdays only. **T**—Through train between Paignton and Moretonhampstead. **V**—Commences April 4th. **W**—Wednesdays and Saturdays only. †—Bovey arrive 10.6 a.m.

1st April to 5th July 1936.

MOTOR OMNIBUS SERVICES

13

(Subject to alteration and should be verified).

MORETONHAMPSTEAD, EASTON CROSS, and CHAGFORD.

(DEVON GENERAL.) (For Tours Nos. 11 and 12.)

DAILY.

		a.m.	a.m.	a.m.	a.m.	a.m.	p.m.	p.m.	p.m.	p.m.	p.m.	p.m.	p.m.	p.m.	p.m.		
Moretonhampstead	dep.	*8***F***15*	*8*30*	*9***S** *0*	*10*25*	10 35	12 10	1 35	3 10	*3***W***30*	4 35	6 10	*7***T***10*	7 25	*8***S***10*	...	...
Easton Cross (for Fingle Bridge)	,,	*8***F***20*	*8*40*	*9***S***10*	*10*35*	10 45	12 20	1 45	3 20	*3***W***40*	4 45	6 20	*7***T***20*	7 35	*8***S***20*	.	.
Chagford (The Square)	arr.	*8***F***25*	*8*45*	*9***S***15*	*10*40*	10 50	12 25	1 50	3 25	*3***W***45*	4 50	6 25	*7***T***25*	7 40	*8***S***25*	...	...
		a.m.	a.m.	a.m.	p.m.	p.m.	p.m.	p.m.		p.m.		p.m.	p.m.	p.m.	p.m.		
Chagford (The Square)	dep.	*8***W***20*	*8*50*	*11* 0*	12 30	2 0	3 30	*4***F** *0*	...	*4***W***20*	...	5 0	*5***G***30*	6 30	*7***T***30*	...	...
Easton Cross (for Fingle Bridge)	,,	*8***W***25*	*8*55*	*11* 5*	12 35	2 5	3 35	*4***F** *5*	.	*4***W***25*	.	5 5	*5***G***35*	6 35	*7***T***35*	.	.
Moretonhampstead	arr.	*8***W***35*	*9* 5*	*11*15*	12 45	2 15	3 45	*4***F***15*	..	*4***W***35*	...	5 15	*5***G***45*	6 40	*7***T***45*	...	...

*—Not Sundays. **F**—Fridays only. **G**—Saturdays and Sundays excepted. **S**—Saturdays only. **T**—Sundays only. **W**—Wednesdays only.

BOVEY, BECKY FALLS, MANATON, and HAYTOR.

(J. POTTER AND SONS.) (For Tours Nos. 68 and 69.)

WEDNESDAYS and SATURDAYS up to May 2nd, inclusive.
WEEK DAYS commencing May 4th.

		a.m.	p.m.	p.m.	p.m.		
Bovey (Station)	dep.	11 10	1 0	2 45	3 35	...	...
Becky Falls	arr.	11 25	.	3 0	.	.	.
Manaton....	,,	11 30	...	3 5	...	...	...
Haytor	,,	*11***a***30*	1 20	.	3 50	.	

		a.m.	p.m.		p.m.	p.m.	p.m.	
Haytor	dep.	...	1 35	...	...	5 40	...	...
Manaton....	,,	11 30	.	.	3 10	.	6 50	.
Becky Falls	,,	11 35	...	...	3 15	...	6 55	...
Bovey (Station)	arr.	11 50	1 45	.	3 30	6 0	7 15	.

a—Commences May 4th.

31st May 1948 to 26th September 1948.

MORETONHAMPSTEAD BRANCH—continued.

UP TRAINS. WEEK DAYS.

STATIONS.	Ruling Gradient.	Time Allowances for Ordinary Freight Trains see page 2. Point-to-Point Times.	Allow for Stop.	Allow for Start.	B Auto. arr.	dep.	B Auto. arr.	dep.	B Auto. arr.	dep.	arr.	dep.	arr.	dep.	B Auto. arr.	dep.	K Christow Freight. arr.	dep.	B 12.50 p.m. Exeter Auto. SX arr.	dep.	B 1.0 p.m. Exeter Auto. SO arr.	dep.	arr.	dep.
		Mins.	Mins.	Mins.	a.m.	a.m.	a.m.	a.m.	a.m.	a.m.					a.m.	a.m.	p.m.	p.m.	p.m.	p.m.	p.m.	p.m.		
MORETONHAMPSTEAD	—	—	—	1	—	**7 50**	—	**8 40**	—	**10 15**	...	...	...	...	—	**11 35**	...	...	...	...	...	...	...	...
Stop Board 12mp.	L.	—	1	1	—	—	—	—	—	—	...	...	...	...	—	—	...	...	...	...	...	...	...	...
Lustleigh	49 F.	10	1	1	7 58	7 59	8 48	8 48½	10 23	1023½	...	...	...	...	11 43	11 44	...	...	...	...	...	...	...	...
Hawkmoor Halt	—	—	—	—	—	8 1	—	8 50	—	10 26	...	...	...	...	—	11 46	...	...	...	...	...	...	...	...
Stop Board 6m. 15½c.	50 F.	—	—	—	—	—	—	—	—	—	...	...	...	...	—	—	...	...	...	...	...	...	...	...
Bovey	50 F.	8	2	2	8 5	X8 8	8 54	8 55	10 30	10 32	...	...	...	...	11 50	11 52	...	...	...	...	...	...	...	...
Brimley Halt	66 R.	—	—	—	8 10	8 11	8 57	8 58	10 34	10 35	...	...	...	...	11 54	11 55	...	...	...	...	...	...	...	...
Pottery Siding	53 F.	2	2	2	—	—	—	—	—	—	...	...	...	...	—	—	...	...	...	...	...	...	...	...
Granite Siding	53 F.	1	1	1	—	—	—	—	—	—	...	...	...	...	—	—	...	...	...	...	...	...	...	...
HEATHFIELD	69 F.	3	1	1	**8 15**	**8 16**	**9 2**	**9 3**	**10 39**	**X1042**	...	...	...	...	**11 59**	**12 0**	12 22	1 3	**1 52**	**1 55**	2 2	2 5	...	...
Teigngrace Halt	70 F.	—	—	—	8 19	8 20	9 6	9 7	10 45	1045½	...	...	...	...	12 3	12 4	C	R	1 59	2 0	2 9	2 10	...	...
Teign Bridge Level C.	—	—	—	—	—	—	—	—	—	—	...	...	...	...	—	—	—	—	—	—	—	—	...	...
Teign Bridge Siding	100 F.	6	1	1	—	—	—	—	—	—	...	...	...	...	—	—	C	R	—	—	—	—	...	...
NEWTON ABBOT	132 R.	4	1	—	**8 25**	—	**9 12**	—	**10 50**	—	...	...	...	...	**12 9**	—	1 21	—	**2 5**	—	2 15	—	...	...

UP TRAINS. WEEK DAYS—continued.

STATIONS.	B Auto. arr.	dep.	K 1.55 p.m. Exeter Freight. SX arr.	dep.	B Auto. arr.	dep.	K Freight. arr.	dep.	B Auto. arr.	dep.	arr.	dep.	arr.	dep.	B Auto. arr.	dep.	G Engine. SX arr.	dep.	arr.	dep.	B Auto. SO arr.	dep.	G Engine SO arr.	dep.
	p.m.	p.m.	p.m.	p.m.	p.m.	p.m.	p.m.	p.m.	p.m.	p.m.					p.m.	p.m.	p.m.	p.m.			p.m.	p.m.	p.m.	p.m.
MORETONHAMPSTEAD	—	**1 55**	...	...	—	**3 55**	—	2 25	—	**5 20**	...	...	...	...	—	**7 0**	—	**9‖ 0**	...	...	—	9 5	—	10‖50
Stop Board 12mp.	—	—	...	...	—	—	2 26	P2 27	—	—	...	...	...	...	—	—	—	—	...	...	—	—	—	—
Lustleigh	2 3	2 4	...	...	4 3	4 4	2 38	2 45	5 28	5 28½	...	...	...	...	7 8	7 9	—	—	...	...	9 13	9 14	—	—
Hawkmoor Halt	—	2 6	...	...	—	4 6	—	—	—	5 30½	...	...	...	...	—	7 11	—	—	...	...	—	9 16	—	—
Stop Board 6m. 15½c.	—	—	...	...	—	—	2 53	P2 54	—	—	...	...	...	...	—	—	—	—	...	...	—	—	—	—
Bovey	2 10	2 12	...	...	4 10	4 12	2 58	3 25	5 34½	5 35½	...	...	...	...	7 15	7 17	C	S	...	...	9 20	9 21	C	S
Brimley Halt	2 14	2 15	...	...	4 14	4 15	—	—	5 37½	5 38	...	...	...	...	7 19	7 20	—	—	...	...	9 23	9 24	—	—
Pottery Siding	—	—	...	...	—	—	C	R	—	—	...	...	...	...	—	—	—	—	...	...	—	—	—	—
Granite Siding	—	—	...	...	—	—	C	R	—	—	...	...	...	...	—	—	—	—	...	...	—	—	—	—
HEATHFIELD	**2 19**	**2 21**	**3 20**	**X 3 30**	**4 19**	**4 21**	**3 55**	**●5 5**	**5 42**	**5 43**	...	...	...	...	**7 24**	**7 25**	C	S	...	...	9 28	9 29	C	S
Teigngrace Halt	2 24	2 25	—	—	4 24	4 25	—	—	5 46	5 46½	...	...	...	...	7 28	7 29	—	—	...	...	9 32	9 33	—	—
Teign Bridge Level C.	—	—	—	—	—	—	—	—	—	—	...	...	...	...	—	—	—	—	...	...	—	—	—	—
Teign Bridge Siding	—	—	—	—	—	—	5 13	●5 24	—	—	...	...	...	...	—	—	—	—	...	...	—	—	—	—
NEWTON ABBOT	**2 30**	—	**3 42**	—	**4 30**	—	5 30	—	**5 51**	—	...	...	...	...	**7 34**	—	9‖35	—	...	...	9 38	—	11‖25	—

NB There was no Sunday service at this time.

31st May to 26th September 1948 (Continued).

MORETONHAMPSTEAD BRANCH.

Single Line, worked by Electric Token or Train Staff. Auxiliary Token instruments on Platforms Nos. 5 and 9 at Newton Abbot. Intermediate Token instrument at Newton Abbot end of the Up Loop at Heathfield. Heathfield and Bovey are Crossing Stations. The Token or Staff Stations are Newton Abbot, Heathfield, Bovey and Moretonhampstead.

DOWN TRAINS. WEEK DAYS.

M.P. Mileage		STATIONS.	Ruling Gradient.	Time Allowances for Ordinary Freight Trains, see page 2.			G		K		B		B		K		B		K		B			
				Point-to-Point Times.	Allow for Stop.	Allow for Start.	Engine.		Christow Freight.		7.25 a.m. Totnes Auto.		Auto.		Exeter Freight.		10.5 a.m. Paignton Auto. W		Freight.		Auto.			
M.	C.			Mins.	Mins.	Mins.	arr. a.m.	dep. a.m.	arr. a.m.	dep. a.m.	arr. a.m.	dep. a.m.	arr. a.m.	dep. a.m.	arr. a.m.	dep. a.m.	arr. a.m.	dep. a.m.	arr. a.m.	dep. a.m.	arr. p.m.	dep. p.m.		
—	—	NEWTON ABBOT	—	—	—	1	—	6‖55	—	7 0	7 41	7 50	—	9 20	—	9 30	10 27	10 32	—	11 15	—	12 50	....	....
1	43	Teign Bridge Siding	100 R.	4	1	1	—	—	7 6	7 20	—	—	—	—	—	—	—	—	C	R	—	—	..	..
1	51	Teign Bridge Level C.	—	—	—	—	—	—	—	—	—	—	—	—	—	—	—	—	—	—	—	—	....	....
2	28	Teigngrace Halt	100 R.	—	—	—	—	—	—	—	7 54	7 55	9 2½	9 25	—	—	10 36	1036½	—	—	12 54	1254½	....	....
3	70	HEATHFIELD	70 R.	5	1	1	C	S	7 27	8 40	7 58½	8 0	9 28½	9 30	9 41	●10 9	10 40	X1043	11 25	11 40	12 58	12 59	..	..
5	6	Granite Siding	69 R.	—	—	—	—	—	—	—	—	—	—	—	—	—	—	—	C	R	—	—	....	....
5	19	Pottery Siding	53 R	—	—	—	—	—	..	..	—	—	—	—	..	..	—	—	C	R	—	—	..	..
5	46	Brimley Halt	53 R.	—	—	—	—	—	....	....	8 3½	8 4½	9 33½	9 34	....	....	1046½	1047½	—	—	1 2½	1 3½	....	....
6	6	Bovey	66 F.	5	2	2	C	S	..	..	8 6	X8 11	9 36	9 37	..	..	10 49	10 51	11 47●	12 20	1 5	1 6	....	....
7	61	Hawkmoor Halt	—	—	—	—	—	—	....	....	—	8 16	—	9 42	....	....	—	10 56	—	—	—	1 11	..	..
8	66	Lustleigh	50 R.	11	1	2	—	—	..	..	8 19	8 20	9 45	9 46	..	..	10 59	11 0	1233 S	T1238	1 14	1 15	....	....
12	28	MORETONHAMPSTEAD	49 R.	14	1	—	7‖30	—	....	....	8 31	—	9 57	—	....	....	11 11	—	12 55	—	1 28	—	..	..

DOWN TRAINS. WEEK DAYS—continued.

STATIONS.	B				B				B				B						B				B	
	Exeter Auto.				Auto.				Auto.				Auto.						Auto.				Auto. SO	
	arr. p.m.	dep. p.m.			arr. p.m.	dep. p.m.			arr. p.m.	dep. p.m.			arr. p.m.	dep. p.m.					arr. p.m.	dep. p.m.			arr. p.m.	dep. p.m.
NEWTON ABBOT	—	2 55	..	..	—	3 5	..	..	—	4 38	..	..	—	6 10	..	..	..	..	—	8 10	..	..	—	10 0
Teign Bridge Siding	—	—	....	....	—	—	....	....	—	—	....	....	—	—	....	....	....	....	—	—	....	....	—	—
Teign Bridge Level C.	—	—	..	..	—	—	..	..	—	—	..	..	—	—	..	..	..	..	—	—	..	..	—	—
Teigngrace Halt	2 59	3 0	....	....	3 9	3 9½	....	....	4 42	4 42½	....	....	6 14	6 14½	....	....	....	....	8 14	8 15	....	....	10 4	10 5
HEATHFIELD	3 4	3 25	..	..	3 13	3 14	..	..	4 46	4 47	..	..	6 18	6 19	..	..	..	..	8 18½	8 19½	..	..	10 8½	10 9
Granite Siding			....	....	—	—	....	....	—	—	....	....	—	—	....	....	....	....	—	—	....	....	—	—
Pottery Siding	..	..	..	..	—	—	..	..	—	—	..	..	—	—	..	..	..	..	—	—	..	..	—	—
Brimley Halt	....	....	....	....	3 17½	3 18	....	....	4 50½	4 51½	....	....	6 22½	6 23½	....	....	....	....	8 23	8 24	....	....	10 13	10 14
Bovey	..	..	..	..	3 20	3 21	..	..	4 53	4 54	..	..	6 25	6 26	..	..	..	..	8 25½	8 27	..	..	1015½	10 16
Hawkmoor Halt	....	....	....	....	—	3 26	....	....	—	4 59	....	....	—	6 31	....	....	....	....	—	8 32	....	....	—	10 21
Lustleigh	..	..	..	..	3 29	3 30	..	..	5 2	5 3	..	..	6 34	6 35	..	..	..	..	8 35	8 36	..	..	10 24	10 25
MORETONHAMPSTEAD	....	....	....	....	3 41	—	....	....	5 14	—	....	....	6 46	—	....	....	....	....	8 47	—	....	....	10 36	—

W—Starts from Newton Abbot on Saturdays.

WESTERN  REGION

Half-Day Excursion Bookings

DAILY

MAY 3rd and UNTIL FURTHER NOTICE

TO

TEIGNMOUTH & DAWLISH

FROM	DEPART					RETURN FARES (Third Class)	
	WEEKDAYS			SUNDAYS		Teignmouth	Dawlish
	a.m.	p.m.	p.m.	a.m.	p.m.	s. d.	s. d.
MORETONHAMPSTEAD †	11 35	1 35	3 15	9 20	1 45	2 6	2 9
LUSTLEIGH †	11 44	1 43	3 23	9 28	1 53	2 3	2 6
HAWKMOOR HALT †	11 46	1 45	3 25	9 30	1 55	2 0	2 3
BOVEY †	11 51	1 50	3 30	9 35	2 0	1 9	2 0
BRIMLEY HALT †	11 55	1 53	3 32	9 37	2 3		
HEATHFIELD †	12 0	1 58	3 39	9 43	2 8	1 6	1 9
TEIGNGRACE HALT †	12 4	2 2	3 43	9 47	2 12		
TEIGNMOUTH ......arr.	12 38	2 24	4 11	10 46	2 40		
DAWLISH .... "	12 45	2 33	4 19	10 54	2 47		

Note.—†—Passengers change at Newton Abbot in both directions.

RETURN BY ANY TRAIN THE SAME DAY.

Children under Three years of age, Free; Three and under Fourteen years of age, half-fare.

The Train Services shewn on this handbill are subject to alteration or cancellation at short notice and do not necessarily apply at Bank or Public Holidays. Passengers should confirm beforehand the service on which they intend to travel.

NOTICE AS TO CONDITIONS.—These tickets are issued subject to the Conditions of Issue of Ordinary passenger tickets, where applicable, and also to the special Conditions as set out in the Ticket, etc., Regulations, Bye-Laws, and General Notices. Luggage allowances are as set out in these General Notices.

Tickets can be obtained in advance at Booking Stations and Agencies.

Holiday Runabout Tickets available for seven days are issued, giving unlimited travel in specified holiday areas.

Further information will be supplied on application to Booking Stations, Agencies, or to Mr. D. H. HAWKESWOOD, District Commercial Superintendent, Exeter (St. David's) (Telephone Exeter 2281, Extension 301, 302 or 303) ; or to Mr. C. FURBER, Commercial Superintendent, Paddington Station, W.2.

Paddington Station, W.2.
March, 1953

K. W. C. GRAND,
Chief Regional Officer.

E9—154 Bartlett & Son, 138, Cowick Street, Exeter Rpt. E9—135

WESTERN BRITISH RAILWAYS REGION

MORETONHAMPSTEAD CARNIVAL

Half-Day Excursion Bookings

THURSDAY, AUGUST 22nd

TO

MORETONHAMPSTEAD

FROM	DEPART				RETURN FARE (Second Class)	Return Times (same day) Moretonhampstead *depart* :—
	p.m.	p.m.	p.m.	p.m.	s. d.	
NEWTON ABBOT	12 44	2 15	4 30	6 5	1/10*	7.0 or 9†30 p.m.
TEIGNGRACE HALT	12 49	2 19	4 33	6 8	1/ 9	
HEATHFIELD	12 53	2 23	4 38	6 13	1/ 6	
BRIMLEY HALT	12 57	2 27	4 42	6 17	1/3	
BOVEY	1 1	2 30	4 45	6 20	1/3	
PULLABROOK HALT	1 6	2 35	4 50	6 25	1/ 0	
LUSTLEIGH	1 10	2 39	4 55	6 29	-/ 9	
Moretonhampstead arr.	1 21	2 51	5 . 6	6 41		

†—*IF THE EVENT IS CANCELLED, POSTPONED OR ABANDONED, THIS SPECIAL TRAIN WILL NOT APPLY.*

NOTE. *—"Special Cheap Day" tickets available by any train after 9.30 a.m.

Children under Three years of age, Free ; Three and under Fourteen years of age, half-fare.

NOTICE AS TO CONDITIONS.—These tickets are issued subject to the British Transport Commissions' published Regulations and Conditions applicable to British Railways exhibited at their Stations or obtainable free of charge at Station Booking Offices.

Tickets can be obtained in advance at Booking Stations and Agencies.

IT WOULD ASSIST THE RAILWAYS IN PROVIDING ADEQUATE ACCOMMODATION IF INTENDING PASSENGERS WOULD OBTAIN THEIR TICKETS IN ADVANCE.

Further information will be supplied on application to Booking Stations, Agencies, or to Mr. D. H. HAWKESWOOD, District Commercial Manager, Exeter (St. David's) (Telephone Exeter 72281, Extension 301, 302 or 303); or to Mr. A. C. B. PICKFORD, Chief Commercial Manager, Paddington Station, W.2.

Paddington Station, W.2.
July, 1957

K. W. C. GRAND,
General Manager.

E9—372 H.D. Bartlett & Son (Exeter) Ltd., 138, Cowick Street, Exeter

15th September 1958 to 14th June 1959.

WEEKDAYS MORETONHAMPSTEAD TO NEWTON ABBOT

UP		Ruling Gradient 1 in	B	B	B	B			B	B	B		B		C	
					Rail Motor				Rail Motor	Rail Motor	Rail Motor		Rail Motor		ECS	
			am		am	am			PM	PM	PM		PM		PM	
MORETONHAMPS'D dep	1	—	7 50	..	8 40	10 15	..	..	1 35	3 15	5 10	..	7 0	..	9† 0	..
Lustleigh	2	49F	7 59	..	8a48½	10a23½	..	..	1 44	3a23½	5a18½	..	7N9	..	..	..
Pullabrook Halt	3	50F	8 1	..	8a50	10 26	..	..	1 46	3 25½	5 20½	..	7 11	..	..	..
Bovey arr	4	61R	8X 5	..	8 54	10 30	..	..	1 50	3 29½	5 24½	..	7 15	..	..	..
dep	5		8 8	..	8 55	10 32	..	..	1 51	3 30½	5 25½	..	7 17	..	..	..
Brimley Halt	6	66R	8 11	..	8 58	10 35	..	..	1 54	3a33	5a28	..	7 20	..	..	..
HEATHFIELD arr	7	53F	8 15	..	9 2	10X39	..	..	1 58	3 37	5 32	..	7 24	..	..	..
dep	8		8 16	..	9 3	10 45	..	..	1 59	3 40	5 34	..	7 25	..	..	..
Teigngrace Halt	9	70F	8 20	..	9 7	10a48½	..	..	2a 2½	3 44	5a37½	..	7 29	..	..	..
NEWTON ABBOT arr	10	100R&F	8 25	..	9 12	10 53	..	..	2‡ 7	3 49	5 42	..	7 34	..	9†35	..
									‡—2.9							

N—Guard to collect tickets and, when necessary, extinguish lights.

15th September 1958 to 14th June 1959 (Continued).

NEWTON ABBOT TO MORETONHAMPSTEAD WEEKDAYS C57

SINGLE LINE—Worked by Electric Token or Train Staff. Auxiliary Token instruments on Platform Nos. 5 and 9 at Newton Abbot. Intermediate Token instrument at Newton Abbot end of the Up Loop at Heathfield. Heathfield and Bovey are Crossing Stations. The Token or Staff Stations are Newton Abbot, Heathfield, Bovey, and Moretonhampstead.

M.P. Mileage M	M.P. Mileage C	DOWN		Ruling Gradient 1 in	C		B	B			B	B	B		B		B
					ECS		Rail Motor				Rail Motor	Rail Motor	Rail Motor		Rail Motor		Rail Motor
					am		am	am			PM	PM	PM		PM		PM
—	—	**NEWTN ABBOT** dep	1	—	6†45	..	7 50	9 20	..	..	12 50	2 15	4 25	..	6 5	..	8 15
2	28	Teigngrace Halt	2	100R&F	..	..	7 55	9 25	..	..	12a54	2a19½	4a29½	..	6a 9½	..	8 20
3	70	**HEATHFIELD** .. arr	3	70R	..	..	7 58½	9 28½	..	..	12 58	2X23	4 33	..	6 13	..	8 23½
		.. .. .. dep	4		..	..	8 0	9 30	..	..	12 59	2 24	4 34	..	6 14	..	8 24½
5	46	Brimley Halt	5	53R	..	..	8 4½	9a34	..	..	1a 3	2a28	4a38	..	6 18½	..	8 29
6	6	Bovey .. .. .. arr	6	66F	..	..	8X 6	9 36	..	..	1 5	2X30	4 40	..	6 20	..	8 30½
		.... dep	7	—	..	..	8 11	9 37	..	..	1 6	2 31	4 41	..	6 21	..	8 32
7	61	Pullabrook Halt	8	61R	..	..	8 16	9 42	..	..	1 11	2 36	4 46	..	6 26	..	8 37
8	66	Lustleigh	9	50R	..	..	8 20	9 46	..	..	1N15	2 40	4 50	..	6N30	..	8N41
12	28	**MORETONHPS'D** arr	10	49R	7†15	..	8 31	9 57	..	..	1 26	2 51	5 1	..	6 41	..	8 52

N—Guard to collect tickets and, when necessary, extinguish lights

Freight Timetable, 15th September 1958 to 14th June 1959.

C50

WEEKDAYS — NEWTON ABBOT AND MORETONHAMPSTEAD

SINGLE LINE, worked by Electric Token or Train Staff. Auxiliary Token Instruments on platforms Nos. 5 and 9 at Newton Abbot. Intermediate Token instrument at Newton Abbot end of the Up Loop at Heathfield. Heathfield and Bovey are Crossing Stations. The Token or Staff Stations are Newton Abbot, Heathfield, Bovey and Moretonhampstead.

DOWN

M.P. Mileage M	C	DOWN		Ruling Gradient 1 in	K To Christow SO	K To Moreton-h'pstead MWFO Christow TThO	K		K	
					SO		TTh O Q		Q	
					am	am	am		PM	
—	—	NEWTON ABBOT	dep	—	9 30	11 15			6 15	
1	43	Teign Bridge Siding	arr	100 R & F	R	R	..	..	6 21	..
			dep							
3	70	HEATHFIELD	arr	70 R	9 40	11 25	..	..	..	..
			dep	—	9 45	11 40	11 40			
6	6	Bovey	arr	53 R	..	11 47	11 47	..	..	..
			dep	—		12*20	12 5			
8	66	Lustleigh	arr	50 R	..	..	..	..	..	..
			dep	—						
12	28	MORETONHAMPSTEAD	arr	49 R	..	12 48	..	..	..	..

UP

UP		Ruling Gradient 1 in	K	K 11.45 am Christow SO	K 2.55 pm Christow TThO		K	K	
			TTh O Q	SO	TTh O		MW FO	Q	
			PM	PM	PM		PM	PM	
MORETONHAMPSTEAD	dep	—					1 51		
Stop Board		L	..	..	..	..	1P53	..	..
Lustleigh	arr	49 F					2 4		
	dep	—	..	..	..	..	2 11	..	..
Stop Board		50 F					2P20		
Bovey	arr	L	..	..	..	..	2X22	..	..
	dep	—	12 5				2 45		
Pottery Siding		53 F	..	..	..	..	R	..	..
Granite Siding		69 F					R		
HEATHFIELD	arr	69 F	12 13	12 33	3 45	..	3 15	..	..
	dep	—		2 30	5* 0		5* 0		
Teigngrace Halt		70 F	..	..	..	..	..	..	..
Teign Bridge Siding	arr	100 F		2 38	5 8		5 8		
	dep	—	..	2 50	5*19	..	5*19	6 35	..
NEWTON ABBOT	arr	100 R & F		2 56	5 25		5 25	6 41	

The last passenger train to travel the entire length of the branch.

41 1962.

THURSDAY, 16th AUGUST—continued

MORETONHAMPSTEAD BRANCH

Sunday School Special—Moretonhampstead to Teignmouth and Return.

7†20 a.m. (ECS) NEWTON ABBOT to MORETONHAMPSTEAD.
To run at the following times. Speed not to exceed 15 m.p.h.

	arr. a.m.		dep. a.m.
Newton Abbot	—		**7†20**
Heathfield		7 35	
Moretonhampstead	**8†10**		—

Load: 10 non-corridor coaches.

8-35 a.m. (Sunday School Special) MORETONHAMPSTEAD to TEIGNMOUTH.
Train No. 1Z11. Speed not to exceed 15 m.p.h. between Moretonhampstead and Newton Abbot. To run at the following times, formed with 10 non-corridor coaches arriving 7†20 a.m. (**ECS**) Newton Abbot.

"**A**" Headcode from Newton Abbot.

	arr. a.m.	dep. a.m.		arr. a.m.		dep. a.m.
Moretonhampstead	—	**8 35**	Teigngrace	**9 32**		**9 34**
Lustleigh	**8 50**	**8 54**	Newton Abbot	**9 40**	**N**	**9 50**
Bovey	**9 6**	**9 9**	Teignmouth	**9 58**		**10†1**
Heathfield	**9 19**	**9 22**	Exminster	**10†20**		—

Light engine and guard thence to Exeter (St. David's).

6‖10 p.m. (LE) EXETER (St. David's) to EXMINSTER.
For times see tabular pages. To also convey Guard, to work 6†55 p.m. (**ECS**) thence to Teignmouth.

7-19 p.m. (Return Sunday School Special) TEIGNMOUTH to MORETONHAMPSTEAD.
Train No. 1Z11. Speed not to exceed 15 m.p.h. between Newton Abbot and Moretonhampstead. To run at the following times.

"**A**" Headcode to Newton Abbot.

	arr. p.m.		dep. p.m.		arr. p.m.	dep. p.m.
Exminster	—		**6†55**	Heathfield	**7 58**	**8 0**
Teignmouth	**7†15**		**7 19**	Bovey	**8 11**	**8 13**
Newton Abbot	**7 27**	**N**	**7 37**	Lustleigh	**8 26**	**8 28**
Teigngrace	**7 45**		**7 47**	Moretonhampstead	**8 42**	—

8†56 p.m. (ECS) MORETONHAMPSTEAD to NEWTON ABBOT.
Speed not to exceed 15 m.p.h. To run at the following times. Formed with stock off 7-19 p.m. Teignmouth Return Sunday School Special.

	arr. p.m.	dep. p.m.
Moretonhampstead	—	**8†56**
Newton Abbot	**9†46**	—

All concerned to note that the crossing gates at Teigngrace and Bovey are to be manned during the passage of these trains. A groundman to be available at Moretonhampstead and the Signal lights at Heathfield and the crossing lights at Teigngrace and Bovey to be lit for the return journey of these trains.

W. J. HARTNELL,
District Superintendent.

Exeter, August, 1962.

Freight Timetable, 15th June 1964 (or until further notice).

PLYMOUTH 852

D.63XX Diesel (Extract from Newton Abbot 702).

Enginemen

Newton Abbot Turn 815

Newton Abbot Turn 834

Newton Abbot Turn 851

Hackney		5.58	**9D79 SX**
	a.m.	a.m.	
Old Quay	6.14	6.50	**9D43 EBV**
Hackney	7.7	7‖12	
Newton Abbot Shed ..	7‖17		
	a.m.	a.m.	
Newton Abbot Shed ..		10‖40	**MWFO**
Newton Abbot Goods ..	10‖45	10.55	**9D05**
Teign Bridge Sidings ..	11.1	11.21	
Heathfield	11.27	11.40	
Bovey	11.47		
Bovey		2.45	**9D64**
Heathfield	3.15	4.10	
Teign Bridge Siding ..	4.16	4.36	
Newton Abbot Goods ..	4.42	4‖47	**0Z33 SX Q**
Newton Abbot Shed ..	4‖52		
	a.m.	a.m.	
Newton Abbot Shed ..		10‖40	**TThO**
Newton Abbot Goods ..	10‖45	10.55	**9D44**
Teign Bridge Siding ..	11.1	11.21	
Heathfield	11.27		
	a.m.	a.m.	
Heathfield		11.40	**9D05 TThO Q**
		p.m.	
Bovey	11.47	12.5	**9D44**
	p.m.		
Heathfield	12.13		
	p.m.	p.m.	
Heathfield		1.30	**9D86 TThO**
Chudleigh	1.55	2.5	
Trusham	2.12	2.40	**9D64 TThO**
Chudleigh	2.48	2.58	
Heathfield	3.26		
Heathfield		4.10	
Teign Bridge Siding ..	4.16	4.36	
Newton Abbot Goods ..	4.42		
Newton Abbot Goods ..		4‖50	**SX Q**
Newton Abbot Shed ..	4‖55		
	p.m.	p.m.	
Newton Abbot Goods ..		5.40	**9D78 SX Q**
Teign Bridge Siding ..	5.46	6.0	**9D64**
Newton Abbot Goods ..	6.6	6‖15	
Newton Abbot Shed ..	6‖20		
Service SX			
	p.m.	p.m.	
Newton Abbot Shed ..		9‖35	**LD SO**
Totnes	9‖55		
0J11 Banker			
	a.m.	a.m.	
Dainton Siding		12‖2	**LD Sun.**
Aller Junction	12‖7		
0J00 Banker			
Dainton Siding		1‖20	**LD**
Newton Abbot West ..	1‖40	1‖45	
Aller Junction	1‖50		
0J00 Banker			
Dainton Siding		6‖55	**LD**
Newton Abbot Shed ..	7‖15		

Service Sun.

For details of trains banked see pages 1 and 2

GOODS TRAFFIC ON THE BRANCH AT ITS ZENITH AND DURING LATER YEARS

Incoming Traffic

MORETONHAMPSTEAD

Coal – for the engine shed, the gasworks and domestic use.
Animal feeding stuffs.
Grain.
Fertilizer.
Food supplies for the Manor House Hotel.

LUSTLEIGH

Coal and coke.

BOVEY

Coal.
Grain.
Fertilizer.
Horses (for the Dartmoor Hunt).

POTTERY SIDING

Coal.
Flints.

GRANITE SIDING

Coal for the gasworks and, occasionally, for the Bovey Pottery.

HEATHFIELD

Coal for Candy's factory.

TEIGNGRACE

Coal – small amounts only.

Outgoing Traffic

MORETONHAMPSTEAD

Cattle, sheep and ponies.
Timber.
Rabbits.
Milk.
Whortleberries (in drums), when in season.

LUSTLEIGH

Micaceous haematite ('shiny ore') from Kelly Mine (intermittent).
Milk.

BOVEY

Farm implements.
Iron and copper ore from the Haytor and Yarner mines respectively.
Timber (mainly for use as pit props).
Pottery products from the Devonmoor Art Pottery in Liverton and other art potteries in Bovey Tracey.
Micaceous haematite ('shiny ore') – small amounts only.
Rabbits.
Milk.

POTTERY SIDING

Pottery products.

HEATHFIELD

Pottery products, bricks, tiles and pipes from Candy's factory.
Ball clay (from Timber Siding).
Lignite ('Bovey coal') for a brief period after World War II (from Timber Siding).

TEIGNGRACE

Milk.
Ball clay (intermittent).

TEIGNBRIDGE SIDINGS

Ball clay.

NB General merchandise, both incoming and outgoing, has not been included above.

Coal being transferred from North Eastern coal wagons in the station yard at Bovey to the lorry of Wakeham & Jeffery, one of three coal merchants operating in the town at this time, c.1930. The person nearest the camera is Arthur Jeffery.

Courtesy of Dave Lewis

A not-untypical scene at Bovey between the wars as a consignment of rabbits arrives at the station. Here, they are being loaded into baskets by a local trapper prior to being despatched by rail to other parts of the country.

Courtesy of Dave Lewis

A study of the cattle pens at Moretonhampstead, which were located at the far (western) end of the station site.

Lens of Sutton

A consignment of timber from the sawmills of George Brimblecombe & Sons of Moretonhampstead passing slowly along the branch near Wray Barton towards Newton Abbot during, or sometime after, World War II. Such movements as this always took place on Sundays, when there was no passenger service, and the timber (obtained from nearby woodlands) would often be destined for coal mines to serve as pit props. However, during the war some of the timber was used for the construction of wooden minesweepers by J. W. & A. Upham Ltd of Brixham and later, in 1957, for the building of the replica of *The Mayflower* by the same company.

Dartington Rural Archive

ENGINEERING AND OPERATING DATA

(a) Pages 244 to 253 are reproduced from the Appendix to No. 5 Section of the Service Time Tables, Exeter Division, GWR – February 1947 until further notice.

(b) Page 254 is reproduced from Alterations and Additions to the Appendix to No. 5 Section of the Service Time Tables, Exeter Division, GWR – February 1947 until further notice, dated March 1952.

(c) Pages 255 to 257 are reproduced from the BR (Western Region) Working Time Table of passenger trains, Exeter District, for the period 16th September 1957 to 8th June 1958 (or until further notice).

(d) Pages 258 to 261 are reproduced from the Sectional Appendix to the Working Time Tables and Books of Rules and Regulations, BR (Western Region), Exeter Traffic District, March 1960.

(e) Page 262 contains a gradient chart specially prepared for this book by Robert Zaple Esq.

(f) Pages 263 to 276 contain a brief account of signalling on the branch by Peter Kay Esq., and also signal box diagrams provided by R. J. Caston Esq. of the Signalling Record Society: the two diagrams of Teignbridge Siding and Pottery Siding & Granite Siding were specially prepared for this book by Robert Zaple Esq.

Photographs of luggage labels and tickets appear on various pages throughout the book.

(Items (a) to (d) in this chapter are reproduced by kind permission of British Railways Board and, irrespective of dates, remain its exclusive copyright.)

MORETONHAMPSTEAD BRANCH.

OCCUPATION OF LINE BY ENGINEERING DEPARTMENT.

The Standard Instructions shewn in the General Appendix to the Rule Book must be observed, as far as they apply.

Three Gangers are appointed for this Branch, as under :—

One from 0 m. 25 chs. to 3 m. 60 chs.
One from 3 m. 60 chs. to 7 m. 60 chs.
One from 7 m. 60 chs. to 12 m. 34 chs.

In order to avoid sending out Handsignalmen in accordance with Rules 215 and 217, when it is necessary to run trollies along the line, or to carry out operations which would render the running of trains unsafe, telephones and Occupation Key Boxes are fixed at places named below :—

Section Newton Abbot East to Heathfield.

Group No. 1 (One Key).	m.	c.
Newton Abbot East Signal Box		
Hut No. 1	–	60
Hut No. 2	1	43½
Hut No. 3	2	28
Hut No. 4	3	8
Heathfield Signal Box		

Section Heathfield to Bovey.

Group No. 2 (Two Keys).	m.	c.
Heathfield Signal Box		
Hut No. 5	4	40
Hut No. 6 (Pottery)	5	19
Bovey Signal Box		

Section Bovey to Moretonhampstead.

Group No. 3 (Two Keys).	m.	c.
Bovey Signal Box		
Hut No. 7	6	79
Hut No. 8	7	72
Hut No. 9	8	40
Hut No. 10	9	0
Hut No. 11	9	57
Hut No. 12	10	48
Hut No. 13	11	39
Moretonhampstead Signal Box		

Telephones in Group 1 communicate with Newton Abbot East and Heathfield Signal Boxes.
Telephones in Group 2 communicate with Heathfield and Bovey Signal Boxes.
Telephones in Group 3 communicate with Bovey and Moretonhampstead Signal Boxes.

The following modifications of the general instructions apply :—

Clauses 18 and 23.—The telephone must be used to obtain the attention of the Signalman.

Clause 19.—The Signalmen at both ends of the section immediately they have agreed to the occupation, must hold down the bell keys of their respective train staff instruments.
The control slide arrangement will not apply.

Clause 21.—When putting the key back the Ganger must turn it to the right until the indication shews No. 1. Having thus restored the occupation key the Ganger must call up the Signalman on the telephone and so inform him, and that the line is safe for the passage of trains.

Clause 31.—It will be necessary for the Pilotman, when distributing Pilot Working Forms, to personally satisfy himself that the occupation key is in the key boxes.

TEIGNBRIDGE SIDINGS.

Shunting.

The Siding on the Up side of the line will accommodate 20 wagons and the Siding on the Down side 30 wagons, and they are connected with the Main Line from both ends. The points are worked from three ground frames controlled by key on Electric Train Token.

The Crossing Keeper must prepare a list of all wagons dealt with at the Siding, and forward it to the Goods Agent at Newton Abbot.

The Crossing Keeper will be responsible for seeing that the Siding gates are kept closed after work has been completed in the Sidings.

Working of Clay Traffic.

Whenever necessary, a brake-van may be propelled from Newton Abbot East for the purpose of picking up loaded traffic at Teignbridge Sidings. The Guard must ride in the brake-van, keep a sharp look-out, and be prepared to hand-signal to the Driver.

The loaded train must return to Newton Abbot East with brake van at rear.

TEIGNGRACE HALT.

Shunting.

Work at the Siding at this Halt can only be performed by Up trains, and any traffic on Down Freight trains must be taken to Heathfield and returned.

HEATHFIELD.

Auxiliary Electric Train Token Instrument.

An Auxiliary Electric Train Token Instrument, for the Heathfield-Newton Abbot East Section, is fixed in a hut near the Up Main Advanced Starting Signal.

The Instrument is provided as an additional facility for the withdrawal of a Token by the Driver of an Up train. Telephone communication exists between the Instrument and Signal Box.

When an Up train is ready to proceed, and the Driver is not in possession of the Token for the Heathfield-Newton Abbot East Section, he must send his Fireman to the Auxiliary Token Instrument to obtain permission by telephone to withdraw a Token.

When the Signalman at Heathfield has obtained permission from Newton Abbot East for the train to proceed, both Signalmen must press in the plungers of their Token Instruments to permit the withdrawal of a Token from the Auxiliary Instrument.

A Token can be placed in the Auxiliary Instrument at any time but one can only be withdrawn by co-operation between the Heathfield and Newton Abbot East Signalmen.

For instructions as to operation of Auxiliary Electric Train Token Instrument by Fireman see the General Appendix to the Rule Book.

Truck Weighbridge Relief Line.

The weighbridge is situated in the Up Refuge Siding.

Engines must not be allowed to pass over the weighing road.

The machine has a weighing capacity up to 30 tons.

Except when it is necessary to weigh traffic, the lever controlling the points for the weighing line must be kept padlocked in its normal position and the key kept in the Weighbridge House.

Immediately the Shunter in charge has completed weighing, the points must be reset in their normal position for the Refuge Siding.

The person in charge must satisfy himself from time to time that the instructions are being strictly observed.

Shunting.

When it is necessary to use the Teign Valley Branch Line for shunting purposes, a brake-van with a man riding in it must be at the Chudleigh end of the wagons.

Messrs. Candy & Company's Sidings.

The straight Siding falls towards the Main Line, and care must be exercised in shunting. After shunting has been completed, the hand-point must be set for the Dead End Siding. Wagons left on the Main Line side of the hand-point to the Dead End Siding must have a sufficient number of hand-brakes securely applied and sprags used.

Fly shunting is prohibited in these Sidings.

Six sprags must be kept 10 yards apart on the incline.

During shunting operations the guard and shunter will be jointly responsible for the safe working, and an appointed porter from Heathfield must be provided to protect the level crossing near the points leading to the Dead End siding.

Working at Chudleigh Knighton Sidings.

For instructions as to working to and from Chudleigh Knighton Sidings see page 113.

GRANITE AND POTTERY SIDINGS BETWEEN HEATHFIELD AND BOVEY.

Work at these Sidings can only be performed by Up trains, and any traffic on Down Freight trains must be taken through to Bovey and returned.

The points are controlled by a ground frame at each place, locked by key on the Train Staff.

A wheel-stop is provided at each Siding, and kept padlocked across the rail.

After work has been completed at the Sidings, the Guard will be responsible for padlocking the wheel-stop across the rail and locking the Siding gate.

ASSISTING FREIGHT TRAINS—BOVEY TO MORETONHAMPSTEAD.

When a Down Freight train requires assistance between Bovey and Moretonhampstead the assistant engine must be attached to the rear of the train.

LUSTLEIGH.

Shunting.

Wagons to be put off a Down Freight train assisted by an engine in the rear must be formed on the van. The trains must stop clear ahead of the Siding points, and before the wagons to be detached are uncoupled the Guard must apply sufficient brakes and sprags on the rear wagons of the front portion. The wagons must then be placed in the Siding by the assistant engine.

When a Down Freight train is not assisted in the rear, wagons must be taken to Moretonhampstead and returned.

Before the engine of an Up Freight train performing work is detached from the train, the Guard must apply sufficient brakes and sprags on the leading wagons left on the Main Line.

Six sprags must be kept at the side of the line between the platform and the facing points.

MORETONHAMPSTEAD.

No vehicle must be detached and allowed to remain on the Main Line.

On completion of the day's service, the coaches must be placed in the Loop Siding and the points set for the Shed line.

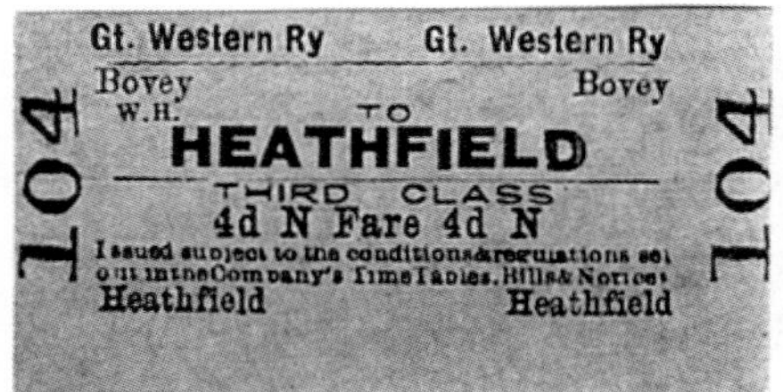

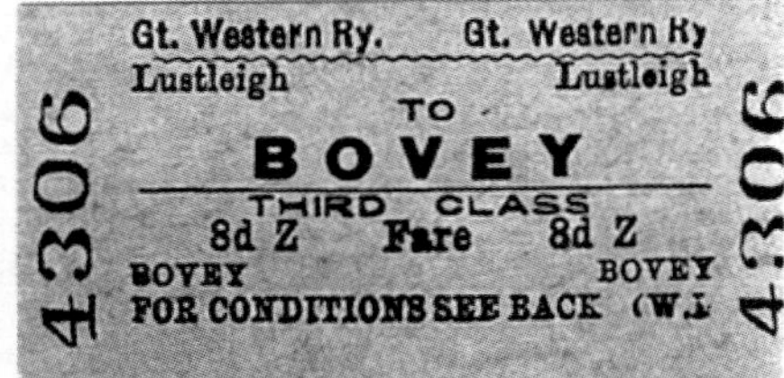

BREAKDOWN GANGS AND CRANES.

Breakdown Gangs Stationed at	For the undermentioned Stations.
Newton Abbot	Newton Abbot to Starcross and Wrangaton (inclusive), Heathfield to Christow (exclusive). All stations on the Moretonhampstead, Kingswear, Brixham, Ashburton, and Kingsbridge Branches

Breakdown Cranes Stationed at	Maximum Lift.	Type.
Newton Abbot	36-ton	Steam.
" "	35-ton	"
" "	15-ton	"
" "	6-ton	"
" "	12-ton	Hand.
" "	6-ton	"

WHERE RE-RAILING RAMPS ARE KEPT.

Station.	Number.	Where Stored.
Newton Abbot	3	On Shunting Trucks at Hackney East, West End, and New Yard
Heathfield	1	Goods Shed.

Re-railing Ramps are supplied as above, and if required at adjoining Stations they may be obtained therefrom on application. They are, however, to be returned to the Stations to which they belong without delay after use.

WHERE ENGINES CAN TAKE WATER.

Station.	Where Situated.
Newton Abbot	Down Platforms and Down Through Road. Up Platform, Moretonhampstead Bay and Up Through Road. Locomotive Yard.
Moretonhampstead	Engine Shed and Yard.

WORKING OF FREIGHT TRAINS DOWN INCLINES.

The points at which trains must stop to release Wagon Brakes are as follows:—

Incline upon which "Stop Board" is fixed	Down or Up Trains	Point where Train must stop to release Brakes
MORETONHAMPSTEAD BRANCH. Lustleigh	Up	Bovey Home Signal.

INCLINES STEEPER THAN 1 IN 200.

MORETONHAMPSTEAD BRANCH.

Incline between	Length of Incline about	Gradient 1 in	Falling towards	Places at which Boards have been fixed and at which Freight Trains must stop to put down brakes.	Modifications of, or additions to, the Standard Instructions.
Newton Abbot and Teigngrace	16 chains	132	Teigngrace ..		
" "	10 "	100	Newton Abbot ..		
" "	12 "	100	Teigngrace ..		
" "	12 "	100	Newton Abbot ..		
Teigngrace and Heathfield	¼ mile	98	Teigngrace ..		
" "	26 chains	70	"		
" "	16 "	172	"		
Heathfield and Bovey	24 chains	69	Heathfield		
" "	9 "	72	Bovey		
" "	13 "	69	Heathfield		
" "	22 "	53	"		
" "	28 "	66	Bovey		
Bovey and Lustleigh	31 "	61	"		
" "	¼ mile	66	"		
" "	28 chains	67	"		
" "	16 "	53	"		
" "	28 "	61	"		
" "	28 "	50	"		
Lustleigh and Moretonhampstead	1 m. 58 ch.	49	Lustleigh	At Moretonhampstead Station near Advanced Starting Signal.	Freight Trains requiring an Assistant Engine from Bovey to Moretonhampstead must have the Assistant Engine attached at the rear.
" "	13 chains	87	"		
" "	29 "	75	"		
" "	38 "	83	"		
" "	23 "	82	"		

GROUND FRAMES AND INTERMEDIATE SIDINGS.

Name of Station or Siding.	Where situated.	By whom attended.	How Locked.	Remarks.
	MORETONHAMPSTEAD BRANCH.			
Newton Abbot	Goods Yard	Shunter	Key in East Box	
" "	Clay Coy.'s Siding	Shunter	" " "	
Teignbridge (Three Ground Frames)	Between Newton Abbot and Teigngrace	Guard	Key on Token	
Teigngrace	East end	Guard	" " "	
Heathfield	South end	Guard	" " "	
Granite Siding	Between Heathfield and Bovey	Guard	Key on Staff	
Pottery Siding	Between Heathfield and Bovey	Guard	" " "	
Lustleigh	West end of Platform	Guard or Porter	Key on Token	

SINGLE LINES AND HOW WORKED.

Between		Method of working the Single Line.	Where Staff, Token or Tablet kept.	Person responsible for exchanging.	Person responsible when aforesaid man is not on duty.	Remarks.
			MORETONHAMPSTEAD BRANCH.			
*Newton Abbot East	Heathfield	Electric Token	Signal Box	Signalman	..	
Heathfield	Bovey	Electric Staff	Signal Box	Signalman	..	
Bovey	Moretonhampstead	Electric Token	Signal Box	Signalman	..	

* Auxiliary Token Instruments are provided on Platforms Nos. 5 and 9 at Newton Abbot and also at Heathfield, fixed near the Up Advanced Starting Signal. See Special Instructions, pages 88 and 114.

CROSSOVER ROADS EXIST AT THE FOLLOWING PLACES.

Station or Signal Box.	Particulars.
Heathfield	Down to Up.

TEMPORARY RESTRICTIONS OF SPEED ON BRANCH LINES.

RULE 218.—On the following Branch Lines Handsignalmen wil not be posted. Warning boards as well as "C" and "T" indicators will be fixed when the restriction of speed commences. The words "Handsignalmen will not be posted" will be included in the notice issued.

Brixham. Chard. Culm Valley. Exe Valley. Moretonhampstead. Teign Valley. Tiverton. Yeovil.

On Goods and Mineral lines where a permanent speed restriction of 15 m.p.h. or less is in force, further speed restrictions will not be imposed nor Handsignalmen posted in connection with Engineering work, unless arrangements are made between the Divisional Engineer and Divisional Superintendent.

SINGLE LINE CROSSING LOOPS.

Stations.	Length in Feet.		
	Up.	Down.	
MORETONHAMPSTEAD BRANCH			
Heathfield	1,721	1,721	
Bovey	553	553	

PUBLIC ROAD LEVEL CROSSINGS.

M. C.	Name of Crossing.	Situated between	Whether a Block Post.	Whether there is a Crossing Keeper, Indicators or Bells, if not a Block Post.	Whether there are Signals.	Whether the Gates are interlocked with the Signals.
6 0	Bovey..	At Station	Yes	Gates worked by Station Staff	Yes	Yes
1 50¾	Teignbridge ..	Newton Abbot and Teigngrace	No	Crossing Keeper, Indicator and Bell	Yes	Yes

COUPLING AND UNCOUPLING ENGINES.

Station Masters and Inspectors are responsible for seeing that Engines are coupled to and uncoupled from Trains.

The Fireman must couple and uncouple the Engine to and from the Train at starting and terminal Stations and also at intermediate Stations on the Main Line where Engines are changed for Locomotive purposes.

At Junction and Terminal Stations on Branch Lines the Traffic Staff will be responsible for this work.

In cases where an ordinary steam engine has been supplied to work a service scheduled to be worked by an auto engine, the Fireman to do the uncoupling and coupling when it is necessary to run round the train.

The following arrangements will apply to the coupling and uncoupling of Engines at the stations named :—

Station.	Work performed by Fireman.	Work performed by Traffic Department.

STATIONS AT WHICH LOOSE SCREW COUPLINGS ARE KEPT.

STATION	No. of Couplings:	
	Type A.	Type B.
Heathfield	–	1
Bovey	–	1
Moretonhampstead ..	–	1

Loose screw couplings are provided as above, and if required at adjoining Stations they may be obtained therefrom on application. They are, however, to be returned to the stations to which they belong without delay after use.

CROSSING OF RAILWAY BY ELECTRIC POWER LINES—continued.

Overhead Electric Power Lines cross the Line at the following Points:—

M	C.	Near	Between	Supply Co. or Authority.	Telephone No.
		MORETONHAMPSTEAD BRANCH.			
4	$9\frac{1}{2}$	Heathfield	Heathfield and Bovey.	Candy & Co.	Bovey 141 or 142.
4	22	" "	" " "	Teignmouth Elec. Light Co.	Bovey Tracey 36.
5	19	Bovey	" " "	" " "	" "
5	49				
7	$56\frac{1}{2}$	Lustleigh	Bovey and Lustleigh.	" " "	" "
11	$60\frac{1}{2}$	Moretonhampstead	Lustleigh and Moretonhampstead.	Torquay Corpn.	Newton Abbot 26.

HALTS AT WHICH STAFF IS NOT EMPLOYED.

No staff is kept at the undermentioned Halts, and the supervision of them comes under the Station Masters at the Stations shewn.

The Station Masters must visit the Halts from time to time to see that the premises are in proper condition, and that notice boards, gates, shelters, seats, etc., are properly looked after :—

Name of Halt.	Station supervising Halt.
Teigngrace	Heathfield.
Brimley	Bovey.
Hawkmoor	Bovey.

STATION ARRANGEMENTS.

NEWTON ABBOT.

Examination of Wagons after being tipped on Electric Power Co.'s Siding.

Wagons before being shunted out of the Electric Power Co.'s Siding must be examined by the Locomotive Department.

The examinations must be made at agreed times daily, and in sufficient time to enable the wagons to be despatched the same night. When the examination is completed, the Shunter must be advised.

It is important that no wagons are shunted out of the Siding until passed by the Locomotive Department.

Shunting Trains on to Moretonhampstead Branch Line after that Line is closed for Traffic.

After the Moretonhampstead Branch Line is closed for traffic, an Empty Coaching Stock Train or a Freight Train may be shunted on to the Branch. After the train has been brought to a stand on the Branch, and the Guard or Shunter has securely applied the van brake, he must proceed to the Signal Box to carry out Rule 55.

The East Box Signalman must verbally instruct the Guard or Shunter when the train may return on to the Main Line.

Working of Clay Trains between Newton Abbot East and Teignbridge Sidings.

Whenever necessary, a brake-van may be propelled from Newton Abbot East to Teignbridge Sidings for the purp[illegible] of picking up loaded traffic.

The Guard must ride in the brake-van, keep a sharp look-out, and be prepared to hand-signal to the Driver when necessary.

The loaded train must return to Newton Abbot East with brake van in rear.

Back Road Sidings, Goods Yard.

Newton Abbot Clays Ltd. Siding.

These Sidings are situated on the Moretonhampstead Branch inside Newton Abbot East Box Branch Home Signal. The connections which are facing to Down Trains are worked by separate Ground Frames locked by key on a lever in Newton Abbot East Box.

When it is necessary to use either of these Sidings the Shunter will obtain the key from the East Box Signalman and when shunting is completed and the Branch Line clear, the Shunter must at once return the key to the East Box Signalman.

The East Box Signalman, after handing the key to the Shunter, must instruct the Driver to pass the Branch Starting and Advanced Starting Signals, which will be locked, at "Danger."

Shunting to and from either Siding is permitted without a Brake Van

After sunset and during fog or falling snow a red light must be placed at the Heathfield end of the wagons.

The Branch Line must not be occupied outside the Home Signal unless the Shunter has obtained permission from the East Box Signalman to do so.

Shunting Movements Goods Yard.

To control shunting movements in the Goods Yard, Klaxon horns are fixed in the following positions:—

No. 1. Opposite Newton Abbot East Signal Box.
No. 2. Goods Yard end of river bridge on the Moretonhampstead Branch Line.
No. 3. Near Starting Signal controlling exit from Goods Yard.

The plungers, to be operated by the Shunter, are fixed in the following positions:—

No. 1. Near Goods Yard Siding Signal.
No. 2. Telephone Box on second River Bridge on Moretonhampstead Branch Line.
No. 3. Goods Yard end of second River Bridge on Moretonhampstead Branch Line.
No. 4. Entrance to Goods Yard Sidings, Nos. 1 and 2.
No. 5. Goods Yard Siding, No. 3.
No. 6. Goods Yard Siding, No. 5.

The Standard Code of Signals for controlling shunting operations, as shewn in the Rule Book, must be observed.

Enginemen must not shunt in any direction until the required code is sounded on the Klaxon horn.

Auxiliary Electric Train Token Instruments for Moretonhampstead Branch.

Auxiliary Electric Train Token Instruments for the Newton Abbot East-Heathfield Section are fixed on Platforms Nos. 5 and 9.

Firemen of Branch trains starting from Platforms Nos. 5, 6, 7, 8 and 9 must obtain the Token for the Newton Abbot-Heathfield Section from the Auxiliary Token Instrument before the train leaves. The Firemen of Branch trains running to Platform No. 9 must restore the Token to the Auxiliary Token Instrument immediately upon arrival.

In the case of Auto trains, the Driver will be held responsible for making arrangements for the Fireman to leave the footplate to perform the above duties.

The Auxiliary Token Instruments must be worked in accordance with the Standard Instructions shown in the Book of Train Signalling Regulations and General Appendix to the Rule Book.

Telephone communication exists between the Auxiliary Instruments and Newton Abbot East Signal Box.

A Token can be placed in the Auxiliary Instruments at any time but one can only be withdrawn by co-operation between the Newton Abbot East and Heathfield Signalmen.

The Firemen of Branch trains running to the Down Through, Main and Relief lines at Newton Abbot East must place the Token on the "Setting Down" post applicable to those lines.

42[illegible] G.W.R.

TO

Newton Abbot

Page 24.—TEMPORARY RESTRICTIONS OF SPEED ON BRANCH LINES.

The instructions under this heading to be deleted.

Page 26.—GROUND FRAMES AND INTERMEDIATE SIDINGS.

Name of Station or Siding.	Where situated.	By whom attended.	How Locked.	Remarks
Amend:—				
Granite Siding	Between Heathfield and Bovey	Guard	Key on Token	
Pottery Siding.	Between Heathfield and Bovey	Guard	Key on Token	

Pages 30 and 31.—SINGLE LINES AND HOW WORKED.

Between	Method of working the Single Line.	Where Staff, Token or Tablet kept.	Person responsible for exchanging.	Person responsible when aforesaid man is not on duty.	Remarks.
Amend:—					
Heathfield/ Bovey	Electric Token	Signal Box	Signalman	...	

LIST OF SIGNAL BOXES—continued. C63

Distance Box to Box		NAME OF BOX	TIMES DURING WHICH BOXES ARE OPEN					Whether provided with Switch
			Week Days			Sundays		
			Opened		Closed at	Opened at	Closed at	
M.	C.		Mondays	Other Days				
—	—	Newton Abbot (East)	—	Continuously.		—	—	—
3	45	Heathfield	6.35 a.m.	6.35 a.m.	Until last train has cleared.	—	—	No.
2	18	Bovey	6.35 a.m.	6.35 a.m.	Until last train has cleared.			
6	14	Moretonhampstead	6.50 a.m.	6.50 a.m.	Until last train has cleared.			

C66

ENGINE LOADS FOR PASSENGER, PARCELS, MILK, AND FISH TRAINS FOR ENGINE WORKING PURPOSES—continued.

Branch Lines.

SECTION		CLASS OF ENGINE				
			B.R. Standard Class 7 (70XXX)	B.R. Standard Class 5 (73XXX)	B.R. Standard Class 4 (75XXX and 76XXX) 78XX	B.R. Standard Class 3 (2-6-2T) (82XXX)
			10XX	4056 4061 4062	43XX, 53XX, 63XX, 73XX	45XX, 55XX
		60XX	4000, 4037, 4073—4099, 5000—5099, 70XX	49XX, 59XX, 69XX, 79XX	31XX, 41XX, 51XX, 61XX, 81XX	36XX, 37XX, 46XX, 57XX, 77XX, 87XX, 96XX, 97XX
				68XX	56XX, 66XX	84XX, 94XX
From	To	Tons	Tons	Tons	Tons	Tons
Newton Abbot	**Bovey**	—	—	—	300 V	250
Bovey	**Moretonhampstead** ..	—	—	—	—	220
Moretonhampstead ..	**Bovey**	—	—	—	—	280
Bovey	**Newton Abbot**	—	—	—	280 V	280

C67

ENGINE LOADS FOR PASSENGER, PARCELS, MILK, AND FISH TRAINS FOR ENGINE WORKING PURPOSES—continued.

SECTION		CLASS OF ENGINE				
Branch Lines.		22XX 32XX	90XX 0-6-0 and 0-6-0T	S.R.—M.7	0-4-2T 14XX 58XX	
		0-6-2T "B" Group	0-6-2T "**A**" Group			
From	To	Tons	Tons	Tons	Tons	
Newton Abbot	**Bovey**	220**Z**	220		140	—
Bovey	**Moretonhampstead**	—	200		130	—
Moretonhampstead	**Bovey**	—	250		160	—
Bovey	**Newton Abbot**	200**Z**	250		150	—

V—Loads specially agreed for 41, 51, 43, 53, 63, 73, and 78XX Class engines between Exeter and Newton Abbot, via Heathfield, in connection with Diversion of Trains emergency working.

Z—Loads specially agreed for 2251—2299 Class Engines between Exeter and Newton Abbot, via Heathfield, in connection with Diversion of Trains Emergency Working.

LOADS FOR RAIL MOTOR ENGINES

The tonnage loads shewn in the "Standard Loads Table" do not apply when Rail Motor Services are being worked by engines of the 14XX, 54XX and 64XX classes, the authorised loads for which are specially laid down separately, in accordance with instructions shewn in the General Appendix, viz. :

Gradient	Rail Motors 0-4-2T	Rail Motors 0-6-0T
	Tons	Tons
1 in 40	72	90
1 in 50	96	120
1 in 60	120	150
1 in 80	144	180
1 in 100	168	210

C72 SPEED OF TRAINS THROUGH JUNCTIONS, ETC.—cont.

NAME OF PLACE	DIRECTION OF TRAIN From	DIRECTION OF TRAIN To	Miles per Hour
Moretonhampstead Branch—The speed of all Up and Down Trains between Newton Abbot and Moretonhampstead must not exceed 40 miles per hour and must be further restricted to a lower speed as shewn below :			
Newton Abbot East	Moretonhampstead Branch	Main or Through Lines	15
Newton Abbot East	Main Line	Moretonhampstead Branch	15
Heathfield (0 m.p. and 30ch.)	Moretonhampstead Branch	Teign Valley Branch	15
Heathfield (0 m.p. and 30ch.)	Teign Valley Branch	Moretonhampstead Branch	15
Heathfield	All Up and Down Trains leaving Station Loop		15
Bovey	All Down Trains entering Up Station Loop		15
	All Up and Down Trains leaving Station Loop		15
Between Bovey and Moretonhampstead	All Up and Down Trains over curves between 7m. 0ch. and 9m. 30ch.		35

MORETONHAMPSTEAD BRANCH

Lighting of Level Crossing Gates

Unless instructions are issued to the contrary, the lamps on the gates will not be lighted from the 15th March until the 30th September, inclusive except during fog or falling snow.

Advice of Running

Stations Heathfield to Moretonhampstead and vice versa, must advise by telephone, the stations in advance the departure time of each train.

MORETONHAMPSTEAD

No vehicle must be detached and allowed to remain on the Main Line.

LUSTLEIGH

Shunting

Work at this Siding can only be performed by Up trains and any traffic on Down Freight trains must be taken through to Moretonhampstead and returned.

Before the engine of a Freight train performing work is detached from the train, the Guard must apply sufficient brakes and sprags on the leading wagons left on the Main Line.

Six sprags must be kept at the side of the line between the platform and the facing points.

GRANITE SIDING BETWEEN HEATHFIELD AND BOVEY

Work at the Siding can only be performed by Up trains, and any traffic on Down Freight trains must be taken through to Bovey and returned.

The points are controlled by a ground frame, locked by key on the Train Staff.

A wheel-stop is provided at the Siding, and kept padlocked across the rail.

After work has been completed at the Siding, the Guard will be responsible for padlocking the wheel-stop across the rail and locking the Siding gate.

HEATHFIELD

Truck Weighbridge Relief Line

The weighbridge is situated in the Up Refuge Siding and has a weighing capacity up to 30 tons.

Engines must not be allowed to pass over the weighing line.

Except when it is necessary to weigh traffic, the lever controlling the points for the weighing line must be kept padlocked in its normal position and the key kept in the Weighbridge House.

Immediately the Shunter in charge has completed weighing, the points must be reset in their normal position for the Refuge Siding.

The person in charge must satisfy himself from time to time that the instructions are being strictly observed.

Shunting

When it is necessary to use the Teign Valley Branch Line for shunting purposes, the engine or a brake-van with a man riding in it, must be at the Chudleigh end of the wagons.

Messrs. Candy & Company's Siding

The Siding falls towards the Main Line, and care must be exercised in shunting. After shunting has been completed, wagons left on the Siding must have a sufficient number of hand-brakes securely applied and sprags used as necessary.

Three sprags must be kept 10 yards apart on the incline.

Stover Siding

Whenever it is necessary for vehicles to be shunted into or out of the Siding through the connection at the Newton Abbot end, the work must be conducted in accordance with Electric Token Regulation 13.

Also see Table F.

TEIGNBRIDGE SIDINGS

Shunting

The Siding on the Up side of the line will accommodate 20 wagons and the Siding on the Down side 30 wagons, and they are connected with the Main Line from both ends. The points are worked from three ground frames controlled by key on the Electric Token.

It is permissible for a road vehicle to draw a maximum of 15 wagons by tow rope in the Up Siding and by the same means a maximum of 16 wagons in the Down Siding ; such working to be carried out in strict compliance with the Standard Instructions relating to the towing of vehicles.

The Crossing Keeper must prepare a list of all wagons dealt with at the Siding, and forward it to the Goods Agent at Newton Abbot.

The Crossing Keeper will be responsible for seeing that the Yard gates are kept closed after work has been completed in the Sidings.

Keys of the Crossing Keeper's Cabin are kept in Newton Abbot East and Heathfield Signal Boxes in case of emergency.

Also see tables F and S.2.

TABLE H.1

WORKING OF FREIGHT VEHICLES WITHOUT A BRAKE VAN IN REAR

Set out below is a list of places where freight vehicles (in accordance with Rule 153/(b)) may be worked without a Brake Van in rear.

One wagon of coal or stores for signal-boxes and stations, or the empty wagon in connection therewith, may be worked without a Brake Van between any two signal-boxes, provided the signal-boxes concerned are not more than one mile apart.

From	To	Line	No. of vehicles and special conditions
Stover Siding	Heathfield	Single	May be propelled when a man must ride in or walk alongside leading vehicle. Must not exceed 25 wagons and speed must not exceed 4 m.p.h.

TABLE A (*Contd.*)

Description of Block Signalling on Principal Running Lines (Dots indicate Block Posts)	Stations, Signal Boxes, etc.	Distance from Signal Box next above		Running Lines			Loops and Refuge Sidings		Runaway Catch Points, Spring or unworked trailing points		Engine Whistles L—long s=short c=crow				Remarks
											DOWN		UP		
		M.	Yds.	Addit-tional UP	Principal	Addi-tional DOWN	Descrip-tion	Standage Wagons E. & V.	Position	Gradient (Rising unless otherwise shown) 1 in.	Main	Relief or Goods	Main	Relief or Goods	
	MORETONHAMPSTEAD BRANCH														
	NEWTON ABBOT EAST TO MORETONHAMPSTEAD														
Electric Token	Newton Abbot East	—	—		⋮										
	Heathfield	3	1052		⋮		CL URS	70 56							
One Engine in Steam	**Bovey**	—	—		⋮	A									
	Lustleigh	—	—		⋮										
	Moretonhampstead ..	—	—		⋮										

4622 2nd · SINGLE SINGLE · 2nd 4622

Lustleigh to

Lustleigh Lustleigh

Moretonhampstead Moretonhampstead

MORETONHAMPSTEAD

(W 8d FARE 8d (W)

For conditions see over For conditions see over

2031 2nd · SINGLE SINGLE · 2nd 2031

Newton Abbot to

Newton Abbot Newton Abbot

S.2 S.2

Kingskerswell Kingskerswell

or Teigngrace Halt or Teigngrace Halt

KINGSKERSWELL or TEIGNGRACE H'LT

(W) 6d. FARE 6d. (W)

For conditions see over For conditions see over

339 2nd · SINGLE SINGLE · 2nd 339

Moretonhampstead to

Moretonhampstead Moretonhampstead

Lustleigh Lustleigh

LUSTLEIGH

(W) 8d. FARE 8d. (W)

ForConditions see over ForConditions see over

TABLE J.1 (*continued*)

Incline between	Length of Incline about	Gradient 1 in	Falling towards	Modifications of, or additions to, the General Instructions for working inclines.
			MORETONHAMPSTEAD BRANCH	
Lustleigh and Moretonhampstead	23 chains	82	Lustleigh	
" " " ..	38 chains	83	"	
" " " ..	29 chains	75	"	
" " " ..	13 chains	87	"	
" " " ..	1 m. 59 ch.	49	"	
Bovey and Lustleigh	28 chains	50	Bovey	
" " "	28 chains	61	"	
" " "	17 chains	53	"	
" " "	29 chains	67	"	
" " "	½ mile	66	"	
" " "	31 chains	61	"	
Heathfield and Bovey	29 chains	66	"	
" " "	22 chains	53	Heathfield	
" " "	13 chains	69	"	
" " "	9 chains	72	Bovey	
" " "	25 chains	69	Heathfield	
Teigngrace and Heathfield ..	17 chains	172	Teigngrace	
" " " ..	26 chains	70	"	
" " " ..	21 chains	98	"	
Newton Abbot and Teigngrace ..	13 chains	100	Newton Abbot ..	
" " " ..	12 chains	100	Teigngrace	
" " " ..	10 chains	100	Newton Abbot ..	
" " " ..	16 chains	132	Teigngrace	

TABLE P

LEVEL CROSSING GATES—OPENING AND CLOSING BY TRAINMEN

The following is a list of level crossings where, in the absence of a crossing keeper, the gates must be opened and closed by the trainmen.

Trains must be brought to a stand well clear of the gates, after which the gates must be unlocked and opened and then locked against road traffic by the Fireman for the passage of the train over the crossing. When the train has passed over the crossing, the Guard (or Fireman in the case of a light engine) must close the gates across the railway and re-lock them, the Driver taking care not to proceed on his journey until he has received an "All Right" signal from the Guard. Enginemen and Guards concerned must see that they are supplied with keys of the gates.

Any defects in the gates or the locks securing them or in the lamps must be reported immediately by the Guard or Fireman to the Station Master concerned.

M. C.	Name of Crossing	Situated at, or between	Remarks
1 50¾	Teignbridge	Newton Abbot and Heathfield	Gates to be operated by trainmen of engineering special trains and other trains not conveying passengers, run outside the scheduled hours of Branch working.
6 0	Bovey	Bovey	

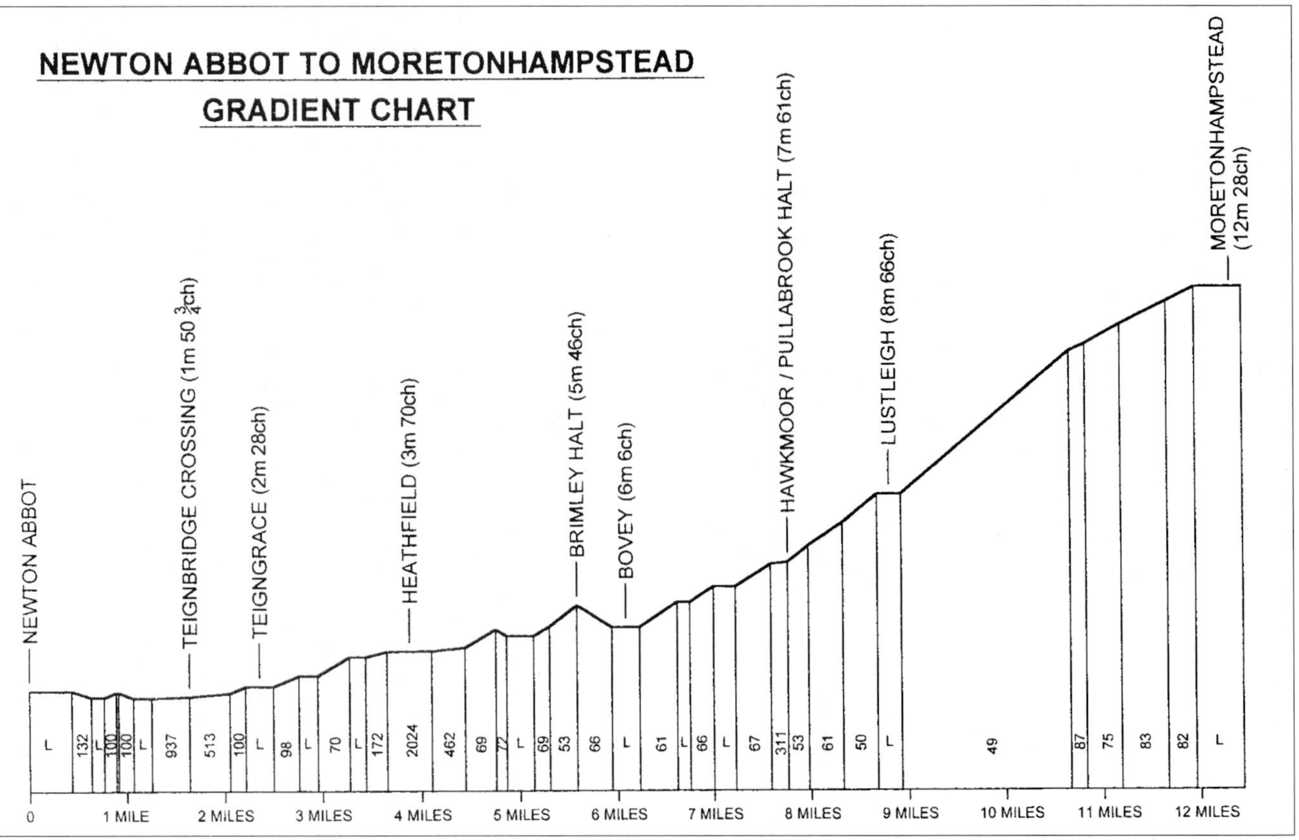
NEWTON ABBOT TO MORETONHAMPSTEAD
GRADIENT CHART
NEWTON ABBOT
TEIGNBRIDGE CROSSING (1m 50 $\frac{3}{4}$ch)
TEIGNGRACE (2m 28ch)
HEATHFIELD (3m 70ch)
BRIMLEY HALT (5m 46ch)
BOVEY (6m 6ch)
HAWKMOOR / PULLABROOK HALT (7m 61ch)
LUSTLEIGH (8m 66ch)
MORETONHAMPSTEAD
(12m 28ch)
L
132
L
100
100
L
937
513
100
L
98
L
70
L
172
2024
462
69
72
L
69
53
66
L
61
L
66
L
67
311
53
61
50
L
49
87
75
83
82
L
0
1 MILE
2 MILES
3 MILES
4 MILES
5 MILES
6 MILES
7 MILES
8 MILES
9 MILES
10 MILES
11 MILES
12 MILES

Signalling/Signal Boxes

When the Moretonhampstead branch opened in 1866 the interlocking of points and signals was still regarded as something for main line junctions only. Thus Colonel Yolland, who inspected the line immediately beforehand, raised no objections against the fact that the branch stations had only unconnected individual levers for the points and signals, except for requiring the starting signals for the passenger and goods lines at Moretonhampstead to be interlocked with each other (see report, Appendix III). At the same time he also insisted on the interlocking of 'Moretonhampstead Junction' in place of the temporary junction arrangements then in existence, and a signal cabin duly opened there in September 1866, albeit only with 'wire-locking' rather than full interlocking. It was replaced by a fully interlocked box, Newton 'C', in 1876.

The first intermediate sidings – Granite Siding and Pottery Siding – had point levers locked by a key carried by the goods' guards, and no signals. However, expectations had increased a little by the time that Teigngrace Siding (1872), Sanduck Wood Siding (1873) and Chudleigh Road Siding (1874) were opened. The point levers were again locked by key, but there was also one signal (in the direction of the facing points) which was wire-locked to give proof that the points were normal. Colonel Rich, inspecting Chudleigh Road, found the idea of this objectionable, because the signal could be put back to danger after the train passed it, and the points could then be moved. (This was true of *all* signals, but the signals here were a long way from the points.) He did not, however, enforce any alteration.

The original 1866 signals on the branch would all have been disc-and-crossbars as per SDR practice, but no photographs are known to exist of these and written/map evidence as to their positions is fragmentary. The SDR changed to semaphores for new works c.1873, and some signals on the branch were, no doubt, renewed as semaphores after this: it is not known whether any disc-and-crossbars lasted until 1892. In most respects the branch, like the rest of the GWR system west of Exeter, remained an '1860s railway' through the 1880s, there being no point in modernising these lines when the change of gauge was pending. It did, however, gain one interlocked signal box – at Heathfield (1882). This was built by the Teign Valley Railway Company and was originally intended to control the TVR lines only, but at a late stage it was decided it should control the broad-gauge line as well – a rather pointless exercise, but the Board of Trade was at the peak of its demands for excessive signalling on minor lines by this date. The signals here were all semaphores.

The branch's signalling was thoroughly modernised in 1892-4 (along with all other lines west of Exeter). The new installations comprised:–

Newton Abbot East SB	–	1876 box (renamed) extended, with new 51-lever frame; full resignalling of station.

Teignbridge Siding GF	–	(New siding opened 1893.) 4-lever covered ground frame, released by key on Staff, no signals.
Teignbridge Crossing Box	–	Crossing-keeper's hut with ground frame inside.
Teigngrace SB	–	New 11-lever signal box with full signalling (not a 'Block Post').
Heathfield SB	–	Full resignalling for new track layout, controlled from 1882 signal box plus a new 3-lever 'Heathfield Ground Frame Box' (released from the SB, and necessary because of point distances and insufficient levers in the SB).
Granite Siding GF	–	2-lever covered ground frame, released by key on Staff, no signals.
Pottery Siding GF	–	Ditto.
Bovey GF	–	Crossing hut with 1-lever frame, released from the SB.
Bovey SB	–	New 17-lever signal box.
Lustleigh SB	–	New 13-lever signal box with full signalling (not a 'Block Post').
Moretonhampstead SB	–	New 15-lever signal box.

All this work was, of course, carried out using standard GWR semaphore signals. Apart from the provision of full signalling at Teigngrace and Lustleigh (a superfluity still often indulged in at this date), the work was done with reasonable economy, the boxes being of the smallest possible size and built of timber with the exception of the lean-to construction at Moretonhampstead. Diagrams of all the stations in their late 19th century form can be found on pages 270 to 276.

Full information on subsequent changes to the branch's signalling installations is given in the tabulation, and only the more important of them need to be noted here. The never-necessary signals and signal boxes at Teigngrace and Lustleigh were abolished at an early date, with ground frames installed in lieu. In contrast, the branch gained an additional signal box – Newton Abbot Goods Yard – in 1911. (This, too, was of dubious necessity, and it only lasted until 1926.) The major 20th century works on the line were the resignallings of Heathfield for new layouts in 1916 (new signal box), 1927 (new frame in 1916 box) and 1943. There was also a resignalling at Moretonhampstead in 1920 (new frame in 1894 box), and work at Bovey for reversible use of the 'up' platform in 1927.

Single Line Working/Operating

Telegraph/Block Telegraph (without Staff) (1866 – 1889)

In accordance with standard SDR practice, the Moretonhampstead branch was originally worked by Telegraph, without a Train Staff. That is to say, the station clerks at Newton, Bovey and Moretonhampstead used the telegraph instruments in the booking offices to send 'Is Line Clear' (etc) messages to the next station. The Board of Trade did not like this system, preferring that drivers should always carry a Train Staff as evidence of the line being clear, so when the M & SDR sent their 'Undertaking' to the Board of Trade in June 1866 it stated that the line would be worked One Engine in Steam Newton to Bovey and One Engine in Steam Bovey to Moretonhampstead. This was an illogical way of describing the system, but the SDR had learnt that this was the best way to placate the civil servants whilst continuing to do things its own way.

At first the 'block' working (as we would call it) had to be done on the ordinary telegraph instruments that were also used for railway and other messages, with the words being spelt out. But this system was producing hopeless congestion on the wires, and in 1867 the SDR began introducing separate 'Block Instruments' for train signalling, which also had the advantage of giving a continuous record of the state of the line. At an unknown date these were introduced on the branch, still in the booking offices at first. (The Newton instruments would have been transferred to the new 'Newton C' signal box in 1876, and those at Bovey were transferred to the new signal box in 1893.)

Bovey was necessarily a 'Block Post' because it had a loop and trains could 'cross' there, though no trains were actually booked to cross there in the first years, and the platform on the second (later 'down') line was sub-standard. (When Colonel Yolland said that Bovey was "ultimately intended for a passing place" he probably meant that the SDR anticipated having two *passenger* trains cross there at a future date.) In 1875 the branch goods train (then Newton – Bovey only), which had hitherto run in the evening after the passenger service had ended for the day, was retimed to run in the afternoon, which meant having two trains on the branch at the same time. The goods spent half an hour shunting at Bovey, during which time the 5.33 p.m. passenger left Newton; as soon as this train arrived at Bovey, the goods departed back to Newton. In 1882 the goods was extended to Moretonhampstead, leaving Newton at 2.55 p.m., and 'crossing' the 5.33 p.m. passenger at Bovey on its return journey. Because there was no interlocking, the two lines at Bovey could be used as necessary; obviously passenger trains used the main platform line in normal circumstances, in both directions. The first booked crossings of two passenger trains were in 1891, *before* the second platform was extended. When Bovey was interlocked (and the second platform extended) in 1893, the two lines became unidirectional 'down' and 'up'. (In 1927 the 'up' platform was, as noted above, made reversible, for passenger and platform staff convenience.)

Lustleigh, and the additional stations at Teigngrace (1867) and Chudleigh

Road/Heathfield (1874), were not 'Block Posts' originally. It is uncertain whether Heathfield functioned as a 'Block Post' on the Moretonhampstead branch after the signal box opened in 1882; probably not, until 1893.

Train Staff & Ticket (1889 – 1901)

By the late 1880s the GWR was unable to hold out any longer against the Board of Trade's dislike of its operating methods west of Exeter. On 25th March 1889 'Train Staff & Ticket' working was brought into use on the branch (the same day as on the Ashburton branch and Lydford – Launceston). The 'Block' working continued as before, but all drivers now had to carry the (wooden) 'Staff', or take a paper 'Ticket' after being shown the Staff, as well. The GWR sent a new 'Undertaking' to the Board of Trade, duly noting that the new working method would be the 'Train Staff and Ticket system in conjunction with the Block Telegraph'. The Staff sections in 1889 were:–

Newton Abbot East – Bovey (Square Staff, red Tickets)

Bovey – Moretonhampstead (Round Staff, blue Tickets)

However, in June 1893 Heathfield was made a Staff station, the new sections being:–

Newton Abbot East – Heathfield (Square Staff, red Tickets)

Heathfield – Bovey (Semicircular Staff, blue Tickets)

Bovey – Moretonhampstead (Round Staff, green Tickets)

A prime motivation in making Heathfield a 'Block Post' and Staff station was that, with the change of gauge, trains could now be run through to/from the Teign Valley line, but only if the junction was a Staff station. (In the event only occasional specials ran through until a daily Newton Abbot – Trusham goods was introduced in 1907, and a running connection to the Teign Valley was not put in until 1916.) Heathfield also had a 'loop siding' on the Moretonhampstead branch in the new 1893 layout, where a goods train could be put out of the way for a passenger train to cross or pass. This facility was made use of immediately in the branch goods' timings. (Not until 1927 did it become possible to cross two Moretonhampstead *passenger* trains at Heathfield.)

Electric Train Staff (1901 – 1940s)

The Train Staff & Ticket system could be inflexible and also meant that only trains carrying the Staff could work the ground frames at intermediate sidings. By the turn of the century the GWR was installing the Electric Train Staff instead on all the busier single line branches. Under this system the (metal) Staffs could be issued as and when required from the electrically-controlled machines at either end of the section. It was brought into use on the Moretonhampstead branch on 14th November 1901, with the same three sections as before. The estimated cost was £493.

When Newton Abbot Goods Yard SB opened in 1911, the number of ETS sections increased to four (Newton Abbot East – Newton Abbot Goods Yard – Heathfield – Bovey – Moretonhampstead). However, because Newton

Abbot Goods Yard box was not open all day, it was also necessary to have 'Long Section' working Newton Abbot East – Heathfield when Goods Yard was shut. This was done using Tyer's Tablet (which was often used by the GWR for this purpose). When Goods Yard box was abolished in 1926, the situation reverted to a simple three sections as 1901 – 1911.

Passenger trains were regularly crossed at Heathfield after the 1927 changes there, and this continued until 1959 (as did passenger train crossings at Bovey).

Key Token (1943 – 1965)

The (Electric) Key Token system, which had been developed by the GWR themselves, worked on the same principles as the Electric Train Staff system, but the 'Token' was much smaller and therefore more manageable for exchanging. It gradually replaced the ETS as renewals became necessary. On the Moretonhampstead branch the first section to go over to Key Token was Newton Abbot East – Heathfield on 25th July 1943. The other two sections were converted subsequently.

The Key Token system facilitated the provision of 'Auxiliary' instruments where drivers could receive or deposit a Token at places more operationally convenient than the signal box itself. The Auxiliary instruments were 'released' by the signalman. One was brought into use at Heathfield 'Up Advanced Starting' signal in 1943, and two at Newton Abbot – on platforms 5 and 9 – on 29th April 1946, for use by the branch passenger trains.

Working after 1959

New methods of working were brought into use north of Heathfield immediately the passenger service ended, on 2nd March 1959. The Key Token working was withdrawn, and Bovey and Moretonhampstead signal boxes were abolished. A wooden Train Staff for 'One Engine in Steam' working Heathfield – Moretonhampstead was introduced, and small ground frames released by the Staff were installed at Bovey and Moretonhampstead to work the points formerly worked by the signal boxes. The Staff became 'Heathfield – Bovey' in 1964, when the line beyond Bovey was closed.

Newton Abbot East – Heathfield remained Key Token until Heathfield box closed in October 1965. It was then converted to telephone working under the control of the Newton Abbot East signalman. The person-in-charge at Heathfield had to confirm by telephone that a train had arrived complete. At the same time the Heathfield layout was converted to hand points, and three illuminated 'Stop Boards' were installed on the approaches to the station. The Heathfield – Bovey section was changed to 'C2' working under the control of the person-in-charge at Heathfield (this was a standard Western Region system of the time, for working without a Train Staff).

Heathfield – Bovey closed in 1970 (the remaining section of the Teign Valley line had closed in 1968), stop blocks were erected north of the Gulf Oil sidings, the last station employee at Heathfield was withdrawn and the residue of the branch became a single section of 'C2' working under the control of the Newton Abbot East signalman.

Signal Box Register

(Includes ground frames existing in the 1893 – 1959 period, but not the individual levers existing in the broad-gauge period, or the small open ground frames installed after passenger closure.)

Moretonhampstead Junction	–	(First box at this location.) Hut with wire-locking. Opened September 1866, closed 1876.
Newton 'C' (Later renamed Newton Abbot East)	–	(Second box at this location.) Saxby & Farmer Type 4 box built for SDR. Opened 1876, closed 25.4.1926. Box extended to 34 feet length 1893. First frame S & F Rocker. Second frame (1893) GWR, design n/k, 51 levers. Third frame (7.5.1911) GWR VT3 bar, 73 levers.
Newton Abbot East	–	(Third box at this location.) Opened 25.4.1926, closed 2.5.1987 (area taken over by Exeter PSB). GWR Type 28c box, 79ft 8in x 14ft 2in x 14ft. GWR VT5 bar frame, 206 levers.
Newton Abbot Goods Yard	–	Opened 10.5.1911, closed 25.4.1926 (replaced by gf). Box design n/k. GWR Stud frame, 12 levers.
Newton Abbot Goods Yard GF	–	BIU (Brought into use) 25.4.1926, TOU (Taken out of use) 1972 (?) (connections TOU). 2-lever open (?) ground frame, released by Annett's Key kept at Newton Abbot East SB.
Clay Siding GF	–	BIU 21.4.1938, TOU date n/k (to hand points). 2-lever open ground frame, released by Annett's Key kept at Newton Abbot East SB.
Teignbridge Siding South GF	–	BIU 1.1914, TOU 10.1965 (to hand points). 2-lever covered ground frame, released by Key on ETS/KT.
Teignbridge Siding North GF	–	BIU 1.1914, TOU 10.1965 (to hand points). 2-lever covered ground frame, released by Key on ETS/KT.
Teignbridge Siding GF	–	BIU 1893, TOU 1.1914 (replaced by South and North GFs). 4-lever covered ground frame, released by Key on Staff/ETS.
Teignbridge Crossing Box	–	GWR Type 29 Hut, opened 1893 (?), closed 14.6.1965 (to hand points/Trainman-worked gates). Signals and gate bolt free, points (BIU 1913) released by Key on ETS/KT. First frame details n/k, second frame (1913) GWR Class 6 4", 6 levers.
Teigngrace	–	Opened 1893, closed 1921 (?). GWR Type 21 (?) box. Frame design n/k, 11 levers. Not a 'Block Post'. (Replaced by ground frame.)
Teigngrace GF	–	BIU 1921 (?), TOU date n/k. 2-lever covered (later open) ground frame, released by Key on ETS/KT.

Heathfield Timber Siding South GF – BIU 1917, TOU 10.1965 (to hand points). 2-lever covered ground frame, released by Key on ETS/KT. ('Heathfield Timber Siding GF' from 1927.)

Heathfield Timber Siding North GF – BIU 1916, TOU 1927 (connections directly worked from SB from 1927). 4-lever covered ground frame, released by Annett's Key held at Heathfield SB.

Heathfield (First box) – Opened 10.1882, closed 1916. TVR design brick box. Frame design n/k, 25 levers. 'Block Post' on TVR line from opening, uncertain whether 'Block Post' on Moretonhampstead line pre-1893.

Heathfield Ground Frame Box – Opened 1893, closed 1916 (connections worked from new SB from 1916). Box design n/k, frame design n/k, 3 levers. Released from SB. Not a 'Block Post'.

Heathfield (Second box) – Opened 1916, closed 10.1965 (12.10.1965 per Weekly Notice, 18.10.1965 per Newton Abbot SM's book). GWR Type 7d box. First frame GWR VT3 bar, 42 levers. Second frame (1927) GWR VT5 bar, 58 levers.

Granite Siding GF – BIU 1893, TOU 9.1967. 2-lever covered gound frame, released by Key on Staff/ETS/KT/Staff.

Pottery Siding GF – BIU 1893, TOU 24.6.1956. 2-lever covered ground frame, released by Key on Staff/ETS/KT.

(Bovey Station was 'Block Post' 1866 – 1893.)

Bovey GF – GWR Type 29 Hut, opened 1893, closed 2.3.1959 (to trainman-worked gates). Released from SB. 1-lever frame.

Bovey – Opened 1893, closed 2.3.1959. GWR Type 26 box, 15ft x 8ft 6in x platform level. Frame GWR Double Twist, 17 levers, relocked Stud 1927.

Lustleigh – Opened 1894, closed date n/k. GWR Type 26 box, 15ft x 8ft 6in x platform level. Frame design n/k, 13 levers. Not a 'Block Post'. (Replaced by ground frame.)

Lustleigh GF – Opened date n/k, closed 6.4.1964. Covered ground frame, frame details n/k. Released by Key on ETS/KT/Staff.

(Moretonhampstead Station was 'Block Post' 1866 – 1894)

Moretonhampstead – Opened 1894, closed 2.3.1959. GWR non-standard brick box, 17ft 3in x 8ft x ground level. First frame design n/k, 15 levers. Second frame (1920) GWR Stud, 12 levers.

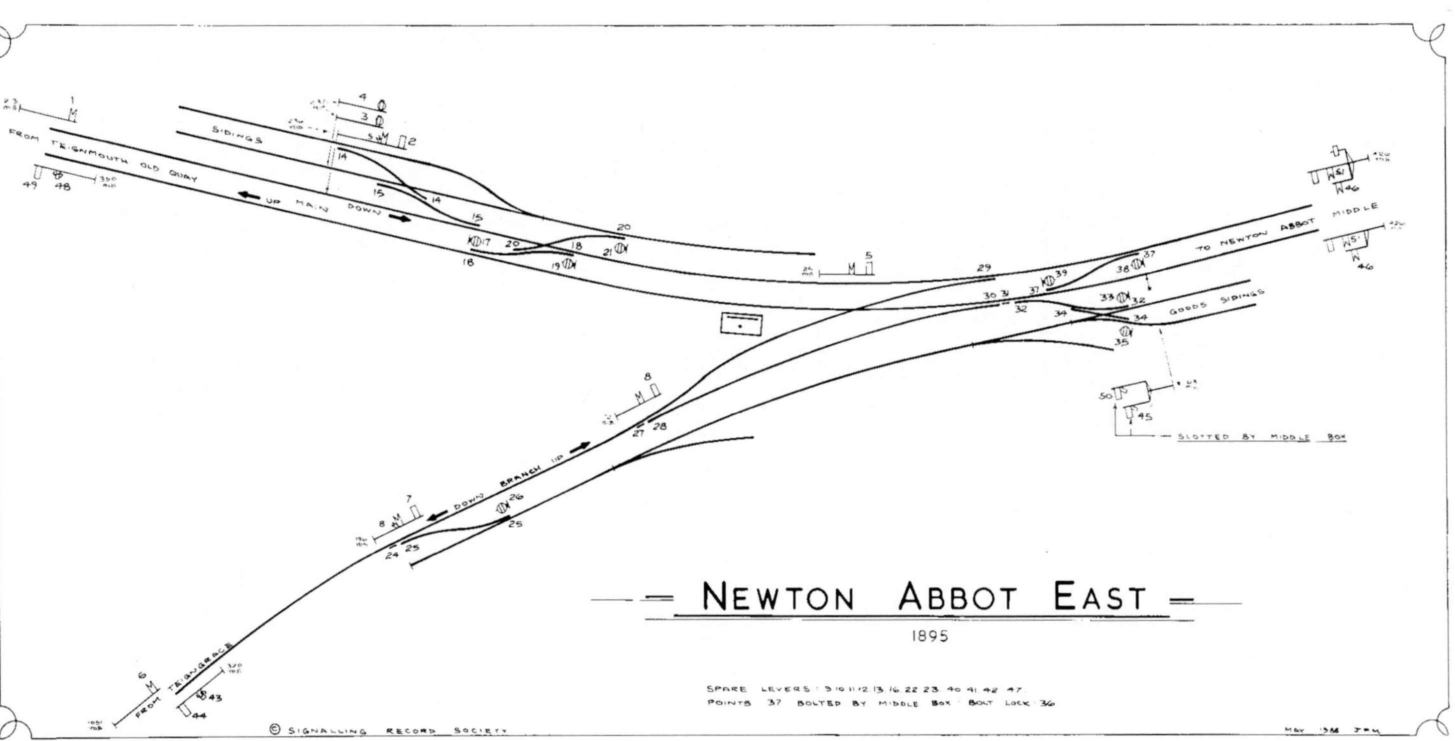
FROM TEIGNMOUTH OLD QUAY
SIDINGS
UP MAIN DOWN
TO NEWTON ABBOT MIDDLE
GOODS SIDINGS
SLOTTED BY MIDDLE BOX
DOWN BRANCH UP
FROM TEIGNGRACE
NEWTON ABBOT EAST
1895
SPARE LEVERS: 9 10 11 12 13 16 22 23 40 41 42 47.
POINTS 37 BOLTED BY MIDDLE BOX: BOLT LOCK 36
© SIGNALLING RECORD SOCIETY
MAY 1988 JPM

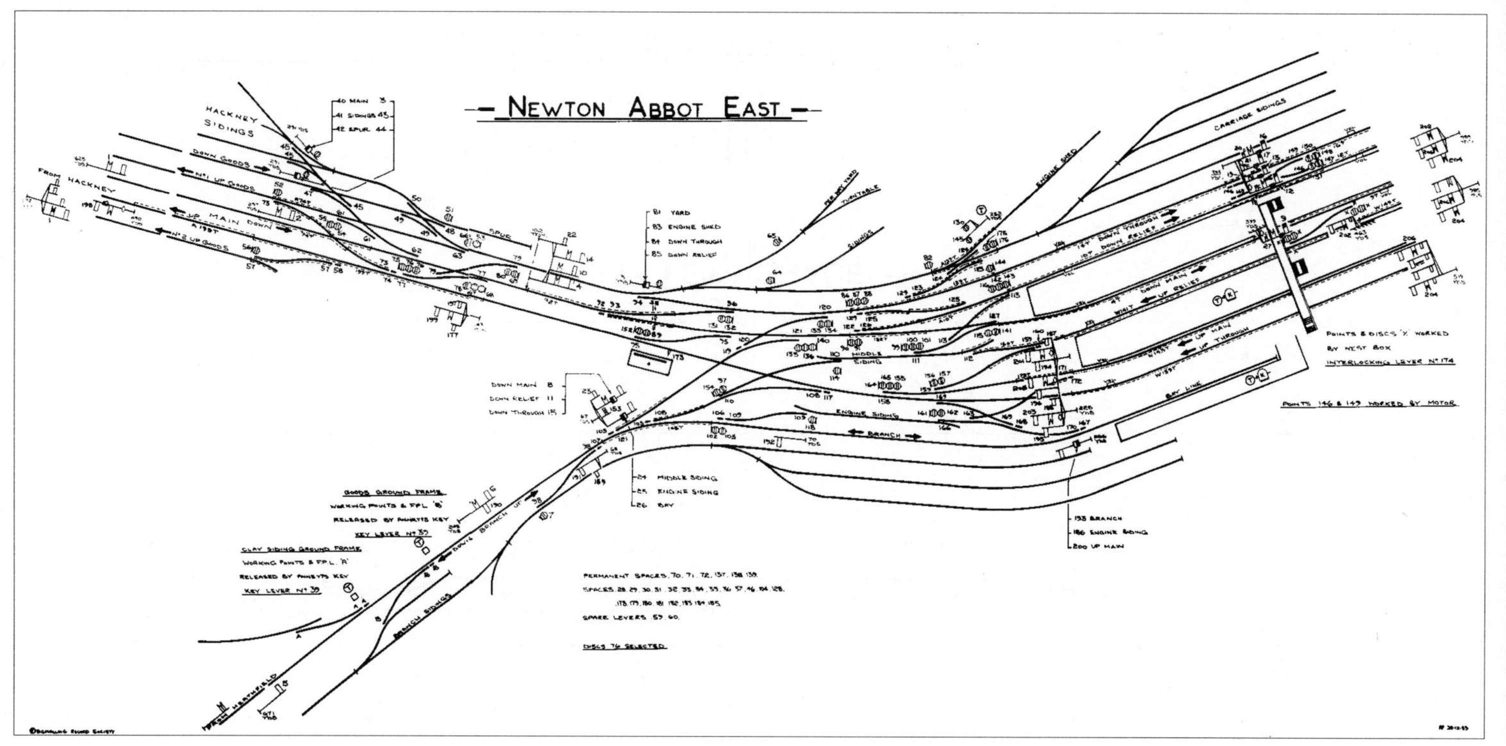

NEWTON ABBOT EAST
HACKNEY SIDINGS
FROM HACKNEY
DOWN GOODS
Nº1 UP GOODS
UP MAIN DOWN
Nº2 UP GOODS
SPUR
40 MAIN 3
41 SIDINGS 43
42 SPUR 44
81 YARD
83 ENGINE SHED
84 DOWN THROUGH
85 DOWN RELIEF
TURNTABLE
SIDINGS
ENGINE SHED
CARRIAGE SIDINGS
DOWN THROUGH
DOWN RELIEF
DOWN MAIN
UP RELIEF
UP MAIN
UP THROUGH
BAY LINE
MIDDLE SIDING
ENGINE SIDING
BRANCH
DOWN MAIN 8
DOWN RELIEF 11
DOWN THROUGH 15
24 MIDDLE SIDING
25 ENGINE SIDING
26 BAY
153 BRANCH
186 ENGINE SIDING
200 UP MAIN
POINTS & DISCS 'X' WORKED BY WEST BOX
INTERLOCKING LEVER Nº 174
POINTS 146 & 149 WORKED BY MOTOR
GOODS GROUND FRAME
WORKING POINTS & FPL 'B'
RELEASED BY ANNETTS KEY
KEY LEVER Nº 35
CLAY SIDING GROUND FRAME
WORKING POINTS & FPL 'A'
RELEASED BY ANNETTS KEY
KEY LEVER Nº 39
DOWN BRANCH UP
BRANCH SIDINGS
FROM HEATHFIELD
PERMANENT SPACES. 70. 71. 72. 137. 138. 139.
SPACES. 28. 29. 30. 31. 32. 33. 34. 35. 36. 37. 46. 104. 128.
178. 179. 180. 181. 182. 183. 184. 185.
SPARE LEVERS. 59. 60.
DISCS 76 SELECTED

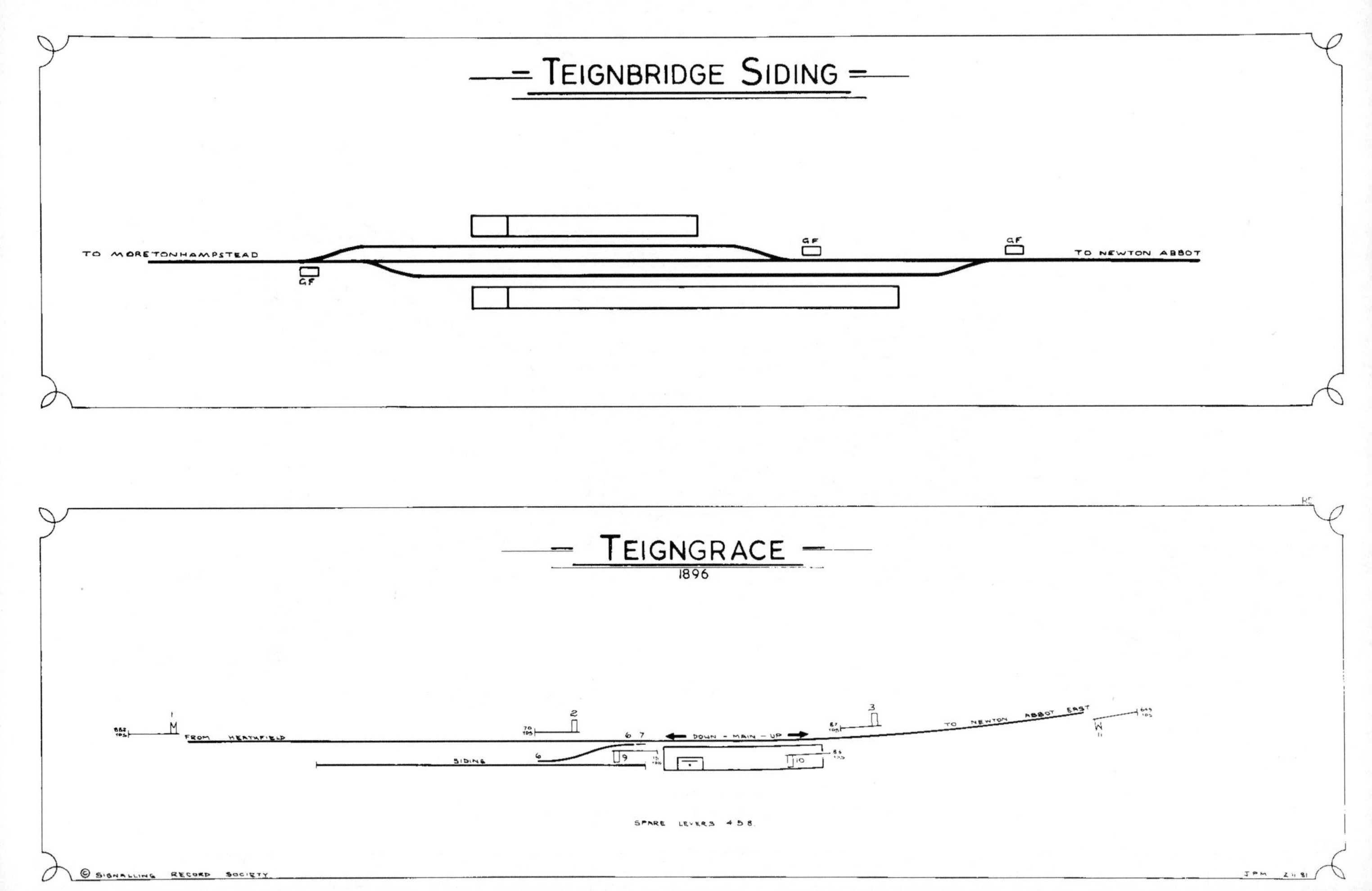
TEIGNBRIDGE SIDING
TO MORETONHAMPSTEAD
GF
GF
GF
TO NEWTON ABBOT
TEIGNGRACE
1896
FROM HEATHFIELD
SIDING
DOWN - MAIN - UP
TO NEWTON ABBOT EAST
1
2
3
6 7
6
9
10
SPARE LEVERS 4 5 8.
© SIGNALLING RECORD SOCIETY
JPM 2.11.81

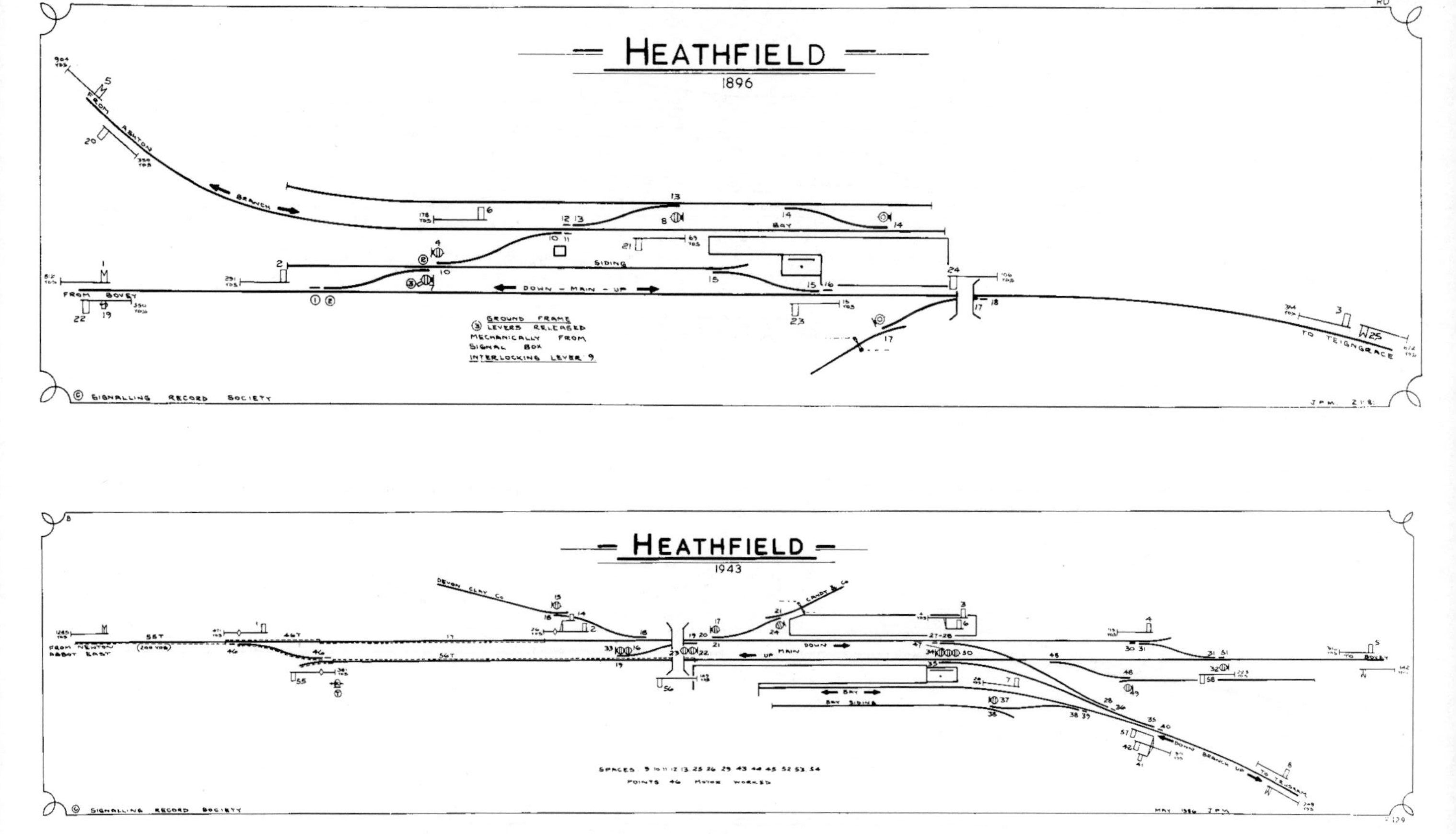

HEATHFIELD
1896
FROM ASHTON
BRANCH
FROM BOVEY
SIDING
BAY
DOWN - MAIN - UP
TO TEIGNGRACE
GROUND FRAME
LEVERS RELEASED
MECHANICALLY FROM
SIGNAL BOX
INTERLOCKING LEVER 9
© SIGNALLING RECORD SOCIETY
HEATHFIELD
1943
DEVON CLAY Co
CANDY & Co
FROM NEWTON ABBOT EAST
DOWN MAIN
UP
BAY
BAY SIDING
TO BOVEY
DOWN BRANCH UP
SPACES 9 10 11 12 13 25 26 29 43 44 45 52 53 54
POINTS 46 MOTOR WORKED
© SIGNALLING RECORD SOCIETY

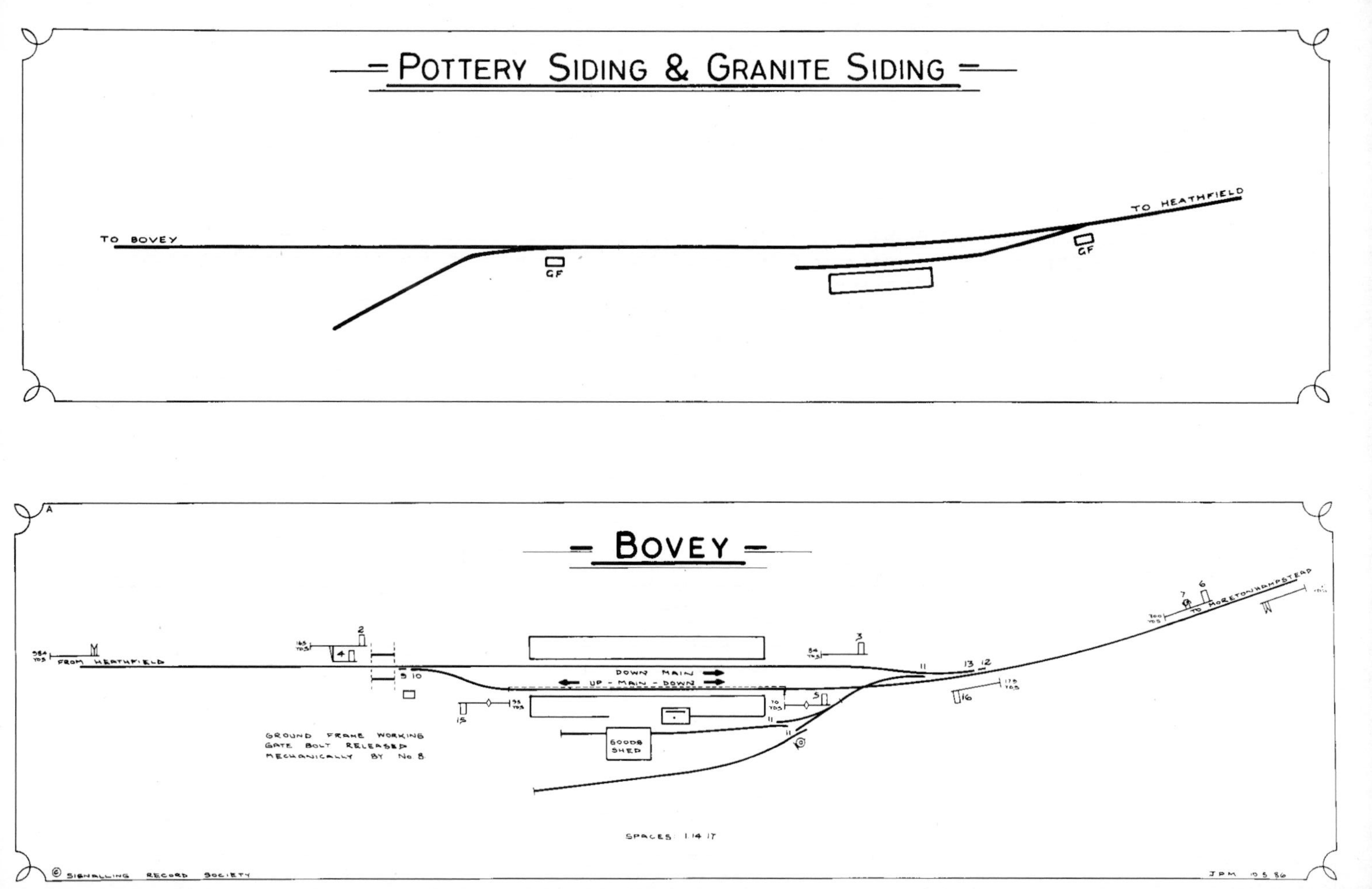
— POTTERY SIDING & GRANITE SIDING —
TO BOVEY
GF
GF
TO HEATHFIELD
— BOVEY —
A
384 YDS
FROM HEATHFIELD
165 YDS
2
4
9 10
15
93 YDS
DOWN MAIN
UP - MAIN - DOWN
GOODS SHED
84 YDS
3
70 YDS
5
11
11
11
10
13 12
16
175 YDS
300 YDS
7
6
TO MORETONHAMPSTEAD
GROUND FRAME WORKING
GATE BOLT RELEASED
MECHANICALLY BY No 8
SPACES 1 14 17
© SIGNALLING RECORD SOCIETY
JPM 10.5.86

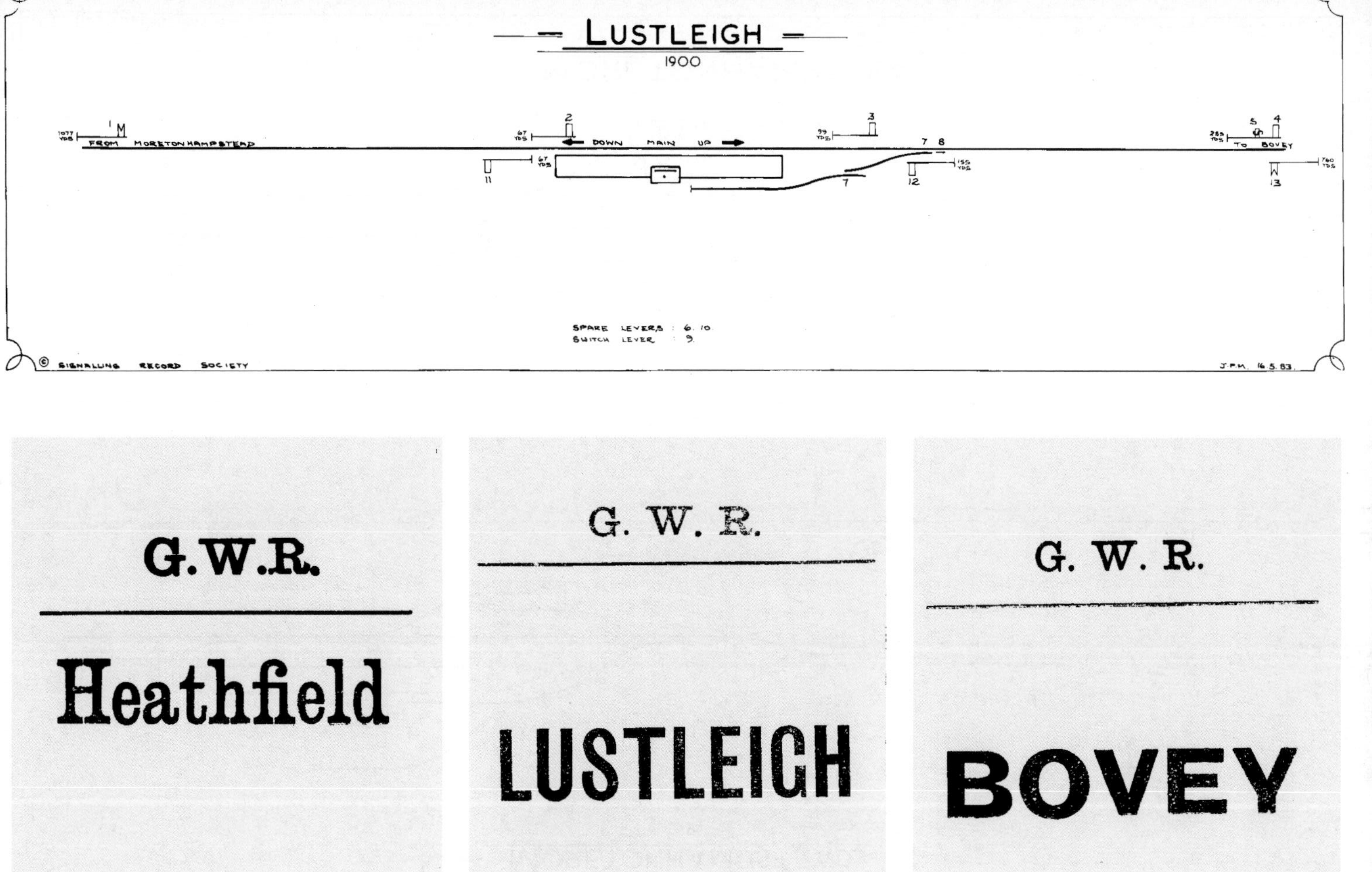
LUSTLEIGH
1900
1077 YDS
1
FROM MORETONHAMPSTEAD
67 YDS
2
DOWN MAIN UP
11
67 YDS
99 YDS
3
7
7 8
12
155 YDS
285 YDS
5 4
TO BOVEY
13
760 YDS
SPARE LEVERS : 6. 10.
SWITCH LEVER : 9.
© SIGNALLING RECORD SOCIETY
J.P.M. 16.5.83.
G.W.R.
Heathfield
G. W. R.
LUSTLEIGH
G. W. R.
BOVEY

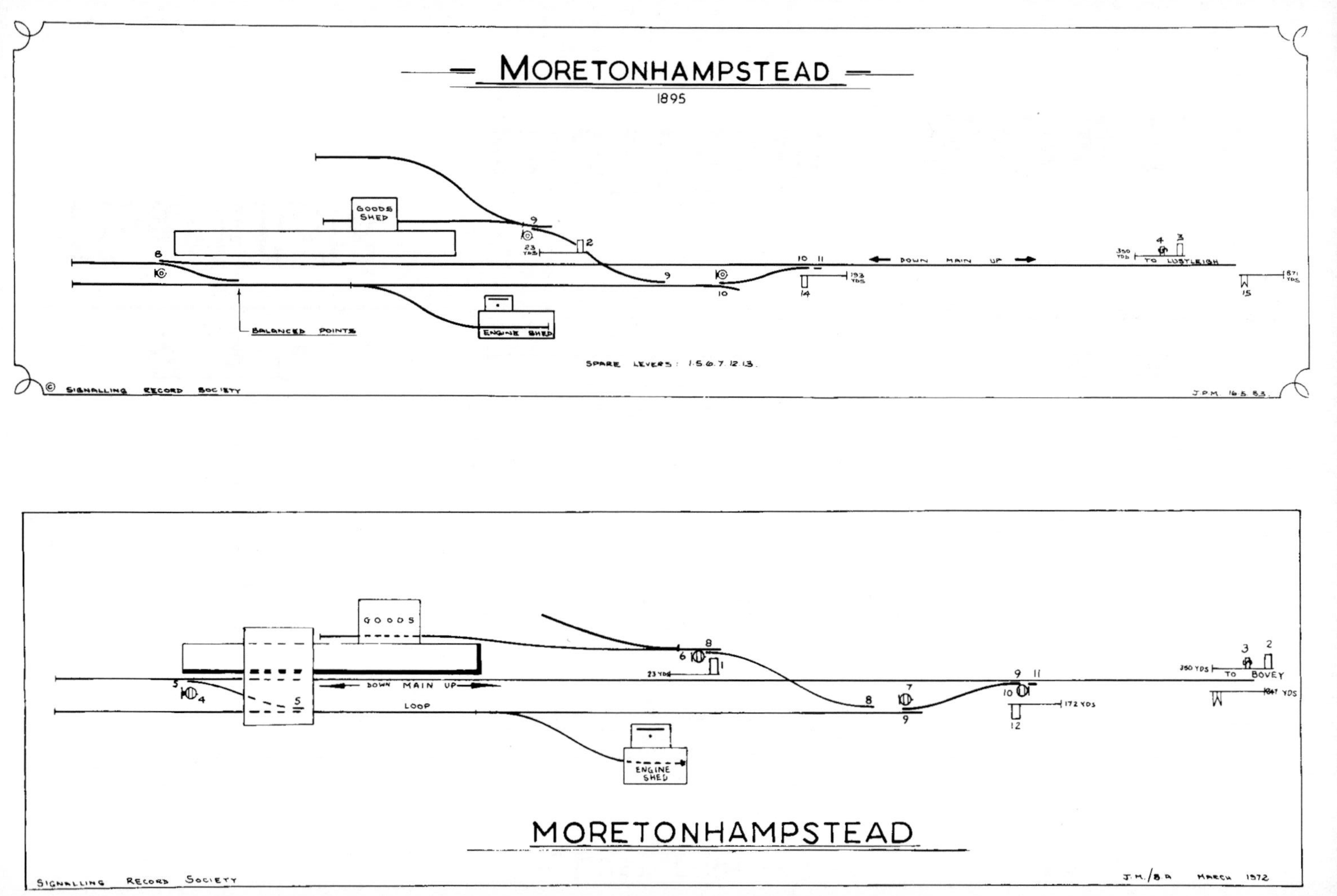

MORETONHAMPSTEAD
1895
GOODS SHED
23 YDS
350 YDS
TO LUSTLEIGH
DOWN MAIN UP
193 YDS
871 YDS
BALANCED POINTS
ENGINE SHED
SPARE LEVERS: 1.5.6.7.12.13.
© SIGNALLING RECORD SOCIETY
J.P.M. 16.5.83.
GOODS
DOWN MAIN UP
LOOP
23 YDS
ENGINE SHED
172 YDS
350 YDS
TO BOVEY
1047 YDS
MORETONHAMPSTEAD
SIGNALLING RECORD SOCIETY
J.M./B.A. MARCH 1972

THE MORETONHAMPSTEAD BRANCH – MEMORIES

Mr Wilf Wright of Truro:–

"Many a GWR branch line has been referred to as a 'family affair' in which everyone knew everyone else, and the hustle and bustle of the main line seemed a long way off. Less vigorous timekeeping, lighter trains and fewer signals all contributed to a comparatively leisured way of life, as exemplified by Cecil Torr in *Small Talk at Wreyland.* Referring to the station at Lustleigh, he states:–

> After the railway came, the trains proclaimed the hours, as most people knew the time-tables approximately, calling the 8.19 the 8, the 11.37 the 12, etc. – odd minutes did not count. As the trains upon this branch were 'mixed', partly passenger and partly goods, there generally was some shunting to be done; but this caused no delay, as the time-tables allowed for it. If there was no shunting, the train just waited at the station till the specified time was up. The driver of the evening train would often give displays of hooting with the engine whistle while he was stopping here, and would stay on over time if the owls were answering back.

The country station was, of course, the gateway to the outside world in the days before road transport became commonplace. It was also a social centre and meeting place where catching up on local gossip was as important as catching the train. It bore witness to the human element in the operation of the railway as well. For example, on the occasions when there was a dance at Moretonhampstead the railway staff at Bovey assisted those people going from there by putting a truck, with a brake, behind the last train. Then, after the dance was over, the party returning to Bovey would push the truck out of the station and ride downhill with the porter controlling the speed with the brake: I can't imagine that sort of thing being allowed nowadays!

To the Wright family, and a number of others for that matter, the railway was quite literally a 'family affair'. After leaving Starcross, where he was second ganger, my father, Jim Wright, moved to Moretonhampstead as ganger in 1919, in succession to a Mr Booth. His gang included Messrs Frank Rice, George Snow and (?) Langworthy, and they were responsible for the 4½-mile section of the line between Moretonhampstead and Hawkmoor Halt, using three- or four-wheeled trollies as a means of travel. Before setting off each morning they would invariably have a fried breakfast in the P.W. (permanent way) hut at Moreton, which was cooked on well-used, but spotlessly clean, shovels over a few hot coals. Of course, they all had their own shovels – no-one would dream of using anyone else's!

The trollies that they used were easily pumped down the line and later, on any given day, would normally be dismantled and returned to Moretonhampstead on a goods train. One of my brothers, Cyril, recalled that on one occasion, when travelling on a three-wheeled trolley, the gang gave a lift to a lady carrying two baskets of eggs to Hawkmoor. Taking one of the curves a little too fast, the trolley then suddenly flew off the line and threw its passengers down an embankment. Fortunately, he said, no-one was seriously hurt – but that certainly didn't apply as regards the eggs!

Two of my other brothers, Bob and Victor, and I also all worked on the railway. Victor started as a cleaner at Newton Abbot before becoming a fireman and then a driver, Bob was another fireman and driver, and my railway career included being lad porter at Heathfield, porter at Lustleigh and, in later years, signalman at Moretonhampstead. In addition, for about four years until the end of the war, one of my two sisters, Edna, worked on the Moretonhampstead line as a guard and, occasionally, took turns in the signal box. So you see, it really was a 'family affair', something that continued into a third generation when Bob's son, Brian, later joined the railway as a cleaner and went on to become a fireman."

Mr Wilf Wright, seen here with his colleagues at Moretonhampstead Station during the final week of the regular passenger service on the branch. From left to right: George Dennis (relief goods clerk), Dave Evans (signalman), Ray Thomas (stationmaster), Wilf Wright (signalman), Jack Tanton (checker), Jim Bennett (goods driver), and Reg Moore (parcels porter).

Courtesy of Wilf Wright

Mary Adcock of Moretonhampstead:–

"My late father, Jim Farr, was employed by the railway for 45 years and for most of that time worked on the Moretonhampstead line.

He first came to Moreton from Brixham as a boy in 1919, staying in lodgings and working as a cleaner. Later, in 1924, he married Kathleen Durston of Lolly Cottage and became a driver in 1941, I believe, the year in which I was born. Over the years he also worked as fireman to Sam Pearce and Walter Aplin.

Another member of the family to work on the Moretonhampstead line was my aunt, who later became Mrs Ellen Perrott. During the war years she was one of the female guards.

I can still vividly remember my father standing by the old black coal range in our kitchen with a blackboard and helping Bob Wright to pass for driver. He also helped Frank Radcliff, who later moved to Exeter, become fireman/driver.

I can also remember the days when cattle were being walked in from Chagford Market and being loaded into wagons at the station. What comes to mind most is the very large horns they had in those days!

Before I was born my mother used to take in railway workers for bed & breakfast, and when I was a young girl she used to say how early they started work in the mornings, cleaning and preparing the engines and doing all sorts of other jobs. She also used to tell me the names of some of the railway workers, and amongst those that I can still recall are Billy Mears (cleaner), Harry Yeoman and Reg Moore (porters), Bob Sawyer, Jack Cornish, Wilfred Wright and Dave Evans (all signalmen at different times), Stan Hawkins (clerk), Bill Horrell and Alf Diamond (guards), Mr Tooley (the stationmaster), and George Snow, Jim Wright and Bill Westlake (gangers). Another one was Harry Yeoman's daughter-in-law, Marg, who worked in the signal box for about three years until the war was over.

It's such a shame that it's now all gone – they were a friendly crowd and it was such a pretty line."

Pamela Lind, formerly of Brimley, Bovey Tracey:–

"When I was secretary dispenser to the Moretonhampstead doctors we used to send the medicines by the evening train to Lustleigh after the doctor had finished his surgery and visits each Saturday. If he phoned the prescriptions late, and they were not ready in time, I used to phone the station and ask them to hold the train, which they always did. Likewise, they always waited for the elderly baker from Bovey Tracey, who did a round in Lustleigh two or three days a week.

On one occasion, when two trains had just left Heathfield for Moreton and Exeter respectively, an old lady asked the guard what time we would reach Exeter. "Oh, my dear, you'm in the wrong train", he said and promptly opened the carriage window and yelled at the Exeter train to stop, which it did. Both trains then reversed back to the platform and the old lady was transferred to the right train.

We certainly got good service in those days."

Shirley Kemp (née Chetwynd) of Bridport:–

During the immediate post-war years I used to travel to and from school at Newton Abbot by train from Lustleigh Station. In the mornings this meant catching the first train down from Moretonhampstead, which arrived at

Lustleigh at 8 o'clock and was regarded as the school and business persons' train. For some, including me, it was invariably a struggle to be at the station on time, but if anyone was seen running towards the station the guard would kindly hold the train. I also remember that when the weather was really cold a fire would be burning in the old Victorian grate in the station office – the only means of heating – and that often the lighted sticks, or even hot coals, would fall out of the grate while the stationmaster (from Moreton) was selling tickets to some of the passengers. Perhaps it was just as well that regular travellers and the schoolchildren had season tickets!

A wintry scene at Lustleigh Station as 2-6-2T No. 4587 stands at the platform with its Moretonhampstead-bound train on 21st February 1947 – a day on which, no doubt, a fire was burning in the old Victorian grate in the station office!

E. R. Shepherd

The early morning train normally consisted of three carriages, although there would sometimes be more on a Wednesday as it was market day in Newton Abbot. Each carriage had separate compartments, with a door at either side (no corridor), and the luggage racks – made of strong rope net with supports – were above the seats. Each window was pulled up or down by means of a heavy strap with holes so that it could be secured on a stud. There were also heavy canvas-type blinds for the dark evenings, and above one of the windows in each compartment was the communication cord with a £5 penalty notice for improper use. Heating in the carriages came from underneath the seats.

At the end of the school day the other children and I used to catch the 4.38 p.m. train home from Newton Abbot, often after a number of us had called at the local fish-and-chip shop before boarding the train. Quite frequently homework was done on the way home, but because of the 'clickety-clack, clickety-clack' of the train the writing was pretty horrible.

On one particular occasion we had a domestic science lesson at school during which we all made rice puddings. These, of course, then had to be transported home on the train. However, after we had all settled into our seats, including a lady in a black coat, the train suddenly jolted for some reason as it was moving out of the station, and shortly afterwards a rice pudding that was up in the luggage rack slowly started dripping onto the back of the lady's black coat. Needless to say, we children all got the giggles and to our relief the lady only travelled as far as Heathfield Station before getting out of the train – unknowingly, with rice pudding stripes down her back. Oh dear, nobody said a word!

Another occasion I remember was when one of us took sandwiches and a bottle of cider on the train for school lunch. For a while all was well, but then about half way to Newton there was suddenly a loud report from the luggage rack: to our horror the cider bottle had exploded, but all the glass remained in the satchel and the cider poured down the back of an empty seat.

Apart from school days, my other lasting memories of the railway are the well-kept station garden at Lustleigh, which often won prizes in the annual railway garden competitions, and being able to enjoy lovely Sunday afternoon walks along the line, particularly in the spring when the primroses were out in full bloom: there were, I would hasten to add, no trains on Sundays at that time."

Mr Colin Pulleyblank of Newton Abbot:–

"I joined the Great Western Railway in 1938 as a rivet boy in the engine repair factory at Newton Abbot, later becoming an engine cleaner in the locomotive running shed and then, in 1941, a fireman.

Work as a fireman on steam engines was hard. I remember getting on the footplate at Newton Abbot Station to work the 1 a.m. train to Paddington, via Bristol, and looking at the tender of coal. It was full (6 tons): when it was nearly empty I knew that we were close to Paddington. Of course, there were other turns than were not so strenuous, such as trips on the Newton Abbot to Moretonhampstead line by auto train (one coach and engine as a 'push-pull'). Here, I remember working the final train of the day. After we had drawn level with the last bus from Newton Abbot (at Kelly Cross, beyond Lustleigh), there followed an exchange of whistles and bus horn. Then the drivers had a friendly race to Moreton: invariably we won!

I also recall that after stabling the autocoach at Moreton we were required to run light engine back to Newton Abbot and that whilst returning one evening we saw the Moretonhampstead fire engine racing towards a burning railway embankment near Lustleigh. I then said to the driver: "I wonder who did that!"

Mr Peter Carrett of Liverton:–

"In the early 1960s I was employed as maintenance engineer (linesman) by GPO Telephones, as one of two people allocated to the Newton Abbot exchange area. We usually worked as singletons, except for difficult jobs or where safety was involved.

On one occasion I had been called to Sandygate to assist my fellow linesman, Sid Saunders, with a difficult job. On completion we decided to return via the Teigngrace road, Sid with the Morris Minor van (SLF 1) and me in the fleet's latest vehicle – a Mini van (308 DLF). We were travelling some 20–30 feet apart and Sid had just crossed the Teignbridge level crossing when a loaded clay truck, which had escaped from a siding at Heathfield, suddenly smashed through both level-crossing gates, passing behind Sid's van and in front – just! – of mine. Meanwhile, as the crossing keeper came from the keeper's cottage to operate the gates, the large diagonal bracing rod from one of them whistled through the air and nearly decapitated the poor guy.

I understand that the truck – adorned with the remains of the two crossing gates – eventually came to rest near the goods sidings at Newton Abbot. Fortunately, there were no injuries and, instead, lucky escapes for all concerned."

Mr Stan Rowe of Paignton:–

"When I started work at Bovey as a junior clerk in 1944 there was a considerable amount of goods traffic to be documented at the station. For a start, all the consignments from the Bovey Pottery – mainly white earthenware made for the various ministries and hospitals etc – had to be recorded, as did the fancy goods produced by the smaller, privately-owned potteries in the neighbourhood. There were also two agricultural engineers in the town, Bowdens and Glanvilles, and both of them regularly received large machinery which had to be unloaded by the station's hand-operated crane. Always a risky business, on one occasion the clutch slipped and porter John Nekola received a nasty wound to the face caused by the spinning handle.

Other goods traffic at Bovey included considerable amounts of coal for

The crossing-keeper's cottage at Teignbridge as seen in 1999 (*above*) and after being restored in 2001 (*below*).

Peter Carrett

Mr Stan Rowe's father, Ronald, also worked on the railway and was a porter at Bovey when this photograph was taken c.1950. *Courtesy of Stan Rowe*

each of the three coal merchants (Wakeham & Jeffery, Frank Harris & Co. and the Co-operative Society), who all operated from the station yard, sackfuls of wheat, barley, oats etc for the nearby mill run by Wyatt & Bruce, and all sorts of other items of a general nature which were then delivered around the town by George Lang with his horse and wagon.

In 1946, whilst on deferred service, I moved to Moretonhampstead as a signalman, a job that also entailed assisting with the unloading of numerous wagons full of animal feeding stuffs for three local agricultural merchants, including Bibbys and Silcocks. These products would then be distributed around Dartmoor by lorry.

Pony sales at Chagford in October of each year brought extra trains to the station and, because only three wagons could be loaded at one time from the cattle pens, I remember that continual shunting was needed to accommodate all the traffic.

The blizzard of 1947, which began on 31st January, saw snow so heavy that within two hours all bus traffic had stopped and the rail service become severely disrupted. For example, the last train from Newton Abbot – normally the 8.10 p.m., due to arrive at Moretonhampstead at 8.55 p.m. – eventually rolled in at 12.30 a.m. As usual, the engine was then put to shed after stabling the one carriage of the auto train, but on arising the next morning, after having slept at the stationmaster's house, I found that the coach was completely buried under a huge snowdrift. It was also so cold that points defrosted by steam immediately froze again and, on realising that we were cut off from the world, the driver, fireman, guard and I played cards for some 12 hours while waiting for a snowplough to arrive.

Three days later relief finally arrived, by which time rations were low and the main source of food was stored potatoes: water came from melted snow! At this time I can also remember that the stationmaster, Mr R. Tooley, who was quite short, could only be seen on the path leading down to the station by his hat moving along, while the platform and line were level with snow, making it particularly dangerous in the dark.

One other thing that comes to mind was that farm accommodation crossings were numerous and sometimes cattle would stray onto the line. This obviously caused problems and on one occasion a valuable animal was killed by a train, which resulted in the ensuing compensation debate going on for several weeks. Game birds from the adjoining woodlands, which formed an orange 'tunnel' over the line in the autumn, also strayed onto the track at times with similar consequences: the ganger making his daily walk lived well!"

Mr Jim Kelly of Hennock:–

"After completing my education at Newton Abbot Grammar School, I joined the railway on 6th October 1947 as the junior clerk at Heathfield Station, where my sister was the senior clerk. The vacancy had occurred there as extra clerical help was required to deal with the 'lignite' traffic from Blue Waters Mine, at Bovey Tracey, which had been reopened as a result of the 1946/47 fuel crisis. At that time the government required industries to accept a quantity of lignite to supplement its normal coal supply, lignite being a form of soft or immature coal. An article in a January 1998 edition of the *Mid-Devon Advertiser* reads:–

> 50 years ago …
> The great opencast workings of British Lignite Products Ltd, at Blue Waters Mine, Bovey Tracey, has been slowed down considerably by the continuous rain, which has turned the place into a sticky sea of a mixture of lignite and mud.

Extra documentation was required at the station to invoice, route and record these consignments which, at their peak, involved as many as 100 coal wagons being loaded and despatched from Heathfield in a day. In fact, Bovey became a mini-boom mining town for a while, and it was even said that certain types of young ladies, usually associated with mining boom towns, had moved into the district!

When coal production returned to normal, nobody wanted to burn lignite, which was unsatisfactory for most industries, and the boom ended as suddenly as it had begun. The end of the lignite traffic also meant that there was no further need for extra clerical assistance at Heathfield, so I was sent to Torre Station, on the then Newton Abbot to Kingswear branch line."

Part of the opencast workings of British Lignite Products Ltd at Blue Waters Mine, Bovey Tracey, in 1947, with mass digging in progress. Known locally as 'Bovey coal', the lignite was despatched by rail from Timber Siding at Heathfield.

Courtesy of Mrs M. Tregoning

Mr Arthur Yendall (the last stationmaster at Bovey):–

"Born into a railway family in 1905, I first came to Bovey as a goods clerk in 1935. However, not long afterwards I was transferred to the booking office at St David's Station in Exeter, and it was not until around 1952 that I was able to return to Bovey, when a vacancy for the job of stationmaster cropped up. I then remained in post until the passenger service was withdrawn in 1959 and subsequently became a 'depot clerk', a task that included attending to the clerical work at Moretonhampstead as well as at Bovey.

As stationmaster I was, of course, in overall charge of the daily running of the station and, in addition, had to attend to much of the clerical work. This was not only very time-consuming, but at times downright frustrating. For example, on one occasion, following a visit from the auditors, I remember that their report highlighted an error that I had made in connection with someone's income tax code; it amounted to one shilling (5p)! At the time I was so annoyed that I immediately telephoned the divisional officer only to be told: "Well, don't worry about that". Even so, it just goes to show how exact things had to be.

Thankfully, some aspects of the job were rather more enjoyable, and I also experienced some rather funny incidents. One was when a ram arrived at the station in the back of a guard's van. After being removed from the train, the ram was tied up in the shed which, at one time, had been the waiting room for passengers taking bus trips across Dartmoor. We then telephoned the farmer to tell him to come and fetch it. However, in the meantime the ram became rather restive and suddenly dived out through the window before escaping into a nearby field – it wasn't injured as it could run alright and, of course, we had the full complement of staff trying to capture it! Eventually, we were successful and then made sure that it didn't escape again before the farmer arrived.

Over the years there were one or two other amusing incidents as well, but the strangest – and most worrying – was the night on which a train 'disappeared'. At the time – one evening in March 1953 – I wasn't even on duty; in fact, I was helping my brother to do some wallpapering. I think it must have been about half past nine when a porter suddenly arrived at the door, breathlessly telling of the train that had left Bovey about an hour earlier and not arrived at Moreton. I knew that the station at Lustleigh was closed at that time of night, so I hired a taxi and began a long search for the 'lost' train to the north of Bovey; this involved driving along dark and narrow country lanes and continually getting out of the taxi at various locations where the line was out of sight from the road – all with just the aid of a small cycle lamp! Anyhow, to cut a long story short, we eventually spotted the train in amongst some trees whilst travelling along the Wray valley. I then got out of the taxi once more, set off towards it – which involved crossing a pretty wide

A photograph of Mr Arthur Yendall taken at Bovey Station c.1958. Seen with him, left to right, are Signalman Derek Aggett, Porter Cecil Fowden and Motor Driver Jack Heale.

Arthur Yendall

Another photograph of Mr Arthur Yendall at Bovey, on this occasion seen attempting to hand an important letter that had been overlooked to the guard of the 10.15 a.m. train from Moretonhampstead to Newton Abbot on 19th February 1959.
Peter W. Gray

stream at one point – and discovered that there had been no accident but that the train had simply broken down. Of course, by this time it was getting rather late, the passengers had already set off on foot to Moreton and then the stationmaster there arrived, out of breath after having walked the line. After that, with the taxi still at hand, arrangements were made for a relief engine to come out from Newton Abbot and then, at long last, it was off home for a mug of hot cocoa and bed."

THE LINE TODAY

At the time of writing, in the early summer of 2004, the branch is still being used as far as Heathfield by the trains serving the ball clay processing plant adjacent to Timber Siding. This, however, is only on a once-weekly basis – on Fridays at around 6.30 p.m. – and throughout the remainder of the week the line lies idle, a situation that seems unlikely to change in the immediate future due to the apparent lack of any efforts being made to attract fresh sources of traffic.

The ball clay itself originates from three pits being operated in the locality by Imerys Minerals Ltd and, after being mined, is transported to the company's processing plant at Heathfield by road. Here, each component clay undergoes a process of shredding before being mixed with others according to the blend recipe; the final blend is then stored separately ready for despatch. However, some of the clay undergoes a form of further processing known as milling, in which it is first dried and then disintegrated into powder. This, in turn, is then bagged, palletised and shrink-wrapped in various quantities, again ready for despatch, or blown straight into empty 47-ton 'powder' wagons stabled in Timber Siding if it is to be sent away by rail. On average, though, only around 5,000 tons per annum are despatched in this manner compared to about 125,000 tons of shredded or powdered clay which is transported by road to Teignmouth Docks for export to various places around the world.

Nowadays the weekly clay train is normally hauled by a diesel-electric locomotive of class 66 (owned by English Welsh & Scottish Railways), which arrives at Heathfield, from Par, already well laden with china clay wagons and with two (occasionally three) empty 'powder' wagons. These empty wagons are then detached and shunted into the siding after the loaded ones have been hauled out, whereupon the train travels back along the branch and joins the main line once more at Newton Abbot. From there, the train then continues its journey to Folkestone en route to the company's store at Gammarello in Italy.

It is hoped that this traffic will continue, and that the line will remain in use, but whatever the future holds it is still possible to recall some aspects of the railway and to visit parts of its route, as indicated by some of the photographs that appear on the following three pages (all taken in 2004 and reproduced courtesy of Karen Lang). Furthermore, thanks to the efforts of railway preservationists, it is still possible to see one of the steam locomotives formerly used extensively on the branch. This is 0–4–2T No. 1466, which is now in the care of the Great Western Society at their site in Didcot, Oxfordshire, and is steamed from time to time, operating with an auto saloon.

As a final event in the story to date, it is pleasing to end on a positive note by recording that the main station building at Bovey has been refurbished and, on 10th April 2004, was officially opened as the new Bovey Tracey Heritage Centre, containing memorabilia of the railway and the town.

The view, something of an eyesore nowadays, looking towards Newton Abbot from the level crossing at Teignbridge, where the two sidings were both lifted in the 1990s. As can be seen, however, the clay loading ramp on the western side of the line is still extant, as is the crossing-keeper's cottage.

Apart from the single line track, the only remnants at Teigngrace are the weed-covered platform (viewed here from the north) and the loading ramp, which lies to the right of where the photographer is standing and is now almost entirely buried in vegetation.

Class 66 diesel-electric No. 66194 runs around its train at Heathfield prior to hauling out the two loaded 'powder' wagons from Timber Siding on 21st May 2004.

A view of the site of Heathfield Station, with its derelict and weed-infested platforms, from the A38 road overbridge. The crossing loop is still used by the once-weekly clay trains, but the short surviving section of track beyond it (leading to the Heltor oil depot) has fallen into disuse.

The main station building at Bovey on 10th April 2004, the day on which it was officially opened as the new Bovey Tracey Heritage Centre. The goods shed also survives, but the former station yard is now covered by a modern housing development.

The course of the line can be reached on the northern outskirts of Bovey and then followed up through a wooded area for $1^1/_4$ miles to the now-dismantled Wilford Bridge. This photo was taken at Southbrook Bridge, the same spot as that used for the lower photo on page 40.

The remains of Hawkmoor/Pullabrook Halt, viewed from the south-east.

The station building at Lustleigh, which has been tastefully restored and extended in the style of the original and used as a private dwelling by Mr and Mrs Mike Jacobs since the early 1970s.

The site of Moretonhampstead Station is still occupied by the road hauliers B. Thompson & Sons (Transport) Ltd, and numerous industrial buildings have been erected here. However, the goods shed (*centre*) and engine shed (*in the background, to the left*) still remain in situ.

APPENDIX I

The Prospectus of the M & SDR Company, July 1862

MORETONHAMPSTEAD AND SOUTH DEVON RAILWAY COMPANY.

INCORPORATED BY THE "MORETONHAMPSTEAD AND SOUTH DEVON RAILWAY ACT, 1862."

(MORETONHAMPSTEAD TO NEWTON ABBOT.)

SHARE CAPITAL, £105,000, in 10,500 SHARES, of £10 EACH.

A Deposit of £1 per Share to be paid upon Allotment.

Directors.

The EARL OF DEVON, Powderham Castle, Devon (Chairman).

ELIAS CUMING, Esq., Linscott, Moretonhampstead, Devon.

JOHN DIVETT. Esq., Bovey Tracey.

WILLIAM ROBERT HOLE, Esq., Park, Bovey Tracey.

THOMAS WILLS, Esq., East Wrey, Lustleigh.

THOMAS WOOLLCOMBE, Esq., Devonport (Chairman of the South Devon Railway Company.)

Engineers.

JOHN FOWLER, Esq., 2, Queen's Square Place, Westminster. | P. J. MARGARY, Esq., Dawlish.

Secretary.

ALEXANDER E. LHOYD, Esq.. Newton Abbot.

Solicitors.

Messrs. WHITEFORD and BENNETT, Plymouth.

Bankers.

The DEVON AND CORNWALL BANKING COMPANY.

London Correspondents, BARCLAY, BEVAN, and Co., 54, Lombard Street.

Messrs. WATTS, WHIDBORNE, and MOIR, Newton.

Messrs. DINGLEY, PEARSE, and Co., Moretonhampstead.

THE population of that portion of Devonshire which includes the Towns of Newton and Torquay, has increased since the Census of 1851 in a greater proportion than in any other part of the county, excepting Plymouth and Devonport, and the consequent increase in the demand for supplies of all kinds at the local markets, and in the trade and business of the District has induced a general requirement for extended railway communication.

In 1858, a Line was projected to proceed from Newton through the Pottery District of Bovey to the rich Agricultural tract which centres in Moretonhampstead and this design being fully matured, and the promoters having secured the cordial support of the land-owners, and obtained promises of material assistance from the Broad Gauge Railway Companies, application has been made to Parliament in the present Session (1862), for an Act of Incorporation, which has been passed without opposition.

The wild and beautiful country near Moretonhampstead on the borders of Dartmoor,—the picturesque old Stannary Town of Chagford, and the romantic scenery in the vicinity of Lustleigh, are celebrated in Guide Books, and well-known to Artists and Tourists; and the pure and invigorating air of this elevated country attracts annually numerous Visitors, to whom, and especially to Invalids suffering from the relaxation of a warmer climate, it offers all the natural advantages which have conferred such celebrity on Malvern.

The Country surrounding Moretonhampstead and along the upper portion of the Line is remarkably fertile, and large quantities of agricultural produce will be brought over the Line to the Markets of Newton and Torquay.

There is every reason to believe that the District is rich in Minerals, including Copper, Tin and Iron, and the Shipment of Ores can at present be effected with facility and economy at Torquay and Teignmouth; Dartmouth, by the completion of its Railway, will afford another port, and from all these places the Moreton District can be supplied with Coal, in addition to that which is brought by land over the Bristol and Exeter and South Devon Railways.

The Extensive Pottery Works at Bovey, and the Smelting Works in course of construction in that locality, in connexion with the well-known Bovey Coal-field, may be expected to contribute largely to the Traffic of the Line.

The arrangements concluded by the Company with the South Devon, the Great Western, the Bristol and Exeter, and the Cornwall Railway Companies, are set forth in the Act of Incorporation.

The particulars and practical effect of these arrangements are briefly stated at the foot of this Prospectus.

It may be fairly presumed that with such large additions to the actual proceeds of the New Line as must result from the rebates granted by the Companies, the undertaking, besides conferring great advantages on the locality, will be highly remunerative to the Shareholders.

The Directors have obtained from Messrs. BRASSEY AND OGILVIE *a guaranteed contract* for execution of the whole of the works, except stations, for a gross sum of £88,500, and these Gentlemen have evinced their sense of the value of the undertaking by agreeing to take Shares for the sum of £29,500.

The Directors have also made arrangements with His Grace the DUKE OF SOMERSET for the purchase of his Canal and the Land required for the undertaking. A large majority of the Landowners on the Line have agreed to accept the Agricultural Value of their land, the amount to be fixed by Mr. JOHN HOOPER, of Chagford, who commands the confidence of all parties.

The Directors have been met in the most liberal manner by the Engineers and Solicitors, who have agreed to become Shareholders to a considerable amount.

Taking into account the nature of the arrangements already concluded, which the Directors feel warranted in describing as being of a very satisfactory description, they see no reason to doubt that the Line can be completed at a cost within the Capital of the Company, leaving a margin applicable for future improvements, consequent on the development of the general traffic.

Sketch of Arrangements with the South Devon, Great Western, Bristol and Exeter, and Cornwall Companies: confirmed by the Act of Incorporation.

The Net Income of the Company will arise as follows:—

1st—One-half of the gross receipts to be handed over by the South Devon Company, who are to work the Line in perpetuity for the residue.

2nd—Twenty-five per cent. of the South Devon proportion of all Through Traffic.

3rd—Twenty per cent. of the proportions payable to the other three Companies, on all Through Passenger Traffic over their Lines.

The Twenty per cent. Rebate to be subject to reduction, and ultimate withdrawal when not required to make up Five per cent. on the Share Capital.

Any surplus beyond Five per cent. on the Share Capital, to be divided equally between the Company and the South Devon Company, who will be at liberty to commute all payments and allowances by the substitution of Five and a quarter per cent. in perpetuity.

The South Devon Company to guarantee Interest on the Company's Debentures until the principal is repaid.

The following Table, intended to exemplify the advantages derivable from the arrangements with the existing Companies, is adapted to the Third-class Traffic for convenience of calculation; but corresponding Rebates will extend to *all* Through Passenger Traffic over the same Lines, and to Through Goods also, over the South Devon Line.

TABLE shewing the Amounts receivable by the Moretonhampstead and South Devon Railway Company, in respect of Twelve Third-class Passengers travelling to the undermentioned Places:

From Moretonhampstead.	Proportion of Local Fares after Deduction of Working Expenses.		Amount of Rebates. 25 ₩ Cent. guaranteed by South Devon Company.		20 ₩ Cent. guaranteed by Cornwall Company.		20 ₩ Cent. guaranteed by Bristol & Exeter and Great Western Company.		Amount Receivable by the Local Company.	
	s.	d.	s.	d.	s.	d.	s.	d.	s.	d.
1. Passenger to NEWTON	0	6	………		………		………		0	6
2. — PLYMOUTH	0	6	0	8⅛	………		………		1	2⅛
3. — TAVISTOCK	0	6	0	11⅝	………		………		1	5⅝
4. — LISKEARD	0	6	0	8⅛	0	3½	………		1	5⅝
5. — TRURO	0	6	0	8⅛	0	10⅝	………		2	0¾
6. — BRIXHAM ROAD	0	6	0	2⅝	………		………		0	8⅝
7. — EXETER	0	6	0	5	………		………		0	11
8. — TAUNTON	0	6	0	5	………		0	6	1	5
9. — BRISTOL	0	6	0	5	………		1	3	2	2
10. — CHIPPENHAM	0	6	0	5	………		1	7⅞	2	6⅞
11. — READING	0	6	0	5	………		2	3¾	3	2¾
12. — PADDINGTON	0	6	0	5	………		2	10	3	9
Total Receipts from 12 Local Passengers, after deduction of Working Expenses…	6	0								
Rebate from S. Devon on fares of 11 Through Passengers			5	8⅝						
,, Cornwall ,, 2 ditto					1	2⅛				
,, Bristol & Exeter 5 } ,, Great Western 3 } ditto							8	6⅝		
Total Receipts of the Company, from the above 12 Passengers, including all Rebates									£1 1	5⅜

Applications for Shares may be made in the subjoined Form, to the Secretary, Alexander E. Lhoyd, Esq., Newton Abbot, to the Solicitors, or either of the Bankers.

Form of Application for Shares.

To the Directors of the Moretonhampstead and South Devon Railway Company.

My Lord and Gentlemen,

I request that you will allot to me ……………………………… *Shares in this undertaking; and I engage to accept the same, and to pay the deposit and calls thereon, when and as called for. And I request you to enter my name upon the Register of Shareholders, as the holder of the said Shares.*

Dated this *day of* 186 .

Name ______________________________

Residence ______________________________

Description ______________________________

APPENDIX II

Schedule of land purchased for the railway as at 26th June 1866

Name of landowner	Payment	Notes
The Duke of Somerset	£8,000 in cash	Land inclusive of the Stover Canal and lower section of the Haytor Granite Tramway.
The Earl of Devon	£5,000 in shares	Approximate value only. Chairman of the M & SDR Company.
Bovey Heathfield Enclosure Commissioners	£230 in cash	Eighteen acres @ £10 per acre plus a further amount for £50.
Devon & Courtenay Clay Co.	£250 in cash	For part of the clay cellars at Newton Abbot.
Feofees of the Teigngrace Charity Lands	£50 in cash	
Overseers of Bovey Tracey	£10 in cash	
Messrs Torr & Jackson	£277 in cash	Property near Moretonhampstead.
Woods & Forests	£10 in cash	Plus £2 2s. 0d. on account of solicitor's costs. Small portion of the bed of the River Teign.
Major Alexander Adair	£135 in cash	Approx. 3 acres of land at Bovey Tracey.
Thomas Amery Esq. (Higher Coombe)	£100 in cash	
C. A. Bentinck Esq. (Indio House)	n/k	
James Buller Esq.	n/k	

W. R. Crump Esq. (Wray Barton)	£900 in shares	Subject to litigation.
John Divett Esq. (Bovey Potteries – Messrs. Buller & Divett)	shares	Value of shares not known. A director of the M & SDR Company.
Rev. John Nutcombe Gould	£645 in cash	Plus £20 tenant's compensation (land at Knowle).
John Harris Esq. (Exeter)	n/k	
William Harris Esq. (Plumley)	shares	Value of shares not known.
? Hole Esq. (The miller at Lustleigh)	£200 in cash	
W. R. Hole Esq. (Parke)	shares	Value of shares not known. A director of the M & SDR Company.
John Nosworthy Esq.	£175 in cash	Plus £100 in compensation and £5 5s. 0d. for surveyor's costs.
Rev. Stephen Nosworthy	£100 in cash	
Miss Shilston	£150 in cash	One whole field at Teigngrace.
? Snow Esq. (Steward Mill)	£20 in cash	
J. Stevens Esq.	n/k	To be paid a max. of £1 per pole for 1 rood, 15 poles.
J. Stevenson Esq.	£60 in cash	Plus an unknown value of shares.
Henry Taylor Esq.	£400 in cash	One field at Bovey Tracey.
J. E. White Esq. (Moretonhampstead)	shares	Value of shares not known.
(Mrs. Wills)	£50 in cash	Tenant's compensation (Caseley Farm).

George Wills Esq. (Kelly)	£633 in cash	
George Wills Esq. (Narracombe)	£450 in cash £50 in shares	Land at Caseley.
James Wills Esq. (Rudge)	n/k	
Thomas Wills Esq. (East Wray)	£1,411 7s. 6d. in shares	A director of the M & SDR Company.
Rev. Mr Woollcombe	£1,500 in cash	Plus £75 tenant's compensation (Ponsford Yeo).

Authors' note: The above schedule has been compiled by reference to the Directors' Minutes Book and other contemporary sources, but is not necessarily complete. In addition, it has not been possible to ascertain the value of all of the transactions, a few of which had still to be completed as at 26th June 1866.

* * * * *

APPENDIX III

Colonel Yolland's Report

Newton Abbot
28th June 1866

Sir,

I have the honor to state for the information of the Lords of the Committee of Privy Council for Trade, that in obedience to your minute of the 22nd Instant, I have inspected the Moretonhampstead and South Devon Railway, commencing at a Junction with the South Devon Railway near Newton Station, and terminating at the Town of Moretonhampstead, a length of 12 miles and 13 chains –

The Line is single throughout, but the land has been purchased, and the overbridges have been constructed for a double Line, if hereafter required – The width of the Line at formation level is 18 feet, the guage is 7ft 0¼ Inch and the space between where there are two lines is 6 feet –

The permanent way is similar to that usually laid down on the broad guage system of Railways. It consists of a bridge rail that weighs 60lbs per linear yard in lengths of 18 and 24 feet laid on longitudinal Timbers of 12 Inches by 6 Inches rectangular Scantling, with transoms and strap bolts, of 6" x 4" Scantling placed at 12 feet apart on the straight portions and 11 feet apart on the curves – The Rails are fastened to the Longitudinal Timbers by fang bolts –

The Ballast is of broken stone and gravel, and stated to be 1 foot deep below the Under sides of the Longitudinal Timbers –

An Engine Turntable has been provided at Moretonhampstead Station – and Sidings have been constructed at Bovey Station which is ultimately intended for a passing place and at Lustleigh and Moretonhampstead Stations –

There are 9 over and 9 under bridges for Roads, and 8 Viaducts over Rivers and Streams; – all are constructed with stone abutments and with either brick or stone arches, or with wrought iron Girders, or Timber Tops –

The largest span is that of an Iron Girder Bridge at Whitelake of 80 feet span – The Girder bridges appear to be well constructed, sufficiently strong, and exhibited moderate deflections when tested, and the masonry generally is good –

The greater portion of the Line has steep Inclines, the steepest being 1 in 48.56 and there are many sharp curves on it. It has been made entirely with horse labor, and should be worked at slow speed until the embankments become thoroughly consolidated – they will require to be closely looked after, especially with reference to the cant of the rails on the sharp curves –

The Junction at the present time at Newton is only a single Junction as the South Devon Railway Company now work over a portion of Single Line there as they are engaged in replacing a wooden bridge over the River close to the Junction by an Iron Girder Bridge – but it is understood that this single Junction is to be replaced by a double Junction with complete signals that will lock the points at the entrance to the Newton Station Yard from the East in the course of two months – Newton is now become so important a Station that I think this double Junction when complete should be looked at –

The Line generally is in good order – The Platforms at the Stations are complete, but the whole of the Station buildings are in a very unfinished state – not sufficiently advanced as to be actually useable – I am of the opinion that their Lordships should consider this as an incompleteness of the "works" that fully justifies the postponement of the opening – but they have not hitherto done so – and it would not be fair to Railway Companies to change the practice without due notice –

The Turntable is in position at Moretonhampstead but the line leading to it, and over it is not yet in order. This is expected to be done by the end of the week –

The arch of a small under bridge at 0 miles 50 chains has not been well turned – it is to be opened out at once, and properly keyed – the rails are to be carried by additional balks until that is done. I observed slight settlements in the N.E and N.W. wing walls for 3 arched Viaduct at Knowle – These should be pointed up and carefully watched. The same may be said of J. Wills occupation bridge of 10 feet span, as regards the wing walls on the West of the Line and of a portion of retaining wall adjacent to it –

Starting Signals are to be put up for the Passenger and Goods Lines at Moretonhampstead Station interlocking with each other – and the Goods Line is not to be used until this is done –

I am of the opinion that their Lordships may sanction the opening of the Line as soon as the Turn Table at Moretonhampstead is in working order – But when the Station buildings are complete, Clocks to face and be seen from the Platforms at the Stations should be provided. I enclose the Undertaking as to the mode of working the Line which is satisfactory.

I have the honor to be, Sir,
Your most obedient Servant

N. Yolland
Colonel

* * * * *

Appendix IV

Chagford: The proposed extension of the line and bus services.

Contributed by Chris Webber of Chagford

During the construction of the railway line between Newton Abbot and Moretonhampstead there seemed to be every possibility that it would be extended to Chagford. The first documentary evidence of this is to be found in the minutes of a meeting of the directors of the Moretonhampstead & South Devon Railway Company held on 2nd November 1864, the following being an extract:–

> The policy of applying in the next Session for an extension of the line to Chagford having been discussed, it was Resolved that not more than £150 be expended in preparing the plans and taking the preliminary steps up to depositing the Bill.

It is not known for sure whether this decision was influenced by the Earl of Devon (the company chairman, who owned estates in the Moretonhampstead/Chagford area) or by some of the inhabitants of Chagford, who may well have made representations to the company following the failure of the Devon Central Railways Company's scheme some three years earlier (see pages 100/101). In all probability it was a combination of both. Whatever, it is known that during the autumn of 1864 surveys were undertaken and that a meeting, presided over by the Reverend Hayter George Hames (Rector of Chagford), was held at The Three Crowns Hotel in Chagford on 17th December 1864 "for the purpose of considering the expediency of extending the Moretonhampstead Railway to Chagford".

At the meeting, which was addressed by the Earl of Devon, it was explained that the proposed extension was just over four miles in length and that the estimated construction costs were £38,000. The earl also intimated his intention of taking shares to the value of the land required by the proposed extension, which was one-fifth of the whole. Then, on the motion of Mr J. Hooper of Withecombe – seconded by Mr Collins of Batworthy – it was unanimously resolved "That this meeting has learnt with much satisfaction that the Moreton and South Devon Railway Company are projecting an extension of their line from Moreton to Chagford and engage to give to the undertaking their united and cordial support". It was also resolved "That a committee be appointed to canvas the landowners and residents in the district for subscriptions for shares, to consist of the Rev. H. G. Hames, Messrs. Ellis, Collins, J. Hooper, Coniam, Osmond and Perryman, with power to add to their number". In response, the committee stated that they would meet at The Globe Hotel on 2nd January 1865.

Unfortunately, before anything further became of the matter, the directors decided that it should be held in abeyance. This was because of the company's dire financial situation, although rather than publicise the fact the directors chose to give another reason in their report submitted at the next half-yearly general meeting of the shareholders (held on 22nd February 1865), of which the following is an extract:–

> In the autumn of last year Surveys were prepared for an extension of your Line from Moretonhampstead to Chagford, for which a Bill was deposited, but the late period at which the scheme was introduced, would not admit of the necessary arrangements being made for proceeding with the Bill in the present Session.

Thereafter no more was heard about the proposed extension. Instead, after the line had been opened to Moretonhampstead in the summer of 1866, a road service was provided between there and Chagford by means of a horse-bus, as explained in the following article that appeared in the April 1868 edition of the Chagford parish magazine:–

> Our South Devon friends are at length to have the privilege of a direct & easy communication with Chagford. The South Devon Railway Co. having announced in large placards on all their stations that an omnibus is to run between Chagford & Moretonhampstead on Tuesdays & Fridays on or after the 14th.

Leaving Three Crowns Hotel, Chagford	9.15 AM	5.15 PM
Arriving Moreton	10.00 AM	6.10 PM
Leaving Moreton	11.35 AM	8.25 PM
Arriving Chagford	12.25 PM	9.15 PM
Fares One Shilling		

> We are confident that this enterprising step on the part of the proprietor Mr Henry Aggett, Three Crowns Hotel, Chagford will meet with the cordial support of our parish and the immediate neighbourhood. Indeed such a spirited undertaking deserves to be well patronised, and the public at large will be sure to maintain that which so much promotes their own convenience. Parties of not less that ten in number can obtain return tickets at single fares from any of the stations on the South Devon Line to Moreton any day (Sundays excepted) by giving one day's notice to E. Compton Esq Plymouth, and from Moreton they can proceed to Chagford by omnibus on reasonable terms, by applying previously to Mr Henry Aggett, who is appointed agent by the South Devon Railway Company for the delivery of goods & parcels in Chagford and its neighbourhood.

In the following month's edition of the Chagford parish magazine there is also mention of an excursion from Chagford to Torquay on Whitsun Tuesday at a return fare of 2s. 3d., but thereafter nothing further appears to have been mentioned in it on the subject. However, in the 1889 edition of *Kelly's Directory* is an entry which states that the omnibus leaves the Globe (Chagford) twice daily from October to June and three times during the remainder of the year for Moretonhampstead, so it is clear from this that the service, by now subsidised by the GWR, was being well patronised.

Two photographs dating back to the 1890s of the GWR horse-bus which ran between Chagford and Moretonhampstead.
Above: Outside the Globe Family Hotel in Chagford.

Courtesy of M. Sheriden, Chagford

Below: At Half Way House, which was about the midway point of the journey.

Dartington Rural Archive

Above: A GWR-owned Milnes-Daimler omnibus photographed outside Rock House (Chagford) soon after the introduction of the motor service between Chagford and Moretonhampstead on 9th April 1906.

Courtesy of Rendells, Chagford

Below: The same vehicle seen in Station Road, Moretonhampstead.

Chapman & Son

Another GWR-owned Milnes-Daimler omnibus photographed at Chagford in Edwardian times, on this occasion at Cross Tree.

Chris Webber Collection

Two studies taken from the forecourt of Moretonhampstead Station showing *(above)* a GWR-owned Milnes-Daimler omnibus waiting to depart for Chagford, c.1908 and *(below)* an AEC charabanc on a lorry chassis with the hood down ready, in all likelihood, for a moorland tour to Princetown and Dartmeet, c.1920.

Courtesy of Peter W. Gray/Chris Webber Collection

Later, in the 1902 edition of *Kelly's Directory*, a William Henry Osborne is listed as agent to the GWR Company, while the 1906 edition states that the omnibus leaves the GWR office (Rock House – now Rendells) twice daily from October to May and four times during the remainder of the year. It also states that the GWR are arranging a motor service between Chagford and Moreton, and this, in fact, commenced on 9th April of that year, when GWR-owned Milnes-Daimler buses were brought into use to fulfil the task. These were garaged in the station yard at Moretonhampstead, from where, some three years later on 12th July 1909, tours across Dartmoor to Princetown and Dartmeet were also introduced by the railway company.

Although strictly outside the confines of this book, it needs to be mentioned briefly at this point that there had been high expectations that Chagford would eventually be placed on the railway map as part of the Exeter, Teign Valley and Chagford Railway. This company had been incorporated in 1883 "for the purpose of connecting the city and port of Exeter with the existing Teign Valley line", and included in its prospectus were plans to construct a branch from Lea Cross (Dunsford) to Chagford. However, the 'usual' problem of lack of finance had led to the company obtaining parliamentary permission to abandon the Chagford branch in 1897 and to change the nomenclature to the Exeter Railway Company. Consequently, Chagford's hopes of a railway had been dashed yet again, but at least it had eventually derived the benefit of a second bus service, this time from the London & South Western Railway Company using, in the first instance, one of a pair of Milnes-Daimler buses. Introduced on 1st June 1904, these ran from Queen Street Station in Exeter and offered a direct connection with the main line express trains to and from Waterloo.

From thereon the bus services operated by the two rival railway companies continued running successfully for many years, but after World War I increasing competition led to the Exeter – Chagford service losing money until eventually being withdrawn at the end of September 1924. The Moretonhampstead – Chagford service, on the other hand, was still being well patronised at this time and would almost certainly have continued being operated by the GWR beyond 31st December 1928 had it not been for the agreement made with the National Omnibus & Transport Co. Ltd already described on page 148.

* * * * *

APPENDIX V

Gauge Conversion

Contributed by Bryan Gibson

Railways built in the early 19th century were initially isolated from each other and the advantage of a common gauge was of no consequence. Rails of Stephenson's Stockton & Darlington Railway were 4 feet 8½ inches apart, but Isambard Kingdom Brunel built Britain's first inter-city main line from London to Bristol to an impressive gauge of 7 feet (eased to 7 feet 0¼ inch before opening). To the Great Western Railway, *this* was standard gauge and Stephenson's was dismissed as narrow gauge or 'Coal Cart Gauge'. Brunel's railway building did not terminate at Bristol, and his Bristol & Exeter Railway, South Devon Railway and Cornwall Railway extended the 'Brunel Gauge' deep into the Westcountry.

As railway building progressed, these different gauges inevitably met, and it was obvious that a national railway network could not be achieved until such time as there was one gauge throughout. Brunel's gauge was undoubtedly superior, but Stephenson's was more widespread. It should be mentioned that not only was 'Brunel Gauge' wider, but the clearance (loading gauge) was higher and wider, so gauge conversion upwards could only be accomplished at astronomical expense.

A common gauge was under discussion as early as 1866, so even then it was evident that the seven-feet-and-a-quarter-inch was doomed. The Great Western Railway made considerable reductions to its mileage of broad gauge (as distinct from mixed gauge) in 1872 and 1874, and by the end of 1875 it was virtually eliminated, with just 8¼ miles remaining. But it then absorbed the lines west of Bristol, which pushed the mileage back up to 275½. This included the South Devon Railway's 12¼-mile Moretonhampstead branch.

The decision was made to extinguish the broad gauge over the weekend of Saturday and Sunday, May 21st and 22nd 1892, by which time there were still 171 miles remaining, all of it west of Exeter. This excluded the mixed-gauge sections, from which the third rail could be removed at leisure. Narrowing was a major exercise and considerable preparations were necessary. Every bolt and screw was taken off, oiled and temporarily replaced. The transoms were measured and the place marked where they were to be sawn through. Where it did not compromise safety, alternate transoms were cut. The ballast was dislodged and, in some instances, a third rail put in at crossings.

Reproduced on page 216 is the Moretonhampstead Branch Service Time Table for April 1892. This is supplemented here, on the facing page, by a Table of Alterations and Amendments set out to match its style. The various cross-references would indicate that the Time Table remained current until the gauge conversion. Also reproduced, on page 310, is the original diagram showing the distribution of men on the branch. It may be helpful to refer to these when reading the following paragraphs. All information additional to

Extracts from the General Instructions and Local Instructions & Arrangements in connection with the Conversion from Broad to Narrow Gauge

Amended and Additional Trains - May 1892

	Thursday 19th				Friday 20th		Monday 23rd		Tuesday 24th	
	B G Goods 1.20pm ex Newton retimed		B G Special (Workmen) 9.55am ex Bristol				Empty N G Passenger 3.15am ex Exeter		Empty N G Special 12.0 midnight ex Bristol	
	arr.	dep.	arr.	dep.			arr.	dep.	arr.	dep.
	p.m.	p.m.	p.m.	p.m.			a.m.	a.m.	a.m.	a.m.
Newton Abbot	—	2 40	3 55	4 5			3 55	4 15	3 40	3 51
Teigngrace	—	—	—	—			—	—	—	—
Heathfield	—	—	4 15	4 18			—	—	—	—
Bovey	—	—	4 23	4 26			—	—	—	—
Lustleigh	—	—	—	—			—	—	—	—
Moretonhampstead	3 17	—	4 45	—			4 51	—	4 25	—

Goods Trains suspended on Friday 20th and Monday 23rd.
All Trains suspended on Saturday 21st and Sunday 22nd.

	Thursday 19th				Friday 20th		Monday 23rd		Tuesday 24th	
			Empty B G Special to Exeter		Empty B G Passenger to Swindon				N G Special (Workmen) to Bristol	
			arr.	dep.	arr.	dep.			arr.	dep.
			p.m.	p.m.	p.m.	p.m.			a.m.	a.m.
Moretonhampstead			—	5 15	—	10 0			—	6 40
Lustleigh			—	—	10 10	10 14			—	—
Bovey			—	—	10 22	10 26			6 54	6 55
Heathfield			—	—	10 33	10 36			7 0	7 3
Teigngrace			—	—	10 41	10 44			—	—
Newton Abbot			5 43	6 35	10 50	11 10			7 13	7 23

B G - Broad Gauge (7 feet 0 ¼ inch)

N G - Narrow Gauge (4 feet 8 ½ inches). This is today's Standard Gauge.

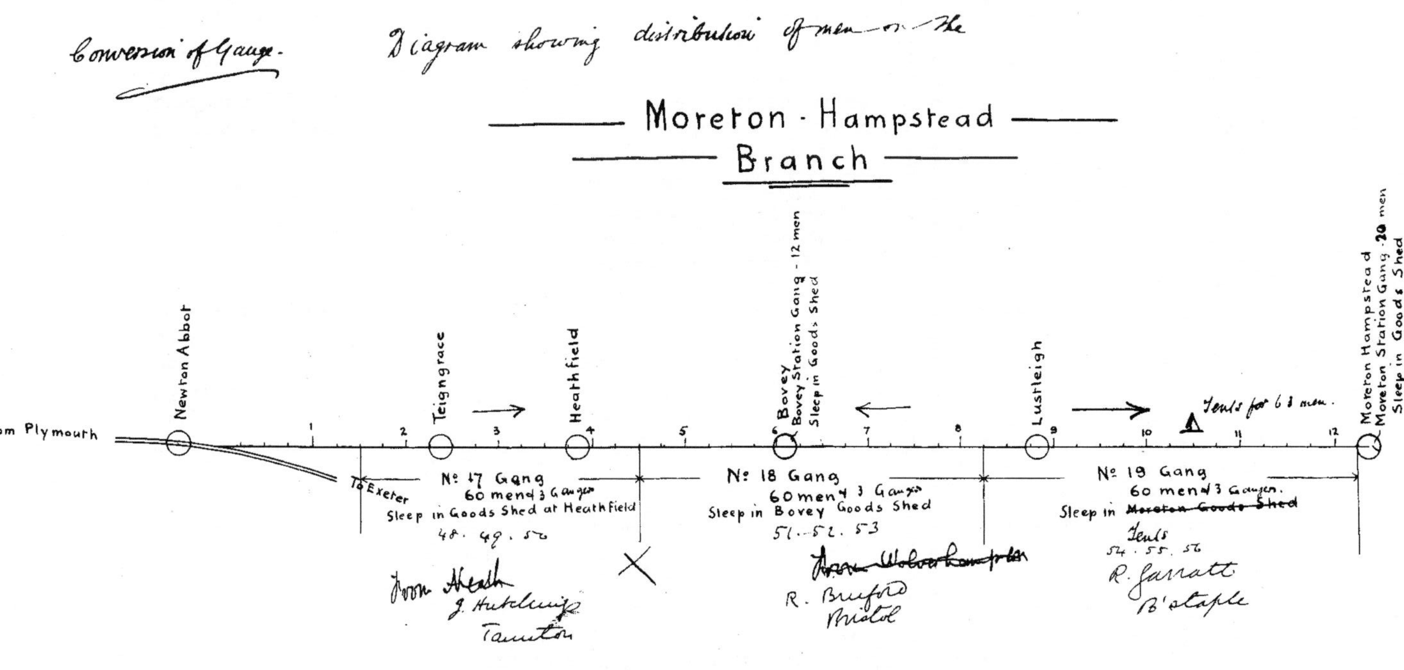
Conversion of Gauge.
Diagram showing distribution of men on the
Moreton-Hampstead
Branch
From Plymouth
Newton Abbot
Teigngrace
Heathfield
Bovey
Bovey Station Gang - 12 men
Sleep in Goods Shed
Lustleigh
Moreton Hampstead
Moreton Station Gang - 20 men
Sleep in Goods Shed
Tents for 63 men.
1
2
3
4
5
6
7
8
9
10
11
12
To Exeter
No 17 Gang
60 men & 3 Gangers
Sleep in Goods Shed at Heathfield
48. 49. 50
J. Hutchings
Taunton
No 18 Gang
60 men & 3 Gangers
Sleep in Bovey Goods Shed
51. 52. 53
R. Buford
Bristol
No 19 Gang
60 men & 3 Gangers.
Sleep in Tents
54. 55. 56
R. Garratt
B'staple

Distribution of Men on the Moretonhampstead Branch.

Some of the information differs from the Diagram (sleeping arrangements at Heathfield and the location of the tents) as it is sourced from much-amended scrip notes which postdate the Diagram.

Gang Number	Officer in Charge	Start at Milepost	Finish at Milepost	Remarks	Inspector Coles' Local Men	Foreign Men	Foreign Gangers (Supervisors)	Platelayers	Smiths and Strikers	Base	Sleeping Arrangements
17 (48-50)	Inspector J Hutchings of Taunton	1 ½	4 ½		4	60	3			Heathfield	30 in the two Goods Sheds. 36 in four carriages
18 (51-53)	Inspector R Bruford of Bristol	4 ½	8 ¼	… then assist Bovey Station Gang	4	60	3			Bovey	Goods Shed
Station Gang	Ganger Maunder				13			2	1	Bovey	Goods Shed
19 (54-56)	Inspector R Garratt of Barnstaple	8 ¼	12	… then assist Moretonhampstead Station Gang	4	60	3			Milepost 10	Tents on the Up Side of the line
Station Gang	Ganger Stanleick				9	10		2	1	Moretonhampstead	Goods Shed
				Totals :-	34	190	9	4	2		

Total Men :- 239

the Time Table is taken from official notices issued by the Great Western Railway, hand-written notes issued by T. H. Gibbons, the divisional engineer based in Plymouth, and cuttings from newspapers and magazines. This was accumulated by Mr R. K. Woodward, the engineer responsible for the conversion of the section of main line between Newton Abbot and Plymouth.

The normal Time Table was operated on Wednesday, May 18th, the 7.30 a.m. goods from Exeter being the last train on which merchandise would be despatched. This arrived in Newton Abbot at 10.15 a.m., allowing for its transfer to the Moretonhampstead branch goods. Use of the train on this particular day was on the understanding that the wagons would be emptied in time for collection on the following day. Traders were warned that any wagons not discharged would be unloaded at their risk and expense. Stations had been given notice that, during this last week, empty broad-gauge wagons should as far as possible be worked to Swindon, sheets, ropes, packing and other articles having been removed and stored so as to be available for use on narrow-gauge stock.

On Thursday, May 19th, the passenger service ran as normal. However, as no merchandise would be delivered, the goods train set out from Newton Abbot at 2.40 p.m. instead of the usual 1.20 p.m. and ran non-stop to Moretonhampstead. In the outward direction it comprised the engine and brake van only. It worked back at the normal 4.30 p.m. but, in addition to conveying the regular traffic, it took away all the empty goods wagons.

The first 'Workmen's Special' was the 12.40 p.m. from Swindon to Falmouth on Wednesday, May 18th. This special was an extra one and was not shown in the General Instructions. It conveyed about 450 men who were decanted at 31 sites throughout the conversion area. A small contingent for the Moretonhampstead branch alighted at Newton Abbot and travelled up the branch on the 8.33 p.m. regular train. The main workforce arrived on a special train from Bristol on the Thursday. To faciliate the loading and unloading of the large number of tools, one compartment in every four had to be retained and labelled for them, the owners travelling in the three adjoining compartments. This special conveyed 462 men for the Kingswear and Moretonhampstead branches, some joining en route at Yatton (34), Highbridge (10), Taunton (136) and Tiverton Junction (3). This train then returned to Exeter, connected with the 3.50 p.m. special from Tondu and took its 483 men to various setting-down points as far as Falmouth. An additional 10 men for the Moretonhampstead branch were supplied by the Cornwall Mineral District. They travelled up from Par on the 10.0 a.m. regular train from Penzance, arriving at Newton Abbot at 3.46 p.m. in time to join the workmen's special.

Friday, May 20th was the last day of the broad gauge. As already implied, there were no goods trains on this day, but passenger trains ran as normal. The last branch train ended up at Moretonhampstead terminus, so it was necessary to work it back to Newton Abbot to clear the branch of rolling stock. It will be seen that this called at all the stations, with stops in excess of the usual 1 – 2 minutes. Inspector Tucker of Newton Abbot was on board and it was his duty to ascertain that each station had been cleared. Having done this, he issued a notice to the respective stationmaster confirming that his was the last broad-gauge train and that the engineering department could therefore take possession for the purpose of converting the gauge. Inspector Scantlebury was on board the last broad-gauge train of all – the 9.10 p.m. from Penzance. He was charged with ascertaining that all broad-gauge stock, including that from the various branches, had been worked away.

As far as possible gangs camped in station buildings, but four carriages normally used on the narrow gauge (i.e. 4 feet 8½ inches) Teign Valley line were used for additional accommodation, being parked at Heathfield Station. Each man was supplied with bedding in the shape of canvas bags filled with straw. Tents were provided in those instances where bases were established between stations. There were 22 locations throughout the conversion area, but only one on the Moretonhampstead branch. Curiously, the General Instructions Book does not show the workmen's trains stopping there at milepost 10, although it is reasonable to assume that this occurred. On the Ashburton branch there were two encampments between stations and the necessary stops *were* specified.

The diagram shows the dispersal of the gangs, each consisting of 20 men and 3 gangers (supervisors). Not shown is the involvement of main line Gangs 19 to 21, the charge of Inspector Jones of New Milford, whose section included the first 1½ miles of the Moretonhampstead branch and a similar length of the main line in the direction of Teignmouth. In addition to the running lines, all the sidings were converted. Each gang of 60 men and 3 gangers was equipped with a total of 443 tools of 28 different types! Those engaged on the Moretonhampstead branch are detailed in a table. It will be noted that 67 men were based at Heathfield but sleeping arrangements were only specified for 66. Perhaps Inspector Hutchings was entitled to more salubrious accommodation off site? The suggested division of labour was as follows:–

	Gang of 44	Gang of 66
Stripping and turning out rails	3 men	3 men
Stripping straps and tie bolts	4 men	8 men
Cutting transoms (2 saws)	4 men	6 men
Lifting rails for slewing	3 men	3 men
Shovelling ballast	1 man	1 man
Slewing	10 men	16 men
Pulling in transoms, ½ inch bolts and tie bolts	6 men	8 men
Packing	7 men	10 men
Flanging 'specials'	2 men	3 men
Narrow-gauge trolleying and cooking	4 men	8 men

Inspectors arranged for three meal breaks of about half an hour each, but the men were required to provide their own food. As an indication of the attention to every last detail, the engineer's office issued the following instruction to every officer in charge (note the 19th century language):–

> In order that the men may have every facility for purchasing bread at places remote from towns, will you please to intimate to any bakers in your locality, that they will be at liberty to come upon the Company's premises, at their own risk, to solicit orders from any men who may desire to purchase of them, and to deliver such bread at any time that may be mutually convenient. They must be given to understand that they must obtain payment from the men, who have to provide themselves with victuals.

The company did, however, supply oatmeal. Four men out of each gang of sixty-three prepared this using the following recipe:–

> In one bucket which will hold about 2 1/2 gallons of water, use 2 pint measures full of oatmeal, mix thoroughly with warm water to the thickness of cream, add boiling water to nearly fill the bucket, stir thoroughly and add sugar (or salt) to taste.

Mr W. H. Wills of Wills' Tobacco, who was also a Great Western Railway director, provided each man with two ounces of the famous Westward Ho! mixture. In the light of experiences at previous conversions, the consumption of alcohol was not permitted.

Having arrived on the Thursday, the gangs were able to start the narrowing of sidings on the Friday whilst the last broad-gauge passenger trains were still running. On Saturday, May 21st, and for as long as necessary on Sunday, May 22nd, work commenced at daybreak (4 a.m.) and continued until dusk. The weather was all that could be desired – fine, without excess of heat and with a refreshing breeze.

Upon completion, a narrow-gauge engine ran to and fro over the section to consolidate the line. The engine used on the branch was based at Exeter and allocated to the section from Exeter to Kingswear, including the Brixham branch. The narrow-gauging of the main line down to Newton Abbot was completed so expeditiously (about 3/4 hour ahead of schedule) that Mr Hammett, the superintending engineer, was able to reach there at 2.30 p.m. on Saturday. Locomotive No. 488 propelled a van from Exeter at snail's pace to enable him to thoroughly test and prove the conversion. As all but 1 1/2 miles of his section was a double line, he had to work his way back to Exeter on the other track, before repairing to Newton Abbot for the night. From 8 a.m. until 11 a.m. on the Sunday, he went over the Moretonhampstead branch in the company of Mr Maggs – the Newton Abbot stationmaster. He declared the line fit for use and a notice to the effect that the line was ready for traffic was issued to each stationmaster.

Passenger trains resumed on the Monday morning and goods recommenced on the Tuesday. Engine drivers were directed to run with great caution until the line was perfectly settled, and Exeter was instructed to have engines and carriages on standby to run special trains in the path of trains from further west in the event of late running. However, the newspaper reports suggest that the conversion work was of such a high standard that such contingencies were unnecessary.

Where possible, replacement narrow-gauge carriages were delivered beforehand. Plymouth's requirement was routed over the London & South Western Railway via Okehampton on Friday, May 20th. To supplement the existing narrow-gauge stock already in use in West Cornwall, additional carriages were despatched to Carn Brea Yard, being conveyed west of Plymouth on broad-gauge 'Crocodile' trucks. Had the Teign Valley line been complete (it did not reach Exeter until 1903), the carriages for the Moretonhampstead branch would probably have been forwarded to Heathfield in advance. In the event, its requirement for two composites (first & second class) and two brake thirds worked down from Exeter early on Monday, May 23rd, in time for the first departure at 7.15 a.m.

The Monday was available for the workmen to complete the narrowing of any sidings and to generally tidy up, and they did not depart until the Tuesday. Their conveyance – a narrow-gauge train, of course – set out from Bristol at midnight and took them home at 6.40 a.m.

In one hectic weekend, in a bygone century, the broad gauge was finally laid to rest and with it the lost opportunity to exploit a grand gauge specifically intended to do full justice to Brunel's inter-city Great Western Railway. Anyone who has seen the demonstration broad-gauge line in action at Didcot will surely be impressed by the sheer size of the locomotive and rolling stock. One cannot begin to imagine how trains would have developed into the 21st century with the benefit of the broad gauge. Would High Speed Trains be travelling faster than 125 mph?

Whilst the broad gauge has long-since gone, there are two pertinent local reminders on the South Devon Railway. Take a look at the unused platform on the other side of the tracks at Buckfastleigh Station and note what appears to be an unnecessarily wide space between the two pairs of rails. Until 1892, both tracks were broad gauge, and this width was needed to accommodate them. The other legacy is in the design of the preserved Super Saloon carriages 'King George' and 'Duchess of York'. Although built forty years after the end of the broad gauge, they are seven inches wider than other companies' carriages to take full advantage of the old loading gauge, thus offering a standard of opulence which could not be matched elsewhere. Consequently, they were restricted to former broad-gauge lines of the Great Western Railway.

⁂ ⁂ ⁂ ⁂ ⁂

APPENDIX VI

Some important dates:–

1847 A preliminary survey, including the marking out of a new line, carried out from Newton Abbot to Okehampton, via Bovey Tracey, Lustleigh, Moretonhampstead and Chagford.

1858 A preliminary survey carried out for a projected line from Newton Abbot to Moretonhampstead, for a newly-formed Newton & Moretonhampstead Railway Committee.

1861 *14th November* – A working agreement made between the Moretonhampstead & South Devon Railway Company and the South Devon Railway Company for the working of the line by the latter.

1862 *7th July* – Royal Assent given to the Act incorporating the Moretonhampstead & South Devon Railway Company.

1863 *10th August* – First sod cut at Bovey Heathfield.

1866 *26th June* – Line officially opened, with intermediate stations at Bovey and Lustleigh.

4th July – First day of passenger services.

8th October – Line opened for goods traffic. (Although the precise date has not been established, Granite Siding was completed at around this time, or shortly afterwards, followed a few months later by the opening of Pottery Siding.)

1867 *16th December* – Teigngrace Station opened.

1872 *14th June* – Teigngrace Siding opened.

1st July – Moretonhampstead & South Devon Railway Company formally amalgamated with the South Devon Railway Company.

1874 *1st July* – Chudleigh Road Station opened.

1876 *1st February* – An Agreement made under which the whole of the South Devon Railway Company undertaking was to be worked by the Great Western Railway Company for a period of 999 years.

1878 *1st August* – The South Devon Railway Company formally amalgamated with the Great Western Railway Company under the GWR and SDR Companies Amalgamation Act of 22nd July 1878.

1882 *1st October* – Chudleigh Road Station renamed Heathfield.

9th October – Teign Valley Railway opened from Heathfield to Ashton, with a goods siding to Teign House (Christow).

1888 *April* – Candy's Siding, Heathfield opened.

1892 *21st/22nd May* – Line converted from broad gauge (7ft 0¼in) to narrow (standard) gauge (4ft 8½in).

1893 Teignbridge Siding opened.

1906 *9th April* – Railway motor omnibus service introduced between Moretonhampstead and Chagford.

1913 Stover (Timber) Siding, Heathfield opened.

1914 *22nd January* – A second siding opened at Teignbridge.

1916 *2nd October* – A new direct running connection between the Teign Valley and Moretonhampstead lines brought into use at Heathfield so as to facilitate main line diversionary workings as well as the daily Teign Valley goods trains.

1927 *11th April* – New station officially opened at Newton Abbot.
June – Heathfield made a crossing station by the provision of a new 'down' loop. A new, 'down', platform also brought into use.

1928 *21st May* – Brimley Halt opened.

1929 *1st January* – The National Omnibus & Transport Co. Ltd which, in Devon and Cornwall, became the Western National Omnibus Co. Ltd with effect from 28th February 1929, took over the Moretonhampstead to Chagford bus service and also those from Bovey Station.
1st March – The Great Western Railway Company purchased the Manor House at North Bovey and converted it into a luxury hotel.

1931 *1st June* – Hawkmoor Halt opened.

1934 A Camping Coach introduced at Lustleigh Station.

1937 *30th November/1st December* – King George VI spent the night on the royal train just to the north of the road overbridge at Wray Barton and disembarked at Moretonhampstead Station on the following morning.

1938 *21st April* – Newton Abbot Clays Ltd Siding opened.

1939 *8th May* – Teigngrace Station unstaffed and demoted to halt status.

1943 *May* – The crossing loop at Heathfield Station extended at the southern end and a double junction with the Teign Valley line installed.

1947 A loading ramp provided at Teigngrace Halt.
November – Moretonhampstead engine shed officially closed.
31st December – Railways nationalised at midnight.

1955 *13th June* – Hawkmoor Halt renamed Pullabrook Halt.

1956 *24th June* – Pottery Siding taken out of use.

1958 *7th June* – Last passenger train on the Teign Valley line (passenger services officially withdrawn on 9th June).

1959 *28th February* – Last passenger train (passenger services officially withdrawn on 2nd March).
18th August – Sunday School Special (Moretonhampstead to Goodrington Sands Halt and return).

1960 *6th June* – South Devon Railway Society's 'The Heart of Devon Rambler' trip from Paignton to Moretonhampstead and return.
August – Sunday School Special (Moretonhampstead to Goodrington Sands Halt and return).

1961 *6th February* – New siding for Geest Industries' banana warehouse opened at Heathfield Station.
4th March – South Devon Railway Society trip from Newton Abbot to Trusham, via Heathfield.
10th August – Sunday School Special (Moretonhampstead to Goodrington Sands Halt and return).

1962 *11th June* – South Devon Railway Society's 'South Devon Phoenix' trip from Paignton to Moretonhampstead and return.
16th August – Sunday School Special (Moretonhampstead to Teignmouth and return).

1964 *6th April* – Goods facilities withdrawn at Lustleigh and Moretonhampstead, and section of line from northern side of Bovey Station to Moretonhampstead closed.

1965 *21st June* – Track lifting from northern side of Bovey Station to Moretonhampstead completed.
October – Heathfield signal box taken out of use.

1966 *January* – New sidings for Gulf Oil (Great Britain) Ltd opened on northern side of Heathfield Station.
3rd January – Bovey Station closed.

1967 *10th March* – Candy's Siding closed.
September – Granite Siding taken out of use.
Motorail traffic introduced at Newton Abbot, using the former Moretonhampstead bay platform 9.
4th December – Last goods train on the Teign Valley line prior to final closure.

1969 *27th/28th July* – H.M. Queen Elizabeth, reviewing the fleet in Torbay, spent the night in the royal train at Heathfield.

1970 *30th April* – Last goods train to Bovey.
5th July – Special diesel multiple unit trips run by B.R. from Newton Abbot to Bovey.
6th July – Section of line from northern side of Heathfield Station to Bovey closed. Track lifting completed on 8th September.

1971 Teigngrace Siding removed.

1972 *5th June* – Heathfield Station unstaffed.

1975 Traffic from Geest Industries' banana warehouse ceased.

1983 *8th/9th March* – The Prince and Princess of Wales spent the night in the royal train just south of Teigngrace, the prince disembarking at Teigngrace Halt on the following morning and the princess (on a separate engagement) at Heathfield.

1988 Teignbridge Sidings taken out of use.

1996 *17th January* – Last 'oil train' (Heltor Ltd) from Newport to Heathfield and return.

1998 *28th May* – After an interval of over two years, a regular goods service was reintroduced between Newton Abbot and Heathfield for the removal of powdered ball clay from Timber Siding.

* * * * *

BIBLIOGRAPHY

A New Survey of England: Devon, W. G. Hoskins (David & Charles, 1972)

A Pictorial and Descriptive Guide to Dartmoor (Ward, Lock & Co. Limited, c.1924)

A Regional History of the Railways of Great Britain – Volume 1: The West Country, David St John Thomas (David & Charles, 1981)

Branch Line to Moretonhampstead, Vic Mitchell and Keith Smith (Middleton Press, 1998)

Branch Lines of Devon – Exeter and South, Central and East Devon, Colin G. Maggs (Alan Sutton Publishing Limited, 1995)

Dartmoor – A New Study, Ed. by Crispin Gill (David & Charles, 1983)

From Haldon to Mid-Dartmoor in old photographs, collected by Tim Hall (Alan Sutton Publishing Limited, 1990)

Go Great Western – Reminiscenses of the G.W.R. main line and branches in Devon, T. W. E. Roche (Forge Books, 1984)

Great Western Branch Line Termini (Volume Two), Paul Karau (OPC, 1978)

Growing Up on the Railway in the South West, Grace Horseman (ARK Publications (Railways), 1998)

Iron Horse to the Sea – Railways in South Devon, John Pike (Ex-Libris Press, 1987)

Let's Explore Old Railways in Devon, Arthur L. Clamp (Westway Publications, c.1970)

Rail Routes in Devon & Cornwall, Chris Leigh (Ian Allan Ltd, 1982)

Railway Motor Buses and Bus Services in the British Isles 1902–1933 (Volume 2), John Cummings (OPC, 1980)

Scenes from the past: 19 – Railways in and around Newton Abbot and Torbay, C. R. Potts (Foxline Publishing, 1993)

Small Talk at Wreyland, Cecil Torr (Forest Publishing, 1996)

Steam in Devon, Peter W. Gray (Ian Allan Publishing, 1995)

Steam on West Country Branch Lines, Peter Gray (Ian Allan Publishing, 1998)

The Great Western in South Devon, Keith Beck and John Copsey (Wild Swan Publications, 1990)

The Hand Book of South of Devon and Dartmoor (Henry Besley and Son, 1874)

The Haytor Granite Tramway and Stover Canal, M. C. Ewans (David & Charles, 1977)

The Haytor Granite Tramway and Stover Canal, Helen Harris (Peninsula Press, 1994)

The Heathfield to Exeter (Teign Valley) Railway, Lawrence W. Pomroy (ARK Publications (Railways), 1995)

The Homeland Handbooks – Volume 8: Dartmoor with its Surroundings, Beatrix F. Cresswell (The Homeland Association Ltd, 1913)

The Moretonhampstead and South Devon Railway, S. C. Jenkins and L. W. Pomroy (Oakwood Press, 1989)

The Moretonhampstead Branch: A Railway from Shore to Moor, John Owen (Waterfront, 2000)
The Newton Abbot to Kingswear Railway (1844–1988), C. R. Potts (The Oakwood Press, 1989)
The Potters' Field: A History of the South Devon Ball Clay Industry, L. T. C. Rolt (David & Charles, 1974)
The Teign Valley Line, Peter Kay (Wild Swan Publications, 1996)
Walking the Dartmoor Railroads, Eric Hemery (Peninsula Press, 1991)
Walking Westcountry Railways, Christopher Somerville (David & Charles, 1982)
West Country Branch Lines: A Colour Portfolio, Peter W. Gray (Ian Allan Publishing, 2003)
'Rail Trail' – a weekly series of articles by Peter Gray appearing in the *Herald Express*

ACKNOWLEDGEMENTS

The authors wish to extend their grateful thanks to all those, past and present, for their generous assistance given in a wide variety of ways during the preparation of this book.
British Railways Board; Dartington Rural Archive; Devon Record Office, Exeter; Heltor Ltd; *Herald Express*; Imerys Minerals Ltd; Kelly Mine Preservation Society; *Mid-Devon Advertiser*; Public Record Office, Kew; Railway Studies Library, Newton Abbot; Signalling Record Society; Stover Canal Society; Watts Blake Bearne & Company Plc; Westcountry Studies Library, Exeter; *Western Morning News*.

Mrs M. Adcock; V. Arthur; Mrs M. Bartlett; C. Bowden; B. Brett; J. Cadoux-Hudson; P. Carrett; L. W. Crosier; Mrs H. Cullum; A. Foster (Imerys Minerals Ltd); D. Frost; Mrs J. George; P. W. Gray; G. Haigh; Mrs S. Healey; G. Howells; Miss V. Huish; M. Jacobs; J. Kelly; Mrs S. Kemp; P. Kingdon (Heltor Ltd); Mrs S. Knapman (Watts Blake Bearne & Company Plc); D. Lewis; Mrs P. Lind; B. Mills; D. Mitchell; W. Mountford; G. Myers (Heltor Ltd); P. Newman (Stover Canal Society); J. Parnell; E. G. Parrott; L. W. Pomroy; C. Potts; C. Pulleyblank; S. Rowe; Mrs E. Rowed; M. Shippam; J. Tapp; Ms. J. Wallace; N. Walter (Kelly Mine Preservation Society); R. Wills; W. Wright; A. Yendall; R. Zaple.

Special thanks are due to the following:–
Bryan Gibson for his detailed information on railway and omnibus timetables, and also on gauge conversion; Paul Karau for permission to reproduce photographs of G. N. Southerden from Wild Swan Publications; Peter Kay for his account of signalling and other assistance given during the preparation of the manuscript; Eric Shepherd for the use of his personal notes and observations on the branch, and also for his editorial work; Chris Webber for his account of the proposed extension of the line to Chagford and bus services.

(Photographs are acknowledged individually in most instances)